Also by Brian Kelly and Mark London

AMAZON

BRIAN KELLY

MARK LONDON

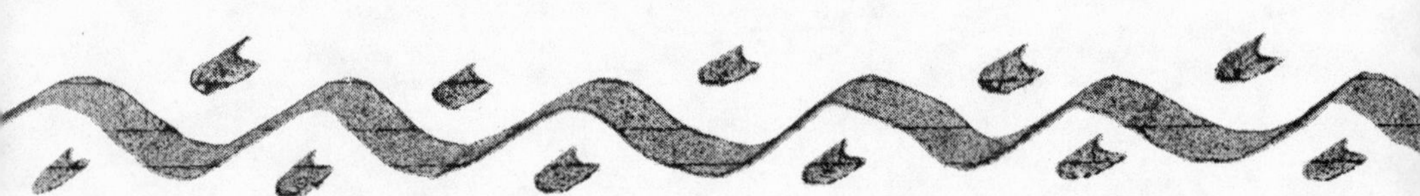

THE FOUR LITTLE DRAGONS

SIMON AND SCHUSTER
NEW YORK · LONDON · TORONTO
SYDNEY · TOKYO

SIMON AND SCHUSTER
Simon & Schuster Building
Rockefeller Center
1230 Avenue of the Americas
New York, New York 10020

Manufactured in the United States of America

10 9 8 7 6 5 4 3 2 1

Library of Congress Cataloging in Publication Data
Kelly, Brian
The four little dragons / Brian Kelly, Mark London.
p. cm.
1. East Asia—Description and travel. 2. Singapore—Description and travel. 3. Thailand—Description and travel— 4. Kelly, Brian,—Journeys—East Asia. 5. Kelly, Brian,—Journeys—Singapore. 6. Kelly, Brian,—Journeys—Thailand. I. London, Mark. II. Title.
DS508.2.K45 1989
915.04'427—dc19 *89-36192*
CIP

ISBN 0-671-55748-3

Some material has been reprinted with permission of the publisher from *Among the Cities* © Jan Morris: Oxford University Press, New York 1985.

We have made every effort to trace the ownership of all copyrighted material and to secure permission from copyright holders. In the event of any question arising as to the use of any material, we will be pleased to make the necessary corrections in future printings.

To Patti and Dania

ACKNOWLEDGMENTS

Among those we wish to thank are the dozens of people who populate this book. They were generous with their time and opened their homes and their lives to two strangers. They did their best to help us understand a foreign culture. The governments of each of the Dragons also did their best to tell their side of the story and, for the most part, made our jobs easier. Particularly forthcoming were Fredrick Chien and his staff at the Taiwanese mission in Washington and Ambassador Tommy Koh of the Republic of Singapore.

We also are indebted to the following friends whom we list in no particular order: Nelson Chang, Carl Chien, John Zagame, H. P. Goldfield, Ann Godoff, Peter Wong, Brenda Chan, Agatha and Timothy Shen, Jay Chun, Sang Yong Park, Bilahari Kausikan, Sharon Tan, Lilly Lin, Shookie and Shimon Ferst, David Lyman, Dorinda Elliott, Adi Ignatius, Ken Sheffer, Tom McHale, Bill Regardie and the staff of *Regardie's* magazine, Mimi Mitchell and the Gordon Brothers.

As always, we are grateful for the enthusiastic support of our parents, and we are particularly appreciative of the scouting missions and guidance of Alan London. Our agent, Rafe Sagalyn, coached this project into reality from the beginning, and our wonderful editor, Carole Lalli, saved us from rhetorical excesses too many times to mention. Kerri Conan kept all the pieces from falling apart.

Finally, while they certainly slowed the progress of this book, we will always be thankful for the arrival in mid-writing of two magnificent little guys who have made us think a lot harder about the future: Daniel Kelly and Scott London.

CONTENTS

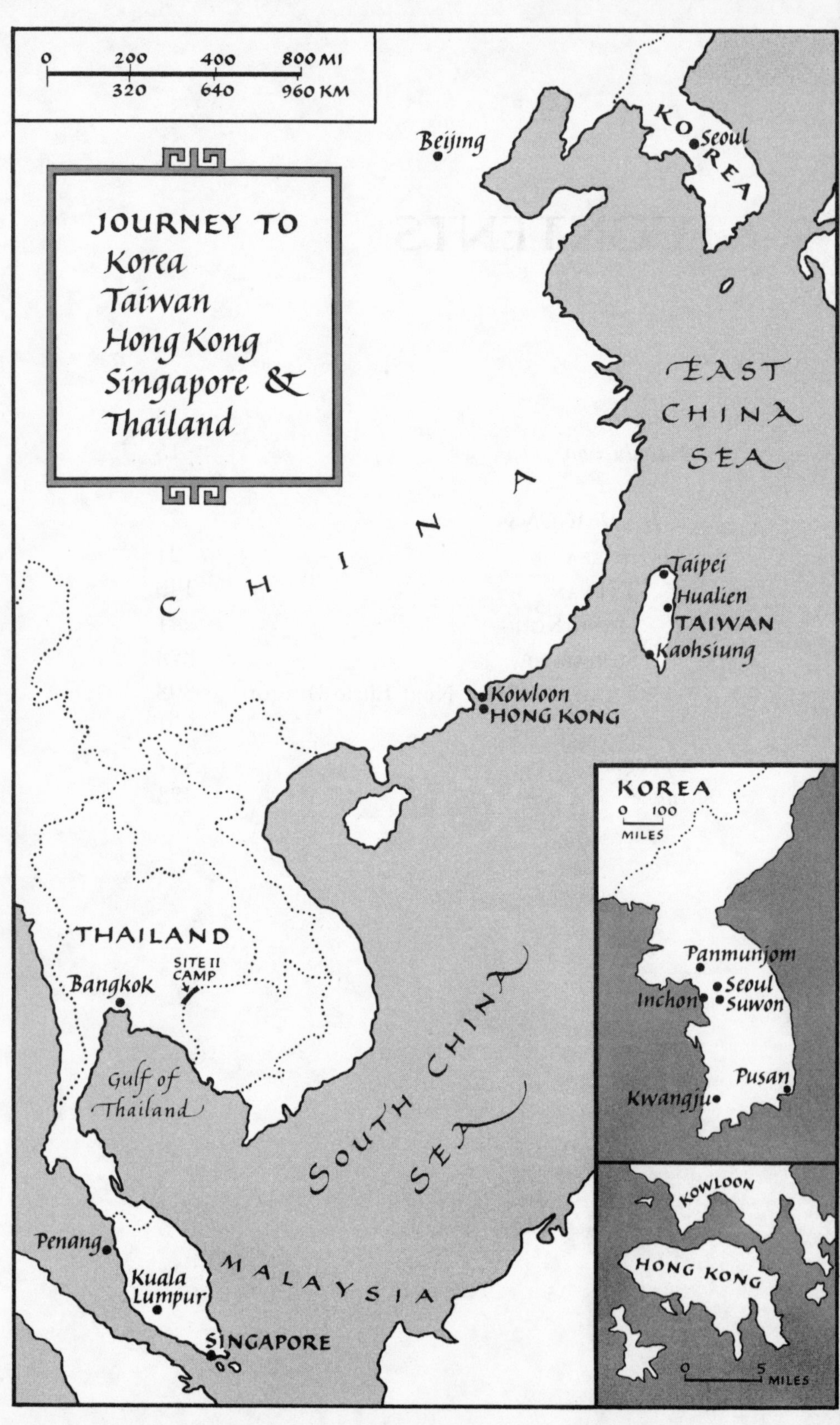

0 200 400 800 MI
320 640 960 KM
JOURNEY TO
Korea
Taiwan
Hong Kong
Singapore &
Thailand
Beijing
KOREA
Seoul
EAST CHINA SEA
CHINA
Taipei
Hualien
TAIWAN
Kaohsiung
Kowloon
HONG KONG
THAILAND
SITE II CAMP
Bangkok
Gulf of Thailand
SOUTH CHINA SEA
Penang
Kuala Lumpur
MALAYSIA
SINGAPORE
KOREA
0 100
MILES
Panmunjom
Seoul
Inchon
Suwon
Pusan
Kwangju
KOWLOON
HONG KONG
0 5 MILES

PREFACE

The Eastern dragon is the spirit of change, therefore of life itself. . . . His voice is heard in the hurricane, which, scattering the withered leaves of the forest, quickens a new spring.

—OKAKURA KAKUZO,
quoted in *Soul of the Tiger,*
by Jeffrey A. McNeely and
Paul Spencer Wachtel

THIS BOOK is about a journey to the New World of Asia. It is the story of how we discovered the people, culture, politics and economics of a region that we came to appreciate as one of the most interesting and important in the world. Most of our time was spent in the Four Little Dragons of Korea, Taiwan, Hong Kong and Singapore. We also traveled to Thailand the next dragon, and, briefly, to mainland China.

The trip was not a seamless one, but broken up into parts over an 18-month period from March 1986 to September 1987. For the purposes of the narrative we have told the story starting in Korea and ending in Singapore. On occasion we have changed the names of certain people. All the events and characters in this book are true.

We traveled in Asia during a watershed period. Each of the Four Dragons was on the verge of major changes. A new, prosperous generation was confronting an older one that had grown up in a world of wants and fears. By the time we finished writing, some of the dramas had played themselves out, others had only paused for intermission.

We've written about the place as it was while we were there. Nothing that happened since we left has altered what we saw and heard. We are convinced that, over the next decades, the only constant in Asia will be change.

INTRODUCTION

ONE DAY during Chicago's frigid winter of 1982, the cranky old Slovak who owned the dry cleaning shop around the corner from my apartment near Diversey and Pine Grove gathered up his excitable dog and headed for a warmer climate. A few days after his unmourned departure—"NO CHECKS! NO CREDIT! NOT RESPONSIBLE FOR ITEMS LEFT OVER 30 DAYS!" was the sign that greeted his customers—a family of Asians took over the shop.

They turned out to be the Kim family from Korea, mother father and three daughters, and immediately some things about the shop began to change. It was open for longer hours, shirts came back with buttons intact, customers were greeted by name and were permitted to pay by check. The mother and father sewed in the back while the daughters, who spoke English well, handled the counter. The girls worked every day after school and all day Saturday. School wasn't so hard, one of them said once. In Korea they had to study much more.

Soon I noticed other small shops in the area being taken over: the Italian shoeman with black polish thick under his nails was replaced by a Korean in a clean apron; the Lebanese jeweler went out of business and a Korean man and woman took over. Angelo's Fresh Hot Pizza was now run by a short swarthy fellow named Duk, whose pizza was, unfortunately, no better than Angelo's.

For someone who grew up in 1960s suburban America, Asian, or more typically "Oriental," meant the occasional take-out Chinese meal from a darkly-lit storefront restaurant. Hong Kong meant cheap plastic toys. Taiwan produced bicycles you hoped you didn't get for Christmas. Korea was a place with a war named after it. Singapore was a city in China, wasn't it?

With these new faces all over the neighborhood I was living for the first time in proximity to people I still thought of as Orientals, as if they were some sort of homogeneous people from a big, ill-defined country across the Pacific Ocean.

At about the same time, the South Side of Chicago was doubled over in agony from the closing of U.S. Steel Co.'s giant South Works mill. From a peak of almost 20,000 workers manning round-the-clock shifts and turning out more hot metal than any plant in the world, the mill had fallen to skeleton crews who kept a few perfunctory fires burning and waited for the inevitable closing of the gates. Once the symbol of smokestack America, U.S. Steel was now an equally vivid metaphor for the changes that were wracking the U.S. economy. But for the tens of thousands of families whose livelihoods somehow depended on the production of steel, and for their larger community of churches and schools and butcher shops, the damage was more than symbolic. In a very short time, the domestic steel industry had collapsed and nobody had seen it coming. The guys on the shop floor were hurting and they were angry. And they blamed the Koreans.

I remember one television news report from a local tavern where a square-faced mill worker talked about having to compete with "Korean slave labor" and people willing to work for "dirt wages." Another man said the union had told him that orders for steel weren't only going to Korea but to "Taiwan or Thailand or some place like that."

Two things stuck with me about that report. At that moment, I was only vaguely aware that they made steel in Korea, or Taiwan or even Thailand, for that matter. And second, here was a report about foreign imports that didn't blame Japan. Not that Japan wasn't already a major culprit in snatching away huge chunks of American markets for everything from autos to televisions, but that was old news. Here were some new players making big gains, and I didn't even know they were in the game.

To me, Asia still meant cheap as in flimsy. Every kid I grew up with knew that the label "Made in Hong Kong" was a likely sign that a plastic rifle or a Wiffle-ball bat would not make it through the rigorous Christmas to New Year's Day break-in period. Somewhere around the time I bought my second Sony television, I began to reassess those feelings and realized that Japan had shed the stigma of shoddiness. But that was where I drew the line. Now it seemed that these other Asians also knew what they were doing.

The manufacturing and marketing might of Japan was already apparent then, though few observers would have guessed that the Japanese were on their way to dominating the world economy. For instance, after years of dismissing Japanese cars as inferior, the auto geniuses in Detroit were finally scrambling to make smaller, better quality cars to compete. "No problem," they said, as if losing half their market share had been part of their strategy all along. They were also closing plants left and right to compensate for that lost market. The economists and the business magazines were writing sportingly about "the Japanese challenge."

But on the shop floors of South Chicago, and a lot of other places in the Rust Belt, the challenge had turned into a rout and the only question was how long would it last? "A lot longer," was the smart answer. These other Asians seemed to represent other Japans in the making.

This new Asia was really three countries—South Korea, Taiwan and Singapore—and the British Crown Colony of Hong Kong. In the parlance of international economics they were the NICs for Newly Industrializing Countries, placing them roughly in the company of such countries as Brazil and Mexico—which is to say well above the struggling Third World but not on a par with the industrialized First World of Japan, Europe or North America.

What they had accomplished was astonishing. In 30 years, each had risen from destitution to prosperity. In the 1950s, after decades of war throughout the region, each had an economy that was indistinguishable from the worst cases of Africa. But from the mid-1960s on, their growth curves zoomed ahead at a 45-degree angle. As a group they could be the most successful countries in the world, and I barely knew where they were.

Then I came across a phrase in an article about Japan in the *New York Times* magazine by Theodore H. White, the journalist who had long specialized in reporting on Asia. This last major piece before his death was a warning to America about the economic threat posed by Japan. White wrote:

> American industry grew up in partnership with European industry, but Japan rouses different fears. Behind Japan ("the Big Dragon," some call it) march the "four little dragons" (Korea, Hong Kong, Taiwan, Singapore) following in its path. And behind looms China and India, desperate as they are to raise their standard of living—at the expense of American standards if necessary.

I told my friend Mark London to pack his bags: It was time for another adventure. We recently had published *Amazon*, about the conquest of the rain forest by the rich and the poor of Brazil and the consequences of that stampede. The Amazon fascinated us because it was a frontier, an unexplored edge. Our months of travel through the jungle were an attempt to answer the questions of how much of the forest was gone and why it was disappearing. It was also a story about how change in parts of the world long ignored by Americans was beginning to come closer to home.

Here was another frontier that invited exploration. Asia and the Dragons seemed to pose similar questions, though they were a cultural mystery, not a natural one. For all either of us knew about them, the people of these countries might have been Indians from the remotest rain forest. Yet more than the Amazon, the Four Little Dragons were beginning to have a profound effect on the United States. From the trade deficit figures to the unemployed steelworkers to the almond-eyed math geniuses at MIT, it was apparent that the world no longer belonged to the Caucasian race. What we wanted to know was, "Who *are* those guys?"

Were they clones of the super-productive Japanese, spoiling to tear their own piece of flesh from the American economy? Was this the coming of the Brave New World where humorless automatons toiled efficiently for the greater good of repressive governments? How was the United States—or, more specifically some 18-year-old kid from Michigan armed only with a high school diploma—supposed to compete with them?

When you added up the populations of the Four Dragons, they totaled about 75 million, which makes a fair-size country, one larger than France, West Germany, Great Britain or Mexico, for instance. Their combined gross national product was $200 billion in the mid-1980s, and growing at about 10 percent a year. Their combined trade surplus with the United States was about $30 billion, half that of Japan. But as one businessman with decades of experience in Asia told us, it wasn't just the Dragons we should be concerned with but their broader impact on the rest of Asia.

"These countries aren't just super economies," he told us, "they are like engines pulling a whole region that easily takes in more than 200 million people *before* you count China."

For instance, tiny Singapore was heavily invested in Indonesia (population 170 million) and Malaysia (20 million). Many businesses in Thailand (60 million) are run from Hong Kong or Taiwan. Lagging farther behind were the politically riven Philippines (60 million) and Sri Lanka (20 million), both with enormous potential and vast cheap labor pools. Then of course there was China, with its billion people waking from a socialist slumber and looking about for guidance.

Sometime in the early 1980s, the people who pay attention to such things noticed that the United States had begun doing more business with Asia than with Europe, the cultural motherland for most Americans, and the trend was accelerating.

"We are about to enter the Asian Century," our Asia veteran told us. "The 21st century will belong to them, not us."

It seemed as though something remarkable was happening. A new world was being created. We decided to go see for ourselves.

Although economics was the source of our interest in Asia, neither of us intended to write an economics text. We set out to tell a story about people. And we would do it the only way we knew how: wander around, meet strangers and ask questions.

A look at the globe made clear that any links among the Dragons would have to be philosophical. The distance from Seoul to Singapore is as great as from New York to the heart of the Amazon. We decided to start in Korea and move south through Taiwan and Hong Kong, ending in Singapore. From the beginning, we realized our greatest obstacle would be language. We were not about to learn the native tongues, as London had learned Portuguese for our travels to Brazil. Chinese was spoken in Taiwan and Hong Kong—though in two dialects as different from each other as English from French. The Korean language, we were told, is unlike any other in the world. At least in Singapore, English was one of the official languages—along with Mandarin Chinese and Tamil.

We also were wary of the governments, all of which were dictatorships of one form or another. Other journalists had told tales of bureaucratic intransigence, restricted travel and even tapped telephones and surreptitious escorts. "These are subtly evil places," was how one put it.

There was one more lingering doubt. The words of one of the first Asia experts with whom we had talked kept returning. He admitted he was skeptical of our ability to succeed.

"These countries are really about China," he said, "and the Chinese can barely understand each other. If a Westerner studied for 20 years, he might have a clue."

Richard Hughes, a renowned British correspondent, wrote about Asia this way: "The foreigner is always an intruder, often tolerated, sometimes liked, often disturbed, seldom accepted."

It was with such baggage already weighing us down that we set off.

BRIAN KELLY

KOREA

THE PHONE RANG. Some guy named Chun from the Korean tourist bureau was down in the lobby. He said he was supposed to show us Seoul. It was 8 A.M.

"Give us a few minutes," London groused. "You're an hour early."

As a rule, neither one of us likes to see the world through the eyes of a tourist bureau guide, but we had a hunch that Korea would be a little out of the ordinary. For starters, we were willing to take whatever we could get. We had arrived late the night before, 14 hours after leaving New York on no-frills Korean Air Lines, one of the world's most efficient and austere carriers. Kimpo Airport had been deceptively familiar—unsmiling customs agents looking much alike throughout the world—and during the taxi ride to the hotel it had been too dark to notice anything except for an occasional neon sign in a wholly unfamiliar language and an eerie proliferation of red neon crosses, like the kind that rise over storefront churches in ghetto America.

The Hilton Hotel was, of course, like all the rest of the world's Hiltons and Hyatts and Westins, down to the complimentary shampoo and the overpriced minibar. That morning we were still comfortably contained in the American businessman's bubble, with a room service breakfast of coffee, toast and scrambled eggs (having declined the "Traditional Korea Breakfast" of beef and turnip soup with seaweed). Whatever was strange about Asia remained, for the moment, outside our room in Seoul.

Not five minutes after London hung up the phone, there was a pounding on the door.

"Who is it?"

"Chun," said Chun, and taking the question as an invitation, barged into the room. He eyed first Kelly, lying in bed and staring dully at the ceiling, then London, emerging from the bathroom in boxer shorts and shaving cream, and started to laugh a deep, throaty *hoho ho HO!* It was a mixture of delighted surprise and contempt, sort of like an evil scoutmaster who has discovered a couple of tenderfeet still asleep on the morning of the big hike. He was a small man for such a big laugh and we wished he'd go away.

Then, apparently trying to control himself, he downshifted to a high-pitched keening laugh. *Hee hee hee hee hee.* Finally he stopped and gave a slight bow of his head.

"So okay. I am Chun. Welcome to Korea. Let's go."

With that he sat down and helped himself to the toast and jam on the room service tray.

Chun wore a tan sports coat, brown slacks, white shirt and brown tie. His lank black hair was shaped like a bowl and bangs fell almost into his eyes, which remained in a perpetual squint behind thick glasses. He was nervous and in a hurry. The smell of garlic hung around him like a force field.

"There is very much to see," he said between mouthfuls of toast.

He had an agenda. First, the Secret Gardens of King something-or-other, then a trip to the duty-free shopping mall, on to the ancient Folk Village and finally a look at the new Olympic Games facilities. This was looking like a problem. We tried to explain to Chun that we were not writing a sightseer's guide; we were trying to find something closer to the soul of Korea, we told him. But it was not clear at that point that we knew what we were talking about and Chun just looked puzzled.

"We're trying to understand how your country became so successful," Kelly started. "What makes people work? What are their hopes, their dreams. . . ."

"Let's go to the Secret Gardens," Chun said.

When he finished his toast, we prevailed on him to take us to the Olympic stadium first, reasoning that the Olympics were at least a common denominator for us and they might have a more sophisticated press apparatus that would allow us to ditch Chun. We took off in Chun's chauffeur-driven black Daewoo sedan and skirted downtown.

Seoul in the daylight is a shock. It is clean, it is new and it is gigantic. The city has oozed its way around and up a series of modest but craggy mountains, giving it the appearance of an overgrown Denver. The downtown is stacked with soaring glass office towers, most only a few years old and others still coming to life under the horizontal necks of construction cranes. A story in that day's Korea *Herald,* one of two English-language dailies, noted that as late as 1965, there were only 18 buildings in Seoul over 10 stories tall. By 1975 there were 127 and now there are 827. The story was typical of many we found in the Korean press in that it sought to reassure readers that their great growth was not an illusion. Even Koreans can't quite believe such statistics as the fact that Seoul had but 12 taxicabs in 1945.

Moving south, we crossed the Han River, once the city limits, but now merely an annoying obstacle in the urban progression. To the right was Cheju Island, an oval of landfill that was fast becoming a second downtown, the location of the National Assembly and stock exchange as well as offices of numerous foreign corporations. Along the south bank of the Han—and extending back for miles—stood a forest of 20-story apartment houses, identical concrete block towers distinguished only by numbers painted in giant circles near the top. Chun said that this area was the largest concentration of apartments in the world, and we were not about to challenge him. Seoul is the fifth largest city in the world with 10 million people (more than 10 times the number it had in 1945) and they have to live someplace.

The preconceived picture we both had of Seoul was of a bleak, gritty manufacturing town, like the industrial nightmare of south Chicago and Gary, Indiana. This was not the case. Even a cursory look spoke of prosperity. Everything was new: the wide streets, the granite-faced subway entrances, the 14 bridges over the Han, the cars on the street. By this comparison, Chicago is the Third World city.

"We rebuild after the war," explained Chun. "There was nothing then."

Seoul, and all of Korea, had been trampled by the Korean War some 30 years earlier. Old photographs showed an overgrown farm town that had been blasted to pieces by some of the fiercest fighting in modern warfare. When the final truce was declared in 1954, few buildings were left standing and the streets were churned to a muddy goo. Those were the days, or so the legend went, when much of the population was reduced to eating tree bark to survive.

It seemed impossible that people who were eating wood a generation ago could have created the spectacle that confronted us at the billion-dollar Olympic complex. Arrayed like a squadron of spaceships were a half-dozen domed sports pavilions and an open-air arena that replicated New York's Shea Stadium. This was the sort of complex that the town fathers of Houston or Kansas City dreamed about. When Los Angeles hosted the Olympics such a construction project was ruled out as much too costly, so the mighty U S of A made do with a patchwork of hand-me-downs.

Not for the Koreans. The Olympics was to be their coming out party and no expense had been spared to accommodate the guests. Much as the world began to take note of the growth of Japan during the 1964 Olympics, the Koreans hoped that the 1988 extravaganza would announce that the Republic of Korea is a nation not to be ignored.

"The games will make us very modern," said Chun. "We clean up for the foreign tourists." Indeed, the clean-up had gone well beyond the elaborate sports facilities, Chun explained, extending to a crackdown on prostitution by closing the famous "barber shops" and the elimination of some of the more exotic market stalls downtown.

"I do not think it is possible now to buy dogs to eat," Chun said with what seemed like a touch of wistfulness. "Dog meat is very hard to find."

Lee Jae-Hong, one of the Seoul Olympic Organizing Committee officials, laughed when we asked about the dogs.

"Well, maybe we are changing a few of the old traditional ways, but not so much," said Mr. Lee. He downplayed the magnitude of the Games.

"We want to show the world that Korea has grown to a size where the Olympics is not such a big deal. We spend, maybe, $3 billion on the games. We can afford that. It will not break our economy."

Mr. Lee, a serious man who spoke English well, was not quite condescending as he told us that we, the United States, had "done okay" with our own Olympics.

"You did a pretty good job with bringing in the private sector to fund the games," he conceded. "We have used some of your ideas. But we still think it's better to have the government more deeply involved. Things move much more smoothly."

This was pretty assertive stuff coming from what we had been led to believe was a typically deferential Asian culture. "They won't look you in the eye and they'll be shy about answering questions directly," we had been told by people who knew something of Asia. Not hardly. The only touch of embarrassment came when we asked about a report that the Koreans had copied their Olympic mascot from Tony the Tiger, the famed Kellogg's Sugar Frosted Flakes pitchman. Hoodori, the cheerful Korean symbol, was a dead ringer for Tony, especially in his earlier incarnations before Kellogg's protested and the Koreans slapped a kind of derby on his head.

"We did have some problems at first," Lee said. "But we have worked them out. It was just that the friendly tiger on the cereal box was really the best kind of tiger for us to use. We changed it a little and everyone is satisfied."

Cartoon tigers, it seemed, were the most compelling item the United States had to offer the organizing committee.

What was most remarkable, grating if you carried any touch of American chauvinism, was that the Olympic complex was virtually finished two years before the games were to begin. Countries the world over have suffered agonizing delays, cost overruns and political turmoil in an attempt to complete civic undertakings such as the Olympics. But here were the Koreans with the whole thing done early, like some obnoxiously ambitious classmate who was handing in his term paper before you had started yours.

Outside, where some of the final construction was going on, we found confirmation of Lee's contention that the Olympics would not make or break Korea. Surrounding the site of the velodrome was the usual assortment of heavy equipment—cranes, backhoes, dump trucks, flatbeds and shovels—only all of it was Korean made. Names like Daewoo, Hyundai and Kia were stamped on the vehicles. Such equipment is only produced by the more advanced nations, and until a few years ago, even in Korea it would have been labeled Caterpillar and Deere. No longer.

As we toured the complex, we came upon a group of old men who had just disembarked from a tour bus, squinting and looking about as if they had emerged from a dark room. Some moved to the curb and squatted on their haunches, gawking up at the 200-foot-tall stadium.

"Farmers," said Chun.

They wore what looked like a uniform: green or lavender silk jackets, billowy white trousers of a gauzy material, brown felt fedoras on their heads and sandals on their feet. They had slight, stooped frames and faces creased and shiny like old leather. Some wore long, wispy white beards. Compared with the young construction workers, who had almost American-size physiques, the old men looked to be from another country.

We started to ask Chun where they were from.

"From the Middle Ages," he laughed. But he was right. They were from the southern part of the country where they had lived their lives in isolated hamlets, tilling the fields with oxen and primitive tools as their ancestors had done for centuries. This bus to Seoul had been a time machine and they were furrowing their brows in amazement at the outcome.

"They like this very much," Chun said as a group of the old men bobbed their heads in presumed agreement. "They do not know what it is for. But they think it is very good for Korea to have it."

It can be naive to ascribe to nations the characteristics of individuals, but something about Korea was becoming immediately clear as we drove around Seoul with Chun as our not always comprehensible guide: These were an insecure people with a big inferiority complex and a burning drive to overcome their status. South Korea, it seemed, was a nation that had been collectively dismissed by some of the world's great powers. Some of the insults, real and perceived, dated back centuries, but they were felt by every Korean.

The history books make clear that Korea has long been one of the great doormats of the world. Conquered a half dozen times, it was a Japanese colony for half of this century. But the Chinese and the Russians have had their turns and even the Americans, who are supposedly here to keep the peace but are increasingly viewed with suspicion.

The feeling of resentment was most evident in any mention of the Japanese who ruled Korea with a brutal hand from 1905 to 1945 after being handed the country as a prize for winning the Russo-Japanese War. The Japanese dismissed the Koreans as an inferior culture—"the garlic eaters" they called them—and treated them as serfs. To this day, Koreans who have lived in Japan for generations are denied citizenship. When Japan began its conquest of Asia in the 1930s, Korea was drained of its resources and its people. All the decent crops were sent to feed Imperial Army troops, leaving rotted beans for the population at home. Korean men were conscripted as laborers while some Korean women were turned into prostitutes to service Japanese soldiers.

As we drove around downtown Seoul, Chun took perverse pride in pointing out the remnants of Japanese colonialism: city hall, the Bank of Korea, and the former governor's palace, now the national museum. The buildings exude a sense of muscular power like brooding samurai with their thick granite walls, iron barred windows and black iron cupolas and domes. There are few early 20th-century Korean buildings left in Seoul because there were few to start with. Any architecture of substance was Japanese.

"The Koreans very much admire the strength of the Japanese," Daryl Plunk, a Korean scholar at the Heritage Foundation had said before we left. "They love the Japanese and they hate them."

They want to be like the Japanese and they want to destroy them.

"Maybe," said Chun, "we will be the next Japanese."

We asked Chun to drop us off downtown so we could walk back to the hotel. The streets of Seoul are explosive. Every block has thousands of people on the sidewalk in a hurry to get somewhere. Below the sidewalk is a second layer of humanity jostling through the subway underpasses that connect most corners. Since pedestrians cross the street underground, the traffic above, while dense, still manages to move quickly. Taxi cabs and private cars—virtually all Korean-made—dart among endless convoys of orange-and-green buses. And everywhere there is commerce. On the streets, in the alleys, in the subway corridors, along the highway overpasses, there are people selling things from booths, shops, stalls, wagons or blankets laid on the ground. A crowd gathered around a man who demonstrated a portable kerosene stove that assembled in 60 seconds, that's right *60 seconds!* Everything is quick transactions. A pedestrian slows down for an instant. Hands over a bill. Collects an umbrella. Or a newspaper. Or a belt.

In one underpass we watched as a man and a woman, both walking at a good clip, appeared headed for a collision. Surely the man would change course to veer just off her shoulder, in the economical way of New Yorkers traversing midtown. No, he wasn't budging. Well, maybe she'd move, in deference. They *were* looking straight ahead. The distance closed until . . . *Wham!* They popped right into each other. The woman, who was considerably smaller, let out a tiny cry as the breath left her. The man grunted but didn't break stride. The woman glared at him for an instant, then moved on. It was our first encounter with the unyielding nature of the Koreans.

At another point, we decided to try the subway. Kelly stood at the token machine counting coins and trying to puzzle the system when a Korean elbowed his way in front and grabbed a ticket. Then, as he turned to leave he noticed Kelly's plight. He plucked 70 won from Kelly's palm, tossed them into the machine then hit the ticket button. With a grunt and a short bow he was back into the game. No smile, no small talk, but a nice gesture.

The subways are clean, quiet and they run frequently. People read the papers or sleep on the upholstered seats. Some wore coats and ties, but most seemed to be working class people. Seoul is a marvelous machine for getting workers from home to job and back, at whatever hour of the day. And everyone on the trains seemed to have work on their minds. Once a drunk got on and swayed into a few passengers while a couple of teenagers in sneakers and dirty T-shirts practiced tae kwon do kicks at each other for a few stops, but everyone was expressionless, eyes averted—models of urban decorum. The only affront, to us at least, was the smell of garlic that by now we realized would be in our nostrils until we left the country.

It also became apparent by riding the subway that virtually everyone in Seoul is Korean. No melting pot here. No white, tan, brown or black skin or any other shade but that sallow hue that is called yellow. This was a homogeneous population that looked alike and dressed alike. Two tall blond white men stood out uniquely. But no one seemed to mind much. No one stared.

Only once when we stood on a platform waiting for a train

did someone seem to notice us—three boys, college students we guessed from their dress, in a train car across the tracks. The window was closed but they were laughing and pointing. Then one started shouting. The words were muffled by the station noise. He began to pound on the window. Finally as the train pulled away we could make out what he was saying. "U.S.! U.S.! Fuck you!" Then he raised his middle finger in the gesture that needs no translation.

Near the hotel, we wandered into a restaurant for lunch. We took our shoes off in the hallway and a young girl showed us into a bare white room and pointed to a low table surrounded by pillows. We sat on the floor and looked at the stark walls and waited. Language, we were quickly realizing, was a problem in Korea if you happened to be a foreigner. The native spoken language is Hangul, a singular tongue that is neither like Chinese nor Japanese but closer to Finnish and Turkish. Koreans even have their own alphabet, said to be a remarkably efficient one with 29 characters, though they continue to use Chinese pictographs to represent sounds. In any case, it is not at all like English and does not lend itself to pulling simple phrases from the guidebook. So we sat, having no idea where we were or how we were supposed to get anything to eat.

After a time, an older woman came in and sat down. She wore an embroidered black robe and her hair was swept up in a twist. She was a large woman with a broad face that may have once been pretty.

"So. You will have lunch?" she asked in English. It was a question, but stated more like a command.

"Yes, lunch."

"Anything else?"

"Uh, not that we can think of."

"I will order for you."

She left the room and left us feeling a trifle uncomfortable about the local customs.

Ten minutes later she returned trailed by two waiters bearing trays laden with crockery. The waiters covered the wide table with bowls and plates brimming with an assortment of vegetables, stews, soups, fish and rice. Our hostess sat down again and gave us a tour of the meal, which included some stringy raw meat, gelatinous-looking squid and gray soup with a chicken wing protruding from the surface, but most of which was some form of kimchi, the spiced and pickled cabbage that was eaten before, during and after the meal.

It became apparent that our hostess intended to stay: She presented a business card, which introduced her as Mrs. Moon, the president of the restaurant, and began to feed us. Deftly using a pair of chopsticks to pluck up bits of food, she presented it in front of our faces, first one, then the other. She was at first oblivious to our discomfort ("What? You don't like Korean food?") but eventually decided to explain.

"In Korea, when you come to a room salon the women feed you. You like women, don't you?" She laughed shyly and put her hand over her mouth.

She asked a lot of questions. Where were we from? Yes, the United States was a very great place. What kind of jobs did we have? Oh, that must pay a lot of money. She was fishing for something.

We mostly wanted to eat, but to the unaccustomed palate, Korean food can be hard to take. There was nothing elegant or subtle about it. The kimchi was fiery, like the result of some Polish grandmother gone mad with the Tabasco sauce. The meat, marinated beef called *bulgoki,* was cooked on a charcoal brazier but came off as tough and stringy as when it started. There were other unidentified dishes we ignored as we quickly arrived at a rule for survival: Never eat anything you can see your own reflection in.

"In the evening," Mrs. Moon continued, "it is the pretty young girls who will feed you. Not the old women like me."

"You're not old," London protested gallantly but insincerely.

Mrs. Moon flashed a momentary smile, a remembrance perhaps of more lustful times, then continued what was increasingly sounding like a practiced pitch.

"No, the young girls are better for you. I have some very beautiful young girls who work here." She pronounced the word be-*yoo*-ti-ful, and said it a dozen times. "They are beautiful girls who would like to meet some Americans. They work tonight. You come back tonight, okay?"

We told her we were very tired, but that maybe sometime later we would come back and see the beautiful girls. She was insistent.

"You must meet them. I think they are upstairs. I will bring them to meet you now. You wait."

So we waited, feeling fatigued and foolish while we drained a couple of bottles of the local OB beer. She returned in 15 minutes with a plaintive smile on her face but no beautiful girls.

"They are very shy. But you come tonight to meet them. I think maybe they will like you and go out with you." Then she actually winked.

We were slow, but the scheme was dawning on us.

"How much?" asked Kelly.

"One hundred twenty-five U.S. for the night," she replied a little too crisply.

We said we'd think about it and left in a hurry with Mrs. Moon calling behind us, "Tonight! You come back tonight!"

At that point all we wanted was a couple of Hilton Hotel beds in a dark quiet room. The map showed that the most direct route was through *nomdaemun,* the market district that spreads out from the ancient south gate of the city. The open-air market is one of the two largest in Seoul (the other being *tongdaemun,* or East Gate), a city of hundreds of markets and hundreds of thousands of small shops where everything is for sale all the time. Need a pair of Reebok sneakers at 4 A.M.? Try any of a dozen downtown subway tunnels. Perhaps a fresh hog's head? There are food stalls in every alley. How about a stainless steel industrial sink? There are plenty of 24-hour outlets.

The South Gate Market was jammed at 4 P.M. Now that lunch was over, food for supper seemed a priority for the thousands of small women in flower-print dresses who poked and prodded at baskets of dried squid, basins of live carp or ropes of greasy sausage. In one half-block stretch, the stalls offered a dozen kinds of dried fish, bags of white and red beans, cooked noodles served from cast iron vats, lustrous red chili peppers, flowers, army boots, plastic sandals, men's suits, bathing suits, T-shirts advertising everything from the Washington Redskins to the Seoul Olympics (that Tony the Tiger ripoff again), ELVIS brand blue jeans, live eels and turtles, inflated beach balls, chrome-plated kitchen chairs and used air compressors.

All the stalls lining the 20-square blocks of the market were open for business; there were no vacant storefronts, practically no vacant sidewalk space. People pushed and shoved their way through firmly, using elbows, hips and knees to gain leverage. Adding to the controlled chaos were deliverymen, most hauling stacks of goods on back frames made of old chairs, some balancing four or five cases of bottled soda on the back of a bicycle. Occasionally a car would try to get through, a feat that seemed impossible. But like a python swallowing a pig, the crowd somehow created a channel as it slithered around the vehicle. Once we nearly tripped over a crippled dwarf who struggled to push a cart of shoes. He, too, moved at his own pace and the crowd made an accommodation.

As we walked uphill toward the hotel, the crowd thinned. Coming toward us was a man staggering back and forth across the alley, bouncing off unconcerned pedestrians, a caricature performance of a drunk. He was a stocky guy about 25 years old, his face puffy and smudged with dirt, his blue shirt torn open to reveal a muscular chest. We gave him a wide berth as he weaved his way up to a stall selling gum, soda and other notions. With a roar and a sweep of his arm, he wiped the contents from the counter onto the street. The owner, a woman half his size, stepped in front of him and started shouting.

The drunk steadied himself and peered at the woman in amazement, then he lunged at her with both arms outstretched and knocked her to the ground, toppling part of the canvas stall around her. This got the crowd's attention and a few people stopped to stare. Someone, we figured, would haul this guy off—and we sure hoped it wouldn't have to be one of us.

We were right. But it was not a good Samaritan. It was the woman who owned the stall. She shook her head clear and bounded to her feet—all five feet two inches of her—like an NFL running back springing from a pileup. She balled her fist and let fly with a sock to the drunk's jaw that could be heard up and down the street. Now people were really paying attention.

She grabbed his hair with her left hand and began pounding the side of his face with roundhouse rights that had him crying for help. Her face was hard and flat like a Mongolian warrior, accentuated by a tight bun of steel gray hair. Her lips were pressed together in a fearsomely cold expression that never changed while her fist made plump, meaty sounds as it splatted into his cheek again and again.

Finally reinforcements came in the form of a couple of

male shopkeepers whose goal seemed to be protecting the drunk from the enraged woman. They sent him on his way, with tears streaming down his face, while the woman put her chewing gum back in order. The momentarily distracted spectators shrugged and hurried off. No big deal.

We walked to the end of the market, taking great care not to jostle anyone on the street. We passed an olive green bus, idling in an alley. The windows were covered with thick metal screens but through the door we could see seats filled with soldiers in riot gear—black shields, flak jackets, visored helmets and heavy batons—all wearing the same flinty expression as the woman shopkeeper. We learned later that a student demonstration had been planned for that day and that the government always responded with force. So, it seemed, did everyone in Korea.

When we returned to the hotel, we discovered that nap time was not to be. An American we knew from Washington had called to invite us to dinner. Chun had called too, four times, but we told him we were in for the night. We had had all the Korea we could handle for one day. We'd have dinner with the American, talk baseball, maybe drink a few Budweisers.

Doug picked us up in his white, four-door Daewoo sedan driven by a former Korean farmer who now earned the astronomical sum of $100 a month. "This looks a little pretentious," he admitted, "but I would never drive myself in this town. Everywhere you go in Asia they say they have the worst drivers. But Korea has the worst drivers."

Doug was a consultant for several American companies trying, with little success, to gain a foothold in the inhospitable Korean market. He took us to dinner at a Japanese-style seafood restaurant where women did not feed us.

"You must have been in some cheap *kiseang* house," he said when we told him of our luncheon. "You shouldn't be in there unless you're with someone who knows what he's doing." The name translates as room salon, he explained, and it is a staple of Korean nightlife. The houses, a Korean version of Japanese geisha houses, are generally used by upper-income business executives to entertain clients and colleagues. They range from expensive to very expensive, with dinner alone often costing over $100 a person for the meal and the privilege of conversing with the hostesses. After dinner is something else again.

"If he wants, the host can wave his hand and say to a guest, 'You like the girl? Take her for the night.' It's one of the great displays of power."

It's also not that common. "Korean men would rather be out drinking with each other. They want to get away from their wives and they like to see a pretty face, but I don't get the feeling they are the horniest people around."

The disease of choice among Korean males is intestinal rather than venereal. Korea has one of the highest rates of stomach cancer in the world and a very high incidence of ulcers. The reason is not complicated. Start with about three heaping bowls of kimchi a day, add enormous consumption of hard liquor—straight Scotch for the rich, potato liquor or rice wine for the common man—and compress it all with the pressure-cooker tensions of a booming and intensely competitive economy and you have a stew that would eat through galvanized pipe.

"Sit in the steamroom of a health club sometime and see how many guys have stomach scars from ulcer operations," Doug said. "It's kind of like a badge of achievement. This is a very hard country. Men are men here, or they pretend to be. There is an attitude that 'we will tolerate any amount of pain to succeed.' Even the wealthy. You see them playing golf in the winter in their shirt sleeves. For God's sake, they can afford jackets."

After dinner we wandered around the downtown nightclub district where the bars—for students, working class or corporate class—were filled. We walked downstairs to one establishment that announced "Karaoke Club." A leering maitre d' inquired whether we would like a table.

"Is this another B-girl joint?" Kelly asked.

Quickly it became apparent that it was not. A man in a well-made suit and unknotted tie stood at the end of the bar holding a silver microphone and singing that lounge lizard standard, "Feelings," only he pronounced it fee-rings. Red-faced and sweating, eyes closed, he hugged the mike and crooned, "Fee-rings, whoa, whoa, whoa fee-rings, again in my hot," to the appreciative howls of his very drunk colleagues, some of whom had tears streaming down their faces. Karaoke bars, another transplant from Japan, feature an open mike and taped background music of popular songs. Patrons are encouraged to express themselves while being backed up by the likes of the Nelson Riddle orchestra or Frank Sinatra's best arrangers.

Groups sat around tables and passed ceramic cups back and forth, all the while seeming to pour a steady stream of *yakju,* a milky, slightly sweet but potent rice wine, from a long-necked jug. The tradition when drinking in Korea is never to pour one's own drink; that would be considered greedy and self-centered. "Even a monk cannot shave his own head," goes the Korean proverb. When you have finished the first round, it is proper to hand the cup to someone else at the table and then fill it for him. Another person will soon pass you a cup and fill it. It is a nice ritual though indifferent to sanitary considerations; it also allows one evil-intended soul in a party to set a very quick drinking pace.

At the workers' bars, the tradition carried on but the drink was *soju,* a clear potato-derived alcohol that tastes like cheap, diluted vodka. The small, brightly lit bars were hot with energy and emotion. While the men drank, they ate snacks of peanuts or dried cuttlefish that came in plastic packs. These were opened not by tearing gently, but by slapping the bag between two hands, causing them to burst with a loud pop. Fists pounded tables to drive home points of argument, flushed faces contorted in laughter or crumpled in tears. Once the doors of a bar burst open, like a scene from a John Wayne movie, and a pack of combatants spilled into the street for a brief and futile exchange of blows that ended with weeping and hugs. The Koreans have been called the Irish of Asia, but that night the term took on new meaning.

At another bar we met a couple of Doug's Korean friends, both government officials with good jobs. They were introduced as Mr. Lee and Mr. Park, names far more common in Korea than Smith and Jones in the United States. We remained on that formal basis throughout the evening.

"I've known them both for a couple of years," Doug explained, "and even though they call me by my first name, they prefer that I use Mr."

Koreans are formal people in some respects. Little brothers defer to older brothers, as do junior schoolmates. Familiarity and friendship among Korean males take many years to earn.

After a dozen rounds of swapped glasses, we headed south through the fashionable retail district called Myong Dong—the carrot that hung in front of at least some of Korea's energetic population because this was where the good stuff was on display. Names like Pierre Cardin, Christian Dior and Sergio Valente adorned gleaming storefront windows that showcased mannequins in contorted poses. The fashions, which were far more common in the windows than in the street, were mostly Western, as were the models. At Shinsegae's, the giant department store, the mannequins were lithe California-looking blondes with spiky coifs and tight smiles.

At 10 P.M. on a weeknight the traffic-free streets were jammed with window-shoppers, mostly men in blue suits or women dressed for success, and sometimes both, arm-in-arm. These were not the uniformed automatons one might expect from the vantage point of the United States. Myong Dong was not exactly Fifth Avenue on Christmas Eve, but it wasn't far off—and in that observation came at least a perverse amount of reassurance. With wealth came wants, it always had, and why should the Koreans be any different?

At the Chosun Hotel disco they had a British disc jockey and a dance floor filled with women in black dresses and pearls. A guy in a blue blazer and yellow Lacoste shirt introduced himself as John-somebody from Taiwan.

"Pull up a chair, gents," he said in English learned somewhere between Choate and St. Paul's. He and his pals—one from Hong Kong, one from Singapore—worked for a big American commodity trading company. They were in Seoul for a meeting and found it "very alive, but not too high class." They preferred Tokyo. We all swapped cards in the best networking style. "Keep in touch," John said when we left.

"One more, one more drink," Mr. Park proposed with determination. Drinking in Korea, we had been told, was an endurance contest. We were enduring. Five of us piled in a cab and headed to the Itaewon district, on the other side of Namsan Mountain.

"Itaewon is where the foreign invaders have always camped," Mr. Park explained. He found no irony in explaining that the U.S. 8th Army was currently headquartered there. Mr.

Park, who was from a well-connected family and seemed a conservative, mainstream sort of fellow, was friendly to us personally, but no fan of the United States. He wanted the United States out of his country politically and economically. He favored the Japanese development model that called for the production of goods for export and protectionist trade barrier at home. He greatly resented the pressure from the United States for Korea to open its markets. The United States, he felt, was just another colonial power that still exercised considerable control over Korea's government.

"Look at what happened at Kwangju," he said.

It was not the first time we had heard the word. Kwangju was a city in the south where there had been a bloody demonstration in 1980 resulting in many deaths. Some Koreans said the U.S. Army was involved.

"What happened at Kwangju?" Kelly asked.

"Not tonight," said Doug. "Don't get him started." Just then the cab stopped in front of a neon-encrusted nightclub and the subject was dropped.

There were 40,000 GIs in Korea and all of them found their way to Itaewon at one time or another. Increasingly, Koreans, too, those with a few bucks in their pockets and looking for a good time, came to this garish strip of nightclubs, bars, hotels and whorehouses. This seemed like the tawdry Asia from the movies.

We headed for the Sportsman's Club, an Itaewon landmark that featured blinking red Christmas lights, soiled red tablecloths and an army of waitresses in short red polyester uniforms and flat white shoes. There were an equal number of GIs and Koreans in the bar, with neither group getting a look at the best the other had to offer. The GIs were large and loud and their shaved heads shone like dunce caps as they grabbed waitresses and terrorized bartenders. "You call this a drink? Put some bourbon in it, you little bastard." They were overgrown high school kids on their first class trip to the big city, showing the same bravado and hiding the same fear.

Doug recognized two Brits he knew, Bob and Alden, at a table near the dance floor.

"You've just missed the greatest good goddamn fight!" Bob greeted us. He was clapping and laughing. "Right there on the dance floor. A couple of these little guys started going at it for God knows why and then their *girlfriends* start fighting. It was a bloody mess. They're pulling hair and screaming."

"It was lovely fun," Alden agreed.

"These people are always fighting for nothing," said Bob. "I'd hate to get in their way when they want something."

We watched the dance floor for a few minutes and London spotted three girls dancing together. He headed off to cut in on them.

"He can forget it," said Mr. Lee. "They want to dance with each other." And once London got close, the three left the dance floor. It was then that we noticed that most of the dancing was among groups of men and groups of women.

"Let's all dance," said Mr. Lee, and with reluctance on the part of some, five men began to boogie to Donna Summer.

Mr. Lee, who had not been too talkative most of the night, was coming alive and turning pugnacious. He was a tae kwon do expert and wanted to start demonstrating holds and pressure points. Fortunately Mr. Park talked him out of it just before he passed out on the table. Mr. Park took Mr. Lee home.

The Brits were still afloat demonstrating that there was at least some starch left in the empire. Someone passed Bob a glass, Korean style.

"Cut that shit out," he said. "Drink your own drink." And so we did.

Bob was, by his own definition, a "silver spoon kid" from a well-to-do family, the product of public schools and bored to death with the stuffy opportunities of London. He had been in the Middle East before Korea, drawn, he said, by the excitement of places that were growing, not dying.

"We're a little farther ahead than you Yanks at learning how to live when things start slipping away. Those guys," he nodded his head toward a cluster of GIs at the bar, "don't even know the empire is over."

At the Catch Me Club we watched a dancer with a sad face. She had big eyes and a turned-down mouth and seemed all out of place in a black sequined top, G-string and high-heeled pumps. We all stared in drunken silence.

"She's a pretty girl," someone said.

"This whole continent really warps your perspective on

women," one of the Brits said. "When you look at one the first thing you think is how much?"

And how much was the question of the night. After midnight events became a blur of strip shows, women squirting beer on each other under a strobe light while second-rate disco played on first-rate sound systems and guys danced with guys until they stumbled out into the street. Huge burr-headed GIs whistled at girls and literally fell down drunk as they tried to make it to the top of Hooker Hill—the only battle you're likely to see in this man's war, son. Old women offered the services of young women and chased us down the street chanting, "Beautiful girls! Anything you want. Oral sex $15. What are you, a faggot?" And some of the girls were beautiful, lurking in doorways, licking their lips and laughing.

We made it to the top of Hooker Hill. "There's a great bar up there," said Bob the Brit. "It's a temple of bad taste."

The Sun Club was a shabby eight-by-twelve room washed in pink light and furnished with couches covered with antimacassars and shawls—a nightmare version of grandmother's parlor. There were a couple of girls there, but it was late and they weren't working very hard. The tape-deck played Bob Seger. ("Sometimes love don't feel like it should. It hurts so good.") Real music not disco. In an odd way, it was kind of homey. Bob ordered a gin and tonic, which he sipped as he sat with his arm around an aging—probably all of about 30—bar girl who was missing one of her front teeth.

"This is the saddest fucking place in the world," he said suddenly, not making clear whether he was talking about the bar or Korea. "It's so beat up and dirty. Nothing nice about it."

He paused and nuzzled the neck of the giggling bar girl with his nose.

"But they make you love it."

After a while, Bob the Brit decided to go upstairs with the woman. She hissed into his ear and pawed his chest. Doug was horrified.

"You must be crazy. She's filthy."

"Oh, she's not so bad. Are you, honey? There's plenty of girls here. Come on along. Enjoy it while you can."

"No, thanks."

"Suit yourselves," Bob said, and went up the stairs.

After he was gone, Alden said, "He pays them real well too. It's like some kind of penance."

We got back to the hotel at about dawn, beyond tired. Out the window we could see apartment rooftops across the street. On one was a man wearing what looked like long underwear. He seemed to be dancing, hopping from one foot to the other, twisting and turning. T'ai chi, probably, the ritual aerobic dance. Many Koreans, we had heard, were very disciplined about exercising early in the morning. But there was someone else on the rooftop. A woman had a long board in her hand, like a 2×4, and she was swinging it at the man. She was chasing him around the rooftop trying to bash him—for what? coming home at dawn?—while he danced nimbly out of her way, no doubt well practiced at the art. Who said this country had no culture? Here was a silent Korean ballet performed in the fabled mists of the Land of the Morning Calm.

We had been in Asia for 36 hours and sensed it was not going to get any easier to understand.

Our search to learn something about the Olympics led us to Lee Yong Ho. He in turn led us to the 10th century.

It started when London was flipping through an Olympics brochure and noticed that Lee had graduated from Amherst College in Massachusetts, where London earned his degree. We decided to see if old school ties were as significant a bond as the Koreans often said and called Lee's office.

"I'll meet you at your hotel in two hours," he said without hesitating.

He arrived precisely on time, looking like an Amherst man of 1959 should look: white polo shirt, pale blue golf sweater, navy slacks, tasseled loafers over yellow socks. He was in fact just coming from a round of golf, an addiction that was beginning to consume the country's elite.

"I'm retiring," he joked without smiling. He explained that he was stepping down as sports minister now that the planning and negotiations for the Olympics were over. A more experienced administrator would take charge.

Lee was an academic by training but he projected the cold efficiency of a Korean executive. He was terse and unsmiling, though willing to cooperate. If we asked a question, he answered.

He had just finished putting together a $300-million deal with NBC for the television rights to the Games. It had not been easy. Executives of the American network considered the Seoul Games a risky bet. The country does not have the romantic allure of Europe, they argued, or the curiosity value of the Soviet Union. The time difference—Korea is 14 hours ahead of New York—would make scheduling difficult. The only thing certain about the internal political situation was that a cadre of radical students and workers would love an opportunity to disrupt the Games and the police would love to bust the heads of anyone who tried. Lee worked out a shared-risk deal where Korea was guaranteed a base sum of $300 million and a percentage of excess advertising revenues. If the Games were a big success, the Koreans could end up making quite a bit more than the $300 million, though some in the government felt the initial figure was too low and had criticized Lee.

"These Games are making people crazy," he shrugged. But like many Koreans we met, he had a sense of pinch-me-I'm-dreaming amazement that he had cut a deal for *any* amount of money with one of the most imposing institutions in the world. Modesty is a Confucian virtue and the Koreans tried to maintain their dignity, but times were so good that many were fairly bursting to tell the world about their newfound fortune—as if the boast might somehow confirm its reality. Lee was no exception.

"There were times when I was sitting in huge offices in New York with all these very serious American executives and I would think to myself, 'This is not so bad for someone who grew up eating tree bark.' "

Tree bark again.

"You didn't literally eat tree bark, did you?" Kelly asked.

"Oh sure. From pine trees. Not the bark on the outside, but the skin under the bark. And sometimes roots, or old bean stems. May was called 'barley hump' month. Sometimes the hump went into June. The crops weren't ready to harvest yet and the winter stores had run out. It was that way most years. When the Japanese ruled the country they left you little. Then through the war years, the crops were bad. No one had money to buy food. You ate what you could grow or find."

"How did bark taste?"

"How do you think? Terrible. The women would boil it into some kind of cake. But it was something filling to sit in your stomach. We didn't know any better, it was the way things were done for centuries. Except in the best times, I think there was always barley hump month. You see, my generation has come a few centuries in 40 or 50 years."

Lee was from a small farming village in the south central part of the country, about 150 miles from Seoul. He said his odyssey from feudal rice paddies to Rockefeller Center was not untypical of many of the country's emerging rank of business and political leaders.

"My generation was different. We knew what it was to have nothing. But we were not like the earlier generations, because we wanted to have more. We grew up hungry and we are still hungry—but it is a different kind of hunger."

It happened that Lee was planning a rare visit to his hometown of Ok Chung and he invited us to accompany him. "You cannot understand what my country is, until you see what it was," he said.

Early one morning we left Seoul on the Kyongbu Expressway, a well-engineered road that goes through Taegu, an industrial city in the central area, and ends in Pusan, Korea's second-largest city and the major port. Even at 7 A.M., traffic was heavy on the road close to Seoul. Trucks laden with machinery and produce almost outnumbered the cars, many of which were driven by blue-suited office workers headed downtown. The Seoul metropolitan area contains about one-quarter of Korea's 42 million people. Pusan has another five million with the other major cities of Taegu, Inchon, Kwangju adding another three million. In all, 15 million people, or one-third of the population, are still considered rural dwellers, though the percentage continues to drop as more and more farmers move to the urban areas.

Once outside the limits of Seoul, the countryside became sparsely populated. Between Seoul and Taegu is mostly farmland, or at least patches of it slipped in among the craggy ridges that form so much of the peninsula. Korea is a hard, cracked country that looks as though someone squeezed the peninsula together into a series of ripples and then baked it dry. The ridges, of ancient limestone and granite formations, are among the world's oldest dating to the pre-Cambrian period. The rock is worn and leeched of minerals, making the one-fifth of Korea that is flat a poor place to grow anything.

But on its own terms, much of the scenery was beautiful. The harsh rocks were softened by fringes of pine, maple and oak trees while the narrow valleys brimmed with white mist. It was for this sight that ancient Chinese poets named Korea "Land of the Morning Calm."

Lee explained that in some places the proliferation of trees was a modern phenomenon, spurred by the resurgence in national pride that came as the country emerged from the shock of the Korean War.

"After the war, whole valleys were scraped bare," he said. "The government started Arbor Days when people were expected to plant trees. Now it is an obsession. We have great reverence for trees because they are one of the only things that grow well here."

We stopped for breakfast at a gleaming orange-and-white roadside restaurant, the equal of anything Interstate 95 in Maryland has to offer, though the English-language menu featured a few puzzling items such as Ham Burger and Jerry Fish. "This is all new," Lee explained. "What you see is the start of the car culture, like you have in the States. Up until maybe two or three years ago, only the wealthiest people could afford a car. Now you see people taking their families for Sunday drives. Not the factory workers yet, but supervisors as well as executives and professors."

We paused at the site of a favorite Korean excursion, Folk Village, which was the closest thing to Disneyland in Korea and a place the Tourist Board's Mr. Chun had been determined we see. The village is a re-creation of life as it has been lived in Korea from the Middle Ages to the 1960s.

The traditional Korean house was a mud-walled, thatch-roofed hut of three or four rooms, built over a channeled floor called an *ondol* that drew heat from the cooking fire and distributed it under the rooms. The windows and sliding doors were made of rice paper, effective at blocking the wind, but not too helpful at keeping the place warm. To keep from freezing, the inhabitants had to maintain their rear ends as close to the floor as possible. For prosperous families, wings might be added to the main house to allow sons and daughters-in-law to move in. Eventually, this arrangement created courtyards, where the farm animals would be tethered. Farming was the sole occupation of practically all of the Korean population until the 1960s.

The folk village was filled with Korean tourists of all generations, and they amounted to centuries worth of stratified layers of rock laid bare in one sample. The grandparents still wore traditional silk pajamas, the parents were in conservative business suits and dresses while the children dressed in knock-off Levi's and genuine Reebok sneakers. A man squatted on his haunches in the dining room of one house as he explained to his son that this was how grandpa sat. The child stared at him blankly. Why would anyone want to squat where there were chairs? For the children, this will soon be the only reminder of the old, hard life.

What began to change the rural culture—and, some Koreans would argue, the mentality of the entire country—was the *saemaul* or New Community Movement. Begun in 1971 by the government of Park Chung Hee, the ingeniously conceived plan played to the Koreans' sense of shame and competition. In the beginning, building materials such as concrete were made available to villages to create civic projects. The villages built schools, waterways and roads—some much more successfully than others. Subsequent awards were based on performance. The villages that did the best, got the most.

"Korea was not always this hardworking country you see now," explained Lee. "We were lazy and after the war, many of us felt defeated. Because of the land reform laws after the Japanese left, it was difficult for a man to own more than three hectares (7.4 acres) of land. There was no incentive to work. In the late 1950s, you are talking about a country where the per capita income was $100 and no one cared. I do not know if it was intentional or not, but *saemaul* was brilliant because it made people care.

"We are very much a shame culture. It is part of the Confucian tradition, that part about doing things so as not to lose face. If your neighbor's children do better at school, you lose face. You are shamed. *Saemaul* converted that feeling to whole towns. One town had a better bridge or school building, so the neighbors tried to do better still. The government was good at recognizing this was happening and promoting it."

New electrical and water systems built by the government followed and eventually highways connected towns that had been isolated from one another forever. Individuals began to rebuild their own homes, replacing thatch roofs with tile and mud sides with concrete. Everyone became involved in the schools. Always schools. Among the mountain valleys, great slabs of white-painted concrete were mortared together to make austere but efficient schoolhouses where government teachers could begin the task of educating through high school all the children of Korea.

The evidence still stands. As we drove south on the expressway we could see the newer blockhouse buildings all over. If it was not a particularly attractive architecture—or any architecture at all—it was certainly practical. Tear down the old, make way for the new. There is nothing sentimental about the progress of Korea. But then restoring 18th-century farmhouses is a luxury reserved for places like the United States, where people aren't in such a hurry.

Yet the *saemaul* towns were positively quaint compared to another modern Korean phenomenon: the industrial city. Coming upon the flat plain that contains Taegu, the largest of these, is like stumbling upon a vast secret army camp as the troops are preparing for war. The city stretched for miles along the valley floor. The sky was riven with tall, thin smokestacks crowned by white plumes. Each stack rose from a pile of square blocks, many the size of skyscrapers turned on their sides. At intervals were relentless rows of apartment houses. They stood at attention, five abreast and 10 or 15 ranks deep, emblazoned with the name of the company whose workers they housed: Samsung, Daewoo, Hyundai—names that at the time were barely familiar to us. These were factories as large as anything in Detroit or Cleveland, yet who were these companies? Weren't the giants of Asia all Japanese names that came attached to cars or TV sets, names such as Nissan, Toyota and Mitsubishi?

We exited the expressway here and, after a few short turns, we were lost. "I was here a year ago and I've never seen some of this," Lee said, grimacing. "It keeps changing."

Many of the roads were still so new they had yet to be paved. We dodged among squeaking tractor trailers piled with six-inch pipe, I-beams, bales of textiles and electric motors. We passed factory gates from beyond which came the sounds of things being made: the grinding and tearing of metal, the hiss of steam, the flat whack of pneumatic hammers and from one a sound like the gentle swooshing of a room full of butterflies—it was hundreds of women at sewing machines.

Two million people live here and they produce goods, not services. Taegu was startling evidence of what makes Korea "an industrial platform," as the economists like to say. The country is ideally suited to making things. Seoul had seemed an efficient factory with its housing, transportation and plants so well-linked. But there were too many distractions in Seoul. There were lots of restaurants and store windows in Seoul; a man's wife might see a dress she wanted or his friends might want to meet him in a bar. In Taegu there was only the company. Here was a super company town—and Lee said there are dozens of smaller ones. These towns take in the raw material to make steel and turn it into the wire, pipe and plates that become trucks and office buildings and videocassette recorders. There are, to be sure, hundreds of shops that make flimsy stuffed dolls and cheap watches and the other effluvia with which Korea is associated in the minds of American consumers. In the recent past, the words Made in Korea were always attached to novelties, oddities, things of little value. They were, one imagined, produced by grim-faced drones who labored in unheated factory lofts and scurried home well after dark to slurp a bowl of soup and collapse until the next shift.

But two things were immediately apparent about Taegu: Those factories were churning out products of much higher value than stuffed dolls, and the lives of the workers were not according to Charles Dickens. Which is not to say Taegu, as opposed to downtown Seoul, gives the slightest hint of offering anything but the barest necessities. In fact, the endless rows of blockhouse apartments, combined with the lingering impression of endless rows of riot-helmeted police, made us think that perhaps George Orwell or Franz Kafka was the more relevant author, though we didn't know enough about the lives of Taegu's inhabitants to say so with any certainty. It only seemed apparent that those lives, while hard and tightly programmed, were not nasty, brutish or short.

After a few tries, we finally found the road to Ok Chung, an increasingly narrow highway that eventually became two lanes of unpaved red clay. We passed through a few cluttered towns—crossroads, really—where hundreds of people on motorcycles whizzed back and forth across the main street, maneuvering amid belching trucks. Farther on, the trucks were rarely in evidence. On the roadside, men stooping under the weight of burlap sacks lumbered along. In the iridescent green rice fields, numerous duets were performed by man and buffalo. The farmhouses were no longer cast from the concrete majesty of the *saemaul* projects. Instead they were made in the centuries-old style of tile roofs perched on gracefully curving eaves.

Some miles after we left the paved road, we came on a construction crew that was chewing at the earth with yellow bulldozers and backhoes, widening the road and preparing it for paving.

"Ah, so progress is finally coming to my home," Lee said. "Pretty soon the roads will be everywhere in Korea."

Ok Chung, though, was not even a crossroads. It was more of a smudge, a hamlet of 30 or 40 houses cradled among pine-furred ridges and a deep-pile carpet of rice plants. Lee's ancestral home was toward the end of the valley, a tiny compound behind a broken fence. A soapy rivulet ran along a path that led to a 40-foot by 15-foot shoebox of a house set atop a three-foot-high concrete foundation. The front was formed with sliding wood frames covered in paper. The four rooms were cubes laid side by side: two bedrooms, a living room and a dining room, all sparely furnished with low tables and ornate chests. Sleeping mats lay rolled in the corners.

Lee's stepmother waded through a squawking flock of chickens to greet him. His youngest sister was there and several cousins from nearby villages. His mother died when he was young and his father had remarried. Now his father, too, was dead and, other than his life in Seoul, this was all the family he had left.

The reunion seemed formal and terse. After just a few minutes of conversation all the men tucked their legs underneath them and sat at the dining room table. The women laid out bowl after bowl of food: several kinds of kimchi, clams in hot sauce, cold squid, soup in which chicken parts floated. We ate with silver chopsticks and drank cool barley tea.

Lee explained that not much had changed since he left more than 30 years ago—and not much had changed in the 300 years before that.

"This is a small farming village, one of thousands like it in Korea," he said. "Life is as it has always been. There is the planting and the harvest. The women cook the meals and the men are served. There is not much to life. Even the good years are not really good years. No one here is going to get rich."

The village now has phone service and electricity—an electric fan swept the lunch table and a radio sat nearby—but in winter, heat still comes from wood burned under the floor. Within the confines of the valley there is not much arable land, so a family only has a few acres. Many farmers survive because prices for rice and other produce are kept artificially high by the government, which is primarily concerned about the political force of the farmers who vote out of proportion to their numbers and have long supported the parties in power. Another concern is that Korea could become dependent on foreign sources of food.

At lunch, Lee asked about crop prices and how the harvest looked, but he seemed quite uninterested. There was nothing about him that suggested he was a man of this place. Life here was slow and all about months of work to make a bag of grain. Even among the shoes lined up outside the house, his polished black loafers danced away from the worn, mud-spattered footwear of his relatives. (Though the greatest contrast was with Kelly's worn-out basketball sneakers, which consistently attracted stares. Koreans may not have been fashion plates, but they were never shabby. Leave it to the Americans to wear shoes with holes in them.)

Lunch was over surprisingly soon. Lee went off to visit graves, first of his mother and father, who shared a plot at the bottom of the valley near the paddies, and then to his grandmother's up the hillside. At each he took off his shoes, knelt and bowed his head to the ground for a minute of Buddhist prayer. Then he made the sign of the cross. The pious display belied his, and many Koreans', less-than-fervent adherence to religious beliefs. As they are in many things, the Koreans are pragmatists when it comes to God.

"In my family we have Buddhist, Christian and Confucian traditions," he explained later. "I'm not sure which we believe in most. I look at it as three forms of insurance. One of them is probably right."

He trudged beyond his grandmother's grave to the top of a hill that surveyed the valley. Standing in a cool breeze he recalled how, when he was 15, he had watched from there as columns of North Korean troops moved into the valley. He had run all night to tell the commander of a South Korean detachment. The south attacked and the result was a battle which destroyed much of the village.

But it was not the past that was on Lee's mind that afternoon. The future was what moved Lee Yong Ho. It was that drive to go beyond the walls of the valley that got him out of Ok Chung in the first place and when he returned, he saw not the soil his ancestors tilled for centuries nor the roads they trod nor the graves that held their bones. What he saw was an investment opportunity.

"What I really would like is to take one of these valleys and put in a resort, with a Swiss chalet hotel. Up there, on the hillside. Picture a chalet. And down there we would dam the stream and flood over all the rice paddies to make a great blue lake. People could come from Seoul for a civilized holiday. Good food, hiking in the mountains. Boating. Maybe someday I could buy up this whole valley and flood it. It would be a great idea, don't you think?"

We drove to the elementary school at Chun San—the center of rural life for neighboring hamlets like Ok Chung—where Lee was to present a contribution to the athletic fund. He was greeted at the entrance with stern, formal bows by a delegation of town fathers: the mayor, school principal, police chief and several prominent farmers. Everyone removed his shoes and slipped on plastic sandals as we marched into the principal's office and sat in an array of stuffed armchairs around a long, low table. Lee sat at the head, looking much different from the others with his styled hair, blue blazer and crisp shirt and tie. The burghers of Chun San wore ample shirts, like Mexican *guyaberas,* open at the neck and untucked at the waist.

There was, for a few minutes, an uneasy silence as a woman poured everyone small glasses of soda or beer. The principal picked up a fly swatter and began hunting flies with fierce whacks. The burghers of Chun San nervously cleared their throats. Finally the mayor proposed a toast to the most famous son of Ok Chung, a man who had left behind the simple rural life and soared to the top of the government in the best tradition of the new Korea.

Lee thanked them and handed over a check, sparking a new round of bows and smiles. The money was to be for expansion of the tennis court that an earlier contribution of Lee's had built in the school yard. The principal said we would all go to see the magnificent new court, but first we had to finish the beer.

No one spoke until Lee began asking questions about the crops. Apples were good, garlic not so good, pepper okay. The population of Chun San had declined from 8,000 to 3,000 in 20 years. How you gonna keep 'em down on the farm after they've seen Seoul? was the lament. Much of what went on in the valley was small-time inefficient farming, the limited acreage making mechanization unaffordable. Serious industrial farming was just being undertaken by some of the giant Korean corporations. Lee mentioned that the Hyundai company was starting a vast plantation built on landfill in the Yellow Sea on the west coast. The burghers nodded gravely. They were part of the one-third of the Korean population still engaged in farming and from their comments it was apparent that they didn't think it was such a good thing for the country to lose many more of them to the manufacturing sector.

When the beers were finished, we walked to the school yard, in the center of which a group of boys were playing baseball using an aluminum bat and a scuffed yellow tennis ball. In the far corner of the yard was an empty tennis court. The net sagged and the clay had not been rolled in months, causing it to erode in a pattern of valleys and cracks. The principal beamed as he stretched out his arms to introduce the court. Lee's face was impassive as he nodded.

Didn't anyone play? he inquired.

Well, of course, replied the principal. Tennis was very popular in Chun San. Just not today.

The problem, Lee gleaned, was that almost no one in town

had a tennis racket. And the relatively few balls quickly found their way into stickball games. He had thought the town might be ready to build a second court, but now he suggested to the principal that his donation go toward equipment. The principal nodded a little too vigorously and smiled the emotionless smile of an instinctive politician.

"They think I'm foolish," Lee said later. "But they should realize it might be good for their kids if they could play a game like tennis. What happens when they get to Seoul? Or the United States? You want to make a good impression if you're going to have ambitions beyond the rice paddies."

When Lee Yong Ho was born in 1935 rice paddies were everyone's future. Korea was a Japanese colony and well on its way to becoming a part of Japan. For centuries the Japanese had dominated Korea, invading and plundering almost at will. After Japan won the Russo-Japanese War in 1905, Korea became one of its spoils. Finally, in 1910, the Japanese coerced an impotent Korean government to formally annex themselves to Japan. There were no protests from the West, where Korea was considered an inconsequential feudal society and suitable meat to quell the hunger of expansion-minded Japan.

The Japanese moved quickly to establish firm control and stamp out any nationalist dissent. Korea was to be one of the feedstocks to fuel Japan's engines of conquest. Particularly in the north, Korea had natural resources; it had a relatively docile work force and a strategic location. Whatever signs of revolt emerged were brutally crushed by the Japanese military police. Over the years, thousands of demonstrators were killed during protests.

By the time Lee Yong Ho was born, Japan was ready to launch its campaign to establish the East Asia Co-Prosperity Sphere and Korea was an early outpost. Japanization was the operative word as the Japanese took firm control over the judicial system and installed a new school curriculum that drilled Japanese language and culture and eliminated references to Korea. The few businesses were Japanese owned and managed with profits repatriated to Japan. Some new roads, rail lines, bridges and ports were built, but their intent was military. Korea became a key staging ground for Japan's invasion of China and as the Japanese war machine geared up for greater expeditions, hundreds of thousands of Korean men were drafted as laborers to fill jobs vacated by Japanese entering the army.

In many ways the young Lee was sheltered from the Japanese and the Second World War by the meanness of his own existence. Times were tough in Ok Chung, as they had always been. "Nothing much changed, season after season," he recalled. "We would sometimes hear news of the war. These great events all over the world. It made us feel very small and insignificant."

When the Japanese surrendered to the Allies in August 1945, Koreans realized just how insignificant they were. Instead of enjoying instant liberation, they were again pawns at the mercy of competing superpowers. In the closing days of the war the tenuous alliance between the Soviet Union and the United States was coming unglued. Korea—much like Germany—was in the middle. As the Soviet army closed in from Manchuria to the north, the United States took quick action to divide the country. The line they drew was practically random and had the effect of isolating all the country's natural resources on one side, but this seemed of little concern. It was, after all, only Korea. The 38th parallel was the agreed demarcation; the Soviets accepted Japanese surrenders to the north and the United States took charge of the south. But the Soviets had dreams beyond administering an armistice. They soon helped Kim Il Sung establish a pro-Soviet, socialist government and began to feed him a significant supply of arms.

The United States was far less efficient. The plan had been to establish a military government that would reconstruct the country, much as General Douglas MacArthur was doing in Japan. The chieftains would be Americans with some experienced Japanese administrators kept on and Koreans only in lower-level positions. The plan may have made intellectual sense, but on an emotional level it offered nothing to a population jubilantly emerging from four decades in bondage and unwilling to submit to anyone else's dictates. The Koreans were going to make their own government whatever the cost and, through an elected legislature, chose Syngman Rhee, a 73-year-old political dissident with a doctorate from Princeton University. For most Koreans, Rhee was the first Korean leader in their lifetimes.

Rhee's ascendancy provided the first twinges of national

pride many Koreans had ever felt. Lee was in junior high school when he heard of this man with a Princeton Ph.D. and vowed that, whatever it was, he would have one. "Here was a Korean—a *Korean!*—who had been to school in the United States, who had talked to President Truman, who had *told* President Truman what Korea wanted. You can't know what that meant."

But if there were such stirrings in the hearts of 12-year-old boys, there was not much happening among their elders. Rhee inherited a demoralized, confused nation with no indigenous economy or system of government; no resources to speak of; hundreds of thousands of homeless refugees from the north as well as those returning from Japan and an increasingly strong military force north of the 38th parallel.

What Lee saw around him was fatalism. People's lives were controlled by forces beyond their comprehension, and that included everything from the rain to foreign armies. It had been that way forever in Korea. So no one worked hard, no one took care of their clothes or their houses. Why bother?

Only one person in Lee's life did not hold such a philosophy. From an early age, his grandmother told him there was something better to life, there was a way to improve. "She had no real education herself, but she knew things about the world. And somehow she knew I could go see that world. She taught me not to give up."

Lee's grandmother did something else for him. She taught him Chinese characters. Koreans speak Hangul, their own language, but in much of their writing the phonetic sounds are represented by traditional Chinese pictographs. There are more than 2,000 such characters and just to read a newspaper one must understand the 300 or 400 most common ones. For a farm boy to have learned them at an early age was a major accomplishment. So when Lee boarded a bus—his first ever—for the five-hour trip to the nearest high school, he was already something of a prodigy.

The Korean War really only lasted for one year—one astonishingly brutal year of armies dragging themselves back and forth across the Korean landscape and slaughtering each other or freezing to death in the harsh winter. It began on June 25, 1950, when hundreds of thousands of North Korean troops poured over the border. They had been given the motive with a statement by U.S. Secretary of War Dean Acheson that indicated that Korea was beyond our sphere of interest. For whatever misguided reason, the United States had decided that Korea was not worth rehabilitating, nor was it of strategic importance. The North had been given the means by the Soviet Union, which generously supplied them with tons of munitions. By the end of the summer, the South Koreans were in a rout. A last-ditch defensive perimeter was set up around Pusan; Lee's village was in a no-man's-land which was overrun several times from both directions. Finally, the battle moved north where it raged until a truce was declared in July 1951.

The country was ground to pulp. Seoul had changed hands four times and was nothing but muddy rubble. Roads, bridges, farm fields and factories were in ruins. Millions of people were homeless. But while war is a horror, it also can be an opportunity. For Lee Yong Ho, as well as many Koreans of his generation, it was both. Those who survived the crucible of the Korean War came out as strong as iron, confident that there was nothing that could beat them.

Lee was sent to Pusan on a college scholarship. He took a train there—his first ever—and remembers the first time he saw a light bulb.

"Someone said to switch on the light and I didn't know what they meant. When they turned it on, I jumped. They were from the city and they laughed at me. But I learned fast."

He lived in a lean-to shack near the wartime campus of Yonsei University and all he did was work. If he wasn't in classes, he was working for the U.S. reconstruction forces. He learned to speak English and won a scholarship to Amherst College, one of several American universities that had agreed to take in Koreans. After days of travel—including his first airplane—he arrived in Massachusetts with $1 left in his pocket.

"It sounds like a story, but it was really my last dollar," explains Lee. He did not speak English well, but he could read and write. "Thank God for essay exams," he remembers. Eventually he made his way to Yale and earned the coveted doctorate, in political science. He taught for a while at the University of Georgia, but like many Koreans he was drawn back home.

The Korea he returned to in the mid-1960s was emerging from a decade of postwar depression. Throughout the 1950s, the economy had gone nowhere, limping along on U.S. aid and a per capita income of less than $100. Corruption was rampant as Rhee proved an inept leader, favoring a few businessmen at the expense of the rest of the nation. Korea was a crippled basket-case nation as bad off as any on the globe. Rhee was brought down in 1960 by massive student demonstrations and Korea had a brief fling with democracy, but the leaders of the Second Republic were not strong enough to hold the fractious nation together. After nine months, a military coup engineered by General Park Chung Hee took control. Park, who was trained by and fought with the Japanese army in Manchuria, quickly set the tone for modern Korea: administrative efficiency and industrialization at all costs.

The Koreans discovered that they had a pool of human capital that, while unskilled, was willing to work long hours at menial, low-paying jobs. Anything it seemed was better than eating bark. The military, variously educated by the Japanese and American armies, provided the first wave of managers, eventually to be replaced by a generation of American-educated technocrats such as Lee. When he returned, Lee found that the mentality had changed. People were willing to work. Forgotten tenets of the Confucian culture were reasserting themselves, principally, that to be unemployed was shameful. By world standards, the Korean economy of the early 1960s was a small geegaw stand, capable of producing only the most trivial products. But for the Koreans, it was, for the first time, *their* trivial economy. A pattern began: If you worked hard, you could do better next year than this year and, most important, your children could be assured of doing better still. A man who knows he will do better each year is a contented man. Non-essentials, like democracy, freedom and control of one's life, could wait.

Lee Yong Ho offered to take us further back into the history of Korea. We drove to Kyongju, the most historic city in the country, seat of the Silla Dynasty that ruled much of the peninsula from 57 B.C. to 936 A.D. It was the Silla kings who, toward the middle of their reign, unified the tribal clans that controlled small slices of the region. Because of the geography, adjacent valleys were often sealed off from one another until they were joined by a network of roads constructed by the Sillas.

Kyongju sits in a wide plain that sweeps to the sea, but is protected from behind by mountains. As we approached the site of the old city, the dominant image was of death. Looming above the tile-roofed houses like giant desert dunes are more than 200 earthen burial mounds covering the tombs of the Silla kings, stuffed with jewels, crowns and statues that make up the royal legacy of Korea. And around the tombs, scattered across the plain, are hundreds of significant sites: the remains of temples, pagodas, forts and palaces. Most of those, too, are introduced by stories of death.

"Here is where the Buddhist monks made their last stand against the Japanese in the 16th century," Lee explained at the site of one restored temple. "They were all killed and the temple was burned to the ground."

Burned to the ground. The phrase is the end of the legend attached to almost every historic site in the country. For centuries, Korea has been one of the most strategic pieces of land in Asia, coveted by dozens of armies that have marched across its soil. Korea was first inhabited some 30,000 years ago by nomadic tribes that wandered from north central Asia—some of the same tribes that also migrated west. Some of the evidence can be found in the fact that the roots of the Korean language are related to Turkish, Finnish and Hungarian. Only in recent history has it taken on some Chinese and Japanese characteristics. The dominant tribes were the Silla to the east, the Paekche to the south and the Koguryo to the north. In one configuration or another, they were usually at war with each other.

From the beginning, this hard land has seemed to provoke the most pugnacious reactions from anyone who encountered it. If the Koreans were not being invaded by foreign armies or engaging in civil war, then individual kingdoms were beset with intrigue, assassinations and coups. The history of Korea reads like a textbook in military strategy, filled with tales of clashes on land and sea; this is a land that has been perpetually crossed and plundered by the dominant regional powers. "When whales fight, the shrimp suffer," says a Korean proverb, but Korea has always maintained its identity and integrity as a nation. From the time the Silla kings united the peninsula in the 7th century, Korea was one country. It ceased to be one Korea only when it was so casually partitioned by the United States and the Soviet Union in 1945.

Among those who dominated Korea were several dynasties of Chinese emperors, the Mongol warriors on their way to Japan in the 13th century and the Japanese themselves, who mounted numerous official invasions and countless pirate raids over several centuries. It was after Korea was devastated by two Japanese invasions in the late 16th century that its rulers turned inward for defensive reasons and the period of the "Hermit Kingdom" began. Nobody in, nobody out was the rule. For two and a half centuries Korea was a decaying feudal culture, a late Dark Ages, stagnant in its development and all but invisible to the rest of the world. It was also a period of relative peace as the great world powers contented themselves with colonizing other parts of the globe. The culture of the West was dominating the world and the Koreans wanted no part of it. Even the Japanese were viewed as too westernized. The Koreans wanted to be left alone and, for a time, they succeeded. They had made themselves so unattractive that for once they had no lustful suitors.

Finally they succumbed to pressure from the Japanese and Americans to open trade. The British travel writer Isabella Bird was among the rare foreigners to travel through the country in the late 1800s. She wrote of meeting the average Korean who felt "the first stress of unsought and altogether undesired contact with western civilization, and resembles nothing so much as a man awaking from a profound sleep."

Suspicions about admitting foreigners proved well-founded. Japan was once again flexing its imperial muscles and soon provoked a war with Russia in 1904. One of the prizes of the Russian surrender, agreed to by the other world powers, was that Japan would take control of Korea, resulting in a virtual colonization that lasted until 1945.

"Now is the golden age of Korea," explained Lee Yong Ho as we walked through a museum of Silla artifacts. He pointed to displays of crowns made of thin gold beaten into foil, no doubt to make a little gold go a long way, and hung with odd-shaped polished rocks. It compared unfavorably to the heft of an English king's crown or the adornments of the Chinese emperors.

"What you see in these display cases is our heritage, but it is not great. Today is the greatest day in our history. And tomorrow will be better than today."

He got no argument about the past. The museums of Kyongju offer small, delicate examples of craftsmanship and some evidence that the Koreans were an inventive people in the early part of the century. But there is no greatness in evidence. Though she never saw what Kyongju had to offer, Isabella Bird wrote of Seoul in the 1890s, "It has no objects of art, very few antiquities, no public gardens . . . and no theaters. It lacks every charm possessed by other cities . . . it has no ruins, no libraries, no literature."

Korea of the 1980s is not far from that description. The attention and public money lavished on making Kyongju a national monument suggested the Koreans' thirst for a heritage, but dig as they might, there wasn't much to find. There were no Great Walls, Forbidden Cities, Taj Mahals. There was the rubble of modest palaces and temples, shards of ceramics, metal work and stone carvings. The Koreans were doing intricate metal casting when Europe was in the Dark Ages. Yet later, during the sustained centuries of European progress, Korea was stilled. When art was flourishing in the Renaissance, when the French were building Paris, the Koreans were withdrawn from the world. Even in its own hemisphere, it had nothing to compare to the wealth or culture of India or China. It was an isolated society unable to defend itself and forced to surrender most of its wealth to one conqueror or another.

We found the golden age of Korea crated on the docks of Pusan, the giant port city southeast of Kyongju. Red, green and blue corrugated metal containers the size of trailer trucks were stacked five and 10 high, row after row along the concrete wharves awaiting the tall cranes that plucked them up and nestled them into the holds of container ships. Like chickens in a barnyard, the cranes bent and pecked, bent and pecked, dropping their feed into the long, broad container ships. The process often went day and night, the faster to make room for the dozens of ships riding at anchor in Pusan Harbor.

Korea's economy was growing at a double-digit rate, consistently among the hottest in the world. Pusan, and the port of Inchon on the west coast, were the clearinghouses for the billions of dollars of goods produced in the factories—the clothing, shoes, TVs, stereos, computers—and the overseas markets that were gobbling them up. And the biggest market of all, the destination for half those ships, was the United States.

"In my lifetime, Pusan has always been busy," Lee Yong

Ho said. "This was our last stand during the Korean War and it was from here that we started back."

Pusan is surrounded by factories, more even than the forest of factories in Taegu. Nearby lies Ulsan, a city that is virtually owned by the Hyundai Corporation, which churns out ships and hundreds of thousands of its phenomenally popular Excel cars. Just to the north is the giant Pohang steel refinery, one of the largest and most efficient steel-making plants in the world and one of the reasons that the streets of Pusan are filled with shops while the streets of Gary, Indiana are shuttered. Downtown Pusan is less stylish than Seoul, more functional and more crowded. With a population of more than five million, it is a densely packed enclave of productivity. Buses shuttled workers from town to factory site, seemingly all day. We visited Pusan on a Friday, yet the parks were full. Lee explained that because the factories were running at such high capacity, sometimes around the clock, many shift workers had time off at unconventional hours.

"Pusan never stops," he said. "People moving, pushing, earning money and spending it in the stores. During the war it was the same, only then we were just trying to survive. Now we are trying to make something great.

"My generation is blessed. We have been through a lot. We came out of the Dark Ages. But in the next 10 years, we will join the advanced world. And we will be proud of it because we have something that I think is very prized in America. We are all self-made men."

That evening we flew on the once-an-hour shuttle to Seoul, a couple of ragged Americans who grew up in comfortable middle-class families surrounded by hundreds of crisply turned out self-made men.

Chun finally caught up with us a few days later. He tried not to let on that he cared, but he was bursting with suspicion.

"So, you are having fun?" he wanted to know. "Find any girls?" He was incapable of smiling without turning the expression into a leer. A dirty old man at the age of 30.

"No, Chun," London replied. "No girls. Only top government officials."

"Such as who?"

"Top officials, Chun. We can't say."

But we needed him to arrange some things for us so we made up some stories about the girls of Itaewon.

"I knew it!" he said gleefully. "We must go back. Together."

Chun was a little distraught. That day's paper brought the news that another 29 barber shops had been closed, bringing the total to more than 1,000 over the past several months. Barber shops in Korea, we learned, will service more than the customer's hair. Other, more personal needs, can be satisfied for an additional fee. But now, in anticipation of the Olympics, the puritanization of Korea was in full swing and Chun feared that soon there would be nothing left for him. No dog meat and no "intimate body massages." What was a guy to do?

Chun had gotten us an invitation to visit Samsung Group, one of the handful of giant corporations that dominate the Korean economy. If Korea was a factory, we thought, we needed to see it from the inside.

We began inside one of the polished granite towers of downtown Seoul, where a stone-faced secretary showed us to a simply furnished reception room. She did not offer us tea, the first time that had happened anywhere in Korea, and, given the early hour, it was the first time the customary jolt truly would have been appreciated. But corporate Korea did not have time for amenities. Corporate Korea was built for speed.

We sat and read copies of the annual report that told us that Samsung, which means "three stars," was a company with $12 billion in sales, enough to list it high up on the Fortune 500 list of U.S. companies. It had increased in size more than 10 times over the last decade and now employed 100,000 people in 18 subsidiaries that made everything from computer microchips to super-size oil tankers. In total, the company accounted for more than 10 percent of Korea's gross national product. With numbers like that, guests could bring their own tea.

Page after page showed pictures of sprawling modern factories filled with the people and machinery to turn out wool, steel, refrigerators, television sets and just about anything else that can be manufactured. This seemed very ambitious for a country that most Americans associate with electronic calculators and other low-tech doodads. There was, in this one annual report, evidence to strike fear into the heart of any working person in the United States. The productive capability of this one company reminded us of old newsreel footage of America gearing up for World War II: sparks flying on the shop floor, smoke pouring from tall stacks, cranes dropping steel ship's plates into place. Then there, on page 15, was something more unusual. Instead of the typical photo of uniformly dark heads hunched over an assembly-line table, there was a shot of blond bouffant hairdos belonging to workers in Roxbury, New Jersey, who were also part of the Samsung family. Here was a bunch of women who looked like everyone's Aunt Dot, churning out color television sets for the greater glory of Korea.

When, five minutes later, a well-groomed young man walked in and introduced himself as Park Byung Mun, general manager of planning and research for Samsung Electronics, we asked him about the U.S. plant.

"That is our first venture in the United States and we are very proud of it. We are giving jobs to Americans who need them. We think we can provide the skilled management to build products in the United States that can be priced competitively. The U.S. worker is not so bad as some people say. The managers . . ." with that he shrugged and waved his head from side to side with a weak smile.

Park was not purposely condescending, but that was his effect. Proud of giving *us* jobs? This was Uncle Sam he was talking about! The mighty United States. Hell, in the 1950s, Catholic schools sponsored "Adopt a Korean Baby" fund drives. The nuns would show pictures of hollow-eyed Asian infants and hundreds of little girls in plaid jumpers would desperately canvas the neighborhood hoping to collect enough coins to pay for a few bowls of rice. Now here was this unintentionally smug corporate hotshot who was not even born until after the war and who got his college education in Decatur, Illinois, talking about how he felt good about helping this Third World country called America.

On the other hand, he was probably right.

"We cannot produce just in Korea," he explained. "We feel the winds of protectionism are going to blow very hard. And if Korea cannot sell abroad, we cannot survive. So we are making investments in the United States to diversify."

And also, he admitted, for reasons of public relations. "It would be the best thing for the United States and Korea to cooperate and not to compete. We think there is much we can teach you."

The New Jersey plant, with 170 American shop workers and 10 Korean managers, was not as productive as a Korean plant, but it was getting better. "I don't know if there will ever be great American factories anymore because Americans don't like to do the same thing for 10 hours a day. But the people we hired were very happy to have jobs and they are good workers."

It was with American management that Park had his quarrel.

"Answer me this," he began. "I have always been amazed that you did not produce videotape recorders. You had the technology in the late 1950s, yet you sold it to Sony. That was a big mistake. Did you underestimate how strong the Japanese would become? I hope you do not underestimate the Koreans."

Samsung's electronics factories were clustered in the town of Suwon, about an hour south of Seoul on the expressway. We headed down in a Samsung car, wedged in with Chun, a company functionary and driver, all redolent of garlic. Chun continued to probe us about our nights out and when we didn't respond, began to express suspicion that maybe we didn't like girls.

Shortly after exiting the highway and driving alongside a series of rice paddies, we arrived at what looked like an army camp. Behind a high barbed-wire fence was a succession of low barracks and larger, metal-sided structures the size of airplane hangars. As we stopped at the gate, manned by rifle-toting guards wearing Samsung uniforms, we could see row after row of buildings separated by tree-lined streets.

Even Chun was amazed at the scale of the place and interrupted his lascivious musings to mutter, "This is pretty great."

Another Samsung guide greeted our car. "Welcome to Suwon Electronics Estate. The largest patory in the world."

The largest what?

"Patory. You know, place to make things. I show you what we make."

The estate covered 370 acres and employed 14,000 people, 4,000 of whom lived on the property. We wandered from building to building and discovered a fully integrated industrial colossus that produced 2.5 million television sets—from two-inch screens to 26-inch—and a million and a half VCRs a year as well as radios, cassette recorders, microwave ovens, car stereos, video monitors, eight-millimeter cameras, dishwashers, heaters, humidifiers and, finally, the only product we would not long before have assumed they were capable of making, electronic calculators—20 kinds. The estate also made most of the component parts for its products, such as glass for the TV picture tubes and computer microchips, among them Samsung's own version of the 256k DRAM chip just invented by the Americans and the Japanese.

We sat in the plush boardroom—the shop boys seemed to get treated better than the executives in Seoul—watching the Samsung corporate film on a Samsung VCR and monitor, listening over the Samsung sound system while our nasal passages were soothed by a Samsung humidifier.

"Samsung Electronics," the urbane, internationally acceptable voice of the narrator explained, "is only 16 years old." It had come from nothing to an expected $3 billion in sales in 1988—with $2 billion of that going for export.

"Samsung," the narrator said, "has done its part to help the Korean miracle."

It seemed a miracle, indeed. How could this phenomenal growth have taken place so suddenly? A conglomerate the size of all but the largest companies in the United States had been established in about two decades. Samsung Electronics alone had grown at a rate of about 60 percent a year from its founding in 1969. The Suwon estate produced cameras for Minolta, watches for Seiko, walkmen for Sony and everything for Sears. At the end of one assembly line, small refrigerators dropped into cartons marked, "General Electric, refrigerators for office or home." At the end of one television plant, sets were stuffed in cartons labeled, "Made in Japan." It was easy to imagine that every piece of electronic gadgetry for sale in every department store in the world originated from this, the world's largest "pa-tory." But of course it didn't, because, as the guide explained, there were a dozen more such estates throughout Korea, some owned by Samsung and some by the other giant Korean corporations called *chaebol.*

We knew at least one secret to the success of these giants. In 1986, developments in the world economy couldn't have been better for Korea. The Japanese yen was at an all-time high against the U.S. dollar, making Japanese goods suddenly very expensive. The Korean won, however, was pegged to the price of the dollar; as the dollar fell, so did the won, and Korean goods became the world's best substitute for Japanese products. U.S. importers were placing orders as fast as they could. Japanese companies, desperately trying to maintain their share of markets in the United States and Europe, were subcontracting jobs to Korean companies that could now make things much more cheaply than the Japanese. At the same time, oil prices had also taken a tumble, and Korea, a big user that had to import virtually all its energy, saw its fuel bills cut in half.

The Samsung executive was sheepish about all this good fortune. "We could be doing even better," he confided. "If we had invested more in bigger plants, we could be producing a lot more. We were very cautious in our planning."

The whole nation seemed unable to believe its prosperity. Over the last 10 years, Korea has had consistently steady improvements in its economy, but this was something else. Every day there were stories in the papers about some new success: giant orders for one company or another, new plants under construction and, for the first time in modern memory, a trade surplus. Many of the stories had that tone of "Pinch me, I'm dreaming" about them as if to reassure readers that they were, in fact, witnessing the period when Korea began to move into the realm of the First World economies.

Then we walked into one of the vast Samsung TV factories and another secret of Korea's success became apparent. In that one room there were about 500 people working, almost all young women about 18 or 20 years old. They wore light blue smocks and white kerchiefs tied around their heads and white cotton gloves on their hands. They sat side by side at 50-yard long tables along which moved the guts of television sets. Each woman was responsible for perhaps five to seven parts. She might solder a circuit board and connect blue, green and red wires at a certain junction, then pass it along to the next woman who would dip a circuit board in molten silver then pass the assembly to the next woman who would add a blue tube, and a blue tube and a blue tube all day long. The only sound in the room was the soft hum of the conveyor as each woman added the fruits of her labor to the boxes that eventually wound their way along several tables and became a completed set.

"Young women are much better with their hands and they have good eyesight," explained the Samsung executive. Each week they are changed to a new work station to break up the monotony of their jobs.

They worked from 8:30 in the morning to 6:30 at night, six days a week. That came to 60 hours a week, which was long even by Korean standards. At 54½ hours, by official calculations, the Koreans had the longest average workweek in the world. The Samsung executive noted that they were allowed to take lunch and several short breaks, bringing their week more in line with the national average. For this they were paid $300 a month, or about $1.25 an hour.

We expressed surprise at the hourly wage. "Yes, I know," he said, "it does seem high, doesn't it? But there is not much we can do about it if we want the best people. This is a lot harder than textile weaving."

"They also get free housing in the company dormitories," our guide pointed out, as well as company medical services and subsidized food. It is, he said, a sought-after job with more applicants than positions. The factory, which was clean and well lighted, certainly wasn't the sort of industrial hellhole that we had been told existed all over Asia.

"They become part of the Samsung family," he said. Unfortunately, many find it necessary to leave home after a few years. The turnover is quite high, sometimes because the women get married, sometimes because their fingers or eyesight give out.

Another Samsung executive had told us earlier that Korea was not nearly as successful as Japan at creating truly family corporations. The average Japanese corporation keeps its employees for more than 10 years while in Korea the number is about three. "Japanese people are so group-oriented," he explained. "They want to belong to an organization and be loyal to it. Everyone is a part of the company and works together. Koreans are more individual. Our managers don't want the shop-floor workers telling them how to run the plant. They want to be the boss. I think that is more like in the States. But I would like us to be more like the Japanese. We have to become more efficient. You know $1.25 an hour is becoming an expensive wage in the world. The Third World is developing. You can get better prices in Malaysia, Thailand, the Philippines, lots of places. Pretty soon the Chinese will learn to do this work for $1.25 a day."

So this was it? Could it be that the Korean miracle was built on the nimble fingers of thousands of sad-faced 18-year-old girls with kerchiefs tied around their heads? Maybe the industrial muscle of Korea was a lot more delicate than we thought—and a lot more sophisticated. If they could make TV sets, they could—and did—make all manner of high technology equipment, the kind that was supposed to form the basis of the new, postindustrial American economy. Only here they would do it for $1.25 an hour and when that became too much, they were already figuring how to either bring the price down or ship out the less sophisticated work and keep the high-value stuff at home. Our question was, What did this leave for the 18-year-old girls in Silicon Valley or Austin, Texas?

The portico in front of the Seoul Hilton was one place to observe, in microcosm, the commercial frenzy that was sweeping Korea. A circular driveway led up to the black steel-and-glass hotel that looked like a curving version of a Mies van der Rohe office tower. From early morning until late at night a raucous interchange of limousines and taxis shuttled an endless assortment of foreign businessmen to some of the most sought-after offices and factories in the world. Being a Hilton, the hotel was favored by Americans, who strode through the lobby in the uniform of blue suits, white shirts and red ties and lugged polished black leather attaché cases. The Japanese traveled in groups, usually three or four, spinning through the revolving doors in descending order of age.

The front of the hotel was a fast-moving place with doormen tweeting whistles and sending cars off with the precision of bosuns on an aircraft-carrier flight deck. On the curb, the well-tailored passengers waited impatiently, checking watches, tapping feet until they were off.

No one moved faster, however, than a distinguished, silver-haired Korean gentleman whom we noticed racing in and out of the hotel on several occasions accompanied by a phalanx of aides. One night about 10, Kelly was waiting for a taxi and watched two elderly Japanese men bid each other good night by bowing repeatedly, each bow returned by one lower until they were both bent perpendicular at the waist. At this moment, the silver-haired Korean burst from the revolving door and almost ran the Japanese down. As they looked up startled, he deftly stepped around them and slid through the open door of a black sedan. He immediately switched on a reading lamp and opened a briefcase as his entourage hurried into the car and one behind it. The doors were slammed and the cars roared off.

"Who was that?" Kelly asked the doorman.

"That's Mr. Kim," the doorman replied, standing stiffly. "He owns the place."

This place and a lot of others, we discovered. The man in question was Kim Woo Choong, founder and chairman of Daewoo Corporation, probably the most aggressive, fast-growing *chaebol* in Korea. If this was the golden age of Korea, then he was one of its ranking gods. For a Confucian country that traditionally reserved its greatest reverence for scholars and has rated farmers and civil servants far above businessmen, Kim Woo Choong represents a new generation of super executives who have changed the equation of respect. The business of Korea, it seemed, was business. We started to ask around about Kim and found some interesting things, including the fact that he has returned the adulation by making business into a religion and hard work into a cult.

Kim is to Korea what flinty, Protestant capitalists such as Andrew Carnegie and John D. Rockefeller had been to America during the industrial boom: role model and taskmaster. The stories about Kim's sacrifice and success have achieved mythical proportions. "If I were asked to choose between my family and my company, I would choose the company," *Korea Business* magazine once quoted him as telling a group of executive recruits. "Self-sacrifice is the first condition for leadership," he says frequently. "Those who enjoy friends, family and hobbies, they can't become leaders." Too much leisure time, he is fond of saying, causes more family problems than too little.

Fortune magazine once called him "the hardest worker in Korea." The 50-year-old executive is said to work seven days a week, often 15 hours a day with five hours for sleep. It is not unusual for his staff meetings to begin at 7:30 A.M. and for his day to finish with the completion of a business dinner at 11 P.M.

An associate once said that at the ritual *kisaeng* house dinners, Kim doesn't drink or tell jokes. "He doesn't even touch the hostesses."

He spends half his time on the road, flying a quarter-million miles a year to oversee Daewoo's 65 offices around the world. His vacations consist of a few long weekends. Kim is the youngest and only college-educated founder of a *chaebol* and unlike his competitors he has resisted the urge to build a vast family fortune. Instead, he has contributed more than $50 million to a series of philanthropic foundations, an unusual gesture for a Korean. "I don't care much about money-making for myself," he told *Fortune,* "because I could do that anytime."

The result has been a company that grew from seven employees in 1967 to more than 70,000 only 20 years later. Its annual sales of more than $10 billion put Daewoo among the 50 largest companies outside the United States. Its development has mirrored that of Korea, with breakneck growth and low profits. "In 1990, when Korea's per capita income reaches $5,000," says Kim optimistically, "that will be the time to go for profits." In the meantime, Daewoo is a patriotic obsession and perhaps more typical of the future of Korea than the other major companies.

Like Lee Yong Ho, Kim was of the new generation that had been created by the hardships and the opportunities of Korea in the 1950s. Born in 1937, he was the son of a teacher who was killed by North Korean troops. After the war, he sold newspapers in Taegu to support his mother and siblings and, most important, he learned how to hustle. After graduating from college on a scholarship, he got a job with a textile trading firm importing yarn and cloth for a small domestic knitting industry. He didn't know much about cloth, but he knew how to sell.

One of the often-told stories about Kim is about the time he was traveling to meet his fiancée in London. He had planned a few stops along the way and in Hong Kong picked up some samples of locally made cloth. On the plane he decided he could find a way to make the same cloth cheaper in Korea. By the time he arrived in Singapore, he had decided to tell cloth buyers that the samples were his. He returned to Korea with several hundred thousand dollars in orders and wrote his fiancée to forget about the wedding.

With a wealthier partner, he started a textile company in 1967 and called it Daewoo, which means "great universe." They began copying U.S.-made shirts "down to the last stitch" and selling them to Japanese trading houses, which in turn sold them to the States. But after studying the Japanese methods, Kim soon discovered he could go around them and sell directly to such retailers as Sears Roebuck, J. C. Penney and K Mart.

The national battle cry was "Export!" and Kim had found one of the best ways to do so. Korea had Export Days and Export Songs. To be an exporter and bring foreign currency into a country that had been bleeding its meager resources for so long was to be a national hero. Accolades and favors followed.

The economists put in place by President Park decided to lavish incentives on exporters—mostly the fattening *chaebol.* Bank loans could be had at a fraction of the going interest rate, the tariff on imported raw materials was waived and the income tax was suspended. For a company like Daewoo, the breaks cut production costs by 40 percent and allowed them to flood the U.S. market with low-priced goods. When the United States slapped quotas on Korean imports, Kim responded by buying up the quotas, often by taking over floundering firms that did not have his access to capital. Soon Daewoo controlled the right to sell almost half of Korea's textile production to the United States.

By the mid-1970s, the government planners were encouraging a shift to heavy industry and Kim was selected by President Park to try to resurrect a failing machinery company. Kim moved into the plant for nine months—"the hardest I have ever worked," he says—but he made it profitable and it became the cornerstone of a huge expansion by Daewoo. Kim continued to bring in batches of top executives, many of them classmates from high school or college, and gave them a free hand at running their departments—decentralization that was not typical of most *chaebol.*

Park later gave Kim a car company to run and a government shipbuilding yard, which Kim did not want. Typical of the iron-handed government-to-business relationship, Park waited until Kim was on a business trip and simply announced that Daewoo would be taking over the yard. To refuse would be for Kim to lose face. The yard at Okpo has since swallowed $500 million of Daewoo's capital but is now considered one of the best in the world, producing ships that are increasingly better designed and cheaper to run—and can be delivered far quicker than from any Japanese yard. With its 1.55 million-ton capacity the Okpo yard exceeds that of all the yards in Great Britain.

Kim even took over the Korean half of an auto-parts joint venture with General Motors. When, after four years under GM management, the company was still in the red, Kim installed Daewoo executives and got the black ink flowing. Now, GM was eager to have Daewoo manufacture its cars for it. It seemed there was nothing Kim Woo Choong could not do. And that was before things got really good.

In the summer of 1986, while the giants of American industry were preoccupied with defending against takeovers, paying out greenmail or plotting leveraged buyouts, the executives at Daewoo's corporate headquarters in downtown Seoul were trying to keep up with success. To be precise, it was 3:15 on a Saturday afternoon, an hour that would find American barons of business on the 15th tee or reading spy thrillers by the seashore. At Daewoo, Saturday quitting time is 3 P.M., but that day the senior executives were all still on the premises, so no one down the line was leaving.

Headquarters is an austere affair. Only the lobby suggests opulence, with its soaring polished marble columns and displays of Daewoo products. The most popular that day were banks of television sets, which showed a bloody kung-fu movie, and a revolving showroom model of the LeMans, the fruit of the GM joint venture. The car was a sleek compact that drew approving grunts from passersby who would nod to each other and say, "Re-mans." We wondered if the marketing men had given any consideration to the fact that the car's name could not be pronounced in Korea.

The Department of Corporate Relations was an open expanse of bare floor lined with a regiment of gray metal desks, each occupied by a man in a white short-sleeved shirt and dark tie. Even for the executives there were no private offices, just desks set closer to the window. We had come on the chance that we could get an interview with Kim. While we waited to meet with his staff, we read company brochures.

The Daewoo story was startling. Its *News from Daewoo* reported record sales, new plants, new products and joint venture deals all in the same issue. One volume from summer 1986 was particularly instructive, containing news of deals with ITT to make telecommunications equipment, with Caterpillar Tractor for forklifts, with Carrier Corp. to build air conditioners and compressors, with Nissan to build minivans, with General Dynamics, Northrop and Boeing to make aircraft parts for 747 passenger planes and F-16 fighter planes. The shipbuilding unit had just won orders worth $320 million. Clothes were being made for such brand names as Van Heusen, Oleg Cassini and Geoffrey Beene. The company was building a cement plant in Africa, a tire plant in the Sudan, a Singapore hotel and a Sumatran highway. Subway-car business was booming and a 250-kilometer per hour train was under development. The company had just bought its first U.S. firm, a computer chip manufacturer called ZyMOS. Overall, Daewoo's export sales had topped $3 billion for the first time. The company was selling bonds in Luxembourg and was part of the first-ever Korean stock offering on the New York Stock Exchange.

The only thing missing was profits. The Daewoo's net income had lingered around $50 million for several years, a paltry percentage of its vast sales. And in some years even those figures were exaggerated thanks to Korean accounting standards that are less stringent than the "generally accepted practices" to which U.S. companies are subjected. The company's debt, on the other hand, was staggering. In 1985, the company paid $250 million in interest. Long-term debt was close to a billion dollars, including $400 million to foreign banks. Looking over annual reports through the mid-1980s, no one could make the argument that Daewoo was a profit-making enterprise.

"You'll find that profits aren't too much of a consideration around here," explained one company executive. "The emphasis is on growth and expanding our capabilities. There will be time for profit later." It was, he noted, the philosophy the Japanese followed in the early days of their industrial expansion.

Nonetheless, there was about this company, as with other Korean companies, an air of astonishing success. Everything was going well. Maybe too well. Here, too, we discovered the same reluctance to talk about success that we had found elsewhere, the same inability to take a compliment. When we would comment about the great days Korea was having, the businessmen would smile and shrug and talk about how far they had to go and what a poor country it still was. Was this just Confucian modesty?

"Some modesty, perhaps, but that's not all," an American executive told us later. "My theory is that when they are talking to Americans they don't want to sound too successful—first, because then the United States will slap tougher trade restrictions on them and second, because they are a little embarrassed that the United States is doing so poorly. It is as if they realize that their success comes at a cost to the United States. When they talk to the Japanese, they boast all the time about how well they're doing."

An interview with Kim seemed doubtful, as he was headed out of the country shortly. But one of his top deputies was willing to see us.

Park Sung Kyou is the man credited with inventing the Leading Edge computer, one of the great business success stories of the last decade. In a matter of a few months from the time it was first sold in the fall of 1985, Leading Edge became the king clone of personal computers, snatching market share from everyone from IBM to the Japanese. It was a remarkable success for the Koreans especially because it relied not just on copying a product and making it with cheap labor, but on some deft design work and skillful marketing.

Park is another Korean-born, American-educated executive. More important, he was a high school classmate of Kim Woo Choong, which is how he got to Daewoo. After earning a degree in electrical engineering from MIT and a doctorate at the University of Texas, Park became a researcher for such industrial giants as Polaroid, where he worked on the autofocus camera, and Schlumberger, where he helped develop a new instrument for identifying oil deposits. At the age of 40 he was just hitting his peak as an engineer with the potential to make a handsome salary when Kim lured him back to Korea.

"I came back to make a contribution," he told us during an interview in his small, unornamented office on the 15th floor of the Daewoo headquarters. "I could have made more money and had more perks if I stayed in the States, but Chairman Kim offered me a chance to make something on my own as well as to do something for Korea. In the United States, you know, the smart people don't make things anymore. They are lawyers and investment bankers, they shuffle around what is already there. In Korea, we still want to make things."

Kim manages Daewoo according to a model more American than Japanese. Although they still sometimes call Kim *tosa,* or master, the way one would refer to a tae kwon do instructor, Daewoo is run by a highly modified Confucian ethic. At the other *chaebol* decisions rest with the patriarchal founder such as Lee Byung Chul at Samsung or Hyundai's Chung Ju Yung. At Daewoo, top executives have almost complete responsibility for their subsidiaries. They make their own decisions—and live or die by them. Park is one of the new generation of Korean executives who thrives on the responsibility and on the accomplishment of making a product—a contrast with U.S. executives who seem obsessed with making deals.

"Chairman Kim gave me a free hand to develop new products," Park explained. "I got Leading Edge because I pushed it. If it hadn't worked out . . ." he shrugs ". . . it would have been my fault."

But Leading Edge did work out, spectacularly so. Park thought there might be an opening in the U.S. market for a Korean personal computer, but he had no idea how to make one. He signed a joint venture agreement with Northern Telecom of the United States to build telephone switching equipment, the manufacturing of which is very similar to PCs. Soon he had a cadre of engineers who could begin experimenting with a PC production line.

Based on his own studies of the U.S. market and the work of a Massachusetts company, Park determined what additions customers wanted from the IBM-PC, the industry leader. They took apart many IBMs and figured out how to make the basic model and add a variety of features.

Customers said the IBM was too bulky, so Daewoo cut the size of the unit by almost half. Customers said it didn't have enough memory, so Daewoo made a 640k board standard. Daewoo added a standard color capability, a quieter keyboard. "We even put the on-off switch in front because people liked it there," Park said. But mostly, Daewoo's model would be cheap—about half what IBM's were selling for.

Park continued to watch the U.S. market and when he saw

the dismal sales dip of 1984, he decided the time was right to start selling an alternative. In a 14-month crash program, the Leading Edge Model D went from drawing board to shipping carton. By the summer of 1985, the units were in the stores and the market ate them up. The most optimistic demand was for 10,000 units a month, but Daewoo's production facilities were soon stretched to the limit, turning out 13,000 units a month.

It was the ideal partnership. Leading Edge, the Massachusetts company, provided the marketing, software and support services. Daewoo provided the engineering and manufacturing at low cost. The venture was not based on new technology, but rather clever application of existing technology.

But wasn't this exactly the problem that would hold Korea back? The ability only to copy and even advance, but not to invent? In the 1950s Japan knew it could only get so far if it copied the technology of the West and so it poured enormous resources into research and development.

"Our R&D budgets are high," Park explained, "but we have a long way to go. We can refine technology. We have the ability to apply it well. But I don't think Korea has the ability to make a breakthrough."

As we left Park's office, we wondered if this was just that same old deceptive modesty or if he was sincere. Somehow it was more reassuring to think that they were just going to copy us. Keep them in their place. With all these Japan comparisons, the thought had occurred to us, Who needs another Japan? Or, more important, Can the United States survive another Japan? We knew these Koreans were tough and hardworking, now we discovered they were clever. What if they proved brilliant as well? Later, we decided they were getting uncomfortably close to just such a combination.

Welcome to the manly art of heavy industry. No girls in kerchiefs here, no white-coated engineers peering from behind thick glasses, this was the stuff of beer commercials. Daewoo Heavy Industries' Inchon factory was a world of thick-wristed guys, dirty and sweating, as they slammed hammers onto metal and made sparks fly. This was metal bending, the skill that made America great, now being practiced by pale yellow men in bright yellow helmets and navy blue jumpsuits. It was an army at work, covering a shop floor the size of a football field. The cavernous room was filled with the burp of rivet guns, the evil hiss of acetylene torches and the clank of an ever-moving assembly line chain. Cranes lumbered overhead moving pallets of steel—Korean steel, made at the world's largest steel mill in Pohang. Real men eat kimchi.

Sang Moon brought us from Seoul to Inchon, the port city 20 miles west that is fast becoming an extension of the sprawling capital. Inchon's fame is in the annals of military history as the site of General Douglas MacArthur's daring amphibious landing during the Korean War. With the North Korean army threatening to push the battered South Korean and U.S. armies off the peninsula at Pusan, MacArthur pulled a classic flanking maneuver by landing 70,000 men on the shore of the treacherous harbor. A bronze statue of the general, wearing his rumpled cap and sunglasses, now stares out to sea, his back turned on the new war taking place at Inchon.

The harbor, on the shallow Yellow Sea, once had tidal surges of 30 feet and its approach was marked by shifting mudbanks and tidal flats. The Koreans have succeeded in turning nature back and have reclaimed the port. Like Pusan, the wharves here were loaded with goods for export. Back from the wharves were more factories, ranked side by side in a show of industrial strength. And back from the factories were the workers' housing, blocks and blocks of company-owned apartments and dormitories that were offered to corporate employees at reduced rates.

"The factory workers get housing, but not the office workers," explained Moon, a young management trainee from headquarters who lived in a cramped apartment with his wife and daughter and commuted about an hour each way by company bus to Seoul. "There is a feeling that the factory worker should be taken care of so that he can be more productive. The office worker is not yet so important in Korea."

Daewoo Heavy Industry workers are among the best paid in the country. For an 8-to-5 day, six days a week, they start at $250 to $350 a month, plus a bonus of one month's salary paid four times a year. Salary bonuses were favored by many Korean companies as a way of sharing profits while keeping fixed costs down.

Moon, a frail sort who seemed even more in awe of the

cacophonous surroundings than we were, took us to the building where they made the forklifts. He was proud of the forklifts and had been talking about them all morning. We followed him through a set of doors as he turned with a flourish and said, "Just like Peoria!"

In front of us lay rows of brand-new forklift trucks, gleaming with that ochre color so distinctive to every construction site we had ever seen. They were Caterpillars, just like they make in Peoria, Illinois, in what had been among America's finest factories, where a sturdy, reliable product respected the world over was produced. Cats built dams in Africa and roads in the Amazon jungle, and were a symbol of the reach of the United States. Now at least some of the famous models were the responsibility of the Koreans. You couldn't tell the difference, but for the small letters on the bottom which announced, "Made in Korea."

In the end, it was probably a good thing. Peoria was going to lose the jobs anyway, mostly to Japan where Komatsu was fast becoming the dominant force in construction equipment. Daewoo formed a joint venture with Caterpillar, taking on manufacturing while the American firm kept the design, finance, marketing and distribution functions. We were discovering that this was the calculus of the new world: a hundred white collar American workers supporting 1,000 Korean blue collar workers. American factory workers didn't figure in. Still, there was perhaps some reassurance that they worked for us, and not the other way around. We designed it, we showed them how to make it and we sold it. They were still dependent on us. They were still copying.

When we left the forklift plant, one of the factory supervisors who was accompanying us suggested we see the diesel engine plant. As a rule, a factory is a factory and we had seen about all we needed to. He insisted we would find it interesting.

At first glance, the diesel plant looked like another license operation with Daewoo turning out truck and bus engines for MAN, a West German company. Engine blocks rode a conveyor to various stations where they were planed and bored to precise tolerances. The difference with this line was that there were no workmen in sight.

"Automated!" shouted the foreman above the whine of machinery. "Two men do what took at least eight."

It was literally so. In a small booth perched above the line sat two men in white coats, facing an array of computer screens, keyboards and gauges. They controlled a series of robots—mechanical arms, really—that bent and twisted over the metal blocks in a programmed series of jerky but precise motions. The robots saved time; they allowed for greater flexibility in switching from one engine model to another and they were able to make the exacting cuts that the Germans, renowned for their metalworking ability, would once have never let anyone else do.

But most important, the Daewoo official told us, the robots were designed and manufactured in Korea, as was the intricate computer software that ran them. They were "invented by Daewoo." He and Moon grinned. It was so easy, and so condescending, to think of them as children who had just revealed a secret talent. Didn't think we could do it, did you, Dad?

While we've been busy buying and selling corporations in the United States, the Koreans had apparently been developing a number of hidden talents. Admittedly this was not cutting-edge technology. The United States and Japan each already had many kinds of industrial robots. But they were getting close to the edge. To have assembled and programmed those hydraulic arms was a remarkable feat and the implications were broad. Robotics was supposed to be one of the great technological frontiers that would make the United States competitive again. We would make the things and learn how to use them so well, one theory went, that we'd be able to build cars and television sets cheaper than the Japanese or the Koreans. But who was kidding whom?

Joint ventures, says Chairman Kim, are the future. Asia will be the manufacturing base of the next century, he says in his speeches; by 2000, it will produce 70 percent of what is made in the world. As he sees it, the United States can choose to participate or not. Daewoo is being created on his theory that the United States is good at such things as developing computer software or other new technology, at marketing and services. Korea is the place to make things. The United States can't make things anymore, he says, because we are not willing to work hard enough. "Today it seems a lot of Americans are working only for leisure," he once told an interviewer. "They work so they can take time off. That is an alien concept in Asia. Here at Daewoo, we work for pride, not leisure."

What the United States offers is a market and advanced technology. Japan protects its own market from the Koreans—or anyone else—and won't share its technology. Kim and other Korean executives are happy to give U.S. companies great deals on labor costs as long as they share their latest secrets. There seems to be no shortage of U.S. companies willing to do just that. But are such arrangements really in the United States's interest? Are we just cannibalizing what little competitive advantage we still have?

At Daewoo, they tell the story of the British shipyard firm that sent a team of consultants over to teach the Koreans how to build boats. They helped Daewoo build Okpo into one of the greatest yards in the world, turning out the most modern boats with the most efficient methods. Soon the yard was attracting orders from all over the world. Not long after that the British shipyard that sent the consultants went out of business.

Over the next few days, we learned about Korean business the old fashioned way: by drinking. As was only hinted in our first plunge into Seoul nightlife, alcohol is the great stimulant of the Korean economy. It numbs the pain of the workingman so he can make it through another 10-hour shift of tedium. But it also binds the office workers, from stock boy to director—each drinking on his own stratum, of course, in a modern tribal ritual that is not so far removed from the tribe.

"Friendship is taking someone home who is too drunk to get there by himself," explained Jae Chun, an American-educated Korean who had made his share of friends.

In a culture where the rule is that a company or a country should be run like a well-ordered family, the temptation to sneak out and let off steam is great. For a foreigner, these liquid business meetings are outings to be endured. Toasts must be given, glasses swapped, songs sung. A drunken, crying jag is a regular event, usually by a single man mourning his unmarried state. A fight or two helps the camaraderie and can often be the catalyst to bring the evening to a close with red-eyed hugs and hard slaps on the back as the revelers crawl into taxis to face home, a little sleep and another day on the corporate battlefield.

And sometimes, between the boasts at the start of the evening and the melancholy at the end, somewhere during the endless pours of *yakju,* beer or Scotch, the truth is told.

It was during one such evening of carousing with several Korean executives that a darker side of the Korean miracle began to emerge. We were at a *bulgoki* restaurant, a Korean barbecue where strips of marinated beef are cooked over a brazier placed in the center of the table. While our dinner sizzled and bubbled on the grill, one of our hosts recognized someone he knew across the room and nodded to him. The well-dressed man in his mid-30s was entertaining a group of friends who laughed and toasted as they sloshed down endless cups of rice wine. Several hostesses in silk dresses sat among them, feeding the men with chopsticks and pouring wine into their cups. By their tone, they had been drinking for some time and showed no intention of slowing down.

Our host, Se Jung, shook his head and muttered something to a companion who only spoke Korean.

"Would you rather be out with them?" Kelly asked innocently. "Looks like they've got a lot more left in them than we do." (London had already inquired about the possibility of being back at the hotel and asleep by 10, which caused the Koreans to grin in amazement.)

Se Jung looked up sharply. "I said to my friend that perhaps we should join their party, since we are already paying for it."

There was bitterness in Se Jung's voice. We pressed him to explain.

"That man is a government official, an aide to a cabinet minister. He has a salary of $400 a month, which by law is capped. That is less than what a skilled worker at a steel mill could make. But you see how he entertains? I see him and others like him at the best restaurants in Seoul. Scotch bottles, pretty girls, the whole shot. So how does he afford it?"

"He's got a rich father?" Kelly tried.

"Better. He has many rich fathers. We call them godfathers. There are many businessmen who are happy to be his friends. They pay his bills, let him sign his name at restaurants. He is a young man in an important position and he is on his way up. He can do them favors. And when he has done them enough favors, one of them will hire him to come work for his company."

Se Jung explained that in an economy where all the major decisions are made by the government, those with special access to that government are in an infinitely better position than their competitors. So the big companies and some of the wealthy smaller entrepreneurs go out of their way to make special friends. We heard stories of generals earning less than $10,000 a year but living as if they made $100,000. Cars and drivers are provided as well as homes, special stipends for "consulting services," and vacations to the United States and Europe.

Relatively subtle, but by our standards corruption in any case. Still, there was nothing like the grotesque blatancy of the Marcos regime in the Philippines, which helped bring about his election defeat. Korea, until that time, had never had a public scandal, though that may have been more a reflection of the government's control over the press. Yet everyone seemed to know it went on. Korea is a society of whom you know, but the contacts aren't the sort of casual, mutually beneficial alliances that American businessmen strike with regularity. The bonds here are sacred brotherhoods, formed in high school, college or the military academy. One has a responsibility to obey one's "elder brother," as a senior classmate is called, just as the elder brother has a responsibility to provide for his juniors. If you came from the right place—one of the handful of schools that matter—it is understood that once you reach a certain level, you are taken care of.

Such cronyism may be widespread, but it is not widely praised, we discovered. There was deep resentment on the part of many middle-class people who perceived that the game was rigged against them. Unless you were part of the elite, you could only expect the scraps that were left over. And the farther down the social order you stood, the less there was left in the end. The problem went deeper in Korean society as well. One night a businessman we were out with turned uncharacteristically morose over the fate of his driver's children. "They don't have a chance," he said. "They are smart children, but they will never go to the best schools and they will never meet people who can help them. They will be well-educated limousine drivers."

Certainly there was an appearance of equality in Korea.

Conspicuous displays of wealth were discouraged, particularly with regard to government officials. When we arrived in Seoul there were stories in the papers about several government officials who had been disciplined for having weddings that were too large. The gap between the richest and poorest was no worse than in the United States and nothing to rival, say, the Latin American countries.

Yet we found discontent and suggestions that the richer Korea got, the worse the problem would become. One of the most articulate critics we met was Lah Jae Hoo, a German and American-educated chief executive of a small trading company that was founded by his father and now exported, among other things, baseballs to the United States.

"There is no doubt that everyone in Korea is doing better," he explained one evening. "But at the top, you have people doing 100 percent better while at the bottom they are doing maybe 10 percent better. We are becoming a country of elites and the pressure is building from the bottom."

One of the main problems he saw was the domination of the economy by the *chaebol.*

"Korea has 4,500 companies who export, yet the top 100 control 90 percent of the exports and the top 10 companies control more than 50 percent. In Taiwan there are maybe 40,000 or 50,000 exporting companies. Everyone there is an entrepreneur."

Korea, Lah thought, had many Kim Woo Choongs hidden away, but did nothing to allow them to flourish. His own company was more profitable than Daewoo, if you looked at profit as a percentage of sales, yet he found it difficult to borrow from a bank. "Ask yourself why did Mr. Kim grow so fast? Because the right people opened the bank vaults for him and said take what you want."

The most consistent criticism leveled at the *chaebol* was their inefficient use of capital. For a newly developing economy, access to borrowed funds was crucial and whoever controlled those funds made life and death decisions. At least in the early days, the decisions were made by a small band of professional economists who were determined to turn Korea into another Japan. The *chaebol* were inspired by the giant Japanese trading houses called *zaibatsu,* companies such as Mitsui, Mitsubishi,

Marubeni, C. Itoh, Sumitomo and Hitachi, which were part of Japan's plan to reconstruct its economy after the devastation of World War II. But Japan had more people and more companies so the domination of a few was not so overwhelming as in Korea. By 1986, the top 10 *chaebol,* including the Big Four of Samsung, Lucky-Goldstar, Hyundai and Daewoo, accounted for almost 50 percent of the country's gross national product, its output of goods and services.

Like their Japanese role models, the firms tend to be large and inefficient, soaking up vast amounts of capital and producing goods at a relatively high cost. One reason Korea has a foreign debt of $45 billion, one of the highest in the world, is because of the voracious borrowing habits of the *chaebol.* Only cheap Korean wages make the price of their goods attractive on a world market. One Korean professor described the country's banks as "filling stations" for the *chaebol,* allowing them to exist with a debt-to-equity ratio of 9 to 1. In the United States, a similar ratio would average about 1 to 1, meaning that for every dollar borrowed, the owners have a dollar of their own invested in the company. Even for the rest of Korean companies the average ratio is about 4 to 1. The result is that large companies make huge interest payments and tiny profits.

The kind of investments that got made were billions of dollars pumped into shipbuilding because some economist has decided Korea could have a natural competitive advantage building ships. And while that may have been true for one or two companies, what usually happened was that each of the giants wanted to get into the same businesses, if for no other reason than to prevent the others from having an edge. So soon all of them were making ships, and cars, and computers, and VCRs, despite the fact that some of the companies performed well in a given area and others did not. Recently, several of the conglomerates were allowed to go bankrupt, though their parts were swallowed by the remaining giants.

"If I can make better use of a bank loan to build a computer factory, I should get the bank loan," explained Lah, citing the pure laws of the marketplace. "In Korea, I wouldn't have a chance. The attitude of the government is, 'We will tell you what is best for you. You just keep quiet and export.' "

Management, too, is a problem. Though Lah admitted he was in no position to complain, he noted that all the *chaebol* with the exception of Daewoo were dominated by executives who had risen by virtue of their relations to the founder. And this meant nephews and cousins as well as sons and brothers. In fact, as the older generation of several of the giants approached retirement, Koreans were poised for a battle for succession that Lah said could rival the television series *Dallas* for family intrigue.

The consequences, predicted Lah, would go well beyond a few disgruntled businessmen. The tight control creates a tiny elite that is not unlike the feudal tribes that ruled Korea for centuries.

There was a host of subcontractors who produced many of the component parts for the conglomerates: diodes for VCRs, auto parts, plastic cases for computers—the thousands of essential but not technically complicated operations that go into making something. It was these suppliers who provided the safety valve for the Korean economy. When times were tough, Samsung did not lay off workers, it merely cut orders to subcontractors, who laid people off or went out of business. The $300 monthly wage at the TV factory seemed generous to the worker until you realized that most of what went into the TV was being made for a lot less.

"The *chaebol* are governments unto themselves," Lah said. "Even if we get political change, how will anyone change these giants? We must remember that it was the mistakes of capitalism that started communism."

Korea's economy was the product of government planning, perhaps more than any in the world. It is at the same time one of the best run in the world and testimony to what a few smart people could do if the politicians left them alone. One of the great legacies of former President Park was to give control over the economy to civilian experts and not to meddle. Through the most repressive days of the military government, the economy operated as though it were in a separate country. We heard foul oaths directed at President Chun Doo Hwan and his cast of military cronies, but no ill was spoken of Kim Mahne Jae, the chief economic planner and by some standards the second-highest member of the government. There was a rational, intricate decision-making process that went on, much as one might find at the top levels of a huge company. Again, the model was Japan, where the Ministry of Trade and Industry controlled the destiny of the giant Japanese corporations; in Korea, it was the Economic Planning Board. Technocrats with advanced degrees from top U.S. universities made the decisions that were crucial to the running of a planned economy: What will be made? Which sectors will be favored? Who gets bank credit? Who gets taxed? How much money can be borrowed from abroad? How much money can be spent on social improvements and how much must people sacrifice?

Simple questions, extraordinarily complex answers. But if economic growth can be considered the standard of success, then in most cases, over a 20-year period, the series of anonymous economists made the right choices. Occasionally blunders were made, such as the campaign to move so fast into shipbuilding and heavy industries that Korea ended up oversupplied at a time when worldwide demand was plunging. That mistake cost a few billion dollars. But gains outweighed losses to such an extent that Korea had to be considered one of the great economic success stories in history, and the period of Chun's rule to be one of uninterrupted high growth.

The key to Korea's success had been a careful progression of steps to add value to the one resource they had: people. When Park came to power, all Korea had was people, an underfed, undereducated population of mostly subsistence farmers with no discernible skills. Through a series of five-year plans, the idea was to use the labor to make increasingly sophisticated, and expensive, products. Whatever goods could easily be produced according to the skills of Korea's workers would be made cheaper. The plan relied on one intangible factor: The labor force would need to work hard. The plan was to move from simple goods that required much labor and little machinery, such as toys and textiles, and then on to metalwork and steel making. The steel would be used to make ships and cars. And the technology that was picked up from the various foreign companies would be used to make increasingly more complicated and higher-priced goods. All the while, the emphasis was on keeping labor costs down. This was critical because it kept prices competitive, important because the other part of Korea's plan was not to sell in the domestic market—they had no money—but to export.

The Koreans had been a presence in the U.S. economy

from the late 1970s, though most consumers were unaware. They were manufacturing goods such as textiles and shoes for familiar American brand names. It was only when Korea started shipping cheap steel and the mills of the Midwest started closing, that Americans began to pay some attention, but the steel crisis had many more culprits than the Koreans. By the mid-1980s, Korea was ready to debut in its own show. Goldstar and Samsung began to export cheap televisions and VCRs under their own names. At first the products lacked the sophistication and style of the Japanese models, but in a remarkably short time, they caught up. And then in the summer of 1986 two things happened: The Japanese yen soared against the dollar and Hyundai began to export a car. The run up of the yen opened the door further to Korea's strategy of undercutting the Japanese on the U.S. consumer goods market it had come to dominate. The Japanese had seen it coming, so they didn't fight too hard. They were looking for a more expensive slice of the market anyway, adding their own value to things such as luxury cars and leaving the cheaper stuff to the Koreans.

The arrival of the Hyundai was equally momentous, because it instantly vaulted Korea into the consciousness of most Americans. After Volkswagen and Toyota, here was another odd foreign name to get used to. But those resilient American consumers were happy to oblige when they saw the $5,000 price tag for a pretty good little car. Helped by a sophisticated soft-sell television campaign, the Hyundai was, within a year, the fastest-selling import in history and it seemed the Koreans were here to stay.

In the United States, headlines finally blared, "The Koreans Are Coming!" But the Koreans knew that they were already here. For the economic planners in Seoul, everything was on schedule, even a little ahead. By 1990 they expected, likely as not, everyone in America would have a Korean VCR, or a Korean television, or a Korean car or maybe all three. Hyundai, Goldstar, Samsung and Daewoo would be household names. Everything was happening just as it was supposed to.

Yet for some of the economists we interviewed, mostly serious young men wearing crisp suits and displaying degrees from American universities on the walls of their modern offices, there was some uneasiness. They were like the minor league home-run hitter who gets his first start in the majors and realizes that he's got to face major league pitching. They were not sure they had all the skills in place quite yet.

"The next five-year plan stresses liberalization," explained Oum Bong Sung, an economist at the Korean Development Institute, a government think tank. "We have to continue to open our markets to foreign goods and we have to make the market system work for us here." He thought that the first products allowed in would be financial services, such as insurance companies, and some farm products. Manufactured goods would take longer.

Like Japan, Korea had made it very difficult for foreign countries to sell goods in their market. The theory was that its fledgling industries needed protection from predatory outsiders who could come in, undersell them and put them out of business. None of the industrial giants cared when Korea was an inconsequential economy. But now there was a question of just who was predatory. In the summer of 1986, the world had stopped treating Korea as a basket case. To the European Economic Community and to the United States it was a potential threat.

The Koreans, who have never had a reputation for being diplomatically astute, nonetheless saw this coming and were trying to head it off. They would have to figure out how to let the United States sell products in Korea or they were going to find themselves shut out of American markets. And as everyone in Korea knew, if they couldn't export, they were in serious trouble.

"We fear protectionist trends in the world more than anything," Oum admitted. "If there is a trade war, we will be the loser."

The world trade system was precariously balanced, as the Koreans saw it, and they needed stability if they were going to be able to follow their strategy of becoming the great producer of mid-priced goods. They hoped to slide in under the Japanese but ahead of low-wage nations like China. They could not afford to have countries slamming the door on their exports.

Domestically, the more liberal economic philosophy meant letting market forces make some of the decisions in certain areas. As it stood, the country's financial system in particular was archaic by rapidly developing standards. The government controlled the banks and the stock market to such an extent that there was no free flow of money. In the United States, the question of which companies can borrow money from a bank or raise it on the stock market is decided by which companies the market thinks are the most creditworthy. In Korea, such decisions were made by the crony network and could have as much to do with where a chief executive went to school as what the prospects for his company were.

The planners knew that had to stop if they expected to truly arrive in the First World, but breaking old habits was going to be difficult. Changing the financial structure meant lessening the economic power of the *chaebol;* Korea was not being run to the advantage of small businessmen. Although there was talk of changing the philosophy and curtailing the big companies, no one was betting it would happen anytime soon.

But for some of the economic deep thinkers, the debate over the power of the giant companies was only a red herring, masking a more fundamental problem.

"You have wealthy executives from big companies fighting less wealthy executives from smaller companies," explained one member of the influential Yonsei University economics faculty. "In the end, they can all make an agreement and go off to the country club together. They have all profited greatly from the so-called miracle. But what about the rest of the country? Will they be satisfied?"

With professional dispassion, several economists, all asking anonymity for fear of being too critical of the government in public, talked about the obvious inequities in the wealth of Korea. Essentially, they said that the country's one resource, its people, had been used at a bargain-basement rate. Now they were restive. Wherever street demonstrations led, there was a grander problem still to be faced. Korea could afford to give people democracy of the sort we had in the United States, but could it afford to give them a decent wage?

In Inchon one day we came face to face with the other great concern of the Korean economists. It arrived on an air-conditioned bus that wheeled into the parking lot of the Olympos Hotel and Casino at about noon. As we stood in the lobby, contemplating whether we would risk $30 to be fleeced by Korean blackjack dealers at one of two casinos in the entire country—both casinos were off-limits to Koreans, since the purpose is to bring in foreign cash, not encourage bad habits—we saw the bus disgorge a file of small, high-strung men in business suits, most carrying Japan Air Lines bags over their shoulders and some wearing terry-cloth beach hats. This could only be one thing. The scourge of Asia. A Japanese sex tour.

Many Koreans fear what some have called "The Second Japan Problem," a condition that must be described somewhere in the psychiatry texts as becoming the person you emulated only to find out that you loathe him. After years of looking enviously at their Japanese neighbors just a short ferry ride across the Korea Strait, after copying their companies and growth plans, their education system and even their microchips, many Koreans were realizing that for a variety of reasons, they did not want to be like the Japanese. We were about to witness one of those reasons.

Built on a promontory overlooking the factory-ringed harbor, the Olympos is a white-washed monstrosity that could be an early version of a Holiday Inn but for the 20-foot-high neon sign on the roof announcing its name, a teasing beacon for the sailors and dockworkers below who could never know the pleasures within. By the appearance of the invading Japanese, those pleasures must be considerable.

Grinning silly grins at each other—some stereotypes have a basis in fact—they pushed their way through the door and into the casino, a small gaudy room that looks like casinos everywhere, and up to blackjack tables, roulette wheels and crap tables behind which stood men and women in tuxedos wearing the bored expressions of casino employees everywhere.

From the airline bags, the Japanese pulled out crumpled fistfuls of won notes that they tossed on the tables like so much wastepaper. In return they were given black, green and red chips—the reds, at about $5, being the lowest—which they began to shower on the green felt tables.

At the blackjack table, two or three men would play while a crowd gathered behind them to watch. At one table, a fellow with a hefty stack of $100 black chips peered at his hole card to the assorted gutteral oohs and aahs of his companions. Finally he made his decision and turned the card up on the table. A six and a four. The dealer showed a queen. He would double down, meaning double the size of his bet and take one more card. It was not the sort of move many players with even a passing knowledge of the game would make. He now had what looked to be $1,000 in front of him. He took his card. A seven. The dealer turned up his hole card. A jack. Sorry, Charlie.

As the dealer impassively swept up the chips, the Japanese burst into laughter. First the man at the table, then his colleagues, who all clapped him on the back. Good show! Tough luck! Big deal! Or whatever they were saying. Neither of us had ever seen someone have so much fun dropping so much money on a boneheaded play.

The scene was repeated around the room. We heard cheers and giggles as towers of chips slid into the coffers of the house. In what must have been 10 minutes, the tour was tapped out. You'd have thought they were trying to lose. Maybe they were.

In groups of twos and threes they trooped off through the lobby and down a set of stairs marked "health club." London, who stood above them by at least a foot, skulked down for a look.

He found a dimly lit corridor, smelling of disinfectant and lined with black doors on either side. From a few of the doors peered small, dark-haired women wearing short white shirts that gave them the appearance of partially clad dental hygienists. In one room, several sat together, reading magazines and smoking. They looked up with hard, hollow eyes, mildly surprised to see a rare American visitor. The clientele they were used to were smaller, kinkier and a lot richer.

"Massagy?" a stout woman who seemed to be in charge asked tentatively. "Thirty dollar, but no fuckee."

It was like a line from a bad Vietnam War movie, but they really did talk like that. How else to get the point across?

More Japanese came down the stairs, some walking straddle-legged, others playfully grabbing each others crotches.

London came back and suggested we move on. As we left, we could see a dozen or so women scurrying from an adjacent building that looked like a barracks. They were heading for the health club, rubbing sleep from their eyes. So what if it was noon? The Japanese libido had to be served.

We learned that more than libidos and bad manners were at stake here. The phrase "the Next Japan" carried with it all the international bad will that the Land of the Rising Sun had been accumulating over the past decade of its ascendancy. In world business and political circles, the implication was almost always pejorative, suggesting that Korea was creating the same kind of lockstep labor force and disciplined executive corps that Japan had used to plunder markets around the world. Would Korea Inc. roll in behind Japan Inc. like some Asian combine to finish off the survivors?

For Korea, whatever their intentions, it seemed that they were about to be punished for spoils they had not yet tasted and they were determined to squelch this comparison whenever they could. We raised the question in a number of interviews, "Is Korea the next Japan?" and were uniformly met with heated denials.

Korea, the argument goes, is not like Japan because it is one-third the size (40 million people v. 120 million), because its economy is less than 10 percent, because Korea must spend a great amount on defense (6 percent of gross national product v. 1 percent) and because Korea is paying off a $45 billion debt to foreign banks while Japan racks up huge surpluses. Korea is not like Japan because the Koreans aren't the same kind of people; they are neither as obsessed with success nor as disciplined in the workplace nor as nationalistic. And finally, Korea is not like Japan because the rest of the world didn't pay attention to Japan while it was sneaking up with its strategy of slashed-price exports coupled with closed domestic markets, but every trading nation on earth was now primed to protect itself against a similar onslaught.

What was similar about Korea and Japan was the uncanny way Korea had followed Japan's growth pattern, moving rapidly through the stages of industrialization to the point where they could make almost anything and sell it cheaply. While it is more open to imports than Japan, Korea is anything but a free trader, throwing up obvious barriers like tariffs and not so obvious ones like complicated import license procedures. Like the Japanese, Koreans saved a huge part of their income, about 30 percent, which was reinvested in businesses. They argued that they were not as disciplined nor nationalistic as the Japanese, but by American standards they were ferociously so.

And it was, after all, American standards that we were interested in. We were not abstractly intrigued by these Dragons of Asia; we wanted to know how they would affect our lives. By that measure, Korea was becoming more like Japan every day. In terms of its trade surplus, Korea was now where Japan was 10 years ago with a surging imbalance that had recently tripled to $8 billion and showed no signs of slowing. Koreans had already helped decimate many American industries and now showed signs of winning control over the high-tech industries many Americans hoped would be our salvation.

What did it matter if Korea only somewhat resembled a Next Japan? We were going to travel through a handful of countries, all of which we knew were running large surpluses with the United States. We knew that Taiwan had a hotter, more formidable economy than Korea and that when Korean businessmen looked over their shoulders to see who was gaining, they worried about places like Thailand. If you put it all together, was East Asia then the Next Japan? And if so, how could the United States withstand another such invasion?

We were not the only ones who were becoming concerned about the fate of the United States in a world that suddenly seemed smarter and more aggressive than we would have imagined. One night after a few drinks and a few bottles of wine we learned one of the reasons the Koreans were so embarrassed about their success: It was because the United States, which some of them really did call "our big brother" was doing so poorly. We were dining with Kang Bong Shik, the general manager of the Shilla Hotel, one of Seoul's best, in the French restaurant on the top floor. Waiters in black tie shuttled a series of courses to our table, an elegant respite from Korean cuisine, which had developed a numbing monotony after about three days.

Kang, whose tall, tailored silhouette would have been at home in any first-class hotel, told us a story of growing up poor that by now had become very familiar. Born in 1930 . . . primitive farm town . . . barefoot to school . . . apple was the biggest treat of the year. And of course the Japanese, who ran the schools, ran the town, ran the country. He was old enough during World War II to realize that the unbearable hardships of those years were their responsibility and grew up hating them. He saw men taken away to labor camps and women to Japanese army whorehouses. Kang remembered the days of watery soups and counting out the grains of rice for each family member, and like every Korean of his generation, he marveled that he could be sitting here with white linen tablecloths, sipping a fruity Beaujolais while the lights of Seoul twinkled in the distance.

As we talked, mostly about business in Korea—you had to know someone a lot better before you could talk politics—it seemed something was bothering him. He wanted us to know that he loved the United States.

"You saved us from the communists," he said. "Many Americans died so Korea could be free. I have thought since then that America was the great hope of the world."

There was an implied "but." He averted his eyes a moment, then called the waiter to bring another bottle of wine.

"I would like to ask you," he started again, "what is wrong with America?"

It was an awkward moment. Unlike many of the people we interviewed, professional opinion givers whose answers would only go so far, Kang was genuinely upset. Unlike the younger generation, he clearly had real affection for the United States. It was apparent, too, that his question was rhetorical.

In his opinion, the United States had almost lost the will to live. Sure, there were great successes in the United States. He visited several times a year and saw the gleaming new downtown hotels in major cities, saw the prosperity. But he knew something was wrong. Why don't we compete?

He had his own ideas, which were not unlike what we had heard from other Korean executives, just delivered with more sincerity and concern.

"I think the American worker is now very lazy. He expects too much and does not give enough work in return. I think unions have done this, unions and drugs. So many people I see in the cities are like dead people. It can't go on."

He looked for some kind of response.

"I'm not sure we know the answer," said Kelly. "I'm not sure we know there's a problem."

"Don't people in America realize how hard the world is?"

And then he told us how hard his own world was. He told us that the hotel he ran, which was part of the Samsung Group, was actually a joint venture. With the hated Japanese.

"With Okura Hotels in Tokyo," he said solemnly. "The Japanese, they are the smartest and best organizers. If we want to be the best, we must learn from them."

But he left us with the impression that he'd rather not learn from them at all.

Down the hill from the Shilla Hotel is the Tongdaemun, or East Gate, market. Despite the heat of the afternoon, we decided one day to see what it had to offer. Before we reached it, though, we came to an area of what seemed like block-long warehouses lined up along Chonggye-ro, one of the main arteries of Seoul, but far enough from downtown that no one would likely go there unless he knew what he was looking for.

As we got closer, we heard a sound like a soft hiss, an insistent *sssssshhhhhh* that grew progressively louder. At the side door of one building we noticed a steady stream of people coming and going, so we wandered in and up a wide concrete stairway. At the top was a corridor so long we could not see the end. On either side were cubbyholes, about 10 feet by 20 feet, and in each of them were women at sewing machines. The sound was now like a wind rushing through the building, increasing a little in intensity and then diminishing, but never relenting. It was the sound of their labor.

We walked the sweltering corridors, up and down the stairs, poking our heads into shops now and then. There were 200 shops to a floor, five floors to a building, 10,000 shops total. With maybe 10 women in a shop, that was 100,000 people making clothes in a two-block area. The buildings were small cities, with noodle stalls, money changers and barbers every few floors.

Our reception was decidedly not cordial. Whenever we would try to talk to someone, we were met with hard stares. No tourists welcome here, no curious travelers hoping to eavesdrop on a quaint slice of foreign culture. This was real life and we could only be an unpleasant interruption. The women at the machines—they looked to be a few years older than the 18-year-olds at the Samsung plant—kept their eyes riveted to their work. Matronly supervisors would glare at us as we backed away. In some of the shops we saw babies fussing on piles of cloth as they were tended by smudge-faced girls.

It would have been an exaggeration to call the scene Dickensian. These were not starving waifs forced to work from sun up to sun down. There are greater horror stories to be found in the works of Lincoln Steffens and other histories of industrial America. Child labor isn't such a problem in Korea because of the strong family structure. Children work, but mostly after school or on holidays. For most families, schoolwork still comes first.

What we were seeing was the bottom end of the Korean economy. It wasn't that it was so horrible, just so hard.

One hundred dollars a month was the wage here, and it was a very long month. These were the people who live in dread that the orders won't come in because someone in Taiwan decided to work for less or another order went to China or someone opened a factory in Thailand where they say no one cares about how long the children work. These were the folks Lah Jae Hoo worried about, the ones who were 10 percent better off this year, while 10 blocks away in the air-conditioned comfort of the Shilla Hotel the captains of industry congratulated themselves on a year of record profits but expressed concern that maybe the wage rate was creeping a little high.

Then too, it was all well and good for Mr. Lah to talk about noble socialist goals, about evenly distributing the wealth and enjoying life. We're successful, but are we happy? he asked of his well-to-do friends. Was anyone here happy? Did the question even enter their minds? The more appropriate query seemed to be whether they would survive. Here they knew instinctively what was meant by a world market for labor. An abstract phrase such as "global competition" could be tossed about and debated in the genteel think tanks of Washington, but here in the sweating shops of Chonggye-ro was where the rubber met the road. Do it fast and do it cheap because in a labor pool of more than two billion Asians—forget the rest of the world—there was *always* someone waiting for the chance to do it faster and cheaper.

As we tried to leave, we found ourselves in a narrow alley jammed with people surging in both directions. These were not the casual shoppers of the market alleys; they were working and God help anyone who got in their way. They shouldered heavy stacks of clothing and used long bolts of textiles as battering rams. As they pushed and shoved against these two ungainly white men, we began to feel claustrophobic. There was a look of tension on the streaming, grim-jawed faces, as if the slightest provocation could set off a fistfight. We were suffocating as we backed up against a wall hoping for a break in the flow.

A mean-tempered storm was blowing in. Typhoon Vera, they called it, perhaps after some Korean War pinup girl. She whipped the wind to a 100-mile-an-hour frenzy along the coast, killing several dozen fishermen as she drove towering waves into shoreline villages. Vera advanced toward Seoul, preceded by sheets of rain that bore down on people hurrying from bus to building.

Yet in some ways the storm was a relief, a welcome midsummer diversion for a simmering city. Vera scoured the grit-laden humidity and the fetid odors that had been accumulating in sewers and subway tunnels for months. She even cleansed the scent of tear gas that lingered downtown. There were no protests while the storm raged; everyone stood in awe of nature. Even the commerce of the world-weary Hilton lobby, where businessmen are oblivious to the ordinary strains of Korean life, was forced to take notice when a particularly ferocious gust blew out the glass revolving doors. Pin-striped bankers shielded their faces with leather attaché cases as glass rained down. A most unpredictable business risk, this nature.

For four days Seoul was even grayer than its normal pallor, enveloped by a kind of sustained gloom that would cause New Yorkers to walk with increasingly slumped shoulders. The Koreans, though, were unfazed, reacting to an unchangeable fact of life with more stoicism than would an American who thinks he can control his environment.

"When you grow up worried if there will be enough dinner, you do not complain about the weather," said a Korean friend. "Maybe soon we will have that luxury."

In fact the weather in Seoul is much like that of New York, somewhat exaggerated. It is colder in the winter, and the hot and sometimes humid summer develops a monsoonlike climate that brings rain across the peninsula once a week and, toward the end of the season, typhoons from the Pacific Ocean.

When the weather cleared we pestered several Korean friends to take us to a baseball game. We needed some fun, though we learned the concept was more serious here. Jae Chun agreed with some reluctance. Baseball had not achieved the same mythical lure as in the United States, where the average male will leap at any reasonable excuse to attend a weeknight game. Jae was surprised when Kelly first mentioned it.

"Baseball?" he said tentatively. "Sure, if you want to. I'll call T.J. I think he knows how to go to a game."

Knows how to go? Has this, too, been corrupted to an Oriental art form? Do they study it? This is a skill a boy acquires naturally. Kelly tried to explain to Jae how it worked. First you go with your dad, forming an inseparable male bond based on having shared legendary pitching performances or ninth-inning home runs. Then you graduate to outings with your pals, outings that consist of searching the crowd for girls in halter tops and drinking beer while under the legal age.

"It's a ritual, Jae. You must do this several times a summer for the rest of your life."

"I'm not sure this will work here," Jae said. "I think in Korea we like to play sports more than watch."

Indeed, along with tae kwon do—the Korean form of karate—wrestling, boxing, soccer, hiking and even baseball, the average Korean kid is pretty active. But if this country was going to make it to the big leagues of spectator sports, they were going to have to learn how to sit and watch. Maybe T.J. would know.

T.J. borrowed his father's car and drove us to Chamshil Stadium, a modern 40,000-seat baseball park 20 minutes from downtown Seoul. It was a great night for baseball. A warm breeze blew across the left-field fence—a boost for those right-handed power hitters—while the Chongo Pintos and the O.B. Bears stretched and sprinted through their warmups. According to T.J., who did know his way around a ballpark, the Bears, sponsored by the biggest Korean brewer, were a powerhouse team while the Pintos, owned by a popular noodle company, were surprising upstarts who had several recent upset victories.

Before the game we dined in a stadium restaurant on noodles covered with a black sauce made of squid ink ("Do not let the foreign guests pay," the elderly proprietor chastised Jae when London reached for the check). There was no beer in the ballpark so we smuggled in two six-packs of OB. We also brought our own peanuts and a traditional Korean drinking accompaniment, dried cuttle fish. We settled into surprisingly comfortable plastic seats—right behind first base—and waited for the great pastime to begin.

Only two things were wrong. First, the bats did not crack.

They pinged. Instead of the hickory wood Louisville Sluggers that defined the sound of a home run with a crisp *thwock,* the Koreans used new-tech aluminum models that emitted an entirely unsatisfying sound like that of a quarter dropping on a sidewalk. The other problem was that there was practically nobody at the ballpark. We got there at 6 P.M. By the starting time of 6:30 there were maybe 1,000 people on hand. The pings of batting practice echoed off the concrete stadium walls unmuffled by human flesh. T.J. explained that many factories or offices didn't let out by 6:30.

The game was fine. The Korean players, muscular but much shorter than American major leaguers, were acrobatic fielders and competent hitters, but few had the power to put the ball very deep. The ballpark hung on them like an oversize uniform. Outfielders on both teams played most batters about halfway in from the fence and not once was a ball hit over their heads. The pitchers were precise, if not particularly fast.

By the fifth inning our attention began to wander. In a beery stupor we lounged in the seats. Jae talked about his impending enlistment in the military. He had postponed the inevitable with two years of graduate school in the States, but now his time had come.

"I don't know, maybe I should try the navy. The army might make me stupid like T.J.," he joked.

"The army will make you a man," T.J. retorted, flexing a solid bicep.

Every male in Korea must serve in the military and it is looked upon as serious business. Korea is a nation in which opposing armies face each other across a truce line. For 35 years there had been a tenuous peace and the military was always in a state of readiness. The situation is complicated and the actual threat from the North difficult to evaluate. Military posturing was important to both North and South Korea for reasons of international as well as domestic politics. The North's intentions were the subject of endless debate in the think tanks and military conclaves of Seoul, Washington and Tokyo.

But to Jae Chun and T.J. Lee, watching baseball on a quiet summer night, the threat was very real.

"Our whole culture has been shaped by war," Jae said. "We don't know it firsthand but our parents do. We have been drilled in it in school. We have seen the pictures of Seoul when it was nothing but mud. Today we hear the air-raid siren tests and wonder if they are real. We read the warnings from the military about North Korean troop movements."

They were both skeptical of many of the wilder claims of impending invasion. Despite the controlled Korean press, Jae and T.J. were sophisticated enough to realize the value to the government of crying wolf at opportune moments.

"The blanket of national security can cover many evils," Jae said. "Especially in our parents' generation, people are willing to give up freedoms in favor of national security. And who's to say there is no threat?"

In the end, Jae said, he and many Koreans subscribed to the unassailable logic of the argument that went: If we take the North too seriously and we are wrong, we have lost something. But if we don't take them seriously enough and we are wrong, we have lost everything.

Part of the problem is that the South Koreans—or anyone else in the free world, for that matter—know so little about their former countrymen. Along with places like Albania, Laos and Burma, North Korea is among the most closed societies in the world—successor to the days when all of Korea was known as the Hermit Kingdom. Few countries have diplomatic relations and most journalists and scholars are barred. For most Koreans, the million-man army of the North—the fifth largest in the world—stands as a terrifying ogre set to pounce unexpectedly.

For T.J., the ogre was a little less mysterious. He had never seen it, but he'd talked to it.

"When I was on duty along the DMZ, sometimes you could talk to the soldiers from the North," T.J. recalled. "At night, when it was quiet you could hear them talking to us. We'd yell back at them, 'Hey, come on over. We got girls here.' At first you think, they probably don't even know what girls are. Then you realize of course they do. They're just some 20-year-old guys like me. And they're Koreans too."

Jae said that among students and, increasingly, the middle class there was hushed talk of reconciliation. Some of the more radical student groups even professed a preference for the supposed egalitarianism of the North over the class system of the South. But even the most radical students chose their words carefully because the subject was enormously sensitive and the penalties for sedition harsh.

"If we have freedom to speak, maybe this is one of the subjects that will be heard," said Jae. "I think most Koreans would tell you that in their hearts, they would like the country to be reunited."

The Pintos staged a rally in the seventh inning and went on to a 4–0 victory, but the game had lost some of its allure. We left the ballpark and went on to a series of bars, talking more politics than baseball. Somehow baseball seemed like a quaint kids' game and in Korea these days it was hard to be a kid.

We drank into the night until Jae was certifiably falling-down drunk, signaling a merciful end to the evening. T.J. slopped Jae into a cab and observed a Korean aphorism. "A friend is someone who has taken you home drunk," he said with a grin. Then he turned with impeccable timing and added, "Jae and I are very good friends."

Early the next morning, suitably hung over, we followed in reverse the road the North Korean army would take into Seoul if push came to shove. The main road to Panmunjom, the site of the truce that suspended but didn't end the Korean War, is the Unification Highway that runs about 30 miles to the border. The trip takes 45 minutes, depending on traffic.

"It's the distance from Dulles airport to downtown Washington," one U.S. military man had joked. "They could invade in taxi cabs."

They could, unless the fortifications along the highway were manned. Cleverly concealed under bridge abutments are gun emplacements with thin slits overlooking cleared fields of fire. The farm fields to either side are bisected by reinforced berms with pillboxes set into the earth. The highway itself is crossed by a curious series of concrete overpasses unconnected to roads. Our driver explained that they are huge blocks meant to be dynamited and dropped onto the road to prevent an armored advance.

Twenty minutes out of Seoul the balance of the landscape begins to shift from rural to military. The road was still lined with pine trees and wildflowers, but the traffic became mostly jeeps and drab olive trucks interrupted by an occasional tour bus. At one point a platoon of Korean infantry, their faces smeared with camouflage paint, emerged from the tree line, startled, it seemed, to find a highway.

At the southern end of Freedom Bridge, a half-mile span across the Imjin River, there were a series of memorials to the Korean War and a snack shop. Just as we arrived, a carload of five Japanese tourists, all corpulent businessmen in the holiday uniform of white short-sleeve shirts, navy pants and white terry-cloth sun hats, parked in the "no parking" zone and clambered ahead of us to photograph one another in front of the marble and bronze monument.

The memorial had the key dates of the war on its base, offering a shorthand history of the fast, furious conflict that left a million Koreans and 50,000 Americans dead. On June 25, 1950, armored columns from the North crossed the 38th parallel. Within a month, the soldiers of the South and much of the population had been pushed back to a precarious perimeter at Pusan. After MacArthur's dramatic Inchon landing, Seoul was recaptured and the Allied forces pushed on to the Chinese border—at which point the Chinese entered the war and Seoul was retaken by the communists. The capital was again recaptured by United Nations and Korean forces in March 1951, and nine months after the whole thing started the two sides settled in for a grinding war of attrition roughly along the 38th parallel. On July 27, 1953, a truce was finally signed.

Beyond Freedom Bridge life was all military. Defensive holes were gouged from the earth and sandbags reinforced every building. In the distance, practice artillery rounds—at least we assumed they were practice—thudded into a hillside. Signs announced encampments for Korean and American units: "Manchu Regiment," "Ninth Infantry/Keep Up the Fire," "This is Manchu Country." As we passed Warrior Base, we saw dozens of hulking armored personnel carriers parked in formation. Painted slogans lined the roadside, like advertisements for the glory of war: "You have never lived until you have almost died." "Life has a flavor the protected never know."

Finally a sign announced Camp Bonifas, "In Front of Them All." Observation posts perched on bare hilltops, campsites were fortified with trenches and sandbagged machine-gun emplacements were manned around the clock. It was, according to a military briefing officer, the only U.S. camp in the world so tightly fortified. Perhaps that was because it faced the only enemy army in recent years to demonstrate a willingness to attack.

In the war between East and West, this is the most volatile border in the world. The South Koreans, who are meticulous at cataloguing every perceived intrusion, claimed then that the North had violated terms of the truce 76,000 times since 1953. Several days before we arrived, there had been an exchange of gunfire across the truce line—a not uncommon event. Memories still lingered of the two American servicemen who were axed to death in 1976 by North Korean soldiers while they were attempting to cut back tree limbs blocking the view from an observation post. Now the United States trims trees with 200 troops and an escort of helicopter gunships.

More disconcerting were the tunnels. In the late 1970s, South Koreans discovered three elaborate, concrete-reinforced tunnels dug far under the DMZ. Each could accommodate the movement of 600 men an hour and seemed an extraordinary expenditure of resources unless intended for use.

Then there was the dam that everyone in Seoul was talking about. South Korean intelligence had discovered that the North was constructing a massive hydroelectric dam just north of the DMZ on the upper branch of the Han River, the same river that runs through the center of Seoul. The most innocent explanation the South could conjure was that the North intended to reverse the flow of the Han to create electric power, the consequence of which would be to dry up key tributaries in the South. But the most malevolent explanation was that the dam was a weapon that could be dynamited to cause catastrophic floods in Seoul. They called it the "water bomb."

The United States has a very visible 40,000 troops stationed alongside the Koreans—along with some not-so-visible tactical nuclear weapons. The total U.S.–Korean army of 640,000, called the Combined Forces Command, is under the authority of an American four-star general. Against this stands a North Korean army of 840,000 with a 3 to 1 advantage in tanks, a far greater amount of artillery and a larger navy. In the past several years, military analysts reported, the North moved 65 percent of its forces closer to the DMZ and increased their level of readiness.

Across the Bridge of No Return is a bulge in the DMZ called Panmunjom, the hamlet that got transformed into a diplomatic meeting center where 35 years of continuing peace talks have taken place. From here, stretching north and south, the 150-mile-long demilitarized zone bisects Korea like a badly made surgical scar. The line is enforced with anti-tank walls, mine fields, barbed wire and a security fence that runs the width of the country.

The centerpiece of the truce site is a bare shed that serves as the conference room. Precisely straddling the truce line is a table covered in green felt; on the days when the two sides meet, it accommodates a handful of military men from either side, flanked by nervous security guards.

The room was empty when we visited with a few other uniformed military personnel taking a tour. But from the windows, North Korean guards peered in impassively, one taking photographs. Beyond the shed we could see the administration building for the North and from its windows more soldiers watched us.

"Now don't cross the line at the center of the room," a U.N. escort officer cautioned with a practiced smile. "We don't want an international incident on our hands."

The laughter was genuinely nervous. Within a relatively few miles of where we stood there were about a million combat-ready troops, frozen in place from a war that never ended and hoping somebody didn't twitch. The greatest threat of war, a U.S. military officer had told us, is from a mistake, an accident that gets out of control. Such as in 1984 when a North Korean decided to defect right at the truce site. Guards followed him across the truce line and a firefight began, resulting in the death of three North Koreans and an American. Close up, the North Koreans seemed truly menacing, the confrontation very real. They are, everyone said, crazy people, unpredictable.

But from an observation post nearby, the conflict took on more comic dimensions. As we looked out over a beautiful green valley, cooled by a gentle breeze that rustled the trees, we could see a village on the North Korean side. It was known as Propaganda Village, the escort officer said, "It's just like a model South Korean rural village—only no one lives there. It's a movie set."

Nearby, the South had its own version, but this was a working farm village where the population was given large government subsidies to work the land for the edification of the North. The village in the South was marked by a 100-foot-wide South Korean flag flying from a 300-foot-tall flag pole that more closely resembled a radio broadcast tower. Recently the North Koreans had installed their own flag and pole—this one almost 500-feet tall.

As we listened to this tale of one-upmanship, we realized that the scene had a sound track. We heard music that could have come from a bad Italian opera played on a cheap phonograph, whiny and haunting, alternately increasing or diminishing as the breeze shifted.

"Propaganda music," the escort officer explained. Through binoculars, he pointed out giant gray loudspeakers. "Sometimes it goes all day."

"What do they say?" someone wanted to know.

"Sometimes it's news or revolutionary poems. Usually it's some hymn to the greatness of Kim Il Sung," he said. "That's all they ever sing about."

He also pointed to a distant hillside where giant Chinese characters had been cut into the stone. It said, "Unification through self-reliance," a quote from Kim Il Sung, the Great Leader of the Democratic People's Republic of Korea, whose presence loomed like a thunderstorm beyond that deceptively sunny valley.

If we were to believe the descriptions of their countrymen in the South, North Korea would be something like a giant Jonestown, just waiting for the Rev. Jim Jones, or, in this case, Kim Il Sung, to order his followers to drink the poisoned fruit punch, invade the South, or carry out whatever other urge moved him. The picture South Koreans drew was composed partly of government propaganda, partly of unpleasant experience and largely of ignorance. If you fear what you don't know, then the South Koreans are rightly terrified.

There are few places on earth about which less is understood than North Korea. The 20 million citizens have taken to heart the historical notion of the Hermit Kingdom and isolated themselves from the scrutiny of the modern world. Accounts by the occasional professor, diplomat or journalist offer some help.

The country seems austere and functional. Yann Layma, a French photographer who traveled there in 1986, shot pictures of modern apartment blocks lined by barren boulevards, revolutionary posters looming over empty streets, ancient steam locomotives and hundreds of workers in lush cabbage fields. He described the 45-story Koryo Hotel—a gift from the people to Kim on his birthday—as having 600 rooms, only 12 occupied. He said there was not a single traffic light in the capital of Pyongyang, nor was there need for one. Citizens are forbidden to own a bicycle or a car.

Yet others saw signs of prosperity. Bruce Cummings, an American academic who visited the country in 1981, wrote that crossing into North Korea from China felt like "one has left a poor country for a moderately well-off one. The fields are deep green and every inch of land is carefully tended; construction projects hum with around-the-clock shifts." He observed the same feeling of time warp others have reported: "The country has an isolated, antiquarian, even bucolic atmosphere, as if one were thrown back to the 1940s." But there are modern hospitals, the people seemed well-fed and he noted that "the elite drive Volvos and Mercedeses and tend to be flashy in showing off foreign consumer items like watches."

What every visitor notes is the omnipresence of the image of Kim Il Sung. From 72-foot gold-plated statues to photographs in every home, North Korea offers perhaps the greatest modern display of a national cult of personality revolving around the Great Leader. He is the sun in the morning and the moon at night, as it were, variously described as the "iron-willed, ever-victorious commander," the "respected and beloved leader" and the "supreme brain of the nation." The history books claim that beginning in 1926—when he would have been 14—he led the guerrilla war that defeated the Japanese. The official press ascribes great feats to him such as helping to unsnarl problems in the construction of roads and creating plans for textile plants. And, it seems, no detail is too small for the attention of the Great Leader. "The attire of our women must be altered somewhat," he wrote in one of his nearly 1,000 volumes of philosophy and instruction. "The long skirts they are wearing are too long. The short skirts that some of our women are wearing these days are attractive, don't hinder movement and are fairly economical in their use of cloth."

If time stopped in the 1940s, it is likely because that is when Kim started. At the age of 34 he emerged as the strongest leader in the Soviet-controlled North. Despite the hyperbole, he had been an effective guerrilla leader during the last decade of the Japanese occupation and this became the prime legitimizing credential in postwar Korea, giving him, in the minds of some, moral authority over the leaders in the South, many of whom had collaborated with the Japanese. Kim surrounded himself with a loyal cadre of fellow guerrillas who had fought the Japanese in Manchuria, alongside the Chinese communists. But while he may have learned some organizing skills and ideology from the communists, from the beginning Kim has stressed Korean nationalism, not international communism.

The government does have a typical Marxist-Leninist structure with a strong party controlling a bureaucracy that makes centralized economic decisions based on long-term planning rather than market forces. Kim has taken some ideas from the Soviet system, some from the Chinese, but has always been careful not to commit too heavily in one direction or the other. What he has created seems to be a system unique to North Korea. For example, the symbol of the Korean Workers Party is a hammer, sickle and calligraphy brush, meant to emphasize the role of intellectuals and technocrats in the party—a group that is scorned by more traditional communist systems. Education seems no less important in the North than the South and worker discipline bears no resemblance to slothful Eastern European communist countries.

Kim's central plank is a philosophy he calls *juche,* which can approximately translate as "self-reliance." As Cummings wrote: "It really means placing all foreigners at arm's length and resonates deeply with Korea's Hermit Kingdom past. . . . *Juche* takes Korean ideas as basic, foreign ideas as secondary." By the 1970s, he said, *juche* had triumphed fundamentally over Marxism-Leninism as the basic ideology of the regime.

Whatever one calls the philosophy, the concept is encouraged by many developing countries who try to keep things homegrown. The realities of world trade and technology would not appear to allow for such a simple solution, though if anyone had the discipline to pull it off, it would be the Koreans. The results so far, those that can be gleaned from a country unwilling to publish economic statistics, seem mixed.

Some observers argue that North Korea is among the most successful socialist economies. It is a land rich in basic resources such as coal and iron ore with a hardworking, educated population driven by an instinct for survival. Agriculture is mechanized and sophisticated. Put on top of that an industrial infrastructure created by the Japanese and you have a formula for success in manufacturing, mining, textiles, steel, heavy machinery and arms—all sectors where the North seems to do well.

Or, at least they were doing well into the 1980s, when advancing technology seemed to be outstripping their natural advantages. Estimates are that the North's economy grew by about 3 percent a year through this decade while the South grew by about 8 percent. Per capita income in the North is estimated at $900 a year, against $3,000 for the South. With twice the population, the South has an economy that is at least four times as large. And the gap is growing.

Among the factors dragging the North down are estimates that it spends almost one quarter of its gross national product on defense—compared to about 6 percent for the South. Military analysts from South Korea claim the North imposes seven to 10 years of military service on young men, shrinking the labor pool considerably. The North appears less willing to deviate from centralized economic planning, even as most other communist countries have experimented with modified market incentives. The North has one of the world's worst credit ratings after a series of bank loan defaults for machinery purchases. And finally, they have no silicon chips, and little of the other high-tech equipment that is freely flowing across most other borders and changing the nature of industry.

This may all change when Kim dies. Or it may not. For years the betting has been that he would be succeeded by his son, Kim Jong Il, or "Dear Leader," in cult parlance. The few photos of the son make him appear to be a middle-aged, round-faced, smaller copy of the father, distinguished by his wildly disheveled hair. But in the South, there are rumors of a discontented military, a discontented stepmother, an ill son. Writing in the *Wall Street Journal* in 1986, Adi Ignatius found a typically ambiguous discussion of the succession question. At last it was settled, but sources wouldn't say which way it went.

"What is most glorious and magnificent in the experience

of our party, gained in settling the question of inheritance of the revolution," wrote *Rodong Sinmun,* the official paper of the KWP, "is that the question of the successor of the political leader has been settled correctly and the organizational and ideological foundation and the leadership system to realize his leadership have been established." But nowhere does the paper say who that successor will be.

The mystery and the unpredictability endure. On four occasions over the last 20 years, the North apparently has tried to murder leaders from the South. In 1974, the wife of President Park was killed during an assassination attempt. In 1983, four cabinet ministers and 21 other people were killed in a bombing in Rangoon, Burma. If anything, Kim Jong Il is thought to be more impetuous than his father. While we were in Korea, he was implicated in the bizarre kidnapping of a South Korean film director and actress, who were abducted in Hong Kong and brought to Pyongyang to upgrade the local film industry. The pair escaped after three years in captivity and reported that the younger Kim, who they thought was running the country, spent much of his time engrossed in his library of 20,000 Western films.

In aphorism-rich South Korea, there is one they should add: Just because you're paranoid doesn't mean there isn't somebody out to get you.

The General agreed to talk to us if we wouldn't use his name. He was a high-ranking army officer who had made the transition to politician, serving at various times as an adviser to President Chun. In fact he was from one of the military academy classes that had spawned most of Korea's current leadership.

The General wore a business suit that fit him well enough, the way a decent tropical worsted might look draped over a block of granite. His square face could have been the sculptor's model for the hard-eyed, high-cheekboned citizens who shoved their way through the subways of Seoul. Even as he shook hands and nodded curtly, there was a controlled fierceness to his movements that advertised him as a descendant of Mongol warriors.

We had dinner in a private room in one of the towering downtown hotels. The General drank a Scotch in two gulps then ordered steak. When the meal came, he slurped his soup while gnawing at a fistful of bread. As he cut his rare meat he held the knife clenched in his palm, as he had learned in basic training.

A friend had arranged the interview, which didn't seem to be going all that well as it became apparent that the only sound in the room was that of The General enjoying his food with open-mouthed efficiency.

Kelly tried the one gambit that seemed to soften all older Koreans. Tell us, he asked, what it was like to grow up in Korea.

"Bean skins," The General replied with a full mouth.

Pardon?

"During the war, we ate bean skins. We lived on bean skins."

The war was the Second World War and the skins were from soybeans grown in Manchuria and crushed for oil at a Japanese-run processing plant. The Japanese shipped train-loads of them to Korea to feed the conquered people they treated as human draft animals.

"In the summer they would rot. You ate as much as you could from the pile and hoped it would last."

He paused and studied a piece of steak on his fork, transfixed for a moment by its fat-marbled beauty. Then he looked up and laughed.

"And now I eat steak!" he said triumphantly. "If I want steak, I have steak."

He returned to his meal, leaving us to contemplate what he must have felt was a self-evident point. It wasn't. London tried again.

"Are you talking about the incredible economic changes that have taken place here?"

The General glared at the question as if it had been asked by an impudent second lieutenant. He exhaled heavily through his nose to clear the stench of naiveté.

"What you *want* to ask me is why the government must be so brutal with the political protesters in the streets."

The thought had crossed our minds.

"The answer is that Koreans have known the worst brutality and we will not let it happen again. We are becoming rich because we are strong. Because we are disciplined. The protests make us weaker. I don't know what will happen, but we have tried democracy before and it didn't work. The problem with one vote for one man is that there are too many stupid men. Even if it comes, we'll see how long it lasts."

Then he stopped himself and set his jaw. "I told you I will not talk about politics. I'll only say that whatever happens, order must prevail."

Few in the Korean military like to talk about politics in public, though since 1960, the generals and colonels have controlled the political debate. The source of stability and repression in modern Korea has been the classrooms of the Korean Military Academy, the Korean West Point. In 1960, the eighth class of the academy, which graduated in 1952, overthrew the country's brief experiment in democracy and installed Gen. Park Chung Hee as president. Nineteen years later, the 11th class, led by Chun Doo Hwan, grew restive and seized control. For three decades, key cabinet, legislative and business posts have been held by former generals in suits.

Despite its power, even experienced students of Korea talk of the military as a mysterious institution. Professionally the Korean army gets high marks as a skilled fighting force. Politically, the military is said to be saddled by internecine warfare, often the result of school days' alliances and rivalries.

The only topic The General was comfortable discussing was "the threat from the North" which was, after all, the reason for his exalted status in society.

"The North has a two-front strategy," he said, reflecting what we understood was official military doctrine. "They will create a guerrilla movement in the South. They have many kinds of special forces troops and we think they want to use traitors from the population. They will create unrest. On the border, they will move fast, sending all their troops at once. If they can take Seoul, perhaps they have won."

Seoul was the prize. If it could be taken quickly, then the South would have to come to terms.

The defense strategy was nothing magic. Stop them early with everything you had. If you didn't stop them in their tracks within a week, you were in trouble.

"We must be prepared to fight at any moment. There is no choice."

But did he really believe the North was as hostile as his propaganda made it sound?

Again, the glare. A pause.

"Their armor, their artillery, their infantry is all forward deployed. They are positioned to move on a few days' notice. Nowhere in the world is there an army so big and so ready to attack.

"And look at the prize. Look at what we have created in the South. Look what they have. The distance between us is greater every year. They think that if they are bold, they can have it."

Wouldn't the cost in lives be extraordinary?

He spoke slowly in words that dropped to the floor like brass shell casings.

"I believe they are not rational."

End of discussion.

Then, surprisingly, The General asked if we would join him for a drink at the rooftop nightclub. He was meeting a friend, an American officer with whom he'd served in Vietnam who was now a businessman. He said he wanted to talk with us a little more about the importance of maintaining U.S. troops in Korea. "The critical balance," he called it. Korean officials choked when President Jimmy Carter announced that the Koreans would be able to defend themselves by the early 1980s and he would start pulling out U.S. troops. A storm of protest from the Pentagon and Capitol Hill reversed the decision, but The General admitted that he and his colleagues have been very nervous ever since.

We had found ourselves groping through many surreal scenes in Korea, but nothing approached the spectacle of the Lotte Hotel nightclub, a Korean version of the international high life. When we got off the elevator, red strobe lights and a disco beat pulsed at us like hot breath. A troupe of topless dancers ran back and forth among tables of dark-suited Korean businessmen leering through liquor-hazed eyes.

We joined The General's American friend, who it turned out was now a lobbyist for U.S. companies trying to sell products in Korea. As the two Viet vets clapped each other on the back, the dance troupe emerged for their next number carrying toy M-16 rifles and attired in strategically ripped military fatigues that exposed generous expanses of bottoms and busts.

They danced to a song called *Nineteen,* an American disco tune with a message, if there could be such a thing, that had once made a brief appearance on U.S. radio stations.

"The average age of a U.S. soldier killed in Vietnam was nineteen," intoned an authoritative voice as the background chorus sang, "N-n-n-n-nineteen. Nineteen. Nineteen.N-n-n-n-n-nineteen."

While the dancers kicked and spun and bent their behinds in the faces of appreciative customers, The General watched impassively. The American whispered to him about the importance of lowering trade barriers and letting U.S. companies into the market.

"N-n-n-n-nineteen. Nineteen."

The strobe made faces leap out of the dark booths. It was an Oriental Gomorah. A silver-haired Korean nuzzled a young woman in a ball gown who might, possibly, have been his wife. Three fat, mustachioed Middle Easterners sat with their chubby fingers on the knees of three prim Korean hostesses. Two Buddhist monks with gray robes, shaven heads and a half-empty bottle of Scotch in front of them giggled and swayed drunkenly. If the student radicals we'd seen earlier could observe this scene, the timetable for revolution might be moved up.

Kelly ventured to have a nightcap with the American at the Hilton bar, a drink neither of them needed.

"The General," he shook his head. "That little fucker's as tough as they come. I saw him operate in Nam. All those Koreans, man, could they take a hurt and keep on fighting. And God help you if they caught you. The NV regulars were scared shitless of 'em.

"You take that little guy sitting there in his suit tonight looking like some kind of diplomat. Hell, if you pissed him off that little fucker'd cut your heart out with a K-bar knife."

He demonstrated the technique.

"*Zip. Zip.* Right out. Thank you very much. Clean as you please. And he'd be smiling all the while.

"But I love 'em. I love that mean streak. They're all great little people, we just have to teach 'em how to behave. Sometimes they're too tough for their own good. Last week I heard about a private who gave a lieutenant some guff in a chow line. The looey beat the guy to death. That's a hard way to run an army.

"Or, take The General. That guy could go a lot farther in this government but he got himself in that shitstorm of trouble before."

How so?

"Hell, don't you know? He was one of the guys who ran that Kwangju show."

A little more than 24 hours later, on a Sunday morning, Kelly headed off by train to find out about that Kwangju show. We had heard the name recited like a mantra by the left. It was, they claimed, the most powerful symbol of what they stood against. Kwangju was a place and an event that represented the culmination of military repression, regional bigotry and American imperialism. For South Korea, it was as if Kent State and the assassination of Martin Luther King, Jr. had come on the same traumatic day.

Kwangju is a city 150 miles south of Seoul where, in May 1980, students and other protesters took over the streets and occupied the provincial capital building. The government responded with a show of force that turned bloody. The accounts vary as to how many were killed. The government acknowledges almost 200. Critics claim 2,000. The most radical dissidents also say that blame for the entire affair belongs to the United States. Depending on how far left one was, the United States either ordered the harsh crackdown or merely looked the other way while frontline troops were mobilized and sent to quiet the unrest. Whatever the reality, it was clear in 1986 that time had made this incident more, not less, powerful. As the voices of protest continued to rise throughout Korea, the name Kwangju was heard with increasing frequency. Each May, the anniversary is marked with violent demonstrations across the country. If the dissidents had their way, it would be the scene, or the excuse, for much more violence to come.

What really happened in Kwangju? Was it premeditated, brutal repression or the legitimate response to a citizens' revolt? There were no authoritative sources to turn to. The Korean government had never publicly investigated the incident—though even if it had, the findings would have been untrustworthy. The swelling opposition occasionally dropped dark hints that, should they prevail, an investigation of Kwangju and an assessment of blame would be high on their agenda. But they offered no coherent story for what had happened over those few days in May. For its part, the U.S. State Department had never made a public statement, though some of the officials with responsibility for Korea have disavowed any U.S. role. Congress had never bothered to inquire into the events that have continued to mar our relations with the people of a key ally.

We had read two private reports on the incident, both compiled in 1985 and each coming to a very different conclusion.

Asia Watch, a Washington-based human rights group, portrayed the incident as a calculated massacre. Their interviews with witnesses provided chilling details that had not been reported anywhere else.

Describing the events of May 19, the report said, "At 10:30 in the morning about 1,000 Special Forces troops were brought in. They repeated the same actions as the day before, beating, stabbing and mutilating unarmed civilians, including children, young girls, and aged grandmothers. . . . Several sources tell of soldiers stabbing or cutting off the breasts of naked girls; one murdered student was found disemboweled, another with an "X" carved in his back. About 20 high school girls were reported killed at Central High School."

When it came to the death toll, Asia Watch was confident of a high number. "[One] source estimated 200 dead and 1,000 injured throughout the city; one reporter personally counted 200 bodies himself, so the death rate was undoubtedly higher: Many estimates now put the death toll at 2,000."

At about the same time, a different version of events was published by Daryl Plunk, a respected Korea analyst with the conservative Heritage Foundation. Plunk saw the events suffering from "great exaggeration and distortion." Based on interviews with government and private sources, Plunk concluded that the incident was a full-fledged rebellion that got out of the hands of the student protesters. There was brutality on both sides, he wrote, but the government made its best effort to keep the situation in control. He said that the government-supported death toll of 191 and 850 injured was the only credible figure and that none of the higher estimates was backed up by any evidence.

The Kwangju incident was "not a deliberate plot by the ROK government to massacre innocent civilians," Plunk wrote. "Given the extent of the insurrection, the death toll was remarkably low."

Clearly this was to be a part of the story where objectivity was impossible. Still, we had to see the place, to find out if the power of the icon was apparent. And there was someone with whom we wanted to talk. Through several sources we had heard about a university professor, Myung Ro Kuen, who had witnessed the demonstrations, who had tried to stop them and who had studied them in the aftermath. We would see what he had to say.

We made the decision for Kelly to take the train rather than fly because an uncomfortable feeling of paranoia was overtaking us. Veteran foreign correspondents had warned us to be careful of exposing sources to scrutiny by government security agents. "You'll be watched," one said. "But nobody's going to bother you. The Koreans are too smart for that. They'll just pay a visit on whomever you interviewed." Trains did not require passports or advance purchase tickets. Korean security officials probably kept track of all foreigners who flew within the country. It was less likely they paid attention to the trains. Or so we thought. Then again maybe subconsciously we were just acting out a certain conceit, pretending we were important enough for the Koreans to care about. We were confused, suspicious and tentative. Paranoia does that to you.

In any case, if anybody from the Korean Central Intelligence Agency cared about such things early on a Sunday morning, it would not have been difficult to learn that a Westerner was heading to a curious place. There was exactly one tall, blond-haired American on the train to Kwangju that left Seoul's cavernous Japanese colonial station at 7:30 A.M.

The clean, air-conditioned train was about half full, mostly with families on the way to visit relatives for the day. There were picnic baskets, crying children and a necking couple. Everyone was clean, well-dressed and well-mannered. If they thought Kelly odd, they didn't show it.

The scenery for the three-hour trip was predominantly small but steep hills covered with pine trees. It was pretty land that masked the fundamental harshness of Korea: not enough arable soil. At occasional breaks in the hills, hamlets had sprung up housing farmers who tended small but lush rice paddies and dried bunches of chili peppers in the sun. They lived in the traditional thatch-roofed cottages with mud sides, their towns seeming to have been untouched by the slabs of concrete that the *saemaul* reconstruction movement had showered on villages we had seen to the north and east. Close to Kwangju, some factories appeared but they too were older, smaller and grimier than what we had seen elsewhere.

This was the province of Cholla, the southwest corner of the Korean peninsula. In the nation's hierarchy, this region was at best second-class. Centuries ago the area had been the heart of the Paekche kingdom—one of the three founding kingdoms of Korea, along with Silla to the east and Koguryo to the north. The Paekche were the most scholarly and religious of the three kingdoms. Some historians claim it was Paekche missionaries who brought Buddhism to the wild pirate island of Japan. The sculpted and painted Buddhas created by their artisans glow with distinctly benevolent smiles, sometimes called "the Paekche smile." The land was not so harsh as that to the north and for a time the Paekche enjoyed what might have been the most serene lifestyle in Korean history. But as any Korean will tell you, softness invites aggression. With Darwinian inevitability, stronger neighbors encroached on Paekche turf until 660 A.D., when the Silla armies, with help from Tang dynasty Chinese mercenaries, overran Paekche and began a tradition of persecution that the residents of Cholla believe endures to this day.

"The Korean Miracle is in Seoul," one labor organizer told us. "In Cholla things have always been the same." When we visited, there were a few textile plants in the region—underwear and socks were the most popular products—as well as some low-end electronics assembly plants. A salary of $100 a month was considered good for a Cholla workingman—about a third of the rate elsewhere.

Some Koreans think this discrimination was one of the factors behind the Kwangju incident. The government needed to make a tough stand against protests igniting throughout the country and only here could they do it without offending important constituencies. The citizens of Kwangju were deemed expendable.

At the Kwangju train station one Caucasian passenger disembarked and looked around in bewilderment at the array of undecipherable signs in *hangul.* A phone booth provided salvation.

"Reverend Chun, please," Kelly tried.

Pause. Followed by a stream of Korean words ending with, "Wait, wait."

A second voice came on.

"Walk ahead maybe five blocks. To tire store. Turn right on little street. Go to white church. Come to back. We wait."

Click.

The streets at this end of Kwangju were something out of the Wild West: dirt roads lined with mud-sided buildings in front of which sat young men who eyed the passing scene with suspicion. Dust-spewing motor scooters crisscrossed among pedestrians who shuffled along with somber faces.

The church of the Reverend Chun was a clearinghouse of dissent. The various Christian churches in Korea—which is 25 percent Christian and growing—had long played a key role in opposing the military government, with Roman Catholics and one branch of the Presbyterians the most active. Prominent priests and ministers had been jailed and put under house arrest for arguing that democracy and human rights were Christian concepts. The Reverend Chun stayed one step off the barricades but used his offices to bring together various parts of the opposition to keep up a dialogue. One of the lessons of May 1980 was that demonstrations can take on a violent life of their own. The reverend tried to insure that one hand in the struggle to reform Korea knew what the other was up to. Through some contacts in Seoul, he had agreed to set up a meeting with Professor Myong.

After about a half hour, a man in a striped polo shirt bounded into the room and stuck out his hand.

"I am Myong. How may I help you?"

He had classic Chinese features, bright black eyes and a trimmed beard—rare for Koreans—that made him look more like a Ming dynasty nobleman than a college professor. His forthright style also seemed from another place—perhaps Ann Arbor, Michigan, where in 1969 he earned his doctorate in English literature, he said, and managed to do some unofficial postgraduate work in the art of political protest.

"Yes, Michigan," he laughed. "That was a very valuable education. I learned that you could change the system if you had faith."

Myong had kept the faith since his return in the early 1970s. He had the physical and emotional scars to show for it, though his exuberance was unbowed. Like The General, he too possessed a quiet power. In 1976, he spent a year in jail for organizing a protest with several ministers against President Park's consolidation of control. In 1978, he and 11 other professors issued a statement about the need for educational freedom; they were all forced to resign their teaching positions. He was one of a handful of people singled out for his role in organizing the 1980 Kwangju protest and served 18 months of a 10-year sentence. He has been beaten, starved, stuffed into cramped cells, but he could still smile and say, "We are winning."

His story of what happened was very similar to that told by Daryl Plunk in terms of the escalating series of events. Where he differed was in his explanation of motives.

In October 1979, the Park regime ended abruptly when Kim Jae Kyu, the head of the KCIA, shot and killed the president during dinner. Chun Doo Hwan, an ambitious young general who headed the Defense Security Command, was appointed to conduct an investigation of the Park murder and used his position to consolidate power within the military. A former commander of Korean troops in Vietnam, Chun used his old military school ties to bring frontline troops to Seoul to help stage a coup in December. While tanks rattled through the capital's streets, several ranking officers were killed and Chun emerged as the strongman. Throughout the spring, students and some workers demonstrated with ferocity unseen since the 1960 protests that brought down the government of Syngman Rhee. Finally, in May, Chun intensified the provisions of martial law and began to arrest student leaders. The reaction was swiftest and strongest at Chonnam and Chosun universities in Kwangju.

"It started with three days of peaceful demonstrations," Myong recalled. "Almost 30,000 students gathered in front of the provincial capital building. They sang and chanted. They wanted political prisoners released and they wanted the government to agree to begin the process of democratization. On Friday, they said that if the government didn't agree, they'd be back on Monday. I have later thought that something about those few days made the military crazy. Maybe it was the speeches of Kim Dae Jung. But a decision was made to respond to the protests with brutality."

At midnight Saturday, the Chun government went into action, arresting student leaders and other opponents, most notably Kim Dae Jung, the legendary figure who had been a thorn in the government's side for a decade, and was hauled in for inciting to overthrow the government. News of the actions swept through the informal network of students and leaders of the Kwangju universities decided to take to the streets immediately. Early Sunday morning they gathered at the gates of Chonnam—where they were greeted by battle-hardened paratroopers who had been moved in the night before.

Student demonstrations in Korea have been a springtime ritual since 1960. Though there is a serious intent to them, some years it seems they are lackluster, as if the current class is merely carrying on the tradition of their older brothers. The chanting and singing had become a rite of passage for young adults; to be teargassed or roughed up by a policeman was a badge of honor. The police, too, treated the protests as ritual, refraining from truly harsh reprisal. During the more violent protests, those who got too close to police lines might be cracked with riot sticks or kicked in the ribs. But deaths and serious injuries were rare. Until Kwangju.

"Something changed that day," said Myong. "The soldiers were very cruel. They beat some of the protesters badly then stripped them naked in front of the other students. The students were a little scared, but they were very angry. They retreated back into the town and started smashing police sentry boxes. The soldiers followed. They were beating students with clubs and stabbing them with bayonets. They were chasing after any young person, going into buildings or on buses and dragging them outside to beat them in public. It was as if they had been told that any young person was the enemy."

Several students were killed in the first two days. Accounts vary as to who was provoking whom. The students had clearly reached a new level of aggression, though their weapons were only rocks and pipes. But in a rare show of solidarity, the citizens of Kwangju began to come to the students' aid. The taxi drivers were first. Eyewitnesses to this new level of brutality, they formed a procession to the municipal stadium and held a protest rally. At the same time a series of rumors passed about the city, some plausible, some incredible. Most disturbing was that the soldiers had been sent from rival Kyungsang province and ordered to smash a communist revolt among the Cholla people. Other rumors had Kim Dae Jung being executed, the death toll reaching 40 and, the most bizarre of all, though one which is still repeated as gospel by many residents, that the soldiers had been starved for several days and given drugs to make them more violent.

"I don't know if they were starved," said Myong, "but I know they behaved the same way as a dog who has been starved and is shown a piece of meat." Myong, a marked man who was moving from house to house to avoid arrest, saw numerous beatings and stabbings and at one point, "soldiers piling bodies in a truck like garbage." But the most graphic description of the violence comes from the Asia Watch report:

"When a mother protested the teasing of her daughter by troops, both were shot dead on the spot. Eleven persons were killed in front of the Hyundai Theater. In one famous case, the troops killed four taxi drivers for transporting students through the city. . . . They even threatened and beat ordinary police who were trying to help the injured lying bleeding and unconscious on the streets."

By late Tuesday, the government had lost control, and to a most ominous force. The dreaded alliance between the students and the workers—and even the middle class—had taken place. Myong saw it happen in a tiny moment: "I saw an old woman gathering stones in her shirt to bring to the students. She said she couldn't believe the soldiers were treating our own people like this. I knew something had changed." The united protesters took over city hall and the local television station and torched police stations. Whatever the motive, a citizens' rebellion was taking place. And then the next day, after a group of rioters stormed a reserve army base and stole weapons, the rebels were armed and started shooting back. At one point students mounted a machine gun on the roof of the Chonnam University medical school and took over the provincial capital. Late Wednesday, the army retreated from the city.

It was at this point that a decision was made to reinforce the army with two regiments from the 20th Infantry Division, a frontline unit stationed along the DMZ. What role the United

States played in this redeployment has been an unending subject of controversy. Under the terms of the joint U.S.–Korean command structure, the U.S. commander has authority over both armies, and supposedly troops cannot be moved without his permission. Critics of the Korean government have used this fact to demonstrate U.S. complicity in the Kwangju violence and to argue that the military government is merely a puppet of the United States. The U.S. position is that first, since the troops were being moved for domestic reasons, the Koreans could do what they wanted, and second, the Koreans didn't say what they were doing until after they had done it. The truth was murky. There has been no official inquiry into the Kwangju incident and no official statement by the United States. It seems clear that unless a credible investigation is held, the issue won't go away. In the minds of many Koreans, the United States will always be a conspirator in the Kwangju tragedy.

With thousands of troops encircling the city, the leaders of the protest movement and the burghers of Kwangju toured the town in stunned silence. "We could not believe how things had gotten out of hand," said Myong, who, with other veteran protesters, joined the religious and civic leaders to form a peace committee. The Committee for Settling the Kwangju Turmoil offered to negotiate between the government and the protesters. Despite the several thousand rifles in the hands of the "citizen soldiers," as Myong called them, they were no match for the might of the Korean army. The committee met with the ragged bands of students, unemployed young men and laborers who occupied buildings throughout the city. Eventually the protesters were convinced to turn in their weapons and surrender to the martial law commander with a promise of leniency.

But on the 24th, rhetoric overcame reason. At a downtown rally, some of the speakers said with convincing authority that if the protesters could only hold out for a few more days, the government in Seoul would fall. Judging by the later reaction of the government in Seoul, the assertion may not have been far wrong. In any event, the protesters believed it that day and all talk of negotiation was abandoned. Sporadic fighting went on for another two days until, early in the morning of the 27th, the troops of the 20th Division moved in. The target was the provincial capital building, the protesters' headquarters, and the army mounted a full frontal assault with tanks and covering fire.

According to Daryl Plunk's account, the mission was successful. "Given the extent of the insurrection, the retaking of Kwangju by martial law troops was a well-planned and well-executed operation designed to minimize casualties and property damage." He said there were 17 rebels killed. Myong's estimate is between 50 and 70. Both agreed that the retaking of the capital ended the uprising.

According to the Korean government, the death toll for the 10 days of fighting was 191—164 civilians, 23 soldiers and four policemen—and almost 900 injured. Myong thinks the deaths should be closer to 1,000, but admits he has nothing to support this claim. Plunk accepts the government's figures and points out that the citizens' committee was allowed to count the dead. Myong said that the Kwangju cemetery contains headstones for 130 people killed during the same few days in May 1980. And around town, he sees the injured, many in wheelchairs or missing hands, feet and eyes. "I have a friend, I call him One-Eyed Jack," Myong says with a bitter laugh. "He got the other one knocked out with a rifle butt."

In the end the numbers probably don't matter. What is clear is that Korean troops ran out of control and whether 2,000 were killed or 200, a great many people died at the hands of the supposedly paternal, Confucian government that was intended to protect them.

"I still can't understand why the government killed its own people," Myong said as we toured the town square where the final assault had come. The provincial capital was newly whitewashed and unmarred by the bullets that had once torn apart its facade. "When it was over, people were in shock and terrified of their own government. After a few days, things had calmed down. But inwardly their hearts burned with anger. They still burn to this day."

Myong was arrested a month later as one of the key organizers of the uprising. He was beaten and forced to confess. For a week, he was crammed into a cell beneath a stairway. "I thought I would like to kill myself if it wasn't against my faith," he recalled. He spent 18 months in jail and was then pardoned.

Although he said the hatred for the military still burns in his heart as well, he now thinks some good may have come of Kwangju. Since then, the police had been careful to minimize violence and as bad as the street fighting got, they used tear gas and truncheons, not rifles. Perhaps Kwangju represented not the essence of Korean brutality but the limits. Tough soldiers had come face to face with killing their own countrymen and said, "Never again." When the repressors lose heart, how can the repression continue?

"The other day, a man from the KCIA came to my house. He asked me not to go to Seoul to sign the professors' protest statement. But he was very humble. He said, 'I know this is not right to do this, but my boss ordered me. It is my job.' "

Still, the problems are not over. And they are deeper than merely giving everyone the right to vote. "You only need to look at what happens in the factories here. People work 14 hours a day for $100 a month. There are many industrial accidents. They live in terrible homes. The wealth is not being distributed. But we are teaching them in night school, even though they can be fired for learning. Those who go to classes become very conscious of their life and Korean history. And student leaders are now going into the factories to organize secretly. That will be the key: the union of students and workers. We saw it here first during the violence and now we will take it to the rest of the country."

Myong had no doubt that the struggle would continue. As we said goodbye, he remembered one more thing. "My eldest daughter," he said with paternal pride. "She's in jail right now for demonstrating."

It was certain that the story of Kwangju was not over, that all its victims had not been claimed. The word caught like a bone in the throat of the opposition and they would not rest until they had coughed it out. Even the moderates made clear that they wouldn't be satisfied until those responsible were punished. If the first act of the Kwangju tragedy had defined the dark, violent side of the Korean soul, then the final act would show whether that soul had grown or hardened.

As he watched the surging discontent in the streets of Seoul in the summer of 1986, The General must have been chewing his steak with unease.

Finally one day we woke up with nothing to do. We had no schedule. No early morning phone call from the peripatetic Chun, no interview with a well-briefed functionary of the economics ministry, no planned tour of the downtown business district. We had, it seemed, exhausted the smothering hospitality of the government of the Republic of Korea. We decided it was time to look for some trouble.

We had come to Korea with official and unofficial agendas. We were perfectly willing to hear the government's version of events, but there was clearly another side to all this. It didn't take a genius to perceive that the country was boiling under the pot lid. Offhand comments from middle-class college professors and middle-level bureaucrats told us that a lot of people weren't buying the government's program. But our strategy was to be both polite and patient before we started asking the unpleasant questions. The furtive trip to Kwangju—if it had been furtive at all—was our first move in that direction. If the government had really forgotten about us, then we could start looking for its harshest critics.

We headed by taxi for Yonsei University, second only to Seoul National University in prestige and second to none in its output of radical student leaders. Through the limestone gates we saw a scene like that on any American campus: a rectangular grass quadrangle was dotted with book-laden students hurrying to class. The men wore mostly dark blue trousers and short-sleeve shirts, the women simple print dresses. But no one lounged on the lawn, no Frisbee football games, no pet dogs or rock music blaring from speakers on fraternity row. Yonsei University seemed all business.

About halfway down the quad, in front of the broad steps leading to the library, a knot of students had gathered to listen to a speech delivered over a wavering loudspeaker by a young man whose long hair was parted in the middle and held back with a white headband. He was animated but barely audible, though his audience still chimed in on cue with chants and cheers. The speech was about "economic imperialism" and, according to what an English-speaking student told us, the United States came in for the brunt of the criticism.

This was how the great Korean ritual of a student demonstration started. We had heard and read enough about the subject to know that for every spring since 1960, while the thoughts of students in other places turned to sex, the students of Korea vocalized their desire to bring down the government. Only once, in 1960, did they succeed. Was this year different?

Some of the old Asia hands said no, it was the same old stuff, a harmless release of tension. But others weren't so sure. They saw a new fervor.

One professor with whom we spoke recalled his own days on the barricades in the mid-1970s. "It was almost a social ritual. The protests were very tame, but it was important to be seen. We'd throw some rocks, the police would throw some tear gas, a few students would be beaten up. Nothing much. But these students, they are more committed. I see that they are willing to cause more pain, and to accept more pain."

Pain was the Korean currency of commitment. "How serious are you?" the government was implicitly asking the students. "Will you take more than a whiff of tear gas? A truncheon to the ribs? A kick to the head?" Already the government was shooting tear gas by the crate, but the students were asking for more. By American standards, even the moderate confrontations featured unacceptable brutality. Policemen trained in martial arts routinely kicked and punched students, breaking bones and splitting skulls. But here was where the sense of ritual entered: Even as the degree of violence escalated, rarely was there a death. Neither the police nor the students used firearms, perhaps in memory of Kwangju. What deaths there were came for another reason.

The students had escalated the stakes with perhaps the ultimate demonstration of pain: self-immolation. Already that year there had been 12 "political suicides." That meant 12 young men had poured flammable liquid on their clothing and skin and ignited it, remaining still while their flesh burned and their bodies went into shock. Often their fellow students stood by and watched. Only a few months earlier, a student at Yonsei ignited himself on the roof of the nearby science building and jumped to his death on almost the spot from which we watched the speeches.

Yet the suicides didn't cause the kind of horror one might assume. The Catholic Church, in keeping with its theology, said in a soft voice that taking one's own life was a sin and tried to discourage others. But we found no evidence that Korean society cared to peer into the dark side of its soul and discover what kind of desperation, or madness, would drive more than a few of its sons to set themselves ablaze for a political ideal.

"They are unfortunate," said one priest of the suicides, "but many people feel they are necessary."

As we imagined the smell of burning flesh, the students, who now numbered perhaps 500, rose from the pavement and began to march toward the university gates, chanting and thrusting their fists skyward. Almost immediately, a row of perhaps a dozen buses parked across the street from the gates exploded with green-clad bodies carrying long black nightsticks. Only in the most extreme circumstances would the police enter the university grounds; today they seemed determined not to let the students leave. In neat phalanxes, perhaps 500 policemen moved right to the curb where they stood with their legs apart, staring straight ahead.

This was the power of the state, muscular and coiled in boots, flak jackets and Plexiglas riot helmets, arrayed against a handful of gawky kids with adolescent acne and bad haircuts. Today the students blinked. Those at the front of the crowd slowed, taken aback by the swift show of force. Whatever they might have had in mind—they were probably going to stop traffic for an hour or so—was not in the cards today. They stayed to jeer the police for a while, then gradually wandered back to school.

We wandered back as well. A friend had set up two interviews on the campus: one with an economics professor and the other with a group of students. In each case, we had agreed not to use names.

The professor taught international economics and finance. Much like business school profs in the United States, he spent a great deal of time in the real world consulting for Korean companies. His sympathies were distinctly not with the left, yet he argued that Korea was headed for some serious problems unless delicate steps were taken to reform the economy.

"Everyone talks about democracy as the great test for Korea," he said. "But whether democracy comes or not, the real test is wages. Who gets paid what is the question, and if we don't have the right answer, it will rip the country apart."

The professor traced the history of the Korean Miracle in precise, unsentimental terms. Success, he said, had come from the proper allocation of capital and labor coupled with well-timed export strategies. Mostly, though, it was a result of cheap, diligent labor.

"We have sold the world our sweat and that has picked us out of poverty. But so far, only a few Koreans have gotten rich. The rest are better off, but not much better off. The time will come when the workers will demand to know, Where's mine? The answer isn't so simple. If we pay higher wages, we run the risk of losing our advantage in manufacturing. We lose out to the Chinese or the Indians or any place else where people will work cheaper. Then we have to make expensive goods and compete directly with the Japanese, and we're not ready to do that yet. So I think that when it comes to demonstrations, the worker is ultimately more important than the student. We may get a democratic vote, but that costs nothing. To raise a steel-worker's salary costs a lot. To let a union start, that costs more than a lot.

"How long can the workers remain content? How long before they want more leisure time? How long can they go seeing a few buy big houses and cars? You will notice there is very little flaunting of wealth here. The rich live in modest houses, fenced like fortresses. They do not try to show off what they have. They realize what happens if you dangle what you have in front of those without. And they are scared. They know that what is really to be feared is not a political revolution, but an economic revolution."

Later that afternoon, we found some reason for the Korean plutocrats to sleep easier. The group of eight students we talked with in a professor's office did not have economic revolution on their minds. These were more or less typical students who, like the majority on this campus of 15,000, usually didn't participate in demonstrations. They were afraid that an arrest record would affect their chances for a good job with a bank or one of the giant conglomerates. They were the products of more or less middle-class families and they were happy enough with winning the right to vote and booting the military out of government. What surprised us was that they also wanted to boot out the U.S. military, which they considered the root of the country's problems.

"History makes clear that the United States has meddled in Korean life since the turn of the century," said Duk, a chubby 20-year-old who considered himself a conservative and, unlike his fellow students, not at all opposed to an authoritarian government. But all agreed with the same version of history followed by the student radicals which said that at key points in Korean history, the United States was there to screw things up. In fact, the deaths of 34,000 Americans during the Korean War notwithstanding, the only nation the students disliked as much was Japan.

Revisionist Korean-American history starts with the end of the Russo-Japanese War in 1905 when, at the Portsmouth Conference, the United States agreed to let Japan colonize Korea in return for Japan keeping its hands off the Philippines. After World War II, the students argued, the United States willingly agreed to Soviet demands that the peninsula be cut in half. They also contrasted the resulting U.S. occupation of Korea with that of Japan. The United States sent General Douglas MacArthur to Japan to restructure the vanquished country's economic and political system—a move that many credit as one of the keys to Japan's phenomenal postwar economic success. In Korea, the United States installed a caretaker command that could not have cared less about rebuilding the economy. On the political front, the United States shunned the Korean nationalists and brought back to power the colonial lackeys who had run the country for the Japanese. The result: the emergence of former anti-Japanese guerrilla leader Kim Il Sung and the permanent partition of the country with Kim as the North's powerful and charismatic leader. The South got a war, 40,000 permanent U.S. troops and a series of leaders that the students assume have been propped up by the United States.

"Sure, you saved us in 1950," a female student said. "But there would not have been a war if you had not divided our country in the first place."

But for a generation of young Koreans, the end of respect for the United States came with the Kwangju incident where, despite denials by the United States, students are convinced that the Eighth Army played a role. In particular they focused on General John Wickham, the U.S. commander at the time, who made several intemperate remarks. At one point he referred to the Koreans as "lemmings" who would follow any strong leader and at another, during the crucial period in 1980 when Chun Doo Hwan was trying to consolidate power, he told the Los Angeles *Times* that Chun had emerged as the clear leader. It was totally plausible then, the students told us, that Wickham knew that the Korean army was going to quell the Kwangju riots with violence and allowed it to happen.

"You have had your hand on our neck for too long," one student said. "You are no longer the Older Brother and Japan is no longer the Older Brother. It is time for you to leave us alone. There should be one Korea—North and South."

It was, at the time, a treasonous statement, punishable by jail if anybody decided to report the student. But no one in that room felt otherwise. After all the years of official propaganda about the evils of the North, after the accounts of a savage war started by their relatives across the border, the students still wanted One Korea.

"You should never underestimate the depth of Korean nationalism," explained our friend who had set up the meeting. "More and more I think it will be a powerful force in changing this country."

If the students at Yonsei were playing at reform, Chang Youn Jae was working at revolution. A few changes in the system would not be enough for this 24-year-old former student leader who was now working to organize industrial workers. The democratic model everyone was talking about here was much like the system in the United States and who wanted that? It was just another form of economic repression, he said.

We met Chang one stormy afternoon. He was in some ways that most unnerving of radicals: soft-spoken and friendly but with a quiet forcefulness that made clear he was utterly sure of the rightness of his cause. He had the kind of wiry build that was made for squirming from the grasp of pursuing policemen, but no extra flesh to absorb the blow of a truncheon if he were caught. He didn't ask that the interview be off the record and he didn't seem to care whether we were journalists or from the CIA. He had already felt the worst the state had to dish out and he knew he could take it.

"I first went to jail during my time at the university," he began calmly. "I was arrested along with a lot of others. But I knew I had to do more. During my trial, I shouted, 'I'm not the sinner! President Chun is the sinner!'

"The guards put me in a special wing for troublemakers.

I threw shit at them through the bars, so they beat me. Then they put me in a solitary cell. Some days I would see no light all day. Then the guards would come in, call me names and punch me.

"I heard stories of other students being beaten and tortured. I had much time to think and become strong."

Chang's mother helped gain his release through a committee of mothers who put irresistible pressure on the government.

"Jail was good for my family. After I came out, my mother said she can understand me, understand the commitment. My father is a former soldier. He used to slap me around when I was in demonstrations. But after he saw what happened to me in jail, he stopped. He still doesn't agree with me, but he respects me."

Chang's radicalism had its roots in school and the church. At university he became involved in the "study circles" students formed to discuss politics and economics. The circles of 20 or so, usually students from the same high school or church, operated as secret societies with senior members selecting younger entrants. They met late into the night in coffee shops or students' homes, often clandestinely if their more prominent members were known to be on police subversive lists. The main purpose was an underground education system. Generally under discussion were books not taught in class. Marx and Lenin led the reading list as did revisionist Korean history. Third World economics was prominent with an emphasis on the nature of dependent economies.

"The older brothers taught us how Korea has always been kicked around by greater powers," Chang said, "and how it is the Korean people who have suffered. Our only hope is to unite the workers against oppression from outside and from inside our country."

The study circles formed the basis for social and political life for students like Chang. The groups, which continue to operate, communicate with each other through an elaborate network of representatives who can mobilize thousands of students into the street in a matter of hours.

Christian churches also have been an important force in supporting radical politics in Korea. Chang, a devout Christian, told us that the teachings of Jesus Christ made clear the need for economic justice. Church groups support him with shelter and a salary as he pursues his organizing activities.

He said he was not a communist, nor did he advocate violent revolution. "I seek justice for all Koreans, North and South. I want a Korean economic system. But change must come and time is running out."

For Chang, too, the most important event in recent memory was Kwangju. "That was the turning point," he said. "It changed the nature from a protest movement to a revolution. It showed us who our real enemy was—all the forces of economic imperialism. We are still a colony of the United States and Japan. We produce for you and you pay us what you want. That has to stop. Kwangju also showed the students the need to organize the workers and the farmers. Just now the students have gone into the factories and fields to work and to reach the workers. The real revolutionary movement is only five years old. Soon you will see the results."

What was becoming clear to us was that rumbling beneath the surface of this grand economic miracle was a discontent that had more to do with economics than politics. The miracle came at a hefty cost, we kept hearing in interviews, and not everyone was paying his fair share. One afternoon we took a taxi to the Christian Institute for the Study of Justice and Development, a think tank funded by several democratic-minded churches that occupied a large house in a wealthy suburb of Seoul. We had been told that these were the people who kept the numbers. If we wanted to understand the forces that were shaping the country, we had to look at the economic statistics. We had seen the government numbers, which were rosy, and we wanted a point of comparison.

Shim Sang Wan, a researcher wearing a white shirt with a selection of pens in a plastic pocket protector, greeted us at the door with an awkward bow and escorted us past a row of offices occupied by men peering through thick glasses at computer printouts. This was truly the revenge of the nerds.

Shim pored through booklets and reports to come up with some of the statistics we asked for:

In 1986, Koreans worked an average 54-hour week, the longest in the world.

The average hourly wage in manufacturing is $1.38. In the United States, it is $13.09 and the work week is 40 hours; in Japan, $6.64 for 41 hours.

Korean auto workers, the royalty of industry, earn $3 an hour, against $18 in Japan and $24 in the United States.

Forty percent of all workers earn less than $115 a month (or less than 50 cents an hour), which is considered the poverty line for a family of four.

Eighty-five percent of females, who are the mainstay of key industries such as textiles and electronics, earn less than $250 a month for 60- to 70-hour weeks.

White collar managers earn $875 a month and technical workers earn $600.

Although the official unemployment figure for the workforce of 16 million is 3.5 percent, about a third of workers are considered part-time or day labor.

Korea has one of the highest rates of industrial accidents in the world. In 1985, according to government compiled statistics, there were 1,718 deaths, 19,824 serious injuries and 160,000 total accidents. The rate is about 10 times that of the United States and Japan.

The richest 20 percent of the country earns 43 percent of the income while the poorest 40 percent takes in 18 percent of the income.

Eight percent of the country received 43 percent of the inherited land.

"These numbers are mostly supplied by the government," explained Shim. "We don't know how accurate they are. For instance, the wage figures are only for companies with 10 or more employees. The smaller companies pay much less."

They were close enough, though. What they showed was a country with a large and growing gap between the rich and poor. The wealth of the nation was rising rapidly, but pay scales were not keeping up—which meant that those who owned capital were doing much better than those who were selling labor. It was, in some ways, not as bad as the situation in the United States, but for a country fueled by a dream of common purpose, the notion of some people doing much better than others was sure to become a problem. For a nation in the process of industrialization, the Korean working class may be the best-educated in history. While the United States, say, or Great Britain had more illiterate and uninformed laborers during their periods of growth, Korean workers seem to have a very clear sense of who's getting rich and why. And when they see that the nation's productivity is growing faster than their own wages, they know their work is being sold cheaper and cheaper. Couple that with a Korean characteristic they call *han,* which roughly translates as inferiority, insecurity or a sense of unease that others are doing better, and you have the foundation for some very unhappy workers.

Yet low wages are believed by Korea's business and government leaders to be the basis for Korea's success. In a country the size of the state of Indiana, with only 15 percent farmable land, factory labor takes on a new meaning. It is for that reason that labor laws are so loose and unions always have been equated with communism and viewed as a threat to national security. One labor organizer explained to us that in the 1950s, the rationale for endless work hours for young female garment workers was that "if a girl doesn't work 18 hours a day, she'll become a prostitute."

Unions were virtually banned through a series of laws that gave the government broad discretion to control them. There was no right to associate, organize and bargain collectively—the tenets of internationally accepted labor rights. There was no minimum wage—only one "suggested" by the government—and few rules on safety in the workplace.

From several underground labor-organizing groups we collected numerous accounts of union busting. In July 1984, at the Bando Machinery Co. near Seoul, three workers who had been forced to work 130 hours in a week collapsed and died of exposure to toxic chemicals. The female garment workers union in Seoul was dissolved by the government in 1981 after it succeeded in forcing employers to reduce the average workday from 14 to 10 hours. During a sit-in at the Daewoo Apparel Co., the union president and 100 female employees were beaten by what the press called "members of the company soccer team" wielding pipes. Eventually the giant conglomerate's chairman personally settled the dispute with an offer of a 12-cents-a-day raise and company medical payments for those injured during the sit-in. At Hanil Stainless Steel Co. in Inchon, union leaders were beaten with pipes and hospitalized for several weeks in 1985 when they attempted to recruit workers.

"The question you have to ask yourself is, Where does Confucianism end and exploitation begin?" said Steven Moon one Sunday afternoon in a hotel coffee shop. Moon, a pleasant silver-haired man in his 50s, was a longtime activist with ties to the student and labor movements. He was the brother of Moon Ik Hwan, a Protestant cleric who was jailed for subversion and has become one of the most celebrated religious figures in the country. Our conversation with Moon and others reaffirmed the idea that whatever happened with the political situation, the greater problem in the long run would be industrial rights: how to split the pie. The solutions would not be easy or painless.

"The Koreans are good workers because they want their children to do better and they want Korea to do better. They don't like unions because they have respect for authority and the authorities have said, 'Trust us. Unions are a bad thing. We will take care of you.' But for all these reasons the Korean worker is one who can be manipulated by those who control the capital.

"What we are seeing in Korea today is not Confucianism with the father encouraging the children to work hard for their own good. What we are seeing is simple greed. It is exactly like the origin of capitalism in England. The owners squeezing the workers and making them think it's best for them. It's an old story.

"The government's fear is the workers, not the students. There was a demonstration in Inchon recently where the factory workers came out to battle the police. Things turned very violent. The workers showed that they are willing to take more punishment than the students because they are suffering more. What the government knows is that politics and economics can't be separated. By opening up politics, they are going to put many unpleasant issues on the table. Korea has an extraordinarily educated proletariat, but a proletariat nonetheless. There'd better be enough to go around. Koreans are not as docile as Japanese."

On one of our last days in Seoul, we decided to make The Call. In our paranoia-fed planning, we knew this one would be the end. We had decided to wait until we had nothing to lose, because once we made this call, we were sure the KCIA would be on our tail, the army would come howling out of its barracks and our passports would be slipped into the shredder.

Kelly had the number on a folded piece of paper tucked in the lining of his toilet kit. He had gotten it from a source in Washington. Fishing it out he dialed and waited, assuming that the various clicks and pops on the line were the signatures of wiretaps cutting in.

"Hello."

"Good morning. Is this the number for Mr. Kim Dae Jung?"

"Who is this?"

"I am an American journalist. I'd like to see if I can interview him for a book I'm writing. I got his number from a friend."

Kelly gave the friend's name.

"Just a minute, please."

Click. Pop. Hiss.

"This is Kim Dae Jung. Why don't you come and have breakfast with me tomorrow morning? My house is in Mapo-ku. Just tell the taxi driver."

"Which taxi driver?"

"Oh, any one. They all know where I live. It's easy to find. There's a big army sentry post on the corner. My guardians. And don't forget to wave to the KCIA. They're in the buildings all around. How about 8 o'clock?"

So much for clandestine meetings.

In Korea, Kim Dae Jung is the king of pain. If suffering is currency then Kim is a wealthy man. For almost three decades he has been the most resilient symbol of opposition to the military regime. For his troubles he has been jailed, beaten, sentenced to death, kidnapped, almost killed on several occasions, exiled and, most recently, placed under permanent house arrest. His survival and, in particular his latest renaissance, made him one of the more legendary figures in world politics.

Writing in his prison diaries, he said, "I have reached this age without once having lived happily. Can we still say that this is living?" He eventually answers with a Korean proverb: "Even if the heavens were to crash down, there is a hole through which to rise up. And even if taken in a tiger's teeth, there is a way to survive."

This ultimate survivor was now the wild card in Korean

politics. Everyone wanted to know what he planned. Would he run for president? Would he violate house arrest and urge his followers into the streets? If he did, would some elements of the military carry out their long-standing threat to kill him? Or was he past his prime, a powerless figurehead issuing meaningless pronouncements from his living room?

Everyone did, indeed, know where Kim Dae Jung lived. When we showed the hotel doorman the address on a piece of paper, he whispered conspiratorially, "Ahh, you're going to see Kim Dae Jung?" The cabbies in line fought to take us there. "Kim Dae Jung! Kim Dae Jung!" they shouted as we looked around uncomfortably.

The winner proudly packed us in the back of his tiny Toyota and drove 10 minutes west of downtown Seoul. He turned off a roaring main street to a quiet, middle-class neighborhood where the houses were surrounded by high brick walls. When he became confused in the narrow, winding streets, he stopped at a military checkpoint where a soldier with an M-16 rifle told him that Kim Dae Jung lived around the corner. He should know. It was his job, and that of the several dozen other troops in the area, to keep Kim from leaving. In the general vicinity there were 100 plainclothes police, two buses filled with riot troops and four KCIA observation houses. This was clearly a man the government took seriously.

Kim lived in a comfortable but not opulent home that his supporters built for him for $100,000. He was not a man alone, with aides bustling in and out all day. The living room, where we waited while he watched Tom Brokaw on the *NBC Nightly News* in another room, was set up like a conference room with a low table flanked by six chairs with a larger one at the head. Despite the house arrest and government surveillance, Kim's house was something of a headquarters for an opposition movement that was growing bolder by the day. Though Kim could not attend rallies, he was said to be organizing many of them and establishing a protest strategy. Occasionally he would record speeches to be played at political gatherings, but those who had seen him speak in person said the tape was no match for his powerful performances. That he could get away with this activity at all suggested to us that the government was softening its position—or losing control.

"Welcome to my home," he said softly as he entered the

living room. He wore cloth slippers and shuffled across the floor with a limp, the result of a suspicious auto accident that almost cost him his life when he was running for president in 1971. "Have you seen all the friends the government sends to protect me?" he said with a laugh as he gestured in a sweeping circle.

"They must care very deeply about you."

He laughed harder. "Yes, they like to keep me very close by their side. They have as many people to protect me as they do for President Chun."

Somehow, he seemed happy with all the attention and the parity with Chun, a man who had tried mightily to have him killed.

He walked to the dining room and sat down at a black lacquer table set with plates of clear soup, scrambled eggs, fruit and tea.

"Please eat," he encouraged with a slight bow. He took a sip of soup, then sat with his hands folded to wait for the questions. Kim was concerned this day about the rising level of violence in the streets of Seoul. He was, he wanted us to know, a man of peace who took no pride in the scenes of students pelting riot policemen with Molotov cocktails. The cycle was escalating. There were probably 1,500 permanent political prisoners and thousands more students temporarily detained. Stories of harsh treatment including sexual torture of women were leaking out and provoking renewed demonstrations. Harsh government responses seemed to encourage more students to take to the streets. Was it just a handful of radicals? Were the police provoking the fights? Could the protesters be controlled?

"Our strength is in two things," Kim began. "Unity and non-violence. Violence is the government's weapon against us. They use it to crack down harder, to drive the middle class away. Some say it is the only way we can show them how strong we are, but I advocate non-violence. My models are Gandhi and Martin Luther King, Jr. In your country, Martin Luther King, Jr. was criticized by the Black Panthers and others. But in the end, they were destroyed by the government and only King realized brilliant success. This government, they took power with violence. They have well-organized military and police. How can stones and Molotov cocktails thrown by students win against such power?

"But if we create a mass of people—500,000, a million people in Seoul—out in the streets, how can government tanks and machine guns attack such people? All the traffic will stop and the world will pay attention to us."

If anything, he saw the violence as threatening to undo the one thing he had spent his life pursuing and now felt on the verge of achieving.

"What I seek is justice. I have seen in my whole life so much injustice, so much of the little man, the poor man stepped on by the powerful. It is my mission to change that."

Kim spoke that way—in round, quotable paragraphs—about his mission or his destiny. Ego was not something he lacked. He also was described as stubborn and uncompromising, characteristics that prevented the various opposition political groups from presenting a unified front to the government. Compromise was not a word well-established in the Korean lexicon and Kim, for all his vision and resilience, yielded to no man in his refusal to give an inch. For a decade, the opposition movement had had two standard-bearers: Kim Dae Jung and Kim Young Sam, a slim, elegant former businessman. The dilemma was, if elections were called, which of the two Kims would be the candidate?

"We will work things out," he said of the other Kim. "My goal is not to be president but to see justice come to the people."

As he talked on, we were not convinced. Kim Dae Jung subliminally projected as much confidence as any politician we had ever seen that he was meant to be the leader of Korea.

He was born in 1925 in a fishing village off the southwest coast of Korea, in Cholla province, a region looked down on by more prosperous parts of the country. Like Lee Yong Ho from Okpo and dozens of other Koreans we had met over the age of 30, Kim grew up in a primitive world where things had been done the same way for centuries. He left the island when he was 13 to go to high school on the mainland and eventually went to work for a shipping company as a clerk. When North Korean troops swept through the country in 1950, Kim was captured. His pregnant wife and child managed to escape and Kim's second son was born in a cave.

"The North Koreans planned to kill me along with all the men of the town. Two truckloads of us were to be driven to a forest where we would be shot. But my truck broke down and that night, the troops were ordered withdrawn."

It was, he said, the first of at least five times he escaped death. "Now when I look back, I think that God saved my life because he wanted me for something."

Like many Koreans, he was converted to Christianity after the war, becoming a Roman Catholic in 1955. Religion changed his life, instilling in him a deep faith and a fatalism. His study of theology caused him to enter politics.

"I learned that Jesus Christ came to liberate poor people and suffering people. He was born into a world where the privileged class exploited the masses, much like in Korea today. He was fighting for them all the time, speaking out and making the government angry. Then he was arrested and sentenced to death for sedition—just like me. He was killed as a political prisoner—almost like me."

He added the two asides casually, as if the coincidence had just occurred to him.

After several unsuccessful starts, Kim won election to the national assembly in 1961. Two days later, President Syngman Rhee was overthrown in a military coup and Kim began his career as the scourge of the generals. He helped form the New Democratic Party in 1967 and three years later was nominated as its candidate for president against Park Chung Hee. A speaker with the spellbinding power of an evangelical preacher, he toured the country tirelessly, attracting audiences that stunned the generals.

During the campaign his car was run off the road by a truck that Kim is convinced was driven by government security men. He suffered a crushed hip, but got back on the campaign trail. When the vote was finally tallied after delays and much suspicion of tampering, Kim had won an astonishing 46 percent. The generals shuddered and Park immediately announced election "reforms" that made direct voting more difficult. He rewrote the constitution to provide for a type of electoral college where professional politicians who were more easily controlled by the government cast the deciding votes.

Kim seized on the government's reaction as a potent issue and began a campaign to protest them. He traveled to Tokyo in the summer of 1973 to seek support for his movement and was on his way to the United States to give a series of speeches when several KCIA agents burst into his hotel room.

"I was staying at the Grand Palace Hotel," he recalled. "The KCIA men said they were going to kill me right there. They had brought knapsacks and they said they were going to dismember me. But just then, my relative who was staying down the hall came and pounded on the door and shouted. They got scared and took me out into a car."

There he said he was "wrapped like a mummy, head to toe" and taken to a boat.

"They tied me to a board and said they were going to throw me overboard. Just then I heard an airplane buzzing overhead. The boat changed direction, but the airplane kept coming back. This happened maybe 10 times. I think maybe it was the United States or the Japanese who did this to save my life. Finally the boat took me to Korea."

There had been some stiff diplomatic protests to Kim's abduction and he was freed. He wasted no time resuming his pummeling of Park and eventually earned a two-year prison sentence for causing a demonstration in violation of martial law.

In 1980, after Park's assassination and Chun's coup, Kim again became the key critic of the government, decrying martial law and calling for the military to hold elections. When the din became too loud, Kim was arrested on May 17 and charged with planning a mass demonstration to be held the next week. His arrest sparked the Kwangju students' protest that led to the explosion in that city. Kim was blamed for that demonstration as well and tried for sedition in a military court.

"On September 17, I was sentenced to death," he said quietly. "It was a moment when I lost all hope. I thought that this was the end of me and the end of Korea."

But typical of the Koreans' continual lack of sophistication when it comes to the ways of world opinion, the generals' action created a potential martyr. Kim's cause became celebrated and diplomatic protests rained down on Seoul. The most potent communication is widely believed to have come through back channels from the White House of newly elected President Ronald Reagan that made Chun an interesting proposal: Commute Kim's sentence and we will invite you to Washington, thereby legitimizing your position. Whatever the deal, Kim's sentence was cut first to life, then 20 years. In January 1981, Chun Doo Hwan became the first foreign leader to meet the newly inaugurated Reagan at the White House.

Still, the prison term was almost the end of Kim. He spent most of his time in solitary confinement, watched 24 hours by guards and allowed only daily 20-minute visits from his wife. He was forced to sleep on the floor and given a half hour outside his cell for exercise. His damaged hip gave him constant pain, he said, but most painful was the denial of books or writing paper.

"I became very depressed. More than ever. For a time, I felt there was no hope."

Eventually his wife won permission for books—notably the Bible—and about one sheet of writing paper each month. Kim taught himself a minuscule scrawl and filled the sheets with 29 letters to his family—essays really—that were later published as *Prison Writings.* Much of what he wrote was anguished self-examination about the futility of his own efforts and the effect it had had on his family. He regretted the time he had spent away from his wife and wondered how his three sons would get jobs or what family would allow their daughters to marry them.

In December 1982, he was permitted to travel to the United States in a sort of self-imposed exile to receive medical treatment. He also became a fellow at Harvard University's Center for International Affairs, where he lectured, wrote and plotted a return to Korea. At Harvard, he also took the time to refine the economic theories that he had first proposed in the 1971 presidential campaign. It is instructive to examine the ideas of the man the Korean military portrayed as a dangerous communist and the virtual godson of the North's Kim Il Sung. As early as the 1970s, he was advocating reforms that would not have embarrassed Ronald Reagan. He astutely criticized the great inefficiencies in the Korean economy that came from tight central control. They were, he said, masked by phenomenal growth rates. But those came from the sweating brows of Korean workers who produced a lot more than they were getting paid for.

"Some Western observers of Korean economic growth regard it as an example of the superiority of a free market-oriented development program," he wrote. In fact, the government "is active in almost every aspect of economic decision making" including prices, wages, interest rates and who gets bank loans.

While saying he "emphatically rejects socialism" as well as communism—"There is no human freedom and dignity in communism"—Kim called for an opening of the economy. He wanted the barriers to foreign goods removed, he wanted the market to determine prices and the allocation of capital, an encouragement of entrepreneurs and a curtailment of the power of the giant corporations. He wanted a new labor policy that let wages reflect productivity gains and that allowed workers some kind of ownership stake in companies. He called it a "mass participatory economy."

He also challenged the assumption that an authoritarian government was good for the economy. "The misleading argument that dictatorship provides political stability must be rejected, for political stability is not achieved by the longevity of a regime but the durability of a political system. Dictatorship invites political instability . . . the seeming stability under dictatorship is like being on a razor's edge. History demonstrates that without freedom, economic development has its limits.

"When the majority harbors strong resentment of an unfair system, radical ideology offers appeal and the young idealists become prey to demagogues."

Yet the generals who ran the country were convinced that Kim was that demagogue. Their hatred of him had passed well into the realm of the irrational. It was rumored that classes at the military academy taught that Kim Dae Jung was the enemy. Some military men had said publicly that they'd rather die than see Kim as president.

"It is not all the military who feel that way," said Kim. "Many know that the government is wrong. They support me. Those who don't, the answer is easy. They have very good lives now. They have power and money. If I am elected, they will have to give that up and become soldiers."

When Kim was allowed back to Korea in February 1985, it was feared he would receive the same welcome as Benigno Aquino, the Philippine dissident who was shot to death on the Manila airport tarmac. But the Koreans had learned some lessons. He was merely brusquely hauled from the airport to house arrest, where he had remained until now, a small but increasingly painful burr under the saddle of the military dictatorship.

Was he afraid? we wanted to know.

"For myself, no," he smiled with sad eyes. "What more can they do? But I am afraid for Korea. I am afraid of the radicals and I am afraid of what the generals will do when they see clearly that they are about to lose their power."

If it all fell apart, he said, Korea could become "a second Vietnam."

The only solution he could see was to walk the narrow line. "Non-violence and unity," he said again. The fatalism was gone from his voice now, the low monotone with which he had told the story of his dark days. His voice rose as he talked about "people power, so many people the government will have to give in."

Millions of people in the streets and one man to rally them, that was the vision of Kim Dae Jung. Then he graciously excused himself to meet with several provincial party leaders who had come to talk strategy with the man they were sure would be the next president of Korea. His shoulders slumped as he shuffled off, until he reached the living room door, at which point his back straightened, he took a deep breath and entered the room.

We awoke on a rainy Sunday to the sound of scissors clanking on the sides of taffy carts. Peddlers wheeled their big wooden carts through the streets of the market district, stopping to cut foot-long strips of bright pink-and-orange taffy for children.

The morning papers were full of news. The government continued its campaign to shut down the "barber shops" that doubled as massage parlors. No doubt the male Korean population was about to begin looking shaggy. At the same time, other illicit pleasures were being curtailed with a raid on 14 bookstores accused of selling "seditious literature." One thousand volumes had been impounded, though the titles—seditious in themselves?—were not mentioned.

There had been a rare gangland-style murder in a *kisaeng* house the day before. The story was played down, but it involved four known underworld figures who were found with their throats cut after a fight that apparently no other patrons had seen. With typical Korean efficiency, 2,500 suspected gangsters had been rounded up overnight and were now undergoing police interrogation.

The historic national palace finally had reopened after extensive renovation. During the Japanese occupation, they had turned the grounds into a zoo. In an incident that we assumed was at least spiritually related, police were still seeking suspects in the firebombing of a Japanese bank.

The lanes and alleys of the market district were not teeming, but they were crowded. Sunday morning or not, Seoul was still at work. Crews of young men in sleeveless shirts were building houses and renovating shops, hawkers touted bargains and skeptical housewives tried to call their bluffs. Didn't these people have homes? We wondered. What about reading the Sunday comics and eating a late brunch? Wasn't there a football game on TV or a softball to be tossed to the youngsters on the front lawn?

Of course, there were no Sunday comics in Korea or, for the most part, front lawns. For the thousandth time we had it pounded into our heads that this was a culture based on work. Maybe they hated their small houses, or maybe they hated their spouses, but an awful lot of people seemed quite content to be putting in a day's work this Sunday. We knew that our friend Sang's 8-year-old son was doing his homework; at that age he was expected to do three hours a night, including weekends *and* summer vacations. Sang, who had lived in the States, wasn't at all sure this was the best way for a kid to grow up, but he knew the competitive pressures and if you fell behind at age 8, you might never catch up.

True, not everyone worked on Sunday. And a lot of Koreans took full advantage of the half-day Saturday. Maybe someday they'd even take the whole day off. We could only hope. Because while we could not help but marvel at what the Koreans had accomplished, we were also frightened by them. It felt like the first day of college when you realized that everybody in your political science class was determined to get into law school and you were just hoping to learn a little something about Thomas Jefferson. Whoops. These guys were deadly serious and not only that, but this was the future.

One of the questions we had set out to answer was whether there was something about the Asians that was different, better, than the Americans. Right now the answer was yes. They were hungrier, they worked harder, they wanted to succeed. But was there anything to emulate here? These people led austere, monotonous lives. A snout full of rice wine and a bar fight was considered a good time. Hunker down and put your kid through college and don't ask questions was what the system told you to do.

If this was what it took to succeed, did we really want it? "In America you work to acquire leisure," Kim Dae Jung had said to us. "We work for the future. You work for the weekend." Damn right. It was the American way. Miller time. Weekends were made for Michelob.

Maybe that was what bothered us about the Koreans. Yet *they're* the ones who are nervous about the future. This was supposed to be the land of cheap labor, yet many businessmen told us they feared those days would soon be over. There were hungrier nations throughout Asia that were now sophisticated enough to get their share. The Koreans were looking over their shoulders while the Americans were looking at their shoes—made, no doubt, in Korea.

But this was too much to deal with on a Sunday morning. We settled in at a noodle shop for bowls of thick, chewy noodles with seaweed and objects of indeterminate origin. Instinctively we reached for the side dish of kimchi to get garlicked up for the day. We chewed and grimaced.

We decided that in the end we didn't like the food, the art, the weather, the manners or the culture. But we liked Korea. The place grew on you as did the people. It was a brutally honest and sincere land trying to survive in a vicious world. Once you could handle their candor, the Koreans' lack of bullshit and pretense was refreshing. They were the kind of people about whom you could say you'd rather have them with you than against you.

As we wandered back toward the hotel to get ready to leave, we passed two scenes that were as symbolic as anything we'd seen of the yin and yang of this singular place. On one block downtown, we noticed a row of maybe 20 young girls wearing plaid skirts and white blouses squatting in front of an office building. As we got closer, we could see that they were scraping at the granite sidewalk with flat metal tools. They all wore orange sashes across their blouses and a man holding a matching orange flag stood nearby. We asked him what was going on.

"Girls' club," he said in faltering English. "They clean chewing gum."

The girls smiled and waved as we walked by, dropping the shriveled fruits of their labor into brown paper sacks.

Not far up the hill were the red brick spires of Myongdong Cathedral, the main Catholic Church in Seoul. Police barricades and fences were jumbled at the bottom of the hill, a reminder of the many demonstrations that centered around the cathedral those days. But on this Sunday, the sinister green buses full of riot police were not in evidence. Mass was in progress and hundreds of Koreans packed the simple structure. In the tiled courtyard, slick with rain, we could hear the gentle sound of muffled hymns and the occasional high trill of the organ. The air felt soft and cool. We saw several couples holding hands on benches and two men engaged in an animated conversation. As we watched, the two men, one in a brown suit, one in blue, stood up, both gesturing wildly.

Suddenly, the man in the blue suit cocked his arm and threw an arching punch that landed with a splat on the side of his companion's head. The man in brown responded with a flurry of chops to the stomach. Now each grabbed the other's lapels and tried to maintain his balance on the slippery tiles while sneaking in an uppercut. They twisted and turned this way for several minutes, legs and arms flying, until a young priest in a long black gown scurried from the parish house and implored them to stop.

The Mass is ended, go in peace, indeed.

TAIWAN

LEAVING KOREA was like skulking away from a scene of domestic violence where throwing plates was about to escalate to carving knives. We were tense and tired after weeks of the aggressiveness and the insecurity, bordering on paranoia, that permeated so much of the country. Once we got to Kimpo airport, our cab was delayed while soldiers meticulously searched each vehicle for, as one tersely put it, "weapons." The mood in the cramped airport lobby was one of barely controlled hysteria as crowds of families surged toward the ticket counters, pushing their piles of bursting suitcases and twine-trussed cardboard boxes. They shoved with the intensity of refugees desperate to make the last plane. But what were they escaping from? They lived here, didn't they?

As flight time drew closer and closer and we got no closer to the check-in counter, we panicked and shamefully involved White Man's Privilege, with Kelly jabbering at an airline clerk that we were important businessmen about to miss a connection. The clerk, apparently not yet realizing who really runs the world, responded instinctively and escorted us past groups of open-mouthed Asians to the passport station. Only a shaggy-haired Englishman deep in the line protested.

"Where the fuck do you think you're going?" he yelled.

"Sorry. State Department," Kelly said, waving his passport. But we both knew how he felt. We wouldn't be getting away with this sort of nonsense much longer either.

Later, we learned that an hour after we left, a bomb exploded in front of the airport, shredding the plate-glass facade and driving shards into the airport lobby. Five Koreans died and dozens were injured. We wondered whether we were getting too old for this kind of fun.

• • •

We tried hard to relax on the two-hour flight from Seoul to Taipei, the capital of the Republic of China, also known as Taiwan. We assumed it would be a short respite; based on what little we already knew about the place, we were sure that paranoia would again be a leading theme.

Our initial dealings with the Taiwanese had been with the staff of their representative office in Washington, where a wide cultural gap became immediately apparent. They were suspicious of us, our motives and our methods, and seemed wholly unused to dealing with the American media. This in spite of the fact that Taiwan's representative to the United States, Fredrick Chien, was widely credited with being one of the most skilled diplomats in Washington. And Taiwan was famous for lavish, all-expense-paid journalistic junkets that tend to attract editorial-page writers from small-town papers and television news directors from Bottom 40 markets. But when we made clear that we were paying our own way, and were therefore independent, they didn't know what to make of us.

It was not until we had had many meetings with Taiwan's Washington press office that they began to agree to our wishes for access to top government officials. But even then, we realized that they had no concept of a couple of journalists asking to wander around their country for a few weeks. Our meetings had a kind of circular argument to them where we would ask for suggestions on where we should visit and they would say that depended on what we wanted to see, and we would say we'd never been there so we didn't know what we wanted to see and they'd say we'd have to be more specific in our requests or they couldn't help us. We sensed that our problem went beyond the language barrier.

A cruel but pointed anecdote stuck with us. One afternoon before we left on our trip, we were having lunch with several members of the press staff of the Coordination Council for North American Affairs (the unwieldy name for Taiwan's diplomatic headquarters) at a restaurant in downtown Washington. We were trying, again, to make them understand that if they wanted us to have an accurate picture of Taiwan, they were going to have to make more officials available to us.

When it came time to order lunch, Clemens Chung said he had a favorite item on the menu.

"Cherder soup," he ordered.

"Turtle soup!" Kelly exclaimed. "I love turtle soup."

"What?" said the waiter.

"Cherder soup," said Chung.

"Turtle soup," Kelly translated. "We'll both have turtle soup."

"No, *cherder, cherder,*" Chung insisted.

"We don't have turtle soup," the waiter offered solicitously.

Chung laughed an embarrassed laugh. We laughed an embarrassed laugh. But no one knew what to do until the waiter finally got the menu and had Chung point to the line which read, "Chowder, New England style with baby clams in a rich cream soup."

"Turtle soup" became our shorthand for a cultural conundrum.

The Chinese have an expression for a good place to be: "Where the sky is high and the emperor is far." It is a phrase that captures the Chinese disdain for regulation, their desire to put distance between themselves and the center of authority and their passion to be left alone. At least by geography, the island of Taiwan, which the Portuguese called Formosa, had been far enough from the emperor to allow for operating room. In the recent past, the "emperor" was Mao Zedong and his revolutionary communist cadres; those who escaped to Taiwan were more traditional rulers, in the form of Chiang Kai-shek and the Chinese capitalists.

Even so, Taiwan is a ludicrous bolt hole: an island the size of the state of Connecticut, dwarfed by the vast expanse of the Mainland 150 miles to the west. On a map, the relationship is not unlike that between Cuba and the United States, though the ideologies are reversed. And like Cuba, this island redoubt has sustained itself improbably as a thorn in the emperor's side for many, many years.

We knew this about Taiwan: It was a country of Chinese refugees, sons and daughters of the biggest dragon of all, which meant that the history and culture of Taiwan belonged to that densely complicated place that Westerners had explored and analyzed and failed to comprehend for centuries. We also knew that its economy was at that moment perhaps the hottest in the world, an exporting marvel racking up foreign exchange reserves of $70 billion and starting to give Japan—with six times the population—a run for its money. And we knew that the mother dragon would dearly love to have these 20 million people and all their energy and productivity returned to the fold.

Taiwan also had a history of bad press. The fault was somewhat its own and somewhat that of the vagaries of politics. Over the years, support for Taiwan became a litmus test for politicians and others seeking hard right-wing credentials; the Taiwanese for a long time had played to that constituency with virulent attacks on the evils of communism. As a result, Taiwan's more vocal friends have tended to be extremists of the Jesse Helms and World Anti-Communist League variety.

We thought of Taiwan as Asia's answer to South Africa, a repressive society barely hanging on against domestic dissent and international rebuke. Our preconception was based mostly on distant memories. When we were kids during the Cold War days, Taiwan was one of a few places that could have caused a hot war. In a more remote variation of the Cuban missile crisis, we vaguely recalled Kennedy winning points from the right for promising to defend two blips of earth called Quemoy and Matsu, those pieces of Taiwan torn from China in 1949.

The recent history of Taiwan is that of Chiang Kai-shek, and in most of our research, he wasn't coming across too well. Most recently, he had been the subject of a best-seller, *The Soong Dynasty,* by Sterling Seagrave, in which he was protrayed as a Chinese Al Capone, an immoral, self-aggrandizing egomaniac. Seagrave accuses Chiang of being little more than a puppet of major crime bosses, especially Big-eared Tu, the eponymous chieftain of Shanghai's drug and protection rackets. According to Seagrave, Chiang was, in fact, a coward and womanizer, and the Soong family, China's equivalent of the Rockefellers, was populated not by statesmen and altruists but by bribemongers and scoundrels. Needless to say, these charges shattered many idols and roused such emotions that Seagrave reportedly received death threats and continues to live in hiding.

Other historians such as Barbara Tuchman and Theodore White portray Chiang as a hooligan and a bumbling statesman. *Stilwell and the American Experience in China* is in large part Tuchman's indictment of Chiang for his selfish obstruction of Vinegar Joe Stilwell's efforts to liberate China and foster some sense of national pride and self-determination. Tuchman chronicles Chiang's behind-the-scene efforts in China and Washington to undermine the American general and argues that Chiang's prime motivating force was not nationalism but egoism, fed generously by Madame Chiang, one of the famous Soong sisters. Teddy White's assessment follows along similar lines. He portrays the founder of Taiwan as a mean-spirited dictator who relied heavily upon a network of secret police and the heavy hand of censorship.

Our preconceptions also were based in the 1984 murder of Henry Liu, a vocal Chinese-American critic of the Taiwan government who was assassinated in Daly City, California. The former head of Taiwan's Defense Intelligence Agency, Admiral Weng Hsi-ling, was convicted of ordering Liu's death. Before his downfall, the admiral reportedly was the second-most powerful man in Taiwan. Moreover, the hit apparently was carried out by members of the Bamboo Gang, Taiwan's contribution to international organized crime.

As of our first visit martial law still was in place, as it had been since 1949. No strikes were allowed, no talk of reunification with the Mainland and a basically one-party system, run by a handful of Chiang's cronies, controlled the country.

It occurred to us that maybe we should have tried harder to appreciate the earthy charms of South Korea. Taiwan threatened to be just as repressive and considerably less charming.

What we got at first was a vision of Virginia. As our plane taxied to the gate we could see the terminal at Chiang Kai-shek International Airport, which is a knockoff of Eero Saarinen's design at Dulles airport near Washington.

The inside was scrubbed and antiseptic with long stretches of empty corridors snaking past empty passenger lounges. The Sunday morning silence was broken only by the hiss of smoothly running people movers and the soothing sounds of piped-in easy-listening music featuring, at that moment, violins inquiring "How many miles must a poor man go?" We glided past a few air-raid shelters and watched a wing of F-5E jet fighters take off in the distance, reinforcing our expectations of a siege mentality. We passed the foreign ministry's reception room. Having diplomatic relations with only 22 countries makes Taiwan eager for visitors, and when they show up, the government is notoriously hospitable. But there were no bands playing this day. Quiet lines formed by the immigration counters where we were punched into a computer that apparently knew something about us. "Ummm, ummm," said the dark-uniformed official, as he pursed his lips and studied what we assumed was our life history on the computer screen. No one comes to Taiwan unannounced.

London's father had told him that on a visit to Taipei in the early '60s, he walked from the airport to his hotel. The runway was in the center of the city, and all the hotels were nearby. Outside of that hub few streets were paved, and his shoes always were caked with mud at the end of the day. Now the airport is an hour out of town.

The scenery was not what we expected from a country sitting on foreign currency reserves resembling those of an Arab oil sheikdom. There were no monorails, no freeway system with intricate arrangements of cloverleafs and flying ramps. Instead, we started on a local road with no lane lines; it was pockmarked with potholes and littered with bicyclists. The zoning here had apparently been under the control of a character of multiple personalities, as factories abutted small houses and rice paddies surrounded all buildings on three sides. Everything looked well-worn and not nearly as well-built as in Korea.

From time to time, set far back from the road, we saw a larger factory, looming in its grayness. Some had Chinese characters displayed on their roofs, but a few had familiar names: RCA, Wang and ITT among them. They were lined up along the highway like planes on a runway. If Korea was a manufacturing platform attached to the side of the Asian continent, then Taiwan was a manufacturing aircraft carrier anchored in the western Pacific.

Occasionally we'd whisk through a town center of a few storefronts that bore colorful signs of Chinese characters. The air on the ground was gray and heavy, although we knew from being in the airplane that at higher altitudes the sky was cloudless. We sensed that protection of the environment was not a national priority.

Our driver was a maniac. He passed cars on the right, often leaving the shoulder and lurching perilously toward the paddies. He maneuvered among scores of scooters if he were being controlled by a video-game stick. He leaned on his horn ferociously, although he maintained an impassive demeanor. He must have learned his trade as an ambulance driver.

Arriving in new and unknown countries on Sunday has its advantages. Everything is at half-speed, or less. There is the opportunity to stroll the streets without the press of traffic and crowds. In this part of the world we had the sense during our Sunday wanderings of being visitors from another planet. Cut off by language and totally unfamiliar with the setting, we felt as if we were moving through the scene in a glass box, unable to really experience anything going on around us. We could look but not touch.

The still-crowded streets of uniformly dark-haired Asians were oblivious to our presence, Westerners apparently being less of a curiosity than we would have imagined before taking a three-hour walking tour in which we saw not a single other Caucasian face.

Taipei on a graying evening was not an attractive place. In fact, for one of the wealthiest cities in the world, it was a dump. The air was filled with noxious fumes and an obnoxious chorus of mechanical noises made by a myriad of scooters and wild cab drivers. Our maniacal chauffeur from the airport had been acting perfectly in character for the denizens of this town who all seemed to enjoy operating just this side of a 10-car pileup. We constantly stood amazed at cars stopping short in major thoroughfares and swerving around as if they were targets of a high-speed chase. The proliferation of motorcycles was merely an annoyance for the auto pilots who treated them as some sort of lower life form to eventually be eliminated by Darwinian selection. Pedestrians, of course, were the very lowest species and crossing the street made us feel like carrion prey.

Taipei's city plan left much to be desired, at least in the older part of town where we walked. Commerce followed no pattern; new high rises loomed over squalid shops. On most sidewalks the parked scooters made it nearly impossible to walk two abreast. We passed grimy but crowded food stalls, more congruous to a debtor Third World country than to a country with one of the world's biggest bank accounts. Still, there were other culinary choices. A familiar red sign glowed across one main street: Wendy's, the fast-food emporium. Only something was wrong with Wendy. True, she had the wholesome pigtails and freckles so familiar to the hungry hunters of America's highways. But her face was black. We suspected that the franchise regulators in the States didn't know about this bit of appropriation. A few blocks away, we saw that McDonald's, too, came in for this sincerest form of flattery.

Two things stood out from our initial reconnaissance: what appeared to be English stores and the barber shops. Both did brisk business even on Sunday evenings, and had this been our only look at Taipei we would have been forced to conclude that it was a city of exceptionally well-groomed citizens, all of whom were fluent in English. The reality was different.

The English stores, clustered by the dozens in the old downtown, were in fact tutoring outlets designed to help students pass their English language comprehension exams so they could apply to study in the United States. With about 27,000 of its students pouring into U.S. universities each year, Taiwan was then our largest source of foreign students.

The barber shops were another matter. There were a truly unbelievable number of them for a city of two million residents, many of whom did not look particularly well-coiffed. Some of the shops had an old-fashioned red-white-and-blue awning, some had one twisting pole out front, others had two or three. Only later were we to discover the true meaning behind this tonsorial epidemic.

On Monday morning we observed a strange mating game played out in the coffee shop of the Hilton. By about 7:30, each table was occupied by a lone Western-looking man in a business suit, while around him a score of waitresses literally ran to see that customers were served quickly. The pace resembled that of traffic on Taipei's streets. Each man looked forlorn as he pored over the baseball scores in the previous day's *International Herald Tribune*. At some point during the meal, a Chinese gentleman in a business suit would join him. Briefcases would open, binders unfold and animated haggling would begin. Here was the bourse of international trade. The Hilton coffee shop, or a dozen like it in Taipei and a few hundred in the other big cities of Asia, was where deals were being made to produce goods to sell in the United States or Europe.

"I want 50,000 dolls that wet their pants," the harried American would say.

"We can make them for $5 each," the Taiwan plastics magnate would reply.

"I can do better in Hong Kong," the American would counter, probably making an educated guess.

"Okay, okay," the Chinese would smile. "Three dollars each, but you have to take 100,000."

"Deal."

And the trade deficit had just grown by a few hundred thousand dollars.

While we watched this ritual, we thumbed through the monthly guide to Taiwan businesses, a giveaway from the hotel. Sometimes you can tell a lot about a place by what it tries to promote. Las Vegas, for example, touts betting parlors and escort services; hotel guidebooks in Los Angeles offer discounts on custom car rentals and expensive boutiques. This book contained thousands of display ads, each with an address for a showroom and a factory as well as a telex number. These were small businesses, mom-and-pop operations specializing in the production of such items as electronically heated toilet seats, digital watches with built-in lighters, pool cues and hundreds of ads for electronic gadgets and handcrafted jewelry. Sprinkled throughout were some higher-end items, like bicycles, computers and yachts.

Few of these items were sold for consumption in Taiwan. All, however, were being contracted for in the Hilton coffee shop over rice porridge (for the seller) and bacon and eggs (for the buyer). What we were witnessing was the transfer of wealth from a country with a lot of whims to one with a lot of ambition.

This, though, was a sideshow. The Americans were jet-age Willie Lomans, only now the middle-age, middle-class salesman was a buyer. As we moved to the lobby, we witnessed the main event.

In the center was a man who looked like Admiral Yamamoto—or the guy who played him in the movies. He stood with his hands balled into fists held waist-high and slightly in front of his body. With his bristly gray hair and clenched jaw, he could have been a weightlifter contemplating a curl. He was watching the elevator doors, which soon opened to spill out a half-dozen Asians wearing well-made blue suits and laughing loudly. He immediately shouted above the din of the lobby, which stopped for a moment. Quickly the half-dozen moved in front of the leader and listened while he issued a few orders in a grunting voice. Then he clapped one on the shoulder and they all laughed much too loudly. Now they were all yelling at one another and clapping one another's backs. Two started singing as they strode, the crew-cut one first, through the parting crowd of the lobby and into waiting limousines.

"The Japanese," whispered a Taiwanese businessman we had met earlier. "They are formidable." His tone was one of hushed awe.

"They are the economic animals of the world."

They are also the Ugly Americans of 20 years ago, the obnoxious, superior, economic imperialists who felt they owned whatever public space they occupied. Now it was the Japanese who moved with the confident air of those who make the rules, while the latter-day impotent Americans watched, bleary-eyed, with uncomprehending surprise.

At 8:25 exactly Daniel Hwang, a 31-year-old foreign service officer who worked for the president's press office, appeared on the scene, breathless and shivering with nervous energy.

"I am glad you are prompt. There are many, many things to do, Brian. Mark. We must be on time." He took off without a response and led us outside. As we emerged, a driver rushed out of a dark sedan with naked flagpoles on the hood and held the door for us. With all the pomp and ceremony afforded petty potentates, we drove the 200 yards to Daniel's office that was practically across the street. It took us 10 minutes in traffic. It would have taken us about five to walk.

"We easily could have walked, Daniel," London offered.

He scoffed. "Walked! We are your hosts."

Daniel's office was in a complex built by the Japanese colonial government in the early part of the century that included the office of the President of the Republic. Soldiers guarded the entrance, but security was vastly different from Korea, where visitors were prohibited from coming within blocks of the Blue House. With little fuss, we were escorted into a waiting room where we watched a procession of young men dressed in blue suits darting in and out of several doors, waving telexes and newspapers and shouting to one another. They matched Daniel's kineticism erg for erg, and after 15 minutes of watching this the phrase Chinese fire drill came to mind.

No one paid us heed. Daniel, who said he usually had about four or five assignments at any one time, explained he had to make arrangements for a group of Dutch filmmakers.

"In Taiwan we are very busy," he said. "We don't have so many people so everybody does lots of jobs."

Visiting between phone calls, he said he would brief us on the country's problems so we could better converse with his boss, the head of the press office.

"We have three problems in this country. Traffic, transport and national identity, which means easing of conflict between islanders and mainlanders. We have a hygiene problem with the small vendors. And we must improve our infrastructure."

"That's five, " we told him.

"Five. Right." And he was gone again.

Eventually, we met Daniel's boss, who politely accepted our statement of purpose: that we wanted to understand Taiwan in a few weeks. It sounded as silly to us as it must have sounded to him. When we had first told our plans to write a book about Asia to an American journalist friend in the States, he asked, "Got a hundred years?" Daniel's boss wished us luck and said anything we wanted, Daniel would take care of. We could go anywhere, see anything. He seemed overworked and harried and not at all the sinister, calculating national security expert we had anticipated. We had been prepared to do battle, demanding our rights and decrying the expected constraints.

"Things are a little easier these days. We're not as suspicious as we once were.

"I hope you enjoy your stay," he said mechanically, and returned to a stack of papers on his desk.

No doubt he caught our surprised expressions, for as we shuffled from his office he called out, "I hope you have come with open minds. Then I know you will be impressed."

Daniel seemed undaunted by our quest for instant knowledge. He hustled us off into a chauffeured car—this one was larger than the one we had arrived in, apparently reflecting that his boss liked us.

"Where are we going?"

"You want to understand Taiwan. You are going to the first place to have this understanding."

We confided in him. "Daniel do you really think it's possible to squeeze all this in, to really get an idea about his place in such a short time?"

He scoffed, "No problem. I am your humble servant."

We cringed as the driver shot into the main thoroughfare without checking for oncoming traffic. He nearly knocked down a helmetless scooter driver and his girlfriend who rode sidesaddle behind him.

Daniel, sitting in the front seat, turned to us. "We have 4.6 million motorcycles in this country. It is a symbol, I think, of how well we have progressed, because 15 years ago we had 4.6 million bicycles."

We asked Daniel why car drivers seemed to have so little respect for them.

"Because I think we are in such a hurry to move forward that sometimes we forget how to be polite," he explained.

Daniel was born in 1955 on Taiwan. He was a "fifth generation islander." Those born on Taiwan bear a certain pride of their legitimacy. Once, the natives of the island practically were excluded from every important aspect of Taiwan's public life. The Nationalists who fled the Mainland and flooded the island from 1947 to 1949 laid claim to its governance, expecting to remain only momentarily before returning to mop up what was left of Mao and his cadres. Even the language they spoke—Mandarin—was different from that spoken by the islander: a type of Fukienese that was brought there by the original settlers. The squatters took over immediately and were tolerated because they had guns and money and no one really expected them to stay long. As time has passed, however, and an older generation has died off the native islanders and Nationalists' children, born on Taiwan, now make up nearly 85 percent of the population. What troubles some hard-liners is that the younger generation, like Daniel, will not harbor a burning passion to recapture the Mainland because it is not their homeland. Daniel told us one of his life's ambitions was to see Shanghai and Beijing, but he stopped short when we asked him if he was prepared to die for that dream. It is because of this uncertain commitment that the Nationalists have been fearful of native Taiwanese attaining power in politics and over the national psyche.

Daniel said that as he grew up he never felt discriminated

against because of his origin. "Taiwan is based on merit. If you're good enough, no one is going to stop you. We are too small a country to exclude worthy persons for silly reasons."

We asked Daniel about his long-range plans. He said he wanted to be an ambassador.

"To where?"

"South Africa."

London grimaced.

Daniel apologized, but for the wrong reasons. "Oh, no, it is very beautiful country. You can live there very well for little money."

We told him of our distaste for its politics.

He smiled. "We cannot be too choosy in our country. There are so few countries who will have diplomatic relations with us. There are only 22 now, and many you may not even consider to be countries. And for the rest, you may not like their politics either."

The diplomatic tide began to turn against Taiwan in 1971 when it was expelled from the United Nations. Observers then felt it only was a matter of time before it lost its most vital link of all—the one to the United States. A collective yelp of pain rose from the island when details of Henry Kissinger's secret China opening were revealed. Finally, on December 15, 1978, Jimmy Carter announced that the new year would begin without diplomatic relations with Taiwan; our new China embassy would be in Beijing. By the time we met Daniel, the roster of countries in which he might serve was topped by places such as Swaziland, Lesotho, Paraguay and the Comoro Islands.

We stopped on a side street in front of what appeared to be a garden.

The driver hurriedly opened the door for us. Daniel ran to our side and apologized—would it be all right if we talked about something other than politics?

"Of course."

Daniel then raised his palm toward the sky and announced, "Good, Brian. Mark. If you want to understand Taiwan you must come here. This is one of the great Confucian temples. You can see all the buildings in all of Taiwan, but you will not understand anything unless you understand Confucius."

We strolled into a courtyard. Daniel told us this temple,

nearly empty that day, is the focal point of the country on September 28 when the president goes there to celebrate Confucius's birthday.

"What do you know already about Confucius?" Daniel asked.

Very little, we told him.

Daniel chuckled. He looked at each of us. "Brian. Mark. Surely you are pulling my leg."

We shook our heads. Then he must have realized that not even at his energetic best could he explain his country to us in a matter of weeks. Or even years.

He removed his jacket and swung it over his shoulder. He shook his head unhappily. "Sit down, please."

He stared at us quizzically. "Surely you must be testing me."

"No, Daniel. We are stupid. It's as simple as that."

"Okay," he readily agreed. "Okay. I will tell you something about Confucius. But you must understand there is so much to tell. It is impossible for you to really know him so quickly."

"Yes, we understand. But Confucius is the one who said that every journey begins with a single step."

He looked confused, then smiled. "Confucius is the greatest man who ever lived," he said with a blunt certainty that was not at all typical of the Asian deference which we had expected.

"Confucius's greatest achievement is the promotion of popular education," Daniel said with the precision of a well-drilled schoolboy. "He was born in 551 B.C. in the state of Lu at the time when education had been the special privilege of the noble class. He taught that knowledge is the most important possession and I think you would say he taught how to be a human being."

Kelly asked Daniel what he meant by that.

"You will see," he said. "You will see it in the way people live."

We stood before a small classroom facing the courtyard and watched a young girl read. "She is here because of Confucius," Daniel said. "I am sure she is from a poor family. She thinks knowledge is the most important thing."

To prove his point, he motioned for her to come out. She ignored him, but Daniel persisted. Finally, she arose and came toward us, her left leg dragging behind. Daniel understood why she had demurred and he profusely apologized for the bother.

He explained to her that we knew nothing of Confucius and asked if she could enlighten us.

Her name was Ho Sho-chui, and she was 25 years old. An embroiderer by profession, she sewed flowers onto tablecloths for export to the United States. Why was she studying instead of working?

"I work very early in the day then I come here to study for night school."

We told Daniel he should delicately ask why she was going to school at such a late age.

She nodded at the translation. "Because when I was young, my family was poor. My leg is bad, and I need to see doctors. I had to work to support my family."

What was she studying?

"Physics. One day I will earn enough money to study abroad. It will take a long time, but I will do it."

We thanked her, and watched as she shuffled back to her desk. "Very typical," said Daniel. He apparently saw nothing out of the ordinary in that remarkable woman.

He continued to lecture. "There are six arts of Confucius: etiquette, music, archery, history, calligraphy and mathematics."

He paused and quietly counted to himself. "Yes."

London disagreed. "No. Riding the chariot was an art. That would make seven." Kelly looked at London in disbelief.

"How do you know that?" Daniel asked.

"We read the encyclopedia, Daniel. I am sure that riding the chariot is an art."

Daniel frowned. "Let me see." He held up his index finger. "I know etiquette or ritual is one. Confucius is very fussy. You must honor tradition when you enter the temple. Music, that is two. You must balance the individual with a temperament, a mentality making you calm down so you can concentrate on what you are doing. Archery—that is bravery. So that is three."

He thought for a moment. "Mathematics—to try your mind, make it sophisticated, meticulous. History is five. Confucius believes if one doesn't know his past, how can one avoid repeating the errors. History, in the mind of Confucius, is just like a mirror."

"Okay. Now what is the sixth?" we asked.

Daniel studied the answer. "The *Book of Changes* is one." The moment he said that he took it back. "I guess that is silly, Brian. Mark. I am ashamed. You are right. It must be horsemanship, the chariot."

We stopped at a pond with turtles all about. "Nearly every temple has one of these," Daniel explained. "The turtles are a symbol of long life. Biologically, the turtle can live 500 years. Confucius himself was not superstitious, but Taoist temples have these symbols. Now in Taiwan and China people have mingled Taoism and Confucius in their minds."

Once on the street again, we were slammed with the noise and traffic of Taipei. With the exception of Bangladesh, Taiwan is the most densely populated country in the world, and it seemed the entire place was in motion.

Daniel picked us up the next afternoon at the hotel. (We had offered to walk to his office, and he seemed offended by the suggestion.) He happily announced that we would have an opportunity to visit a "national treasure."

We had heard that one of Confucius's direct descendants lived in Taipei, and we had requested an interview with him on a laundry list of things to do. We hadn't thought much of it; frankly, we had expected an audience with a wizened saffron-robed man who would grunt a few truisms and take his leave of us.

"But he is far from here, so you will see some of Taipei before we arrive."

Again, we were struck by how dull the cityscape was. None of the buildings was more than 20 stories, and Daniel explained that was because Taipei sits in an earthquake zone. "There have been more than 80 tremors already this year," he said. Taiwan also sits in the Asian typhoon belt, and in 1986, typhoon Wayne killed nearly 100 people in the central part of the island.

"There are an awful lot of barbershops," London told Daniel.

He seemed not to hear.

"It doesn't make sense, Daniel, what's going on with all the barber poles?"

He blurted out a confession. "We are proud of them. They are a consequence of a hardworking society. We are proud that our per capita income is enough to allow people to do this sort of thing."

Clearly, we had struck a chord. "Daniel, that's very impressive. But what are they?"

He looked surprised. "You don't know? Brian. Mark. You are testing me again."

We shook our heads.

He translated for the driver who gave us a look in the rearview mirror of barely constrained amazement.

"They are places of relaxation," Daniel offered.

"Oh?"

He told the driver to turn in to a side street and proceed slowly. "You can see that some have one pole, others two and sometimes you can see three poles."

We noticed that the windows of the single-pole places were clear. The double poles had mirrored windows with shoe-shine boys sitting out front. We did not see three poles.

"What's the difference?"

Daniel searched for the official explanation. "One pole is for a regular haircut. Two poles means you can touch but not too much. Three poles, anything goes."

We jotted that down.

The ornate gray building was the headquarters of the Examination Yuan, the government branch that oversees the salaries and testing of civil servants. We were led into an all-white reception room with large open windows that let in noise from the streets. Three portraits hung on the walls—Sun Yat-sen, Chiang Kai-shek and his son, Chiang Ching-kuo, the president of the country who died shortly after our visit. Sun and CKS peered severely into the room, no humor there. These were men of fire-tempered steel who had survived decades of war and treachery on the Mainland in their attempts to control the destiny of the Chinese people. In contrast, CCK, who had grown up under the shadow of his father and in the relative peace of the island, had a cherubic face, a sheepish smile and a bemused what-am-I-doing-here look about him. But we had come to understand that the expression on the portrait was out of date. In recent years, CCK had found himself in the middle of a power struggle between the country's more progressive businessmen who wanted Taiwan to liberalize its political system and its relations with the rest of the world and the old guard warriors who thought that now was the moment for increased vigilance and a reaffirmation that China would one day be reunited—under their rule. The understated CCK was displaying a savvy that broke down Taiwan's dependence on his father's lingering shadow and turned the country's attention to an enlightened agenda based on international commerce.

Taiwan's government is divided into five branches or *yuans:* the Executive Yuan (headed by the president), the Legislative Yuan (the Parliament and the National Assembly, which chooses the president every six years), the Judicial Yuan, the Control Yuan (a formal watchdog or inspector general branch) and the Examination Yuan. The division of powers was the brain child of Dr. Sun Yat-sen, who founded the Republic of China on January 1, 1912 and whose idea was to combine Western-style branches of government with the traditional Chinese divisions. Of course, only one branch really had counted since 1949 when CKS took over.

Daniel explained that Sun Yat-sen had added the Control and Examination Yuans to the traditional Western branches of government because China had been ruled for so many years by emperors and there was no assurance that capable public servants would emerge. Sun's idea was to etablish an independent oversight branch and those officials would be tested and selected by the Examination Yuan.

We asked why Confucius's descendant was selected for this particular job.

"Because he is so highly regarded," Daniel said, "and he gives respect to the Examination Yuan. He believes that. . ."

Daniel stopped short and jumped to attention. He muttered, "Please stand up, Brian. Mark."

We hadn't seen our host enter.

K'ung Teh-cheng quietly shuffled into the room and right up to us, barely giving us time to stand to greet him. He was a white-haired man in a dark blue suit with a gray cardigan underneath. After greeting Daniel, he sat down. Daniel remained standing, nearly in a trance.

We asked Daniel if we could begin the interview. He came to.

"Yes. I am not sure you know how important this man is," he whispered.

Daniel was right. K'ung Teh-cheng was the 77th direct descendant of K'ung Fu-tzu, better known to English-speaking ears as Confucius. To Taiwan he is the physical link with the glorious history of China. To the communist regime he stands as an obstacle to its claim to being the rightful and logical heir to the soul of the Chinese people. Being so new to the country, we couldn't tell if K'ung actually was a figurehead to be dusted off for visitors or an active participant in the country's life. We also could not define our reaction to this man; frankly, we were not sure if we were meeting the pope, the president or Oral Roberts.

K'ung was born in 1919, four months after his father died, which indicates how precarious this direct lineage has been. He smoked a pipe through yellowed teeth.

In English, we gave Daniel our first question, which had to do with our observation that each of the countries in which we were interested—Korea, Taiwan, Hong Kong and Singapore—seemed to have one common denominator: Confucianism. Singapore, Hong Kong and Taiwan, being Chinese cultures, clearly clung to the teachings of his ancestry. And Korea probably is the strongest non-Chinese adherent: The design of the South Korean flag consists of the yin and yang symbols (the male and female cosmic principles) and trigrams (groups of three lines) from the *I Ching* or *Book of Changes*, perhaps the foremost of the Confucian classics.

We asked K'ung how a way of thinking nearly 2,500 years old could be so vital today.

Daniel muttered, "Good question."

K'ung spoke at length, sucking on his pipe and using it to make a point. We had no idea what he was saying, but he spoke with passion and measured his sentences carefully. When he finished Daniel said, "He thanks you very much for coming."

Daniel obviously was frightened by the prospect of translating this interview. He had been hoping K'ung would have his own interpreter. We told Daniel that with his translating this promised to be a very short interview. He apologized to us and asked K'ung if he could write notes on paper as he spoke. As a precaution, London turned on his tape recorder. Then we asked the same question.

K'ung responded, "The reason that K'ung has been so easily

accepted by the people is because he provided the basis for people to deal with daily lives. What he taught 2,500 years ago still provides the basis for the way we live our lives today.

"For instance, Kung emphasized loyalty to one's duty and loyalty to one's country. This is not so far off from what today's leaders emphasize." He waited for Daniel to translate.

"Forgiveness is another foundation of K'ung's teaching. One should not impose on others what they would not do themselves.

"And there is an emphasis on thoughtfulness. In winter we do not want to be cold, so we must think of a way to make others not cold. If one does not want to be hungry, one must think of the stomachs of the impoverished."

He paused for Daniel, then continued the litany of what some might consider bland truisms had his ancestor not been their author. "If I want to have others' respect, I must respect them. And honesty: Your word is your word."

Although Daniel had pointed to Confucius's promotion of education as his greatest gift, others believe that his articulation of social relationships stand out as his most important contribution to Eastern thought.

These teachings are symbolized by the Chinese character *jen,* which has been translated as love, virtue and, roughly, humanism. It forms the basis of what is probably the best-known of Confucius's sayings: Do unto others as you would have others do unto you. (Confucius actually used the negative voice, "Do not do . . ." when he said it.)

After *jen,* the most important concept to Confucius was *li,* which is a term embodying all of the interactions between people, a social order. Those who point to Japanese discipline and acceptance of a hierarchy as a secret for that country's success cite another of his sayings, "Let the prince be prince, the father father and the son son."

Yet, this seemingly rigid social order should flourish, according to Confucius, in a meritocracy; that is, princes should not be born but princeships earned. In this regard, Confucius espoused revolutionary thought in a time when noblemen passed on power to their heirs; a superior man, not a nobleman, should be the social paradigm.

Known as the *chün-tzu,* the superior man blended the concepts of *jen* and *li* together to arrive at the notion that wise men, not blue bloods should govern. Confucius himself said, "To govern is to set things right. If you begin by setting yourself right, who will dare to deviate from the right?" The superior man was one who had mastered the six arts that Daniel had listed for us.

K'ung said that the concept of *chun-tzu* and communism were incompatible. (He wanted us to know right away what he thought of the government on the Mainland.) "I categorically rule out that communism and Confucianism can coexist."

We wondered why.

"K'ung can only survive where men are free to think and govern themselves. In K'ung's time if a poor man wanted new clothes and didn't have the money for them . . . he shouldn't steal them because he is afraid of the law but because of his conscience. K'ung said if you wanted to enforce a law you must give people the reason and the reason must be right."

K'ung accused the communist government of destroying the social structure that his ancestor had espoused. In Confucian societies, the family, not the state, is the vital social unit. For this reason, it is not uncommon to see four generations of a family living together; social security for the elderly is the responsibility of the offspring. Then, too, courts are of limited usefulness in a Confucian society; disputes are better handled by a complainant's plea to the family's elder. Businesses often are structured in proportion to the number of functioning family members, as each division is headed by a brother-in-law or a cousin.

Confucius and his most famous disciple Mencius, who lived 100 years after him, taught that the state should be subordinate to the individual. Confucius summarized the relationship between the state and its subjects as follows: "From emperor down to the common people, all, without exception, must consider cultivation of the individual character as the root."

K'ung explained that the government on the Mainland was "anti-humanitarian." He said, "The individual is not free to become an individual and is only part of the state, much more than the state is part of the individuals."

He stopped Daniel in midtranslation and cut pieces of a cake and insisted that we eat. "K'ung said that it is very Confucian to be hospitable to your foreign visitors," Daniel translated.

We asked K'ung if he ever thought of returning to the Mainland.

He put down his plate and fork and spoke with his mouth full. "All the time," he nodded. "All the time."

He spoke slowly. "Every patriotic Chinese, no exception, looks forward to the day China will be reunited. But only under two conditions: under traditional Chinese culture and the teachings of K'ung and under the principles of humanitarianism."

K'ung was born in Shantung province on land believed to be in the family for 2,500 years. He was educated as a Confucian scholar, as he has educated his son. In 1949, he fled with the Nationalist government to Taiwan, and he said he never harbored doubts that one day he would return home.

He explained, "You must remember that 35 or 40 years to a nation with a history of 5,000 years is nothing. It is a second on the clock. K'ung has been tested for 2,500 years and he is strong. Communism has been here for 40 years and it cannot survive."

Daniel told us that it would be polite if we would take our leave. We demurred. Our original question was still on the table.

"Why does it appear that Confucianism provides the basis for probably the strongest economies in today's world? Why is it still so vital?"

Daniel told us we already had asked that question twice. Kelly sternly told him to translate and not to editorialize. "But he may be insulted," Daniel warned.

K'ung asked what was going on. Daniel translated, and, it seemed he apologized, wanting K'ung to know that he had warned us not to be repetitious.

K'ung nodded as if he understood the challenge. Then he instructed Daniel to translate slowly and carefully. "One reason is loyalty, which I spoke of before. K'ung teaches that individuals acting together as a family can accomplish much.

"And K'ung taught that the individual is most important, and the individual becomes good by education. Teaching and love of learning, that is very important. K'ung said, 'To learn and relearn again, isn't it a great pleasure?' "

He suggested that many Westerners really did not understand what Confucianism is; he found many people believing him to be a priest or a philosopher. "K'ung taught a way of life. Many current religions have similarities, but K'ung taught that virtue is for your own sake, not to please the gods. K'ung taught that the here and now, not the hereafter, is what is most important."

And yet, as the here and now has changed Confucianism hasn't.

Daniel was furiously scribbling Chinese characters. He looked up. K'ung was smiling.

"Yes," K'ung said. "That is why K'ung is so adaptable to these times. Technology changes machines but it does not change human beings. K'ung believes that there are principles that make a human being a human being. The principles do not change even if the times do."

Daniel stood up and told him we had to leave. We were about to argue, but K'ung rose and told us how much he enjoyed the visit. As we exchanged pleasantries, we heard a car's brakes screech.

"One more question," Kelly asked. "What would Confucius have said about the way people in Taiwan drive?"

His face collapsed into a smile. K'ung did not have the answers to all questions.

Our journey of extremes took us on the night of having met the great teacher to Snake Alley, a transplanted part of old China in the Wanhua district of Taipei. As a guide for the journey—all of about 10 minutes by cab—we had secured the services of Linda Lu, an executive from our hotel who had offered to give us her special city tour that would involve snake blood and counterfeit watches.

The crowded neon-lit street gets its name from the principal merchandise on display. Poisonous snakes traditionally are revered for their blood, which is believed to be the stuff that makes a man a man. Because we had a barbershop visit on our agenda, we thought we could use a lift.

Many different varieties of snakes hung from the tops of the stalls dripping blood into puddles on the streets. Hooded cobras, vipers, green tree snakes, black snakes. Other snakes were coiled in cages waiting to be slit open, though at some stalls the cobras sat on the open counter and swayed rhythmically within what seemed to be comfortable striking distance of passersby. More reassuring though no more appetizing were the snakes that lay twitching on sizzling barbecue grills. In the depth of the stalls glared televisions showing dog fights-to-the-death and Japanese sumo wrestling, all being watched by families whose eyes never left the screens as they sucked bowls of noodles into their mouths.

"You go on ahead," said Linda, as a rack of fake Gucci handbags caught her attention. "I hate snakes."

We watched an ambitious vendor shoot his hand into a cage and pull out a dark gray serpent. He held it close to Kelly's nose and taunted him, then held it to his crotch like a trainer waving smelling salts before a fallen athlete. He swung the reptile like a lasso, partly to get the attention of the passersby and partly to prove his own virility. Something snapped and the snake went limp. He suspended the snake from a rope and slit it from top to bottom with one smooth stroke of a razor blade, lifted the tail and squeezed dark red blood into a small glass. He added green bile from the snake's gall bladder and gave the concoction a swish.

"Here, you drink this and you make love like a snake," he offered to Kelly.

Kelly declined, telling the hawker that his personal recipe was deer's penis, another alleged virility enhancer. The vendor pointed across the narrow street to where that delicacy was being sold.

We really had no time for love potions. We had shopping to do. Even among our friends who didn't know the difference between Taiwan and Thailand, there still was an understanding that we could get cheap Rolexes where we were going. Taiwan's reputation as the king of copy had spawned a cult following among the ranks of America's factory outlet shoppers. And the prize catch in the sea of copycats was a $14,000 gold Rolex with diamond numerals that we heard could be fetched for about $20.

We already had plenty of indications that we would be successful in our search. Despite a well-publicized government crackdown against counterfeiting, all we had to do was cross the street from our hotel to the yellow arches of a nasty-looking hamburger stand that hoped to be McDonald's. We purchased hardcover books for a fraction of their price in the States, the international copyright laws being no hindrance to publishers here. We knew the Fila socks and shirts we were buying could not possibly be sold for a fifth of their normal price if they were genuine, but they looked great. In the early 1980s, the U.S. International Trade Commission estimated that 60 percent of all counterfeit goods sold in the States were made in Taiwan.

Three reasons often are given for why Taiwan persists in violating every trademark and copyright law known to man. First, only now is Taiwan's legal system beginning to catch up with what the world generally calls intellectual property rights. And, because of the plethora of small-to medium-size industries, there really isn't much capital available for research and development in areas such as design and marketing. Buyers in the United States and elsewhere want the knockoffs and are prepared to run the risk of marketing phony goods in their native countries. The type of merchandizing allows a businessman to quickly find a source for a product that may be particularly hot so that he can ride the wave of a fad.

Companies whose legitimate products have been threatened by copies have pressed Taiwan's government to enact and enforce anti-counterfeiting laws. A new industry also has developed—private detectives who trace these products to the source and blow the whistle. The government uses these captures to make a showy display against copycats, but foreign competitors question its resolve to really crack down.

We set out to find the Great White Rolex. We started with an advantage. For as long as he could remember, London's father had returned from his trips to Asia with an arm laden with watches for every friend and relative he could think of. London himself never wore a watch, which caused his father to question his heritage.

Linda Lu was London's father's watch scrounger. After our foray into man-making potions she suggested that we go buy some timepieces.

To divert any attention we might have drawn, we left Snake Alley by way of a temple across the street, lit some incense and dropped coins into jars. Then we slipped out the back way.

"Hurry," said Linda, holding open the door of a taxi.

We asked her why the spylike m.o.

"We could go to jail," she said. Then she added, "You, too. The detectives always watch the tourists."

The taxi ride lasted 20 minutes and took us to the old part of town. We slalomed through the sidewalk traffic, our watch scout searching the alleys for her contact.

She spotted a man across the street who craned his neck to the right.

"Come on," she said. "This is it."

We had heard about the subtleties of the East, but this was taking the equivalent of a jaunt to K mart to the extreme.

We left the main street to a darkened alley where we could make out the figure of a young girl about 50 feet ahead. We walked quickly to her, and she grabbed Linda by the arm and led her upstairs to an apartment.

It was a small place, where we could sit in the living room and see the kitchen, dining room, bedroom and bathroom, which is all we did for 15 minutes while our watch scout spoke heatedly with the mother of the young girl.

We asked what was going on.

"They do not trust you," Linda said. "I am trying to tell them you are not policemen."

The discussion continued, and all of a sudden the mother let out a loud "Ah" and left the room.

"What happened?" we asked.

"She is going to get the watches."

"How did you convince her we were not cops?"

Linda pointed at London. "I told her who he was."

We remained puzzled.

"I told her he is the son of a man who loves watches."

In front of us lay hundreds of watches—Rolexes, Cartiers, Movados and so on. The retail value of them, if they were real, would have been well into six figures.

The woman held London's hand.

We asked why she was doing that.

"Your daddy is a very important man here. She wants you to be welcome," Linda said.

London was humbled. Halfway around the world on the second floor of a decaying hovel his father had achieved heroic stature. That thrill was even greater than the one we got for copping a $14,000 diamond-studded Rolex for $26. Of course, when we had returned to the States, London's father told him he had overpaid.

There are two pieces of the Chinese legacy that Taiwan possesses and the communists covet. One is the aging form of

K'ung Teh-cheng and the other is the treasure in the National Palace Museum, the world's greatest collection of Chinese art and antiquities that the nationalists spirited out of the country when the communists took over. Both are symbols of legitimacy, powerful totems that represent tangible proof of China's history. But while Confucius represents a lineage of ideas that the communists may find incompatible with their own system, the treasure is universal. Its thousands of crates of pottery, sculpture and painting represents 5,000 years of Chinese accomplishment. Where it sits, the Taiwanese will argue, must therefore be the legitimate capital of the Chinese. And where it sits today is in mountainside vaults on the edge of Taipei. To find out how it got there, we went to see the man who stole it.

Dr. Han Li-wu, who is 85 years old, keeps a spacious suite of offices in a downtown high rise. The display board in the lobby announced that the suite housed, among other organizations, the Asia Foundation and the Taiwan chapter of the World Anti-Communist League; Dr. Han was one of the founders. At the time, the League, which has occasionally made shadowy appearances in newspaper accounts of Third World counterrevolutionary movements, was suspected of having played a role in funneling money to the Nicaraguan contras. We assured Han's aides that we were there to talk about history and would let current events take care of themselves.

"Dr. Han is very proud of his work fighting communism. It is his life," one of an endless stream of sober-faced aides told us, as we were ushered through the spacious offices to a formal sitting room.

From a side door emerged a man considered on the Mainland to be one of the great war criminals of the Chinese revolution: the slight but rod-straight figure of Han, a porcelain smile spreading across his face as he offered a characteristically limp Chinese handshake.

His skin was smooth and shiny as oiled wood and his hair was still dark—the result, he said, of four spoonfuls of sunflower and sesame seeds a day. He spoke in precise English, though with a slight lisp because of the gleaming dentures. His eyes were unclouded circles of hard, black obsidian.

We asked if it was true that he was still under a sentence of death on the Mainland.

"Yes, yes. I am a criminal," he beamed. "I have heard that Mao said his greatest loss was the collection."

He smiled and nodded to himself for a long minute, savoring again the triumph of a lifetime.

Then perhaps forgetting why we were there, he began a monologue on two subjects that presently concerned him: politics in the Philippines and the Chinese takeover of Hong Kong in 1997.

"The world must make the Chinese keep their bargain to leave Hong Kong alone," he was saying as London rolled his eyes at Daniel Hwang.

"He is an elder," Daniel whispered. "You must be polite."

"*You* must be polite," London corrected, and tried a provocative question to snap Han out of his reverie:

"But as far as the treasure goes, Dr. Han, why does it have such importance? Why should the communists care about what is only the product of the ruling class?"

"You could not be more wrong," he answered. "Art is a universal asset. It can be very powerful, because it appeals to the highest sensibilities of the people. And it appeals to their sense of history and pride and beauty.

"The danger is that the communist leaders would exploit this treasure. Just imagine if these works remained on the Mainland. They would have been destroyed, over and over again. One day the communists are concerned with history. The next day they say there is no history before Mao. These treasures are delicate things. They cannot live by whims."

From Han and others, we learned the story of the odyssey of the palace treasure that sometimes seemed closer to a Hollywood script than real life.

It was after the fall of the Manchu dynasty in 1912, after almost 300 years of imperial rule, that which had been the emperors' art collection was opened to the public. From the time of the Sung dynasty in the 10th century, the emperors of China had been diligent about accumulating the best art and craftsmanship from their vast domain. Pottery, calligraphy, carvings in wood, jade and ivory, jewelry, bronze work and paintings were all amassed for the pleasure of the imperial family. Some of the treasure was functional, such as intricate dinnerware or lacquered jewelry boxes, but some was historic, such as a silk cocoon found at the site of a 5,000-year-old Neolithic village. All of it had been for the eyes of the privileged only.

With great anticipation the Palace Museum in Peking was opened on "Double Ten" (October 10), 1925. One of the most forbidden caches in the Forbidden City was displayed to a curious public, which for centuries had been denied access to the greatest creations of their culture. With the end of dynastic rule, China's politics and culture were undergoing a tremendous transformation, which began as a step toward republicanism and ended in chaos. The art exhibition lasted about as long as the political stability.

In 1931, the Japanese invaded Manchuria and their attempt to extend their domain over the rest of China became a foregone conclusion.

Two university students in Peking—Na Chih-liang and Wu Yu-chang—who had conducted an inventory of the collection since its opening read the tea leaves and prevailed upon the museum authorities to let them pack up the cream of the collection in case it had to be moved quickly. In 1933, that escape took place. On the night of February 4, they supervised the loading of 19,557 carefully packed crates of treasures onto trains bound for the foreign concession district of Shanghai. They stayed there until December 1936 when they were taken to the nationalists' stronghold in Nanking.

There, Han, who was the founder of the Sino-British Association and who had been in charge of local refugee areas, entered the picture and was put in charge of the evacuation project in the summer of 1937 when full-scale war broke out between Japan and China. The crates were divided into three batches and scattered through the countryside.

The first group of boxes went to Changsha, the provincial capital of Hunan, 420 miles southwest of Nanking. For three months the crates sat safely in the basement of the university library. Then came the Japanese bombardiers. Fortunately, only a day earlier Na had sent the collection to adjoining Kweichow province and stored it in a private garden under climatic conditions that would terrify a curator. After a short respite the pieces were taken to dry caves in Anshun, and they remained there for six years as war raged.

The second trove of 7,000 boxes escaped Nanking a month before the Japanese army's infamous rape of the city. Only ravenous coyotes and pit bull terriers could have wreaked more pain, suffering and indignity on the city than the Japanese soldiers who violated as much personal property and as many women as they could find. The treasures would have had a short life had they been found.

Instead, they had been taken to the remote town of Paochi in Shensi province where they arrived on a journey often interrupted by Japanese terror bombing. As the invaders neared, Wu directed an escape over the Chinling Mountains, a journey of 100 brutally hard miles that took over a month to make. Then, on through torrential rains that washed out all the roads to the small town of O-mei in Szechuan province. The trek lasted 19 months. Despite the harsh weather and the rough journey, not even a teacup was damaged. Ironically, the entire batch nearly was ruined in O-mei as fire destroyed the town but spared the temple where the collection was stored.

The third batch of 9,369 crates left Nanking just as the Japanese entered the city. Han commandeered a British steamboat to carry them up the Yangtze River to Hankow. The Japanese neared and Han decided to move to Chungking, another 600 miles up the river, but that idea was abandoned once it became apparent that no significant urban center was safe from the Japanese. Instead, the collection was sent to a small river town called Lo-shan, where it lay unloaded, because boatmen could make far more money transporting refugees. In September 1939, another disaster almost befell the treasure. As it finally was being unloaded the ropes broke and the cargo raft careened downriver. Luckily (some say miraculously, due to a huge statue of Buddha that overlooks the river at Lo-shan), the raft got caught on a sandbar and was saved.

The treasures, safe by late 1939 in Anshun, O-mei and Loshan, stayed there until after the war when they were gathered in Chungking and then sent to the nationalists' new capital of Nanking. Nearly 15 years after they had been packed away in the dead of night, they finally were put on display to the public. They had escaped the war unscathed.

This peace was short-lived.

Civil war raged through the country, and the communists

sieged Nanking. Again Wu and Na decided to pack up and leave. This time the destination was Taiwan. And again art had to compete with refugees for space on boats. The problem that faced the relic rescuers was to chose among the treasures. They could not afford to take the entire collection, so they chose what they believed were the real prizes. Han was able to send 772 crates and some museum personnel on the ship *Chung-ting* that left Nanking on December 22, 1948 on a voyage that left all of the passengers miserably seasick. Another 3,502 crates left two weeks later. And finally, 1,248 of the remaining 2,000 crates they had decided to take left Nanking for Shanghai barely ahead of the communist advance and then to Taiwan through mine-infested waters.

Han recounted to us the reception that awaited the treasures in Taiwan. "Nothing." He stored them in sugar warehouses in Taichung, chosen because it was on the driest part of the island.

"But it was hard to get people interested in them. Hard to get money to show them. I remember a government official who asked me your question, 'What's the use of having them?' "

Han managed to eke out an $18,000 grant from the Asia Foundation to build a small display center, which proved to be a Mecca for scholars around the world. Although the center had a capacity to display merely 200 of the nearly 250,000 pieces it strengthened Han's resolve that what he, Wu and Na had brought was the most significant treasure that existed in the East. When the government saw the enthusiastic reception for the collection on an American tour in 1961, it collaborated with Han to build what became the National Palace Museum.

Sunk into the hillside north of the city like some bombproof military bunker are the vaults that contain the heart and soul of Chinese culture. The collection numbers 650,000 pieces and is growing each year from purchases in auction houses around the world. Only a relative handful of the vast assortment is on display at any one time, laid out in glass cases along the modern, temperature-controlled halls of the building.

We toured the museum one afternoon, along with a usual array of fidgety Taiwanese school children in worn uniforms, regimented Japanese school children in crisp white shirts and navy trousers or skirts and awe-struck older Taiwanese up from the south on holiday. These were some of what museum officials say are three million visitors a year.

One wall of the lobby is devoted to a time line of the 5,000 years of Chinese history, a record of a civilization based on the produce of its artisans: the oracle bones that collected on bits of bone and shell the wisdom of the Shang dynasty from almost 2,000 B.C., a period of relative tranquillity after centuries of war had swept back and forth across the land; the ritual vessels of the Ch'in dynasty emperors who united China in 221 B.C.; the remarkable multicolored pottery of the T'ang dynasty in the seventh century and the tremendous works of the Sung dynasty, an uncharacteristically tranquil period that is known as the golden age of literature, landscape painting and calligraphy.

Julie Chou, the director of acquisitions for the museum, reveled in her role as tour guide.

"This is the most important collection of Chinese art anywhere," she told us. "It is perhaps the best collection of art from a single culture anywhere."

It was her job to make it better. She was enjoying her assignment because Taiwan's wealth and the renewed sense of the collection's prestige combined to allow her to purchase virtually any major piece of Chinese art that appeared on world markets.

"We had to leave behind hundreds of thousand of pieces, although we believe the best pieces were brought here. Now we have a budget that allows us to compete with any buyer anywhere in the world. What we want we get."

The collection now has enough pieces that if it were changed twice a year, it would take 30 years for all the pieces to be displayed. Yet Chou said that she frequently goes on buying missions, usually to Hong Kong or Macao. "It's funny how pieces from the collection, left behind, find their way to the auction houses. We don't ask where they come from when we're buying."

The mainland Chinese, it seems, have recently become interested in restocking their own collection and often try to compete on the open market.

"They do not have the resources," Chou said, allowing herself a slight smile.

Much of what is for sale now was smuggled out of the

Mainland over the past 40 years, especially during the Cultural Revolution though much valuable art was destroyed then nonetheless.

"We lost things we will never see again," Chou said bitterly. "The students knew nothing. They smashed anything they could find. And now the communists say, 'No, no, we didn't mean it. Art is good.' Well, it is too late. I am only grateful for how much we have taken out. If not, I don't know what would remain."

We stood over a jade bowl with flower inlays from the Ch'ing dynasty. "This is a nice piece although not nearly as valuable as some of the pieces from the Sung. Jade is very popular with our tourists because they can get a sense of its value in the market."

We asked if there was a Mona Lisa of the collection.

She shook her head. "Not really. For some scholars the most valuable are some paintings like this one. It is called *Traveler in the Mountain Path.* The Sung dynasty landscapes are very valuable."

She pointed out the fine detail and shadings on the silk and paper scroll paintings that used techniques at least comparable with European art of the same period. An unknown artist painted *The Palace Musicians,* a T'ang dynasty (A.D. 618–906), masterpiece of figure painting. The artist Li Ti did *Buffalo Boys Fleeing a Storm* during the prolific Sung dynasty (960–1279) and the monk Chü Jan painted *Seeking Truth in Autumn Mountains* about 975.

Chou said that most of the luminous porcelains came from imperial craftsmen. The museum owns 23 items of the 11th-century Ju ware, out of a total of 34 pieces recorded in the world. Wall after wall was lined with the distinctive blue-and-white Ming dynasty (1368–1644) porcelain and the brightly colored works of the Wan-li (1573–1620) period.

There was a whole room of miniature carvings, most of which, Chou told us, had been gifts to the Emperor Ch'ien-lung (1736–1795), who apparently had a passion for them. All sorts of materials were used: rhinoceros horn, bamboo, fruit pits and wood.

The most remarkable piece was a softball-sized orb of ivory carved with figures and a lattice design. At first glance, it was a standard museum artifact, an intricate piece of craftsmanship that evokes a nod of admiration for the time and patience it must have taken to complete. But the ball was not so simple. It was really 17 balls, one inside the other, each covered with the same figures and lattice designs of the layer preceding it, each able to rotate freely and all carved from a single, solid piece of ivory. The ball was the work of three generations. Day after day of practically microscopic carving, handed down from father to son to grandson until it was perfect enough to present to the emperor.

We had seen other pieces of astonishing intricacy—a bronze tripod with 500 characters cast on its legs or an olive pit that has been carved into a replica of a royal barge complete with movable windows and a cabin containing chairs, tables and eight figures—but none so striking as the ivory ball. Within, perhaps, was the Chinese enigma. How was it made? Even after Chou explained the process, we couldn't figure it out. Why was it made? For a Western mind, it didn't seem to serve any purpose beyond the first layer. It sat on display in an emperor's salon, among many other small treasures. Wouldn't just one delicately carved ivory ball have been enough? Three generations of a family's labors were devoted to a moment of pleasure for the emperor and his guests.

The most popular piece in the museum was a carved jade replica of a cabbage head with a grasshopper sitting atop it. The piece is the size of a fist and is realistic enough to tempt one to slice it for slaw. The artist had shaded the cabbage from dark at the base to light at the leaf tips by meticulously following the natural green and white lines of the jade stone. The jade came first, Chou explained. The artist saw what he had to work with and fit his subject to the color of the stone. It was as if he had merely coaxed out a cabbage that was already lurking within.

We walked over to an extensive display of small porcelain cups with a chicken design. "One like these," she said, "recently sold for one million dollars at a Sotheby auction. We have several like that. In fact, we must have thousands of pieces worth at least a million dollars."

As best as can be divined, the actual collecting began during the Sung dynasty, although much of the art itself is much older. Pieces arrived in the Forbidden City, the emperor's inner sanctum, by confiscation, gift, inheritance or purchase. Many of the pieces inventoried by Wu and Na from 1925 to 1933 were fakes that led them to believe the emperors were not all connoisseurs—or that no one in the palace would risk telling them that their art was ersatz.

Most of the collection remained intact throughout the centuries except during the Boxer Rebellion, a time when the acquisitive English were furnishing the British Museum with ill-gotten masterpieces from around the world, and at the beginning of this century when the last emperor, P'u Yi, sold or gave away what he could to buy favors.

Chou stopped before a jack ax or *ch'i,* really a ceremonial hatchet. "This is very old, from the Chou dynasty, about 1,000 B.C. It is a priceless piece, not only because of its art, but because this is our heritage, our culture."

But because of this, Chou explained, the collection is unlikely to be seen outside of Taiwan anytime soon.

"We can't trust it to leave," she said solemnly. "I think the communists would like very much to steal it back. Certainly no one would insure it."

So for now one can only imagine the length of the waiting list for tickets at the Metropolitan Museum of Art or the Art Institute in Chicago. This symbol of a culture in exile is, itself, an exile.

Like Korea, Taiwan's economy has been shot from a cannon, achieving in the last two decades what most countries could not attain in a century. The popular perception is that it was founded in 1949, much as America was discovered in 1492. Yet natives were there to meet Columbus, and many people were in Taiwan to meet Chiang Kai-shek.

The island originally was settled by aborigines whose descendants still inhabit the eastern part of the island. About 1,500 years ago came the Hakka, an ethnic Chinese group that had made its way to Fukien and Kwangtung coastal provinces, then formed the cadre of a Chinese diaspora throughout Asia.

During the 15th and 16th centuries Taiwan grew in importance because of its strategic location; it served as a haven for pirates who preyed on the Japan-China trade that passed close to the island. These hijackings angered the trading nations, who decided to retaliate. Not surprisingly, Japan took the initiative, led by Toyotomi, a warlord, whose attempt to conquer the island failed nonetheless in 1593. Then came the Dutch who actually succeeded in establishing a settlement and three forts. Some historians give these Europeans, and not the British of Hong Kong, credit for introducing opium to the people, a habit that soon drifted to the Mainland and eventually wreaked havoc on China.

As the Ming dynasty came to a close in the mid-17th century, after a quarter millenium of power, Taiwan became embroiled in the power play that engulfed China. A swashbuckling sailor named Koxinga was left in charge of the Ming forces in their fight against the marauding Manchus. He was a respected general, but the odds were against him and ultimately he was forced from the Mainland and sought refuge in Taiwan—a path that was followed about 300 years later by Chiang Kai-shek when he found himself in similar circumstances. Once there Koxinga booted out the Dutch and established a throne, which was later held by his son and grandson. Koxinga died shortly after his arrival in Taiwan, where he still is revered as a liberator of sorts. Neither of his offspring was up to his level of leadership though, and in 1684 the Manchus brought Taiwan into the fold.

It was a mostly forgotten island until the mid-19th century when Western trade with Asia began in earnest. Still, Taiwan was best-known as a place to avoid. British sailors who were unlucky enough to end up on Taiwan's shores found themselves subject to torture and imprisonment by natives they understandably regarded as savages. Yet, as the Opium Wars brought about an opening of trade, Taiwan too became more tolerant of foreigners, at least those from the West.

The Japanese never forgot about the island and never lost their desire to own what might be seen as a natural extension of the Japanese archipelago. When, in 1872, a Japanese ship sank off the coast of Taiwan and its surviving crew members were murdered by the aborigines, the Japanese military clamored for revenge. Instead, diplomacy won out with the Chinese emperor making a formal admission that the aborigines were beyond his governance.

But domestic pressures in Japan were building to such a point that the military felt that the only way to relieve them was to make a conquest, any conquest. Korea and Taiwan were considered. Taiwan won. A Japanese military expedition landed on the island and stayed until the Chinese emperor paid them to leave. Japan was entering its most militaristic phase, with visions of empire stirring in the heads of the ruling elite. China, for all its size and wealth, was a nation of astonishing vulnerability. The Japanese had watched the European powers exploit China for decades and now wanted to bring the game closer to home.

Finally, the dam broke in 1894 when Japan invaded Korea, a Chinese protectorate, and wouldn't leave without getting some real estate for their troubles. In the Treaty of Shimonoseki, a year later, Japan received the Ryukyu Islands and Taiwan.

As conquerors go, the Japanese were not all that bad during this period. Taiwan's experience was far less brutal than that of Korea. The Chinese were accepted as a higher order and they benefited from the Japanese mania for regimen. Colonial rule brought Taiwan into the modern age, creating an infrastructure of roads and railroads, schools, hospitals and industry. The conquerors insisted that everyone speak Japanese but that was fanciful because the island always was—and still is—linguistically fractionalized between the original Fukien-speaking settlers and the Mandarin speakers from the Mainland.

For a half-century Japan ruled Taiwan, until October 25, 1945 when, in the aftermath of World War II, Taiwan returned to China. Sort of.

The history of modern Taiwan begins with Sun Yat-sen, a medical doctor who was educated in Hawaii and Hong Kong. From a base in Japan at the beginning of this century, Sun organized secret societies whose aim was to overthrow the feudal rule of the Manchus and establish a republican government in China.

Sun's concept of republicanism already was commonplace in the West, but it was downright revolutionary in a country that had been ruled by an imperial class for thousands of years. The modern age had loosened the reign of isolation and ignorance fostered by the imperial family. The underpinnings of the corrupt Manchus were rotting and Sun Yat-sen was able to set in motion forces that would sweep them away—although those same uncontrollable forces would also ensure Sun's own failure and the success of the communist revolution. Sun was able to put military might behind the country's yearnings for nationalism, partly through his fabulously wealthy father-in-law, Charlie Soong, and partly through his dealings with the Soviet Union.

Sun's political philosophy is popularly known as the Three Principles of the People, namely nationalism, democracy and economic socialism. Nationalism was important for the return to China the spoils stolen by foreigners and to compensate the Chinese for the accompanying indignities. Democracy did not necessarily mean a political structure, but rather the need for all Chinese to learn to read and write. The socialism that Sun advocated was simple: Those who tilled the soil should own it, and the government had to assume responsibility for industrialization.

Yet, Chinese factionalism and jealousies were to prevent Sun from consolidating power. The country was in a state of anarchy with an impotent central government unable to affect the domains of the warlords, whose private armies had sprung up to fill the power vacuum. The post-monarchy period left the country in shambles.

Throughout this period Sun came and went from power, his strength derived from the military leaders, warlords and secret-society kingpins who backed him.

The Kuomintang Party (KMT) that Sun organized in 1914 was joined by the Chinese Communist Party (CCP), formed in 1921, to espouse a program of ridding China of foreign influence and unifying the country. Sun actually began to see success in 1924 with the promulgation of a national constitution that promoted the values of an equal society. At the same time, a military academy was set up on Whampoa Island in Canton to train officers loyal to the government, and Chiang Kai-shek was chosen as its first commandant. Two of the main strategists of the communist revolt, Chou En-lai and Lin Piao, were among the first cadets.

All this momentum died suddenly on March 12, 1925 when Sun Yat-sen succumbed to liver cancer. The alliance between the KMT and CCP disintegrated. Chiang, who had spent four months in the Soviet Union studying its new government, had become virulently anti-communist, and he led a murderous purge of the KMT to rid it of any Soviet influence. The communists were driven from the cities and forced to flee to the countryside—which, as events proved, was exactly the right place for them to be.

Chiang actually came close to unifying the country by his early victories over the warlords who controlled fiefdoms throughout China. Yet, this success was not to last because he had the CCP and the ravenously land-hungry Japanese breathing down his neck.

It was not until the outset of war with Japan in 1937 that some unity returned to China. By that time Mao and his cadres had completed the Long March, a 6,000-mile epic trek to the refuge of the barren northwest after government troops drove them from their stronghold of Kiangsi. The Japanese, meanwhile, were firmly ensconced in Manchuria to the northeast, but for the time being they were not advancing. There was relative peace and the nationalist government in Nanking was bringing China into the modern world. A new constitution was being enforced as was a modern code of laws. Improvements were made in the army, public health, transportation and, most important, education. But it was in education that the increasing conservatism of the KMT began to surface; the fundamentals of Confucianism were reinforced as the guiding principles. Chiang was asserting himself as the stern ruler and he was losing the support of the intellectuals.

Chiang was also devoting his attention to domestic intrigue and ignoring the threat of Japan outside the borders. Following the course of most Chinese emperors, Chiang attacked the enemy within the kingdom—in this case the communists. It was a policy that endured until one of history's more curious events occurred in December 1936. Chiang had ordered two army commanders to attack communist positions. The generals refused, saying that they were more concerned with Japanese advances. When Chiang flew to the northwest to personally issue the orders, he was kidnapped by one of his subordinates. To his rescue came Chou En-lai, who arranged for Chiang's release with the understanding that the KMT leader would stop fighting communism and start fighting the Japanese.

That was enough to keep Chiang's hands full. World War II devastated China, and Chiang, operating from a provisional capital deep in central China in the city of Chungking, constantly dickered with America's General Joseph Stilwell, who considered his counterpart to be a pompous buffoon. Yet, led by Chiang's savvy wife May-ling Soong (known to the world as Madame Chiang) and her brother, T.V., the China Lobby in

Washington succeeded in ousting Stilwell before the war had ended.

Once the Japanese surrendered, the nationalists raced the communists—who by now had assembled an army of almost a million men—to claim territory and arms abandoned by the Japanese. Within months the country was firmly split into two camps. Both sides had victories to claim, but the tide began to turn in favor of the communists in 1948. Large-scale defeats of the nationalists, who lost some 400,000 men in Manchuria alone, spelled out the inevitable. The final blow came between November 1948 and January 1949 at the Battle of Hsüchou when the nationalists lost 500,000 men and their equipment. Only time stood between the communist armies and the nationalist capital of Nanking.

As 1949 wore on, the communists mopped up the rest of the country, and Chiang and his followers took their art and gold to the island of Taiwan.

One of the benefits of traveling through young countries is the opportunity of finding people whose personal histories offer stirring examples in microcosm of the drama of nation building. In Korea, we had found Lee Yong Ho, who had jumped from the 15th century to Amherst College in a few moments. In Taiwan we traveled to the country's second city—the industrial seaport of Kaohsiung—to meet a man eager to superimpose his life story on the tableau of his nation's history.

W.P. Chuang was born on December 5, 1939 in the Manchurian town of Mukden, now called Shenyang. His father worked as a civil engineer for the Japanese Royal Company, which built the railroad through Manchuria.

"But I hated the Japanese," he told us. He looked carefully around the nearly empty employee cafeteria at China Steel, Taiwan's largest steel maker, whose plant we also had come to visit. He whispered to us, "I hate them now. Bad people. Animals." He paused, "Fortunately they lost the war."

W.P. said his recollection of World War II was limited because he was only a small boy then. "I remember right before the unconditional surrender we were bombed every day at the same time, at 3:30 in the afternoon, by your B-29s. For a year. We saw only silver dots in the air, very high. And four silver lines. We just heard the explosive sounds. Boom. Boom."

He banged his teacup on the table for emphasis. "The Japanese always run for cover when the bombs come. But not us. Not the Chinese, because it was not our business. But bombs have no eyes, and Chinese get hurt."

W.P. warned us that we should hurry and publish our book. "You will have competition," he declared. "I am thinking of writing my history. You will see, it is very exciting."

W.P. was a thin, wiry man filled with the sort of kinetic energy we were beginning to assume was a national trait. He stabbed the air to make a point; he grabbed his throat and scowled to express disgust.

He had been assigned to escort us around China Steel, but it became obvious that he had been harboring a story for a long time. And even though he didn't want us to compete with him, he couldn't keep his tale under wraps. "When the surrender happens it becomes the only moment in my life when I have known peace. It was about one week. Between August 14, 1945 and August 22 or 23. My family was living in the country because of the war. We were poor.

"But not hungry," he added quickly, establishing the difference between an honorable and dishonorable existence at the bottom of the barrel. "Never hungry. My grandmother had a farm. My father tried to run a small stand, but he was no businessman.

"In that week the Japanese were gone. No more war. The Russians still had not come. It was hot, but it was quiet. I remember the quiet. Peace. Peace."

The respite was to be short-lived, as another invader stormed Manchuria. "The Russians." Chuang grabbed his throat as if he were gagging. "I hate the Russians. More than the Japanese.

"My father was on a bicycle when they came. They took his bicycle, his fountain pen, his watch, his eyeglasses. They raped. They looted. Women tried to camouflage, dress as soldiers.

"The Russians were cossacks, countryside people. Stupid. Dumb. The soldiers couldn't distinguish between pumpkin and watermelon. They used no fork, no spoon. Just hands. Filthy people."

He pretended to spit in a gesture of contempt.

"Bad people.

"The Russians took all the Japanese soldiers and the young Chinese men and rounded them into cattle cars and nailed the cars shut and sent them to Siberia. As the cars passed, piece by piece they picked up the rails and loaded them on and took them to Siberia."

W.P.'s family, with no home or possessions, went back to the countryside.

Conflict followed them, as this was the beginning of China's civil war, and Manchuria served as the bloody central theater during the early years. W.P. said that the Russians had turned over abandoned and captured Japanese weapons to the communists. He told us his family had no antipathy for the communists. "But we had to hide, because if they found out my father worked for the Japanese. . . ." He ran his index finger across his neck.

There was a lull in the fighting in 1946 due largely to the mediation efforts of General George C. Marshall, sent by President Truman to see if he could dampen a war that was of little interest to a country celebrating victory over the Japanese and the Germans. Yet, peace broke down in 1947. At first, the nationalists scored impressive victories. W.P. remembered fighting near Mukden when the nationalists enjoyed their finest moments during the war, before the communist armies led by Lin Piao challenged them for control of Manchuria.

He held up his left hand to show us a scar on his palm and near his knuckles. "Glass. I walked through a small village just after the fighting and cut myself. It was winter and there was no medicine so I just pulled it out and cried."

In terms of lives lost, the civil war was nearly as devastating to the country as World War II. W.P. summarized his recollections. "During civil war too many people died. At that time life meant nothing. A lot of fighting. A lot of big battles. A lot of people died."

When the nationalists controlled Mukden his father joined them as a civil engineer. He was assigned to build an airstrip in the city of Tsingtao.

"Finally, that city is taken by the communists, and we are captured. We tried to get permission from their government to move to Shandong, and we got a note and we used the note as a passport but instead we decided to go to Peking.

"We went to a small fishing port and we paid a captain gold to take us to Qinghuangdao. Almost 50 people in a small boat. It was winter. Cold. Very cold. I remember, it snowed a lot. This was one time in my life I was hungry. Hungry so I thought I might starve. We thought the trip would take two days. It takes six days."

We asked him why he didn't travel by land.

"Land? Land was captured by the communists."

He continued his journey. "We go from Qinghuangdao to Tientsin by ship, by steamer, then to Peking by rail."

W.P. said that they had gone to Peking to collect back pay that the government owed his father. Once there, his father was asked if he wanted to follow the government.

"What choice does my father have? He stays, and he dies. My father has no idea about a nationalist or a communist or any political thing. He just wants to have a job. And there is a rumor that the communists want to capture everyone who served under the Japanese, and that is true. A lot of people were murdered, buried alive. He had no choice. No choice. My father really didn't have any politics. He was just scared."

In early 1949, the communists made their final push toward Peking. W.P. and his family went to Wuhan and then to Canton, as the south was the final harbor for the nationalists.

"1949, August, my mother, my brother and sister are together. We are given tickets and taken on an air force aircraft to Taipei. It was a C-46. U.S. made.

"Remember, I told you there were 50 people on the boat. Only five—my family—came to Taiwan. The others stayed on the Mainland, because they say they are tired of fleeing. They say, 'We are Chinese and look, even when we are controlled by Japanese they do nothing to us. So what can the Chinese do?' "

We asked W.P. what Taiwan was like when he arrived.

He laughed. "I didn't know anyone in Taiwan. First day I came here I cannot understand what they say. They speak Taiwanese, and we speak only Mandarin. But my father can speak to them because he speaks Japanese. We can communicate in Chinese by writing but not by speaking."

He recalled the chaos of the country at the time. "Taipei had been bombed by the United States and there was a lot of debris all over, bricks and glass. Broken buildings."

And it was crowded. Within the first year, two million Mainlanders had fled to Taiwan to be dumped atop a native population of six million.

W.P.'s family remained in Taipei only a short time. His father took them to the city of Tainan on the west coast, where he was assigned to build an airport, and began the task of remaking here what they had over there.

W.P. said that even now he finds it hard to believe that he has come such a long way. "When I tell my children this, first they look at me and say 'We do not believe this.' This is a story, a fairy tale, just like a Grimm fairy tale, Andersen fairy tale. The lesson I try to convince my children is that your intellect, your mind can be yours forever. No one can take it away. When we left the Mainland, we were empty. But my father is an engineer and he can flee to a free land and be a free man because he has something in his mind and he can use this to develop a skill and earn for a family."

Yet he also voiced a concern. "My children study very, very hard. There is much pressure on them to get into a good university. I think 70 percent of all children wear glasses."

We ask W.P. if he'd like to go back to Mukden.

"Yes. Very much."

"Why?"

"It's my, what do you say? Hometown?"

Did he think it was possible?

"In the near future there is no way. But many times when I travel I meet people from PRC and we become friends. We talk. They believe the same thing: We must be unified. And we all believe one other thing: Time will cure everything."

During much of our time in Taiwan we did battle to keep ahead of the reams of literature that we received. The Taiwanese have a fondness for books and pamphlets chronicling their existence, as if somehow a critical mass of paper will assure that they will not someday be washed into the sea by the communists and forgotten to the world.

Had we packed up all the handouts throughout our trip we could have filled a couple of suitcases. Instead, we skimmed what we were given by whatever ministry or company was on our agenda and left a trail of rubbish wherever we went. Often, a polite secretary would come running after us to let us know that we had forgotten some document. Daniel was, at first, taken aback by our inattention. Then one day, we decide to keep that day's collection of literature and asked him to carry it around. He got the point.

Which is not to say there weren't some gems. For example, the *Annual Review of Government Administration of the Republic of China,* which looked like a particularly offensive work because of its weight, was one such find. It started out:

"The Republic of China, situated in East Asia, is bounded on the east by the Pacific Ocean, on the west by the Pamirs, on the south by Nepal, Bhutan, India, Burma, Laos and Vietnam, and on the north by the USSR."

Bhutan? Pamirs? We continued reading.

"Although it is the world's most populous nation, China has a density of only 60 persons per square km. . . ."

Something was not right. We knew that Taiwan was so crowded that a sniffle could spread so fast it could mutate to a type-A flu bug in a matter of a week. Peace and quiet were illusory concepts here while 60 persons per square kilometer would be virtual solitude.

There was also the matter of the map. There in green was the tiny island of Taiwan, with a label for "Taipei, capital of the Republic of China." And there to the left, in the same green but shaded with cross-hatching and stretching halfway around the world was the land called simply "Occupied Territories."

Then the pamphlet began to make sense. "Since moving to Taiwan in 1949 the seat of the Central Government of the Republic of China has been based *temporarily* in Taipei."

K'ung's view that 40 years is a mere second in history is pervasive. China has not been lost forever to the winners of an indigenous revolt; it's just been occupied by squatters. For this reason, talk of making Taiwan an independent nation was considered a treasonable offense on Taiwan. Independence from what? the old timers asked contentiously.

The flame—some say the fiction—has been kept alive for 40 years. That less than 20 million people will one day rule over one billion is an idea whose power has not waned through these years of military retreat followed by diplomatic defeats.

The keeper of the flame for much of this time was the man who watched it go out in the first place—Chiang Kai-shek. On December 8, 1949, he established the Republic of China on

Taiwan for what he assumed would be a very short period of time.

The islanders no doubt wished him well in his reconquest, because they largely resented the invasion of mainlanders. Taiwan, because of Japanese occupation, had been seen as a bastard child by the rest of China. After the war, the nationalist officials on the island led a repression campaign against islanders who were accused of cooperating with the Japanese or supporting communism. It was likely that after a half-century of Japanese rule, most of the islanders had had some contact with the Japanese—and were thus subject to punishment. A lingering fear and resentment met the wave of new arrivals in 1949 who spoke a different dialect and had no more respect for Taiwan itself as a soldier for the day's foxhole. All the nationalists wanted out of Taiwan was a place to rest.

Yet the moments of respite turned into months and years. As time passed, the Battle of Kumingtou, fought on the island of Quemoy on October 25, 1949, grew in significance. It was there that the nationalists beat back a furious communist attempt to wipe out the front line of defense of Taiwan and establish the island as a base for an invasion. When the smoke cleared even the communists had to accept that the boundaries of coexistence most likely had been drawn. The communist army, though not well-trained or equipped, had exploited its advantage of numbers when the fighting was on land. But on island fortresses, the calculus changed in favor of the defenders to the point where the communists, with a weak navy and air force, would have had to pile the beaches high with their dead if they hoped to rout the nationalists. As time went on, the nationalists dug in deeper still.

During the Korean War, Chiang received a welcome visitor, when Harry Truman stationed the Seventh Fleet between the two Chinas and increased economic and military aid to Taiwan. The U.S. Navy's role in discouraging invasion is thought to be as important a comfort to Taiwan as the invasion of Normandy was to France. China's antagonism toward the United States magnified the symbolic importance of Taiwan, these also being the days when the "who-lost-China" question caused finger-pointing throughout Washington. This was prime time for the China Lobby, whose most prominent voice was Henry Luce's *Time* magazine and included many of our country's most notable right-wingers such as Senator William Knowland of California and New Hampshire newspaper publisher William Loeb. The goal of this loose federation of like-thinking anti-communists was to keep the pressure on our government to isolate the Mainland (popularly known as Red China) and to maintain the facade of the inevitability of Chiang's return. Long after China entered the mainstream of world politics and Taiwan that of the world's economy the residue of the lobby lingered. Friendship for Taiwan still indicated a particular mind-set.

On the island itself the public enthusiasm for the return home was not allowed to die. There was some hope in the mid-1950s that Peking would renounce the use of force against Taiwan, but this was blown apart by daily artillery bombardment of Quemoy beginning in 1958. Only the threat of U.S. naval intervention and the softening of Soviet support for Peking's militancy quieted the guns.

The fiction of transiency on Taiwan survived in the structure of its government. The Legislative Yuan had 760 members elected in 1948, and by 1986, only 323 remained (14 members were in their 90s, and 105 were octogenarians). The National Assembly, elected in 1947 with 2,961 members, was down to 972 by 1986. The reason for the atrophy was that the legislature purported to represent all provinces in China, and obviously no elections could be held while the voters were under Peking's rule. Finally, the government, realizing that politicians do not live forever, altered the local election system in favor of one that provided greater representation to Taiwan.

Throughout Taiwan's formative years, however, only one branch of government counted, that being Chiang himself. And he was as hard-line as they come.

Born in 1887 in the coastal province of Chekiang, Chiang was active in Sun's republican movement to overthrow the monarchy. His youth combined revolutionary politics and gangsterism; China in the early 20th century was a country of turf battles. Chiang developed a skill of ingratiating himself to power brokers, and developed into the ideal front man for these unseemly forces.

Yet, to even suggest a darker side to this man is to arouse blind anger among his loyalists who worship him as a liberator of his people. After Sun's death, Chiang, who had married the sister of Sun Yat-sen's widow, tried to consolidate power among the factionalized warlords, and he emerged as the recognized leader of the nationalist forces during World War II and the civil war.

Chiang was a spartan soul, given to long quiet walks and exposition of his thoughts on the vitality of classical China. In the 1930s, he promoted the New Life Movement, which was aimed at modernizing China while at the same time keeping alive its Confucian traditions. In a sense that is the atmosphere of Taiwan today, a modern society strongly clinging to its Chineseness.

When it came to reconciliation with his enemies, Chiang was a bear. The young patriot who had engineered Chiang's kidnapping in order to refocus military efforts against Japan spent the rest of his days under house arrest. And toward his enemies, the communists, Chiang articulated his thoughts as the three noes: no negotiations, no compromise and no contact. He enforced his policies through a legal system based on martial law that controlled the press, political parties and travel. It was not until the 1980s that Taiwan's citizens could even travel directly to Hong Kong, lest they be contaminated by the communist presence there. The police and army operated as heavy-handedly as anywhere in the world in stifling dissent and taking political prisoners in the process.

Chiang died on April 5, 1975 and news of his death was accompanied by a sudden cloudburst that the superstitious Chinese have interpreted as outpouring of divine tears.

When we traveled through Taipei, the memory of Chiang loomed over the city in several ways. Most evident was the spectacular blue-roofed tomb and museum that dominated the vast public square under construction. A decade-long project, the square was lined with an opera house and museums built on a grand scale and, at the end, atop a rank of stairs, the white-marble mausoleum of Chiang. Inside a gigantic statue of Chiang sat in a pose not unlike that of Abraham Lincoln in his own memorial. For posterity, the fierce, treacherous Chinese warrior was smiling over the city like some kind of benevolent paterfamilias.

But more than a decade after he passed away, Taipei was finally showing signs that Chiang was actually dead. His memory was revered, but politicians—in particular his son—seemed to feel for the first time that if they disobeyed his dictates his arm would not reach at them from the grave. Perhaps the most startling message that he was gone for good was contained in the newspaper accounts we saw of a fistfight on the floor of the Legislative Yuan. Premier Yu Kuo-ha was about to tell his colleagues about the glorious economic results of 1986, and he started with an old Chinese proverb: "Spring is on earth and all is so refreshing."

All of a sudden one of the opposition party members rushed to the podium shouting, "You are but an interim premier," and all hell broke loose. The day before a free-for-all had broken out for 30 minutes, and ended only when the national anthem was played.

The reaction from everyone we spoke with was one of amusement and even pride. Only a short time before and the disruptive legislators might have found themselves in a locked small room with no windows. But the climate we encountered was vastly more casual. A political springtime freshened the air. In December 1986, an opposition party had won 12 legislative seats and 11 in the National Assembly. (Only 100 out of 323 seats in the Legislative Yuan were open to election.) The election had been preceded by two demonstrations at the airport to meet the plane of a returning dissident who was not allowed to land. Despite property damage no one was hurt at the incidents, and no crackdown followed.

Instead, the government tolerated the victories of the opposition candidates and allowed them to take their seats, bruised though they might have been. Indeed, the KMT appeared to be turning away from the model of a Soviet Politburo to follow the lead of a democratic system with one dominant party, like Japan or Mexico, which can bend with the wind to cover most of the territory oppositionists might occupy.

Chiang was succeeded by his son by his first wife, Chiang Ching-kuo. He was a physically unimpressive man who had lived in the shadow of his father. Pictures of them together portrayed a tall, lean CKS, often with a visionary look in his eyes, trailed by a round-faced, round-bodied CCK wearing a golf jacket and baseball hat. Even when he was in his 50s, CCK looked like an overweight adolescent in the presence of his father.

CCK graduated from Sun Yat-sen University in Moscow

at a time when the Nationalist Chinese were leaning toward a Soviet-style government. But even as his father was pulling away from the Russians, young Chiang became a member of the Communist Youth Corps, lived in Moscow until 1937 and brought home a Russian wife, thereby creating the political irony of an eventual Russian first lady of one of the world's most virulently anti-communist countries.

Many hard-liners had hoped that Madame Chiang would replace her husband, as she was seen as a die-hard opponent of communism and a fan of authoritarian rule while her stepson's background created some particular problems among Chiang's faithful.

CCK and Madame Chiang reportedly remained at odds, even after the rift with his father healed. CCK quickly became a general in the nationalist party and served as his father's personal assistant and a kind of internal security czar in growing Taiwan. CKS eventually made his son minister of defense and passed a message to all, including his wife, that the leadership would pass to him.

After his father's death (there was a short interim between the presidencies of the father and son), CCK confounded both his allies and critics by liberalizing Taiwan's political system from atop. The hard-liners were aghast at his steps intended at ending martial law and hints that the Taiwanese might be allowed to visit their billion or so relatives across the strait. His choice of a native-born Taiwanese as vice president was a selection his father never would have endorsed. He preempted the opposition by hinting that many voices could be tolerated. He appeared to be an astute scholar of Asian politics which, in the case of Korea and the Philippines, taught that flexibility and strength were not necessarily incompatible.

Businessmen gleefully jumped at the chance offered by the apparent leniency of CCK; the most flagrant display of this attitude is the open secret of Taiwan's near $2 billion annual trade with China, most of which flows through Hong Kong. The government occasionally made a showy display of nabbing some merchants—in the summer of 1985, four businessmen were convicted of trading with the enemy (the charge: "attempting to overthrow the government and having applied means to it"), one receiving a jail term of 12 years—but such profitable activity often prompted the government to evoke a policy of three other noes: see no evil, hear no evil, speak no evil.

An amusing albeit bona fide test of the myth of the Mainland occurred in May 1986, when a pilot of Taiwan's China Air took his $60-million 747 cargo jet and two fellow crew members to Canton during a scheduled cargo run from Bangkok to Hong Kong. Upon landing in Beijing the pilot announced he had made the inaugural flight between the two countries. Unwilling to believe that a man could voluntarily defect to the Mainland, the Taipei government floated rumors that agents of evil had boarded in Bangkok and commandeered the jet. What apparently happened is that the captain wanted to be reunited with his aging father.

Thus Taiwan and the Mainland were forced into a rare display of public diplomatic contact. Perhaps seeking a public relations edge, Beijing quickly told the world it wanted to make arrangements with Taiwan to return its property and people. But under the three noes Taiwan couldn't talk to intermediaries. (The last time the two sides talked was on May 10, 1946, when Chou En-lai met in Hankow with KMT military minister Hsu Yung-chang to try to negotiate an end to the civil war.)

How to be practical and save face?

Taiwan originally proposed that Hong Kong's Cathay Pacific Airways, which flies to both China and Taiwan, act as its representative in the negotiations. China refused but gave in on its demand that the talks be held in Beijing. Taiwan then appointed a negotiating team of mid-level executives from China Airlines and insisted it was a private carrier—which, by most definitions, it is not. They met in Hong Kong with officials from China's state-owned CAAC (Civil Aviation Administration of China), which Taiwan in turn pretended was a private business concern. Thus the fiction was maintained and the plane was turned over to Taiwan in Hong Kong.

Hopes that the legacies of Mao and Chiang would reconcile over an airplane hijacking quickly were dashed. Taiwan resented the opportunity the event gave Beijing to appear reasonable. Beijing, however, was unable to make Taiwan look intransigent, and in the end the affair passed quietly and without a major thaw in relations. Yet we could sense that a rapprochment of sorts had to be imminent. CCK appeared determined to bring his country into the international commercial arena, and he clearly understood that a prosperous populace, which he was developing, no longer could be galvanized behind shibboleths of a time gone by. We were pleasantly surprised that our preconceptions of this place might be outdated.

Our fascination with this game of subtle diplomacy between Taipei and Beijing led us to ask the government for a meeting with one of its most prized possessions, a wiry air force pilot by the name of Chen Pao-chung. With a net worth of $1.6 million, he was one of the newest millionaires in a country where such a distinction was beginning to have meaning. And all he had done to earn his money was to fly his aging MIG-19 fighter plane out of China and into Taiwan—with a stopover in South Korea.

In the propaganda war, there is no greater catch than a pilot and his plane. Taiwan long has offered a generous standing reward to any member of the Chinese air force who will defect with his aircraft; so far the government will confirm 10 who have made the escape.

Chen Pao-chung arrived at the coffee shop of the Lai Lai Sheraton precisely at 2 P.M., accompanied by an air force escort officer and a translator. A slight man in his mid-20s, he wore a well-cut gray suit, blue shirt and blue-striped tie. The open-mouthed bow of the waiter when Chen sat down made clear that we were in the presence of a celebrity. He solemnly ordered tea while we made a few introductory babbles about how grateful we were to have him take this time and the translator told him God-knows-what and we all stared at our tea for a while.

Then London asked if he had seen the movie *Top Gun,* at that moment a Stateside box-office bonanza that made clear, with the accompaniment of a driving rock score, just how cool it was to be 20 years old and flying a very fast plane.

Chen looked down with a smile and said in Mandarin, "Number One movie. I've seen it twice."

"Do girls chase you too?" London asked.

Chen lowered his eyes and smiled to himself as he took off his jacket, loosened his tie and rolled up his sleeves. Then he turned to London with a big white-toothed grin, shrugged and said, "No, but what else do you want to know?"

Fighter pilots, it seemed, shared certain similarities the

world over. It would not have surprised us had he then inquired in a Texas twang if we wanted to get liquored-up and chase some honeys. He had that same combination of nervous awareness and easy confidence you'd find in the ready rooms of aircraft carriers with "USS" painted on the bow. On a relative scale, he was just like any hotshot fighter jock who strapped himself into an F-14. In his own world, Chen was a stud and he was just learning what that meant. No wonder the town of Tanjin, China had been too small to hold him.

"When I was in school I was taught that there is a beautiful island that was ravished by nationalist soldiers, and it was the students' responsibility to recover the island," said Chen. He grew up wanting to be a pilot. "I wanted to help in the fight to return Taiwan to China," he told us. As a student he attended gliding school and became an excellent gymnast. "Good training for a pilot," he said. He decided to join the air force because of his love of flying and because pilots were the highest-paid members of the armed forces.

Chen said that as a boy he really had no politics. Because Taiwan's defeat stood as a national goal, it was his goal. But he said he began to develop doubts about his government in 1981. "As I grew older I began to see problems with the system. The communists had opened society under Deng, so it was easy to see these problems and have these doubts."

Political doubts are not exactly grist for air force locker-room conversation, and Chen held these feelings to himself. "I thought it would be dangerous to tell even my family or girlfriend."

By 1984, he made a decision to leave China, but he had no plan. "By then I was living a very good life. I had a girlfriend. The food was very good. I had benefits."

He was stationed in Kwangsi province, flying reconnaissance missions over the Vietnam border. He considered defecting then but chose not to. "I felt loyalty to my government. I know that must sound crazy, but we had fought a war with Vietnam, and I felt it was my duty to serve."

But as a reconnaissance pilot, he learned many of the evasive skills that he later would need to escape from the air force. And when at the end of 1985 he was dispatched to Manchuria, he hatched his escape plan.

"At first, I wanted to leave right away. But I decided to

wait for the Chinese New Year to visit my family and my girlfriend. I wanted to leave all of my money with my mother. And I did not want to defect before the new year because the government might punish them during that time." He spent the holiday with his parents and three siblings in Hopei province, never letting on to his audacious plan.

On the morning of February 21, 1986, Chen woke up at 5:30 A.M. "I had slept very well the night before because I thought it would snow, so I would not be able to fly. But at dawn the weather cleared."

His mission that day was to fly reconnaisance over Mongolia, just he and one other plane. He was to keep radio silence and fly behind his partner in a blind spot.

"I had planned my break-off maneuver for a year," he said. "By peeling away and flying low I would avoid detection from the other plane and ground radar would not pick me up."

Traveling at 950 miles per hour at 30 meters, Chen created quite a stir over the countryside. "I flew right over an air force base but it was snowed in and they could not catch me."

Expert in China's radar detection system, Chen was nevertheless greatly afraid of what would happen when Korean radar picked him up. "I knew Korea's air force flew F-4 and F-5 planes, which I learned well from training. I could avoid them, but there would be too many very soon."

About 200 miles from Seoul, Chen was picked up by four South Korean jets. "I waved my wings and gave them thumbs up and they gave me thumbs up."

His jet was escorted to a Korean air force base, where the air was filled with sirens and the field surrounded by tanks. "A major came up to me and saluted, but he spoke no Chinese so I had to wait."

Chen told his hosts he wanted to see Taiwan's ambassador to Korea and he announced that was where he wanted to live.

"Did you know about the reward?"

He scoffed. "No, it was a big surprise. I put it all in the bank, then I gave most of it away to charities."

Taiwan's policy forbids Chen from flying again. He is studying to take his university entrance exams.

We asked him what he liked about Taiwan.

"I don't need to get in a long line to buy something. I can

take a long trip around Taiwan, when I want and stay where I want."

Then he smiled. "And there are many swimming pools."

One of the differences between Taiwan and, say, France is that people go to France for a vacation, to relax, to soak up the culture. People go to Taiwan for one reason, and most of the foreigners we found looked as if they'd been through the cash register several times. The businessmen in the Hilton looked spent, and no doubt they probably were from the long flight to Taiwan. But there also was an in-the-trenches air about them, as if the deal-makers had remained home and sent the workers. After all, the differences between manufacturing a shoe in Taiwan and one in South Korea may be a fraction of a penny. Someone who could think in such terms had to be sent on the trip.

That Taiwan is off the beaten track for high level businessmen and free-spending tourists came through to us on a trip to Hwalien on the east coast. We were to depart at 7:00 A.M., but not enough tourists had been gathered, so we waited at the Taipei airport for an hour. There wasn't much browsing we could do at the newsstand, so we made chitchat with our fellow travelers. Not one of them had come to Taipei as a destination; it was just for transit. There are Francophiles and people who lather at the mention of Rio but there appear to be few Taiwaniacs.

In a way that may be unfair because Hwalien is as pretty a place as exists on anyone's map—a rugged mountainous coast knifing into a blue sea. The Taiwanese claim its airport is the only one in the world made entirely of marble; this is quarry country. And after the stagnant, dirty air of Taipei, Hwalien is a cleanser for the lungs and the eyes. But a country desperate for tourists can ruin even the finest sites.

We again waited in the airport for an hour or so until another planeload of visitors arrived. Then we set out on a bus to Taroko Gorge, an idyllic canyon of sharp walls cut by a pastel-colored stream. We chose Hwalien for what we thought would be a leisurely daylong tour.

Once the bus entered the gorge, it stopped frequently for vistas and to allow passengers to buy souvenirs, film and the like. We began to detect a pattern. At each concession stand our guide, who had come to dislike us from our displays of impatience at the airports, stopped for her take of the action before moving on.

She apparently had negotiated with the merchants how long we would stop at each vista and how much of a kickback she would get on the sales. She let us loiter at rather prosaic stops; at some spectacular moment she hustled us along. Our browsing time did not depend on Mother Nature but on human nature, i.e., greed. Consequently we saw more Chiclet boxes and soft drinks than mountain orchids. At one stop the two of us took an unscheduled detour and hiked up a rock embankment to visit a small monastery. The guide told the waiting busload of obeying passengers that we were disrupting the schedule and threatened to make everyone miss the highlight of the trip—the excursion to the jewelry store.

While it was still late morning, our guide announced we had to leave. We careened down the mountain to make up for our tardiness and pulled into a roadside restaurant-cum-jewelry shop, where she announced we would be spending the next two hours. That is, we'd get to gaze longer on ersatz jewelry than on one of the world's great natural wonders.

"Two hours!" London complained. "We came to see the gorge, not to buy jewelry."

She scowled at the impudent Americans. We tried to stir up some discontent from our fellow travelers, but many of them were placid Japanese who, in any event, didn't know what we were talking about. As for our fellow Americans, they had come to Asia looking for bargains. They could bring home postcards of the gorge to prove they were there, but bargain jewelry presented a great opportunity. Our guide's relentless strategy continued as we were served one of the worst meals imaginable: cuttlefish, stringy pork, the parts of chickens that move, cold rice and bitter, cold tea. The plan obviously was to get us away from the table and to the display cases as quickly as possible.

Our fellow travelers bolted in a hurry to browse and eventually buy. The guide was no small factor as she embarrassed people into buying, stuffing jewelry into their camera cases and telling them that they must buy or be arrested for theft. Ha, ha. This to a bunch of tourists who weren't quite sure if Chiang Kai-shek was dead or not. As we boarded the bus we saw the jewelry store owner dole out to the guide her share of the take.

Our last stop was to see an aboriginal dance exhibition. We thought this might be a welcome respite from the hustle, because the aborigines present a uniquely Taiwan tradition. There still are more than 250,000 descendants of the original 19 tribes that settled Taiwan perhaps as long as 10,000 years ago. Mostly they dwell in the mountainous central region and along the east coast. Hwalien is the hub of the largest group, the Ami, which number about 50,000. As with the native cultures everywhere, the aboriginal culture is losing out to the public education system and, of course, television. In a country now repairing decades of fissures between islanders and mainlanders, the oldest natives of all seem to be shunted aside. Statistics show that their unemployment is higher and life expectancy lower than the ethnic Chinese. They still are in demand, however, for the tour groups that pass by and for whom they perform many of their traditional rituals, including dances for harvest, marriage and the other rites of life.

Our group settled into the small amphitheater and performed a dance exhibition by young women in gaudy skirts and feather-studded headpieces. All was well until our guide grabbed members of the group by their arms and hauled them onto the dance floor. Out of the audience arose her Polaroid-armed partner who danced to the tune of the cash register, snapping pictures and offering them for sale at $8 each.

We tried to explain to one of our dancers that we liked her very much but did not want to pay to prove it. The guide jerked her away to more promising waters.

We decided to take the train back to Taipei lest we be forced to have to tip the pilot to let us out at the gate.

The second-largest city in Taiwan is Kaohsiung, a gritty seaport on the southern coast that serves as the exit for the billions of dollars of goods that Taiwan disseminates to the world. Even though it enjoys a tropical setting, the city is shrouded in the grayness of Hamburg or Rotterdam, proving that the Eastern economic miracle can be just as ugly as the Western one. Many sections are filled with the junk of scrapped ships and discarded merchandise. Along the waterfront stands the largest ship-breaking facility in the world, whose end product is rusted steel. Next to the dead hulls lies the country's largest industrial complex.

China Steel is an anomaly in Taiwan, yet it also is emblematic of the country's industrial might. Unlike Japan and Korea, Taiwan does not produce many proprietary products that most of us would recognize, like Sony televisions or Hyundai cars. The economy is populated by thousands of small producers, each of whom will slap an American brand name and a Made in Taiwan label on their finished work.

Part of the reason for the paucity of the giant companies is that the Taiwanese suffer from a packed-luggage mentality. If the word comes that they are free to cross the Strait to return home they very well could not carry an auto factory. This sense of transience, though it fades rapidly every day, still shows itself in the fantastic savings rate of 30 percent (cash can be packed into luggage) and in the lack of enthusiasm for capital-intensive industries (machine tools cannot).

Part of the reason also is cultural. The famous Japanese ethic of teams working together, which has had some success in Korea, just doesn't stick in Taiwan. W.P. Chuang, our friend from China Steel, had two Chinese sayings to explain why: "One Chinese can beat 10 Japanese in brainpower, but 10 Chinese cannot beat one Japanese—because they cannot agree." And, he added, "Ten Japanese speak with one voice. Ten Chinese speak with 20 voices, out of both sides of their mouths."

But there came a time in the late 1960s when Taiwan's government decided that for national security and developmental reasons, a large integrated and world class steel mill was imperative. Once mobilized, this plan came to fruition on target and up to expectations. What was floundering as a sunset industry in the United States became a sunrise industry in Taiwan.

Most of the department managers at China Steel spent some apprenticeship in the United States and they exhibited Chinese pride at besting an older brother.

"Only three or four American steel companies can compete against us," said W.P. who took us on a tour of the plant in Kaohsiung. "Even U.S. Steel, their main business is no longer steel." He chuckled at the absurdity of it.

W.P. added that Taiwan's location made China Steel's feat the more remarkable. "We are the only tropical mill in the world that makes money." We disagreed. In Brazil we had seen blueprints for a network of steel mills in the Amazon located right at the source of the ore.

W.P. scoffed. "Even if they don't have to pay transportation, Brazil steel cannot compete with us. Brazil people are very lazy. Lazy. Chinese people work very hard."

We told him one of the advantages he had was a non-union labor force.

He shook his head violently, "Sure we have unions. But no strike. This is warfare."

We walked over to the harbor area where there were huge piles of waste dust. Workers wore wet hand towels on the lower half of their face to keep out the deadly powder. W.P. surveyed the apocalyptic scene of men raking the residue of industry. "This is why you Americans give up," he said. "You cannot tolerate a lot of dirt."

That, and something called the Occupational Safety and Health Administration, we told him. He didn't understand.

We pointed out that the dust probably was deadly and that concerns about pollution control had had a profound impact on U.S. industry. Pollution was not considered a problem in Taiwan.

He shrugged. "That is the price."

Our jeep took us to the blast furnace, a vision of the inferno containing blackened human forms with profiles ablaze. Chiang Ma-chou, a 29-year-old foreman, was shoveling coke into the furnace. We commented on the heat that was slowly broiling our faces, but Chiang didn't seem to understand.

W.P. knew what we were talking about. "Hot, hot," he clamored.

But Chiang was as unaware as if he were sitting on an office couch.

Chiang told us that after military service he went to vocational school to prepare for his trade, which he plied for five years. His salary was N.T. $23,000 per month or about U.S. $600. But because of his exceeding production goals, he received a bonus equal to 25 percent of his salary.

We asked if it was a onetime bonus or regularly paid.

"Always," W.P. chimed in.

Then it's salary, not a bonus, we said.

"No, no," said W.P. "They tell the men how much to produce and they do more. Always."

He translated for Chiang, who looked at us as if we had questioned his manhood.

We asked him what he did with his money.

"I give it to my mother and father. They live with my wife and son and me and also with my brother and sister."

We told him it must be a pretty crowded house.

"Confucius," W.P. interrupted, as if we had missed the road sign.

How well do you live, we asked.

"I have a television, videocassette recorder, refrigerator and motorcycle. Now I am looking for a car."

How is your production this year?"

"Better than last year."

So you expect more money?

He smiled broadly.

What will you do with it?

"Maybe find an *yi tai tai.*"

W.P. turned to translate, but none was needed. We had heard the phrase on numerous winking, elbow-to-ribs occasions. *Yi tai tai* was literally "junior wife," or mistress. It was at least the stated goal of most upwardly mobile Taiwanese men we met.

There was a goldfish pond next to the blast furnace.

We asked W.P. about it.

"For luck, of course. This is a dangerous job, and we feel the fish protect us. They keep the evil spirits away. Also, it is made of slag. Many people think slag is dangerous. No danger. We dump the slag in the channel to make a man-made island. Maybe one day we use the slag as a stepping-stone to return to the Mainland." We laughed at that thought, but he did not seem to share the joke.

We continued walking through this sprawling industrial city.

The various lines—the cold-rolling mill, the cutting line, the wire mill—were run from small clean rooms lined with computer terminals and manned by business school graduates. W.P. explained that in Taiwan, making steel was a prestige job that attracted some of the brightest students.

W.P. pointed out the plate mill. "All of our equipment comes from a famous U.S. company. But now it goes bankrupt."

He held his neck. "And we must make it ourselves, or buy from the Japanese."

We told him we didn't recognize the name of the company.

He stopped and looked at us in shock. "It built guns on your ships *New Jersey, Missouri.* A great company. Great. I don't know how you let it go out of business."

Our last stop was the research and development laboratory to meet Dr. K.H. Cheng, its director, via Purdue University.

"Steel is a very old technology," said Dr. Cheng. "The only way you can improve is by making better quality and selling it at the same price."

We asked how he compared China Steel's technology to that of the United States. "In many areas we can do in 30 minutes what takes four or five hours in the United States."

But as with most people we met who made such comparisons he stopped himself, and made sure he had not implied any insult. "You must understand we had a great advantage by starting so late because we made our capital investment in a time when technology had changed so much and yours was obsolete."

We asked him about the models for technology.

"Japan, of course. Nippon Steel has 3,000 people in the R & D. We have only 170. The Japanese originally learn their technology from you and make improvements. We learn from the Japanese and make improvements. One day someone will learn from us. Probably the Mainland."

Back in Taipei, we sought out the founder of China Steel, Y.T. Chao. Everyone who ever has worked for China Steel has a work number indicating when they joined the company. W.P.'s number is 941. Y.T. Chao is number one.

By way of introduction, he asserted, "I am honored to be the founder of China Steel, the most efficient steel mill in the world."

By the time we met him, Chao was the chief economic planner for Taiwan, but his affection for China Steel was undiminished. He saw his creation as one of the symbols of strength of Taiwan's economy. "American mangement philosophy is too shortsighted. In public companies you retire at 65. You are struggling for what? For personal ambition and high salary. After you retire, you have no long-term relationship with the company. You are not interested in the long-term view."

There is another reason Chao will always be linked with China Steel: His nickname is Ironhead. Some say that is because it is shaped like a steel block. Others say it is for the toughness he showed in creating a world-class steel mill from nothing.

"My personal story is very simple. I am an engineer. I received my university education on the Mainland. I came to the United States in World War II to work in the factories. I worked in Buffalo, in Harrison, New Jersey, in Springfield, Vermont and in Springfield, Massachusetts. I had a chance to observe your industry.

"Allow me to tell you the truth, my dear American friends. Your productivity, your diligence, your hard spirit is gone.

"I can remember when I worked there on my first night I was too tired to even change my clothes. Recently, I went to the United States, and for productivity there is no comparison."

We asked for examples.

"China Steel produces 500 metric tons of steel per man. This includes the chairman down to the sweepers. An American integrated steel mill is 300 metric tons at best."

Chao was a controversial sort among the Taiwanese. He forcefully advocated internationalizing the economy and opposed the squatter mentality that eschewed capital investment. Still, as an economic planner he rated high marks for his country's performance under his tutelage. Taiwan had rocketed to the top with him in the cockpit. We asked him how he would cure problems if he was the economic planner for the United States.

He smiled at the thought. Clearly he was not unprepared to answer. "I have a program. The American economy is in danger."

What Ironhead offered was a tough prescription containing some of the standard nostrums: cut government spending, create new technologies, reduce social welfare costs— "If you have too much mercy for the old man you will have suffering for years to come." The weakening of unions should be encouraged, too many foreigners were taking up space in American universities and not enough of a priority was placed on the importance of research. "Doing research is a hard job. Nobody who does research can become a millionaire quickly. In America everyone wants to be a millionaire overnight."

What it came down to, he said, was a change in national attitude. "You must change your mentality and talk about productivity and quality. You have too much confidence in your past."

He scoffed at the notion that the age of American economic hegemony had ended. "You have the pioneer spirit. You have the guts. You can take these risks.

"We are just the opposite. We are very conservative, very diligent with a hardworking spirit. But we compromise. We are very flexible. One day we can live like a king. The next day we can live like a beggar.

"And we live much more dangerously than you. Taiwan is like a small shrimp in the ocean. All the big sharks can swallow us up. We manage a small boat on very rough seas."

Already the sharp-eyed Chao was seeing increased whitecaps on those seas. "Today we have certain economic advantages, but we know they will not last. We also have signs of trouble. In steel and other conventional industries, the technology is mature. Other countries are learning and catching up. Therefore, all of our conventional technology should be phased out in favor of high-tech industries.

Chao cited examples of textile plants, electronic plants and plastics factories packing up one night and moving to Malaysia or India. "There was no technological advantage here anymore, and our labor became too expensive. Look at Japan. Twenty years from now they will not be the auto kings anymore."

This was a lesson in the shifting nature of economies that was becoming apparent to us as we traveled. The dragons were spawning. China Steel feared the low-cost labor on the Mainland; investors in labor-intensive industries like shoemaking were turning to places like Thailand to place their capital.

"I know this firsthand. My son studied at MIT. He started a garment industry here. You know where he is now? Sri Lanka.

"Economic development is dynamic. It never gets in an equilibrium state. There is no respect for borders, only profits and the economies of production. Big economies or little economies. They can't stand still. There is no way to resist this."

The heart and soul of Taiwan's economy is the little guy. By way of example, between 1966 and 1976, the number of manufacturing firms in Taiwan increased by 150 percent, while the average size of the individual enterprises, measured by the number of employees, increased by less than a third. In Korea, the situation was the opposite. The number of employees in each company increased by 176 percent. Hyundai, Korea's largest *chaebol,* is about three times as large as Taiwan's 10 largest private firms combined.

The roots of this egalitarian economy were planted during the land reform initiated by Chiang shortly after his arrival on the island. Chiang wanted to end landlord abuse that kept tenant farmers impoverished and to devise a system that would spark higher agricultural output to feed the island's suddenly increased population. The government itself sold land on favorable credit terms to the farmers who worked it and forced landlords to do the same. In return, the landlords received stocks and bonds that could be cashed in with proceeds used to develop urban industries. The reforms shifted rural landlords into urban businesses and gave small farmers the opportunity to purchase the land they worked. The system had built-in incentives for both sectors to use their financial and physical resources efficiently.

Nonetheless, in those early days Taiwan was entirely dependent on the United States for raw materials for farming and manufacturing. A major change occurred in 1958 when the government decided to bring Taiwan's economy into international markets by promoting exports. The Taiwanese knew early on that a country their size and with their lack of resources would have to export aggressively to survive. When U.S. aid stopped in 1965, the government had to find alternative sources of capital, which it did by taking advantage of the Chinese predilection for saving.

The changeover to an export-oriented economy coincided with a global economic boom in the mid-1960s. Textile industries led the way as Taiwan provided a cheap source of labor for quality goods. The government's reluctance to follow Japan's example of fostering several behemoth corporations to dominate the economy led to an epidemic of small- to medium-size firms, all looking beyond Taiwan's shores for their markets.

The practitioners of this economic ethos can be found everywhere. One afternoon, paging through the directory of

Taiwan manufacturers in search of a suitable company to visit, we decided to see if we could buy pool cues wholesale and commandeered a cab to Nankang, an industrial suburb of Taipei. We passed scores of somber factory buildings, squat and functional, and headed along a dirt road lined with row-houses, some of which were factories. Outwardly, there was nothing modern or efficient about any of this. The main streets were crumbling, the side streets were a muddy rubble. Down one such street was the most famous pool-cue maker in Taiwan. This great factory had no more equipment than a telex to receive the orders and a telephone to tell the manufacturer in Taichung how many pieces to make. The entire block was lined with similar distribution centers, connected in turn to a network of small manufacturing shops across the country.

This block, and hundreds like it, was the objective of U.S. buyers. Like the fellow from Chicago whom we met at the hotel the night before. He was there to purchase hearing aid devices because the labor costs were one-tenth of what he paid at home. He admired his suppliers, "These people are amazing. They will haul in the whole factory over a weekend to fill a last minute order."

He told us that he had transferred nearly all of his production facilities to Taiwan.

"Why not all?"

"Because we're willing to give them all but the most technologically sophisticated things we make. If we showed them how, they'd copy them in a minute and we'd be competing with our own knockoffs."

Another day we went way out of town past the airport to that confusing entrepôt of industrial and rural development, where factories are surrounded on three sides by rice paddies. We passed young men hauling oversize logs on the backs of motorcycles; we saw yards full of geese next to brand-new metal-sided warehouses.

The building we entered was not new. It was a drafty cold structure with concrete floors and walls and no such frills as company emblems or fountains. There was, however, a new Mercedes sedan parked out front.

We met George Lin in the "showroom" that doubled as a conference room and sleeping room for the weeks when things got very busy. Lin, a native of Taiwan, started in the bicycle business in 1972 almost by accident: He was working in a small electronics factory when he got a call from a friend telling him he had an order for 8,000 bicycles that he needed help to fill.

"So I helped him out," said Lin. "I had never made a bicycle before, but I bought a few and took them apart and figured it wasn't so hard. Then I stayed in the business. The fitness craze in the United States was just starting and I saw what it could mean for us. In 1971, all of Taiwan exported 20,000 bikes. Last year we exported 10 million. Our factory alone exported 150,000."

Lin had seen his opportunity and raised $25,000 from four friends—Chinese businessmen would rather borrow from friends or relatives than banks—to start his own company back in 1981. He started making money from day one. He produced bikes for famous brand names in the United States and Europe. We asked him why he didn't try to become one of the giants of the industry and sell under his company's name.

"I have no interest in the marketing side. It is so cultural, and I don't want to fight that battle. I make all the money I need."

Lin was enjoying a growing customer list from buyers who used to go to Japan. "Japan and Korea, we can compete with them. They like big orders, but that means little flexibility. We have huge flexibility, and that's important in our business. Each year there is a theme to bicycles, they are very fashionable—health, recreation, return to nature, microlight—you have to be able to change with the fashion."

As a small company, Lin could respond to those changes, which he said he found to be an attribute more important than size.

"The way I grow is to increase sales and keep the same labor force. This is not what you think—not increasing productivity, but adding value. Quality is very, very important."

This was a big change for Lin. "I remember in the 1970s when you could sell anything with two wheels, but not anymore. People want quality."

Yet success had not come easily. Lin worked 16 hours a day, six days a week. And, he laughed, "It doesn't give me much time to spend my money." When he is not at the factory he reads 20 or 30 trade publications to keep up with the changes in the industry.

We toured the factory, starting at the end of the assembly cycle, where a white-coated worker was slapping on a "Made in Taiwan" sticker. Lin explained, "That is a good symbol for you. It used to be a small sticker and we put it on a part of the bike where we didn't think it could be seen. Now it's big and up front. We are very proud of our work."

It was the end of a shift and Lin greeted each of the 50 workers by name as they departed. He observed, "They aren't like the Japanese, you'll find. They go off by themselves, not in groups. The Japanese will all follow a guy with a flag. You can't even get three Chinese together to argue."

We heard a lot of that throughout our time in Korea and China, comparisons to Japan. The Koreans held up the Japanese as models to be beaten; they're good but not so tough. The Chinese held them up to be weirdos; maybe they're successful but who would want to be like them?

Lin told us that the Koreans could get to be tough competitors. He said that the Mainland was decades behind as far as quality. We asked him about Singapore, and he laughed. "My Australian customers call the Hitler of Asia. I don't know what to think of them. They are strange."

The American counterpart of Hsiao Fang-tsai, ceramics entrepreneur, undoubtedly sports gold chains on various appendages, drives a pastel-colored foreign car and has his hair cut by someone other than himself. The only bow to luxury we could discern on Hsiao was the end tape of cloth lining his pockets, awkwardly announcing England to be the origin of the fabric of his not-quite-properly custom-made trousers.

Hsiao's factory, merely an amalgam of several small houses, stood in Taipei's suburb of Peitou. To get there we left behind the glimpses of the prosperous future of the island and stepped back into a place of one-lane roads, shanties and occasional meandering cows. As in Korea, these vestiges of underdevelopment are apparent if you look past the glamor of high tech to the industries which are as old as the places themselves. Ceramics was one of those trades.

Hsiao got his start in crafts from his father, who made

decorative hats during the Japanese occupation. He told us that his family had come to the island 150 years ago from the province of Fukien. (Every native Taiwanese made a point of telling how long their family had lived on Taiwan.) He remembered that the most chaotic period of his life was when the mainlanders invaded the island after the war.

"I personally had no problem because my father was a disciple of Sun Yat-sen and looked to the Mainland as his fatherland," he said. After Hsiao's father died he moved from his home in Taichung County in central Taiwan to attend school in Taipei. We asked him when that was. "In the 46th year of the Republic," he responded.

Hsiao said that he learned ceramic engineering at school and then worked in a tile factory to learn business skills.

"In the 61st year of the Republic, I started this business. Now we have 50 employees. My goal is to become the largest in Taiwan," he laughed impishly as if such ambitions were supposed to remain unspoken.

Yet, he told us that his plans may be stymied by competition from the fatherland. "In the low end of products I cannot compete with them because their price is much better," he said. "But as quality becomes more important they cannot compete with me."

He took us through the various houses that make up his factory. A barefoot man used a wheel to create clay forms.

"What he is doing," Hsiao instructed, "will become this." He walked over to an eight-foot tall decorative vessel. "This takes 45 days to make and will sell for about U.S. $3,000."

We watched a woman painstakingly etch designs into a small vase. It would take her a week to put in the designs and finish painting. At the end the piece will say, "May all your days be springtime and as pretty as the flowers of spring.'"

In another building we saw vases made from molds. Hsiao commented, "This is the practical part, the mass-produced part, where we will lose out to competition."

Kelly asked Hsiao how profitable his business was. He pretended not to understand. He rubbed his thumb against his index and middle finger, and Hsiao blushed. The Taiwanese say that each successful businessman keeps eight sets of books: one for his wife, one for his mistress, one for his investors, one for his partners, one for the bank, one for the tax collector, one for his accountant and the real one—which he keeps in his head.

Hsiao told us he could not remember any sales figures. "Only my accountant knows," he professed.

We asked if the accountant worked nearby.

Hsiao shook his head vigorously. "Far away. Very far away." He shrugged his shoulders. "Sorry."

On the day we wandered over to the New World Trade Center, we found a contigent of American business writers on a government-sponsored junket touring the facility. We tagged along with the group. The sprawling just-completed convention center complex was one of the few actually modern buildings in Taipei, all green glass and reinforced concrete with interesting angles and shapes that must have been designed by a genuine architect, as opposed to the rest of Taipei, the plans for which appeared to have come out of a civil engineering manual.

The director of the center, Shih Tan-hsu, was lamenting to the group that he had had spectacular success in renting out only the second through sixth floors. Someone asked why he was apologizing.

He spoke in a precise, British-accented voice just like the late actor James Mason. "Those floors were easy. Those are for Taiwan companies wishing to export. The seventh floor is the tough floor. Those are for companies that want to import into Taiwan, you Americans. We rented out only 10 of 131 rooms on that floor."

Someone asked what products he felt Americans could sell to Taiwan on a competitive basis. He thought a moment—a bad sign—then replied carefully, "Toothpaste. Shampoo. Refrigerators. Airplanes."

A government guide added almost wistfully, "Weapons."

We had heard the sentiment before, though the visiting journalists seemed startled. There was a widely held view in Taiwan that the United States didn't have much in the way of products that local consumers wanted. It was hard to separate what was genuine and what was a convenient fiction crafted by a country that spoke of the need for free trade yet saw how successful the Japanese had been at keeping their markets closed and allowing homegrown industries to prosper. Intuitively, it seemed, the Chinese knew that the xenophobic Japanese model was not the best way to do business, but change was painful.

Still, what was truly remarkable to the Taiwanese was that whatever the market restrictions, U.S. companies seemed so unwilling and inept at trying to crack the local markets. It was as if the Taiwanese were playing a sly courting game where they were willing to let down their defenses, but only to a persistent suitor. The United States had proved disappointingly flaccid.

We went up to the seventh floor. The entire center was more like a retail mall with small showrooms surrounding an atrium. From above, the lower floors had a carnival atmosphere with music and laughter and lots of foot traffic—U.S. buyers, Taiwanese sellers engaged in the eternal dance of business.

The seventh floor was a dark mausoleum.

"What about the 10 rented rooms?" London asked.

Shih looked puzzled. "I guess no one is interested today."

The tremendous trade imbalance we have with Taiwan has a curious ancestry. In the early 19th century, Britain, too, suffered the scourge of too much money going out and too many foreign goods coming in. The insidious solution they devised looked like caked mud yet produced peace and dreams like no other substance the Chinese ever had known. The magic substance was opium, and much to Britain's delight the Chinese took to it like, well, addicts to a drug.

What Britain would not tolerate at home—a stupefied population—it tried to foist on China. And when the emperor complained, the Brits reared up and practically shoved the drug down the national throat. When the Viceroy of Canton burned 20,000 cases of British opium in 1839, the English decided this deserved escalated retribution. They declared war on the Chinese.

The Opium Wars of 1839-42 and again 1856-60 are infamous in Chinese history; each resulted in a kowtow to the West. The First Opium War ended with the Treaty of Nanking, which gave the British sovereignty over Hong Kong and other parts of China. The outcome of the Second Opium War included the legalization of opium and the liberal opening of China to foreign merchants and missionaries.

Hidden deep within the export psyche of Taiwan must lie the insecurity bred by these lessons of history. World trade exists in a dog-eat-dog world, and not for a moment should anyone doubt that one country's trade surplus is another's ambition. Sugar-coated with diplomatic niceties like "trading partners" and "economic allies" the commerce still flows closer to the Opium War model than the polished tables of the GATT negotiators in Geneva. Our Taiwanese friend who called Japan the "economic animals of the world" clearly understood this. And during our visit to Taiwan we saw our own country, desperate to bring trade back into balance, engaged in a modern-day Opium War that let Taiwan know just how precarious their fabled strength really is. After all, if the ports of Long Beach and New York closed to Taiwan's Evergreen container ships, one might begin a deathwatch over the island.

To learn about this brewing trade war, which was typical of pressure the United States was trying to apply throughout Asia, we met with the general directing Taiwan's trade strategy—Vincent Siew, the country's top trade negotiator, an enormously powerful position in this export-oriented economy.

What almost became Mr. Siew's Treaty of Nanking began on October 16, 1985, when President Reagan announced that Taiwan had agreed to improve access to its market for American wine, beer and cigarettes. Barriers such as high tariffs and distribution controls had kept out American products. Taiwan's Tobacco and Wine Monopoly Bureau had unchallenged control over how Taiwan's $840 million annual output of those products would be priced and distributed.

The United States Trade Representative's office reveled in the good news of a compromise over this issue. On a similar issue involving barriers to tobacco exports, Japan had kept a solution at bay for seven years, using a tactic that had come to be known as the "Japanese Stall": talk, talk, talk, smile a lot, then say no. USTR officials had feared that Taiwan would take a hint from the Japanese and drag out the negotiations, thereby forcing the United States into a public relations nightmare: having to make a loud case for forcing the Taiwanese to import a potentially harmful product, cigarettes.

Taiwan had read Clayton Yeutter, the newly appointed trade representative, as a man good to his promise of backing tough talk with swift action. Meanwhile, there were other trade issues to fight, such as threatened U.S. quotas on textiles and machine tools, both of which are far more vital to Taiwan's economy.

"At the time of President Reagan's announcement I thought the issue was over," Mr. Siew told us. "But I was wrong because the issue was much more than the price of tobacco, as I was to learn."

Cigarettes, wine and beer were a great bone to throw to the United States, a gesture of cooperation that might help to shield Taiwan from the storm of protectionism that Taiwan felt certain was coming. And Siew really didn't think anyone would care that much about letting the United States come into the three markets.

In the summer of 1986, a shift occurred in the delicate balance of the relationship of our countries. The problem was textile import legislation sponsored by Congressman Edgar Jenkins, the strongest protectionist bill to be taken seriously in many years. Taiwan's representative to the United States, Fredrick Chien, correctly read the advance of the trade brigade, and he crafted a preemptive textile agreement with voluntary quotas. Taiwan's concessions, along with similar moves by Hong Kong and South Korea, helped to take the steam out of Jenkins's bill, which was nonetheless passed by Congress, then was vetoed by the president, and finally expired on a veto override by a mere eight votes.

At about the same time an ugly portent appeared in Taiwan. The newspapers began to react against implementing the October 1985 agreement on wine, beer and cigarettes. The outpouring of anger in the press coincided with the visit to Taiwan of Sandy Kristoff, one of the USTR negotiators assigned to work out the details of the agreement. "It was an unwelcome intrusion," said Siew. "The press, which I never understood to be concerned with the health issue, made the negotiations difficult."

The press reports made much of America's demand that Taiwan dismantle the state-run monopoly that controlled the sale of the three products. The United States was taking a harder line than Siew was used to, and the press, no longer in the government's tight grip, was reacting with surprising outrage at being told how to run Taiwan. The U.S. pressure was being called another "Opium War," a term that dredged up painful memories for the Chinese. The West was again trying to force unsafe products on them for its own commercial gain.

USTR was not sympathetic and in no mood to make concessions. The United States was being battered by a swelling trade deficit, and protectionist fervor was growing in Congress by the day as congressmen returned to their districts to campaign for the November elections and heard cries of anguish from unemployed manufacturing workers. The White House was strongly against protectionism, but it was increasingly coming to feel that it had to take a few tough stands to head off a worse alternative, such as some of the protectionist legislation still brewing in Congress. Taiwan, it seemed, would be the test case for backing tough talk with action.

In Washington, Chien was getting cable traffic from his government that mirrored the public's objections. "There never was any wavering by the government of the commitment we made," said Siew. "Once we made it we had to honor it. But we had to find a way to do so in order that the public reaction be satisfactory."

It was an awkward time for both sides because neither, it seemed, had wanted this issue to get so far out of hand.

On August 29, Chien wrote a memo to Yeutter summarizing the state of outstanding trade matters. Machine tools and textiles were close to agreement. But, he warned, peace was threatened by the cigarette issue. Siew said he didn't sleep for two days during the textiles negotiations and didn't want to repeat that experience.

By the beginning of October talks had broken off. Siew had come to Washington to give USTR what he called his best and final offer on the mechanics of allowing American products to compete fairly with domestic brands. Then, in a standard negotiating ploy, he went home, expecting the United States to come running after him. But much to his surprise, no one came. He said, "Then I knew we could expect retaliation."

The staffers at USTR believed that the Taiwanese were adhering to an old Chinese saying, "Do nothing and all good things will be done." There was a great deal of frustration over the three major components of the original agreement: price to be charged—whether the American products could fairly compete—distribution and promotion.

On distribution, USTR wanted direct access to hotels and

nightclubs. Taiwan was proposing rules that would have given the Monopoly Bureau control over access to the most important of the country's 70,000 retail outlets, including hotels and nightclubs.

Taiwan also feared a promotion blitz by the U.S. marketing giants such as Phillip Morris. They wanted restrictions on print advertising and a prohibition of free samples. And here was where the opium analogy was potent: Flooding the market with sample American cigarettes could be seen as an immoral temptation for Taiwan's youth.

Arguing the other side was, of course, an American tobacco industry, which claimed that Taiwan's attempt to create a moral dilemma for USTR was just a negotiating tactic. One U.S. tobacco industry executive had called the health issue "a canard. We found it amusing that the Taiwanese government, the largest seller of cigarettes in Taiwan, was preaching to us about health."

USTR undoubtedly appreciated the conundrum it faced: export smoke or export nothing at all. Its spokesman acknowledged that "It wasn't our best public relations case. But there were a couple of factors that made it possible to avoid. The monopoly system was outrageous. One of total control. Cigarettes, wine and beer are three products in which the United States can be very competitive worldwide. And finally, we had a commitment from Taiwan and we had to follow through and see that they lived up to their word."

Siew told us he tried one last compromise strategy: to accept USTR's position on beer and wine and put a confrontation on cigarettes off to another day.

However, he suspected what USTR's response would be. He believed that the tobacco industry was applying the same heat to the USTR as his government was receiving from the Monopoly Bureau and from local governments, which received substantial revenues from the sales of these products. And he knew that in the case of Phillip Morris, which makes both Marlboro cigarettes and Miller beer, a partial solution was unacceptable. These companies packed impressive lobbying clout, and the inaccessibility of some foreign markets stuck in their craw.

By October 9, Siew knew that USTR was not going to accept any form of agreement except unconditional surrender. He smiled, "I never had a negotiating session where each time the other side's position became tougher and tougher." USTR informed Chien in a telephone call that Presient Reagan would soon announce that he was invoking section 301 sanctions. A very pleasant day in October 1985 had now given way to a nightmarish day in October 1986.

Section 301 is the ICBM of the U.S. trade arsenal. Just the thought is enough to scare most trading partners, especially one as dependent on our markets as Taiwan. The sanctions are provided by the Trade Act of 1974 and go into effect when the president makes "a finding of unfairness." The administration then estimates how much trade revenue has been lost by being shut out of a particular market and moves to prohibit an equal dollar amount of the country's goods from entering the United States.

In Washington, Chien scrambled to get out of the way. He met with high-level officials at the departments of State and Commerce and the National Security Council. Each of these meetings was off-the-record because of U.S. restrictions against official contacts with Taiwan, even in the face of imminent trade war. But his point was the same: Such sanctions could cripple Taiwan at a crucial period in its history. The issue was not just trade but national security. The sanctions could cause economic and political disruptions. Chien and Siew desperately needed more time to work out a compromise between Taipei and Washington. But they knew that time was running out.

On October 27, Yeutter announced that enough was enough. "A year has passed and Taiwan has not honored its agreement," he said.

His message was delivered in the tough language that had become his trademark. "This administration will not tolerate broken promises, nor will we allow our trading partners to erect unfair trading barriers to U.S. goods and services. I have instructed my staff to begin immediately drafting appropriate retaliatory measures."

Taiwan was having a collective tobacco fit.

"The press in Taiwan was in a frenzy," one American businessman told us. "They were very much against the government acceding to the U.S. demand. They felt we were meddling in internal policy far beyond what the scope of trade laws should be—and with products that even we considered hazardous to their well-being."

Siew was hearing many voices on how to respond. On one side were the chauvinists who objected to the U.S. infringement on Taiwan's sovereignty; this was the dominant position in the press. Local government officials added fuel to the fire by arguing that they could not do without the revenues that were being passed to them from the Monopoly Bureau.

Opposing them stood the new breed of technocrats, whose view of the world is dominated by economic and political realities. This group did not underestimate Yeutter's resolve. They feared that the USTR, under pressure from private industry, would make an outrageously high finding of the potential market for beer, wine and tobacco, and that a like amount of Taiwan's exports would capriciously be chosen for retaliation. Vital industries such as textiles, shoes and plastics would be targets of U.S. sanctions.

The multiple warhead of 301 sanctions allowed for sanctions against diverse products, and this was an unacceptable risk to those who wanted peace as soon as possible. The peculiar nature of Taiwan's economy makes it especially susceptible to across-the-board sanctions. As we had learned, most of Taiwan's exports to the United States come from relatively small factories. Businesses with average working capital of $1 million and fewer than 100 workers constitute 95 percent of the island's companies and employ 70 percent of its workforce.

USTR had little sympathy for the intricacies of Taiwan's plight. The free traders in the White House had decided that it was time to back tough talk with at least the threat of protectionist action. "Once the president said there was a problem, that was it. We had to go back at them with more," its spokesman said.

Siew understood that a new level of toughness had been reached. He gave Chien his marching orders: surrender. Better to concede defeat before casualties occurred.

But that wasn't good enough. On November 10, Chien had a breakfast meeting with USTR officials and he was served a large portion of crow. He was told that the U.S.'s "bottom line" position, which he had come prepared to accept, was no longer on the table. The United States was going up the ante, and if Taiwan wanted peace, it would have to meet it.

USTR apparently had anticipated Chien's offer to capitulate. Its spokesman said, "We felt that Taiwan expected us to compromise and accept a high sales price as well as restrictions on distribution and advertising. But there was no way we could do that. There already was a feeling that USTR had stretched a bit too far, and if Taiwan was unwilling to meet us in our original position, then we were going to go back to where we were comfortable."

Where the United States was comfortable was with everything. USTR made a take-no-prisoners demand for immediate and total access for U.S. manufacturers of beer, wine and tobacco.

Chien, who had a reputation as the master of pragmatic politics, was stymied. He knew that USTR would make a take-it-or-leave-it proposal that Taiwan had once found objectionable. The public reaction in Taiwan was already one of outrage; he could only guess at the outcome if the United States tried to humiliate the government into accepting stronger demands. To the Chinese, "face" is a vital asset that one does not lose willingly; now Chien feared that his country's face was about to be put in the vise.

He decided that the best strategy was to stall. Not the Japanese stall; it was too late for that. He needed to buy time—let emotions die down and allow the hard-liners in Taipei to ruminate over the consequences of a full-scale trade war.

What Chien feared most was USTR's announcement of the penalty list—the products that would be targeted for retaliation. All hell would break loose in Taiwan when the news came out. He figured that the American tobacco industry was telling USTR that Taiwan was a potential market of $500 million for the three products, which meant that few pockets of Taiwan's economy would be spared. He responded to USTR that such a market size was ridiculous, though he had no way to challenge the sophisticated studies of the tobacco industry. He told USTR officials that they were being used by the tobacco industry, which saw a declining domestic demand and was desperate to create new markets abroad. Taiwan, he said, was the victim of "the last gasp of a dying industry."

Chien began to win small victories. His efforts to keep both sides in their respective conference rooms started to pay off. What he needed was more time to negotiate. Chien and USTR officials came to an understanding that it was not really punishment that the administration wanted but simply to pry open the markets.

Meanwhile Chien tried to educate himself and then his countrymen on the power of Section 301. He brought in a team of lawyers and lobbyists to explain the sanctions, and he became certain that they were not to be taken lightly. He sent a flurry of cables home explaining the gravity of the situation. Siew understood it, and with Chien's help he began to persuade his colleagues that starting a trade war with the United States was a foolish venture that could not succeed.

In early December Chien got the administration's "new bottom line," and it was as drastic as promised. There would be no compromise. Taiwan would roll over and open the wine, beer and tobacco market completely or the 301 stick would come down.

Siew wasted no time in accepting the terms. The Monopoly Bureau would have no authority over imports. American companies would have total access to all distributors. There would be few restrictions on advertising. And free samples could be distributed on the streets.

When Chien signed the agreement in Washington, he made an uncharacteristically harsh statement. "I sign this agreement with a heavy heart . . . I sincerely hope that both sides will take lessons from the negotiating history of this case. It is also my sincere hope that the USTR will not use this case as a role model for future negotiations with our side."

Siew told us that the tobacco war had taught him how difficult his job had become and how complicated world trade had become. At home he now had to contend with public opinion, something that never had been a factor. That, of course, urged him to take a nationalist position. On the other hand, he had to deal with USTR, which also had a public opinion problem due to rising protectionist sentiment in the United States. And he was caught in the middle.

"We have inherent problems in negotiating with the United States," he smiled. "Our surplus makes us an easy target. You know it is almost an embarrassment of riches. And we do not have access to GATT to voice our complaints. Finally, we are not as politically important to you as Japan."

He said that one of the ways he envisioned tackling this problem was with the high-profile buying missions that Taiwan was planning to send to the United States. Periodically, Taiwan sends a group of officials to tour the States with one purpose: to buy American. Their itineraries often are the home bases of favored congressmen and senators. One Taiwan official had told us his country imported more apples from the United States than any other country. "It's not that Chinese like apples," he smiled. "It's that we like Senator Evans [of Washington] and Senator D'Amato [of New York]."

"But even that creates a problem," Siew said. "When we say we want to buy from you that means the price will go up. Americans are not as competitive as, say, the Europeans. Then our people criticize our government as a sucker because of the 'Buy American' policy."

Siew, unlike Y. T. Chao, did not lecture us on the foibles of the American economy. Rather, he complained that we lumped Taiwan with Korea and Japan, which he characterized as "totally closed economies." He said he believed Taiwan was unfairly singled out in the tobacco negotiations.

He added another concern. "You pressure Japan to revalue the yen. Korea, for some reason, you don't pressure. And Taiwan, you pressure a lot. But that is not fair. It is not fair to our small and medium industries who cannot absorb this revaluation."

We told him that we felt he protested too much. After all, Taiwan then was sitting on a more than $70 billion pile of foreign reserves, second only to Japan.

He shook his head sadly as if we had misunderstood. "Foreign reserves is a result of our foreign exchange control policy. It is not fair to judge our economic strength by foreign reserves. In fact, it has become a handicap because a huge money supply, if mishandled, becomes a threat for high inflation."

We asked him why the savings rate was so high, why indeed was Taiwan choking on money.

"I think there are two reasons. People don't want to invest in new areas. High tech means high risk, and people do not have the knowledge to evaluate that risk. We know how to run a footware factory or a textile factory but it is very complicated to run a high-tech industry."

We would have thought that the team captain of the world's most adept mercantilists would be chortling over his good fortune. Wrong.

Siew said, "The future really looks gloomy. There is rising trade protectionism. Our small industries won't put enough money into research and development. Our technology transfer is too slow. And lastly we still are exporting low-value textiles, footware and sporting goods. Korea is exporting high-value consumer durables like cars and VCRs. How can we compete?"

Siew said there was an answer. "We must liberalize our economy. We must internationalize it. We must become a partner in the world trade rather than a target. If that happens, and our mentality at home changes to confront competition, then we will be all right."

The dilemma that Vincent Siew and Y. T. Chao faced was how to convince the economic leaders that they had to change horses in midcourse, at a time when Taiwan led the race by a healthy margin. The assets that brought Taiwan out of the Third World—cheap labor, especially—threatened to send it reeling back. That is, these technocrats stood certain that if the economy did not retool itself Taiwan would find itself competing with Sri Lanka and Malaysia, and even the Mainland, and would come up short.

To staunch the propensity toward low-tech, labor-intensive industries the government in 1979 sponsored the development of the Hsinchu Science-Based Industrial Park, 40 miles southwest of Taipei near the willing labor pool of two of Taiwan's best engineering colleges. The government promised tax holidays, venture capital from the state and low-interest loans to anyone who set up shop there. The goal of the site's planners was to create the Silicon Valley of Asia in Taiwan. The plan was not as farfetched as it seemed, due mainly to the tremendous human resources available to the 70 or so concerns that established factories on the 5,000-acre locale.

One of these companies, Mitac, introduced the world's first Chinese character computer keyboard in 1976, which may not seem impressive until you consider that the Chinese language has more than 5,000 characters. The breakthrough was the brainchild of Mitac's founder, Matthew Miau, who like nearly every entrepreneur at the park was educated and trained in the United States. Miau's return home stood as a symbol of hope for Taiwan, because each year it sends about 27,000 students to the States. Taiwan cannot endure such an uninterrupted brain drain.

K. P. Chew, a Mitac vice president, told us that he expected the growth of the computer industry in Taiwan to attract some of the expatriates.

"The quality of life here always is improving. The way of life is becoming much more relaxed," he said. "There is no reason engineers cannot work and live here as well as in the United States."

These companies were banking on that perception, and the government apparently was willing to commit $400 million in the next decade in incentives and improvements to the industrial park.

The economies bespoke the reason. K. P. Chew explained, "Here we pay engineering graduates $600 per month, and senior engineers $2,500 per month. In the States we would have to double that. And because of the nearby colleges we have a ready pool of workers."

While we were in Taiwan, Mitac was introducing its Viso computer in the States, an 11-pound, fully IBM compatible desk-top model, selling for $1,200.

"At the trade show in Las Vegas we had dealers offering us cash for the floor models," said K. P. happily.

He said that Viso's success would only add to Mitac's phenomenal rate of 46 percent annual growth since 1982. "And there are others here who consider that no growth at all," he added. Yet, he said he realized that the world of computers was so competitive that there were no assurances of long-term success. "We have about a one-year advantage on the Japanese and other local companies with this model. Then we'll get lost in the crowd."

We asked him if he saw the Koreans as competition. He frowned noticeably. "They make great low-cost copies. They don't innovate at all. But once they know how to make your product, you cannot compete with them."

Then we asked what was becoming to us the most depressing question of all: What role will the United States play in this arena?

"R & D," he said. "You're not as cheap as before, but no one develops innovation like you. Your research laboratories are still valuable. Then once you develop it, you can't compete with the world in making it."

Even to the untrained observers of Taiwan's people and press it was possible to tell that the country was choking on two disparate commodities: money and filth. Newspapers constantly posed the question, "What do we do with all our money?" And then, "Isn't the air and water getting too dirty?" It didn't seem to occur to anyone to connect the two thoughts.

We saw stories claiming 19 of the island's 21 rivers were polluted. One newspaper account told of a young woman who tried to commit suicide by jumping into the Tan-shui River, which has a 40-mile stretch in which no living creature survived. The woman had second thoughts after diving in and quickly swam to shore. She was quoted as saying that being in the river was a fate worse than death.

The air is so polluted that 17 percent of the year it is considered harmful to health. Waste treatment plants barely exist. The country suffers from the harmful by-products of an increase in the number of factories from 5,623 to 62,474 in just 30 years.

The money problem was caused by the great trade surpluses that had the central bank soaking up a reserve fund of 70 billion foreign dollars which sat with no place to go. The Taiwanese financial system was primitive for such a booming economy and couldn't figure out how to properly distribute capital. The huge surplus threatened to wreck the economy if it wasn't properly controlled.

This notion of Taiwan killing itself with success was very much on the mind of an American lawyer we had drinks with one evening. He had been in the country three years, which he thought put him at a dangerous time. "You've gotten over the first impressions, but you've got another seven or eight years before you get to a new level of understanding.

"But for you guys it's like you've just landed on another planet," he added charitably.

"Never forget that under the tie and the Mercedes, these are the Chinese. They are a different culture. The signposts of the West do not appear—Judeo-Christian, Roman, Greek. They have Confucius and they think a lot of what we have is crap. They see us as barbarians and don't forget that.

"First, you should notice the distribution of income. That is miraculous." In fact, Taiwan often is cited as perhaps the most economically egalitarian country in the world. In 1952, the income of the richest 20 percent of the population was 15 times that of the poorest 20 percent. But the spread has narrowed to the less than four times, which is considerably better than the United States.

He continued, "Then focus on distribution of capital. That is horrendous. Remember that 15 years ago this was a farm economy and it wasn't even thinking about trade surpluses. The average person borrowed and still borrows money on the curb market—the *wei.* The girls in my office do it. They make a pool on payday and people bid for it. All debts are paid off by the Chinese New Year."

What this use of capital has wrought is an unsophisticated banking system that literally is buried under a ton of money. In 1985, there was a scandal involving the island's largest credit unions that highlighted many of the primitive financial practices, including postdated checks, borrowing in employees' names without their permission, and the use of fraudulent accounts. As details emerged there were three suicides, eight attempted suicides and at least a dozen divorces to protect the assets of spouses.

More prosaically, the mountain of money is hardly working for the country. Banks practically beg the notoriously frugal population not to save, and they only pay 2 percent interest on the accounts. Yet, money is not being spent on capital-intensive industry because of the economy's distaste for them and the subliminal national sense of transience: You just can't pack up an auto factory and take it with you, either back to the Mainland or to Paraguay, if things should ever come to that. Much of the money is used to buy U.S. Treasury bills, and the central bank "sterilizes" the currency by printing money and removing it from circulation by various debt instruments. The memory still is strong of the Shanghai lesson, the KMT's experience in the late 1940s when hyperinflation destroyed the nationalists' currency. The consequence is that industries seeking financing to modernize outdated plants and equipment or move into high-tech products are left without a source of funds.

Our lawyer friend called Taiwan a "millionaire squatter." The country teems with urgency and, consequently, prosperity. But it does not bespeak historical certainty; that is, no one will bet you that his or her grandchild will become president of Taiwan, because no one stands ready to guarantee that there will be a Taiwan in 50 years.

There is only one date that counts in Taiwan's future, and that is June 30, 1997, when at midnight, Hong Kong becomes a part of China after 150 years of English rule. In order to cut this deal China promised to observe "one government, two systems" for 50 years.

Hardly was the ink dry on its agreement with Britain than the Chinese prime minister Zhao Ziyang offered the same terms to Taiwan. "Our proposition of one country, two systems after reunification is most reasonable," he declared. "We are deeply convinced that the great cause of reunification of the motherland will succeed."

This is the great dilemma that Taiwan faces in the coming years. Practically, there is little rationale for reunification, as Taiwan's economy plays in a different league from China's. But independence is out of the question for fear it would provoke China, further isolate Taiwan diplomatically, and dash the dreams of Chiang Kai-shek's followers. The Mainland's leaders have suggested that Taiwan's declaration of independence would be followed by invasion.

But keeping the political myth alive has its own baggage. Daniel Huang spoke longingly of wanting to see China, and W. P. Chuang hoped his children would see his homeland. Taiwan's government knows that if Hong Kong's transition is a smooth one then the pressure for reunification will intensify. It also fears Hong Kong's failure and the prospect of five million Hong Kong Chinese hunting for apartments on Taiwan. For dollars and cents reasons Taiwan shivers because Hong Kong is its third-largest trading partner, and it will have to discover another conduit for the illicit trade with the Mainland.

Some see reunification as inevitable and the two sides compromising their positions. There are many who fear the power of such a union. There are just as many who fear its very existence.

Our trip to Quemoy began somewhere around 4:30A.M., although neither of us could swear to events of that bleary morning. We were traveling with the military that, the world over, seems to get started before the sun comes up. When we got to the airport, we realized the army considered Quemoy to be serious business. We had to sign a statement saying we would submit material about Quemoy for prior approval. We also agreed not to mention troop strengths or gun placements. (Since the *New York Times* had recently revealed both facts we figured we'd just use their numbers.)

On the 727 with us was a military representative from Paraguay and his attractive wife, whose short skirt and high heels probably would have been too much to keep Latin troops in line, but did not cause a murmur of lust among the full complement of Taiwanese troops aboard. The flight, due west from Taipei and aiming at the heart of China, brought us to the island that was Taiwan's first line of defense in an hour and a half.

Major General Hsieh Kuo-shu, who we understood to be the second ranking of the 20 generals on the island, met us at the airport. We were impressed with our status, and told this to Colonel Soong, a military attaché who had accompanied us from Taipei. He advised us not to get carried away with self-importance. "He is second from the bottom," the Colonel laughed.

M. G. Hsieh, as we were told to call him, took us into a mountainside vault that was the heavily fortified headquarters of the Chinmen (the Taiwanese name for Quemoy) command and then to a briefing room adorned by one of those austere portraits of Chiang Kai-shek sporting his pencil-thin mustache and ethereal gaze. While we waited, Colonel Soong let us know that he considered Chiang Kai-shek to be "one of the gods." As proof, he cited the sudden cloudburst that appeared at the moment of the Gismo's death. We thought of wisecracking, but the Taiwanese hadn't much of a sense of humor on this subject.

Then he took us for a ride. For the first time in Taiwan we had a feeling that we were in a pleasant, unhurried place. In the distance we could see light sandy beaches, and the road was lined with shade trees backed by small farms. On closer inspection, however, we learned that all is not what it appeared to be.

"Nice place for swimming."

The general shook his head. "No. It is dangerous. The beaches are mined." He turned to his driver and told him to stop. Then he pointed toward the water, and we could see that the sand also was sprouting rows of anti-tank spikes.

"No one goes swimming," said Colonel Soong. "This island is not for recreation. You must consider the sea to be Free China's Great Wall, and we are here in case the communists come over it."

At the intersections of the roads stood camouflaged pillboxes manned by soldiers holding anti-aircraft guns and reading the skies. At occasional guard posts we saw sentries wearing gas masks, which could not have been a pleasant way to spend an eight-hour day.

Yet it seemed so peaceful. The fields of soybeans, corn and sweet potatoes looked like those in any other town, except for the cement posts with metal spikes that grew among them like weeds.

"What are those for?"

M. G. Hsieh smiled. "For paratroopers." He squatted above his seat in the van and pointed to his bottom. "They sit on the spikes when they come from the sky."

The general explained that most of the fortifications were buried in underground tunnels that crisscross through the island's spine of mountains. "We are proud that although this is a defense installation, people can live ordinary lives. They can farm and have businesses too."

The government has made a concerted effort over the past 20 years to make Quemoy a livable place for its 50,000 nonmilitary residents. In fact, word about Quemoy had filtered across the water to Fukien province in China, which sits about a mile away.

"We get about a 100 refugees a month," said M. G. Hsieh.

"What do you do with them?"

"We give them toothpaste or a small bar of soap and send them back. Usually, we also give them a meal."

But if this is an outpost for freedom why don't you take them in and let them be free?

Colonel Soong answered. "If we allowed them to live here or in Taipei, then word will get out and they will come in the millions."

Why was that all right in 1949 and not now?

Colonel Soong scowled. "Now we don't have room, the resources. The answer is not for them all to come to freedom but for freedom to go to them."

Colonel Soong offered that he was such a patriot that even when he traveled abroad he would not drink Tsingtao beer.

At the museum commemorating the Battle of Kumingtou on October 25, 1949, which history has shown to be the nationalist's last successful stand, the conflict is portrayed in a score of enormous paintings, each depicting a crucial moment. Because of the sorry state of the communist navy, their 20,000 soldiers crossed the narrow strait in 200 fishing boats. Fifteen thousand nationalist soldiers dug in for the defense. The battle was joined at 2:00 A.M. and lasted in a seesaw fashion for 56 hours. In the end 6,000 Communist troops were killed, 12,000 captured. The nationalists lost 1,500 men.

M. G. Hsieh told us that were the communists to try again today, they would be successful. "They could take this island if they wanted," he said. "But we would make them pay dearly. We figure that for every one of our dead we could kill five of them." Troop strength on the island is estimated to be 125,000 men.

Our hosts took us to their underground headquarters, a series of tunnels carved in cool granite.

"Sometimes we do not come out of here for days," said M. G. Hsieh. "And when it is hot we are happy about that."

The idea of an underground city makes sense from a logistical point of view, but also it was dictated by history. In 1958, China began heavy bombardment of the island on a daily basis, reducing it to a flattened beachhead. It was this escalation of tensions that entered into the 1960 presidential election with both Kennedy and Nixon using the plight of Quemoy and its sister island Matsu, 150 miles to the north, as bellwethers in the fight against communism.

Nearby, the army maintains a psychological war museum that came about when the bombardment ceased and a war of words began. Both sides had replaced the explosives in their shells with pamphlets. Colonel Soong analyzed some of the propaganda for us. "Basically, what they send is meant to exaggerate any bad news about Taiwan, to brag about their own accomplishments and to try to stir up a homesick feeling. We try to show them what we produce."

Pamphlets still passed back and forth but in balloons rather than artillery shells. In the baskets went a variety of consumer goods: calculators, raincoats, pens, watches, socks and towels. M. G. Hsieh explained how Taiwan got the better end of this deal. "Our target is bigger than theirs. Because of the winds it is hard for them to land the balloons on Taiwan or Quemoy. We have all of China to aim for." Each year, Taiwan sends over 100,000 pounds of geegaws of the free world by these means. The balloons have a timing device that is supposed to make them explode at a prearranged point. Sometimes, though, they malfunction; one reportedly landed intact in Finland.

There was one other means of message transport: Tupperware-like plastic containers.

Colonel Soong exlained that the Tupperware drop gave an unfair advantage to fishermen who were more concerned with a catch of consumerism than the real thing. An entire class of fishermen had sprouted, specializing in the catch of plastic containers filled with goodies.

Colonel Soong said that the Free World's monopoly of Tupperware gave them an advantage in this phase of psychological warfare. The communists were forced to compete with handmade sailboats. Colonel Soong displayed an oversize bathtub boat with a sign proclaiming, "The American imperialists brought the people of Taiwan disaster and colonialism."

Snaking out from the central tunnels were a series of increasingly narrow passageways that ended at the beach facing Mainland China. Here sentries watched day and night for some sign of infiltration from the giant looming slightly more than a mile away. Through the high-powered binoculars we could see large villa-type houses that Colonel Soong assured us were merely phony facades. ("No one on the Mainland has houses like that," he said.) We could see batteries of loudspeakers aimed at those on Quemoy's shores, the weapons of a propaganda war that it seemed was waged more for symbolism than anything else. We could see small fishing boats.

We stood on an island that was no more than a grain of sand in the sea. Before us was the biggest dragon of all, silent yet restless. Our hosts watched not in fear, really, but in sorrow. For they had been banished from this rich and complex land.

Such a short distance away lay the treasure of their history. As much as they may quell the lust to know themselves by knowing their land they cannot really do so. They have brought with them a living legacy of Confucius and another living legacy of art. They have accomplished in a generation that which the entire continents of South America and Africa have not approached in a century. When they arrived in Taiwan in 1949 there was a strong feeling that if they did not make it they would die.

Now they stood on the brink of their own century, a time when their examples of hard work, diligence and single-mindedness caused the world to look to Asia for the secret to prosperity. They were causing the world an uneasy sense that the dynamism of this part of the world was too much for Europe to handle and perhaps, in the long run, the United States.

But they lived nervously. Just as Korea suffered from a massive inferiority complex, Taiwan mourned its head being separated from its heart. Both confronted the reality of an armed border that left them divided and vulnerable. Their triumphs were day-to-day and in the end, many felt they were unfulfilling. Even the poorest folks we spoke with suspected that there was something more to nation building and national well-being than per capita income and gross national product statistics. People here were running faster than anywhere else in the world. Unlike our impression of Korea, we sensed that this country, with its remarkably balanced distribution of income and atrophying feeling of political isolation, could continue its forward movement without much disruption. A sense of optimism was settling over the country. Korea was proud but still paranoid. Taiwan justifiably brimmed with self-esteem, a national trait that appeared to grow under increasingly enlightened leadership.

HONG KONG

EAGER TO ASSUME the posture of Old Asia Hands, we filed through Hong Kong immigration fortified with the few words of Mandarin Chinese that we had picked up in Taiwan. We had been warned several times that Chinese from geographically disparate parts stood as good a chance of communicating with each other as a battalion of Hungarian soldiers and the hostesses of a Haitian dance hall. But we shrugged off that advice, suspecting that China's reputation as a nation of a thousand tongues was exaggerated in part to impress Westerners with the complexity of their culture. After all, these languages share a common alphabet, albeit one with thousands of pictographs, many imperceptibly different from a dozen others. So we figured the Mandarin we knew had to be somewhat similar to the Cantonese spoken in Hong Kong.

We already had dropped any pretense of understanding many aspects of this world. We were certain that all of our friends in Taiwan went home after hours of serious conversation with us to an evening of laughs over our buffoonery. Yet, we were willing to mispronounce a few words of Chinese at least to show we were making an effort.

In Kai Tak airport in Hong Kong there stood around us a swelter of Westerners anticipating entrance into the mysterious East, and among them we figured we'd stand out as travelers rather than tourists. The lines were long, as Hong Kong, unlike Korea and Taiwan, stands out on the world map of worthwhile destinations. The flight board displayed an international stew of locales—from Canton to Male to Zurich. The incoming passengers seemed remarkably oblivious to the effects of the abrupt landing in Hong Kong, or unlike us, they had not looked out the window. Kai Tak airport sits amidst a thicket of skyscrapers, any of which from the window of the plane, looks as if it could tear the wings off an incoming aircraft.

The energy of the arrival pack inexorably pushed us toward the counter where we would be asked where we were staying and what we were carrying in the form of luggage as well as diseases. London waited patiently to get back his passport from an immigration officer who looked like a teenage boy in his oversize black uniform. He scanned a tome that resembled a Chinese phone book then studied London with a squint that was more brusquely businesslike than the suspicious glares we had encountered in Korea and Taiwan.

"*Shay, shay,*" said London, eagerly showing off his linguistic prowess.

"What?"

"I said *shay, shay,*" he repeated, certain he had just thanked the man.

The immigration officer, unimpressed, waved his hand for the next arrival. He turned back to London, who now proudly believed he had accomplished his first conversation in Chinese.

"Sir, in Hong Kong we say *M'goi. Shay, Shay,* I think, is the sound a girl's dress makes when she is dancing." He turned to the business at hand. "Next."

That minor crash into the language barrier further convinced us that we were going to need help getting through Hong Kong. We had to find an agent, a scrounger, a fixer, an eyes and ears. Unlike Korea or Taiwan, there was no welcoming government or gargantuan corporation waiting to sell us their version of reality. Hong Kong is a city where people mind their own business and resent anyone asking about it. Even the geography of the tiny place was baffling in its detail. To call the whole place Hong Kong is a bit misleading, because that is only the name of the principal island. What the world thinks of as Hong Kong actually consists of 235 islands, a tongue of land called Kowloon and a lump, growing out of both Kowloon and China, known as the New Territories. Hong Kong Island is only about 50 hilly square kilometers of the British Colony of Hong Kong, which totals 1,062 square kilometers.

Outside the airport, we took places on the cab queue and determined that our first order of business would be to decide on Our Man in Hong Kong. As if to reinforce the wisdom of our decision we pronounced the Marco Polo Hotel in a half dozen ways and inflections before making ourselves understood to the driver.

The Marco Polo fit in the middle of an enormous commercial complex hard along the edge of Kowloon's shoreline, a Herculean stone's throw across the harbor from Hong Kong Island. We had chosen to stay there because it was relatively affordable and because it was available. Hong Kong is home to some of the great hotels in the world—the Regent, Mandarin and Peninsula would make anyone's list of the top 10—but they stood outside our price range. Also, we were able to reserve a room in the Marco Polo, no small feat in a city notorious for its "No Vacancy" signs. Confucius says, "The traveler who touches Hong Kong without a confirmed reservation has an infirm travel agent."

We had pruned our list of candidates to represent us to three possibilities: a wealthy husband and wife business team whom London knew through their friendship with his father; two Israeli brothers whose reputation as lady-killers and doyens of local culture (they actually drank snake blood at Snake Alley) had come to our attention from the female employees of the Taipei Hilton; and a local businessman named David Wang.

We wasted no time in setting up appointments, starting with dinner with the married pair who warned us to save our appetite. They gave us a room number and time to meet them in a place called the New World Centre.

To get there we ambled through the indoor city that included our hotel. The site, which had once been the working docks of Hong Kong and was now some of its most expensive real estate, strung from the Star Ferry Terminal along the waterfront for nearly a mile: It included our hotel and two others as well as more shops than would fill a medium-size American city. Known as Ocean Centre, Ocean Terminal and Harbor City, the complex also contained three major office buildings and a United Nations of restaurants. It is said that one could live his whole life resplendently along the shores of Kowloon's wharf and never need to venture outside. The floors shined, and the stores glittered with high-priced designer goods that defied Hong Kong's reputation as a bargain basement. This was classy consumerism, part of the Colony's effort to get rid of its discount image.

The whole empire reportedly was owned by one man who at the time was undergoing a name change. Known to the world as Sir Y. K. Pao, this refugee from China repeatedly made everyone's shortlist of the world's richest men. However, as the date for Hong Kong's return to China approached this megamillionaire let it be known that he preferred to eschew his British colonial title and instead to be called by his birth name—Yue-kong Pao. It occurred to us fleetingly that this palace of pander will eventually be part of a country where reportedly 20 million people still live in caves.

Finally, we emerged from the cavern of shops and stood at the top of the stairs leading to the Star Ferry, the link between Kowloon and Hong Kong, which was also owned by Yue-kong Pao. More than 400 times a day these well-tended green-and-white wooden boats cut a path through ocean liners tiered like wedding cakes, rusty tankers and somber junks to connect the high-rise commerce of Hong Kong Island to the mainland of China. Until the Cross Harbour Tunnel opened in 1972 everyone and everything went back and forth by ferry. Now, cars could pass under the water, though we already wondered who would want to drive in Hong Kong. Still, the 39-ton ferries, which can carry a full complement of 580 commuters, tourists and daydreamers, make the eight-tenths of a nautical mile jaunt in about 10 minutes.

We walked down the steps toward the ferry station and turned left past a well-stocked drugstore and McDonald's. On the next block stood a low-slung YMCA, obviously occupying a piece of real estate that, if sold, could buy gym shorts and a T-shirt for every young Christian man in America. Next to it berthed the Peninsula Hotel, a grande dame of Hong Kong's inns. Its once matchless view of the harbor had been stolen by a museum under construction, but its elegant demeanor appeared intact. We recognized the fleet of green Rolls-Royce limousines; we had seen some well-appointed arrivals at Kai Tak climb into them. We passed chauffeurs idly buffing headlights and strode into the airy lobby. Remnants of late tea lingered on some of the small tables occupied by people of leisure. A bellboy held a small blackboard with Chinese scrawl and rang a bell to announce the message. We had passed into a quieter time. The British would say that after our jostle of Korea and Taiwan we finally had reached a civilized place. But after the hustle of Korea and Taiwan, the Peninsula was more like a wax museum, quaint but hopelessly unrealistic.

We took the underpass and came out in front of the opulent Regent Hotel, which was born in 1980, 52 years after the Peninsula, on a landfill that assured it an unobstructed view of the harbor and of Hong Kong. Three doormen snapped to attention to let us in. Our rubber soles squealed on the polished marble as we headed toward the lobby bar and its panoramic view of the skyline, Victoria Peak and the harbor. We sat and swallowed the awesome sight, one which had inspired florid prose in so many writers who struggled to capture the essence of Hong Kong. One of the best passages came from Jan Morris's visit in 1974 when she had stood atop Victoria Peak and looked from there down across the Colony to where we sat and beyond. She wrote,

> The kingdoms of the world lay before us. The skyscrapers of Victoria, jampacked at the foot of the hill, seemed to vibrate with pride, greed, energy, and success, and all among them the traffic swirled, and the crowds milled, and the shops glittered, and the money rang. Beyond lay the ships in their hundreds, like a vast fleet anchored in the roadsteads from Chai Wan to Stonecutter's Island, here a supertanker, here a cruise ship, there a warship all a-bristle with their attendant sampans busy beside them, and the junks and tugs and pilot boats hurrying everywhere, and the hydrofoil foaming off to Macao, and the ceaseless passage of the Star ferries backwards and forwards across the harbour. Across the water lay Kowloon on the mainland: deep among its structures ran the great gash of Nathan Road, violent with advertising, and off to the east the airport protruded brutally into the harbour, and sometimes a jet threw itself screaming and smoking into the sky.
>
> Beyond it all again lay the hills of China, but these my guide ignored. His eyes were focused, intense, almost fanatical, upon that brilliant pulsation at our feet, like the most diligent of landowners surveying his inherited estate. "You may not like it," he said. "We don't ask you to like it. We don't expect you to like it. But you must admit it works."

A strong sense of purpose hit us as we floundered through yet another gallery of shops, this one connecting the Regent to the New World Centre. In spite of the teams of strollers around us—some shopping, some just ambling for exercise—there seemed to be a reason for all this; the opulence wasn't wasted on making vacuous impressions as in a garish, overpriced and thoroughly awful tourist restaurant. The shops were busy, the goods fine, and the prices not too dear. The shops were not some subsidized facade making a statement, "We are a Third World country, but this is what we can become." These malls and hotels truly stood for Hong Kong—Jan Morris, we believed after less than a half-day, was right; busyness and business abounded. And yet among these hundreds of people we felt that no one was pushing us. You could take it or leave it. Hong Kong didn't care.

Too bad, because we quickly became lost. We rode two banks of elevators and opened three fire doors to find stairwells before emerging into a quiet hallway with numbered doors. No kitchen, no maitre d', no matchbooks or toothpicks.

We were the last to arrive at the dinner party and were introduced around by our hosts, who were in the textile business, one of the mainstays of commerce in Hong Kong. The guest of honor was a young man from New York City who apparently bought Ultra-suede fabric in large quantities. We met a couple we thought had flown in from Goa, but they didn't say a word throughout the meal. There was a hardy fellow from New Zealand who was twice the size of his wife, although her voice was deeper than his; they bred animals that eventually became Ultra-suede, but we never were sure if that meant sheep or cows. Kelly sat next to a young Chinese named Benny King whose pink pastel Ultra-suede sports coat seemed inspired by *Miami Vice*. On his other side sat an older man who we took to be his godfather. And London sat next to Bacon Lee, the proprietor of a tailor shop in the Peninsula Hotel.

A butler appeared from a door we hadn't noticed and methodically carried in dish after colorful dish. The lazy Susan made its turn carrying shark's fin in soup, chicken tendons glistening in oil and a steamed fish as big as the plane that had brought us from Taiwan. London had warned Kelly about his friends' culinary sophistication; he still remembered attending their wedding when he was 12 years old and marveling about the strangeness of some of the 22 dishes he had eaten. For London, who had spent his first dozen years nurtured by hamburgers and tuna fish sandwiches, that banquet remained as a gastronomic epiphany.

"We represent the Ultra-suede association in Hong Kong," Leon whispered to London by way of explaining the odd group. "Our guest of honor is a very big buyer."

"But Leon, you're not even in that business." Leon still runs his textile company in the States, specializing in what the trade calls gray goods, although the product —basic unfinished textiles—is not particularly gray or good. Every night he leaves his home on Victoria Peak at 9 o'clock and travels to his stockbroker's office in the central business district of Hong Kong and opens a telephone line to the States, alternating calls between his broker and his textile office. He remains on the phone until dawn, then goes home and sleeps until early afternooon.

Leon laughed. "This is Hong Kong. You know, we Chinese are in every business as long as there is money to make."

"But what do you know about Ultra-suede?"

He pointed to his wife who wore a beige Ultra-suede dress. She also dangled a few pieces of jewelry that suggested that Ultra-suede had been very good to them. "I know whatever Diane tells me. She knows it is hot now. Hot." He stole a look around the table. "Look at Benny King. He's a nightclub owner. Chicago, a few blocks from here. Benny understands that this is the year for Ultra-suede."

"And next year?"

Leon chewed a chicken tendon, a dish we had decided deserved no more than a quick probe. "Next year, Mark, probably will be different. You see, next year our friends from New Zealand will still be farmers. Our guest from the States—I don't know this—he probably will still be buying Ultra-suede. But we will not be selling. We will move on to something else, something hot. You see, Mark, there isn't much time."

Leon was talking about July 1, 1997, the day the People's Liberation Army will lower the Union Jack over Hong Kong and raise the red flag of China.

Leon and Diane had no fear of that day, mainly because they had American passports and a big house in Westchester County. Their only concern was whether they could make enough money before then to never have to think about what would be the Ultra-suede of 1998.

It was not the first time they had to contemplate a change in scenery. Both had come to Hong Kong from Shanghai in the early 1950s, part of a wave of immigration that is credited with saving the Colony. After the rise of Mao, Hong Kong swelled with hordes of refugees who arrived to find nothing but tin-roofed hovels. The place reeked with humanity and stood on the brink of suffocating itself.

Then an unusual breed of immigrants started appearing in the area, hailing from Shanghai, which had been China's most cosmopolitan and enterprising city. Richard Hughes, the longtime correspondent of the *Sunday Times* and the *Economist,* noted that these new arrivals had something to give, an ethos that energized the bloated Colony and reversed the slide toward helplessness. He wrote:

> Then came the big operators from Shanghai, those Chinese who have made brutal capitalism pay in one lost colonial enclave, and who preferred to re-invest what they had been able to salvage in another capitalist enclave rather than accept the blessings and opportunities of Maoist Marxism-Leninism.
>
> They were, the Communists said, rats leaving a sinking ship, and they were swimming hard to another ship which, if not already foundering, had sprung a thousand leaks and was rotten—ready for the breakers. But Shanghai money and enterprise, plus the industry and talent of the humbler refugees, kept the second ship afloat and put it back into freebooting business, still improbably flying the Union Jack and still faithful to the RN discipline, protocol and traditions.

Diane and Leon counted among their friends the truly rich of Hong Kong, not because they all had made a killing under British protection but because they had all grown up together, and they had all fled together. Now ironically, they were going back together.

"Oh, sure, sure," said Leon. "Diane is very important in China. She has a hotel supply business, and she is there all the time with her customers."

A successful businesswoman in the notoriously male-dominated East?

Leon scoffed. "You know her a long time, Mark. How many

men you know that are smarter than Diane? Here people respect your ability. More precisely, your ability to make money."

Diane complained that we weren't eating enough and that Leon was talking too much. She was making a heroic effort to establish some *esprit de table*, with little success. The Goans stayed noncommunicative. The farm couple from New Zealand appeared jolly but seriously perplexed by what was being put on their plates; they murmured to each other with painful expressions, but told Diane that they loved the food. They sat next to Benny King's godfather who hid behind dark sunglasses and had no discernible knowledge of English. Kelly managed to wrangle an after-dinner invite from Benny to Chicago, and also managed to set up an appointment at Bacon's tailor shop. He considered these to be significant accomplishments, and they were. In a town teeming with nightclubs and tailors, we now had our own. Very efficient. Very Hong Kong.

"There is a magic about 1990 right now," Leon continued. "What happens then will determine if we can live out the following seven years as we are used to. And what actually happens won't matter. Perceptions will matter. What is believed in 1990 will become a self-fulfilling prophesy for the last seven years."

"How so?"

"If people believe that China still wants economic reform, then we won't stop even to glance at our watches."

London asked, "And if the signal is different?"

Leon smiled. "You just arrived today. You haven't seen the newspaper advertisements for passports?"

"No."

Diane finally cut in. "You know the game you played as a child. Musical chairs? Hong Kong is one big game of musical chairs. No one is sure when the music will stop. Some leave now, some will leave later, holding onto every day when they can make an extra dollar."

Leon interrupted. "You know what the rate of return here is? You know what it means to stay open an extra month, to get one more order—today of Ultra-suede—for the States?"

"No."

Leon's wrist went limp, and he shook his hand as if it hurt. The waiter misunderstood and began clearing away the plates. Diane let him know we weren't finished yet.

• • •

Leon and Diane offered to drive us to Chicago in their Rolls (there are more of these cars per capita in Hong Kong than anywhere else), and when we opted to walk they told us to ring them for whatever we might need and slowly disappeared down the floodlit drive of the Regent.

We decided that Leon and Diane wouldn't do as our reps in Hong Kong. In a way they were too smart and certainly too successful—we needed a fuller picture of the town than we could get in the back seat of a Rolls. We also wondered what happened to Benny King. He had invited us to his nightclub, given Kelly his card and stolen away undetected. His rabbi, left behind, explained in English, which he had not spoken all night, that Benny had some non-Ultra-suede business to attend to.

We walked up the garishly neon-lit Nathan Road and peered down even gaudier side streets where the signs stretched so far that those from one side overlapped with those from the other and created an endless canopy of flashing colors. They call this stretch the Golden Mile, because the world offers nothing that could not be bought in the street-level shops or in the storage rooms and factories above them. Lights blazed on every floor. We entered some stairwells and could hear sewing machines; up a flight in an ivory factory a wizened old man bent double over a white snowball in which he was entering exquisite details of four monkeys—see no evil, hear none, speak none and do none. It was after midnight, and commerce took no pause.

We were tired and tempted to return to the Marco Polo. But we knew from experience that would be a mistake; we always pushed ourselves for as long as we could find something to explore. There would be plenty of downtime, plenty of time on the telephone and waiting for appointments to be made.

Chicago lay just off Nathan Road on a narrower street whose signage was no more discreet. A line of teenagers stood outside waiting to get in. On the whole they parodied an age gone by—skinny boys with their hair slicked back wearing sunglasses and cigarettes dangling from their mouths; the girls wore tight, shimmering dresses that caricatured Oriental hookers from American B-movies. Only the sailors were missing. Clearly, these children had watched too much American television and served as proof that our greatest export—low culture—didn't show up on any ledger sheet.

If there was anything Chinese about the disco we missed it. Done in black and white to evoke the ambience of Capone, the pulsing beat and flashing mirrors reminded us of a dozen outdated discos we had seen from Phoenix to Hartford.

Bobbing and weaving our way through teens jacking up their libidos to the voice of Cyndi Lauper, we found Benny and the boys at a large round table in a corner. He glanced up at us, then did a double take and groaned as if he hadn't expected to see us ever again. Normally, a host would ask his guests to sit. Benny didn't.

He pointed to an adjacent table, crowded with young men staring intently at the dance floor. He shouted to one of the teens at his table, who stood up and shooed the kids away then ordered us some beers.

After a few Benny came by.

"Sorry guys," he shouted above the din. "I didn't think you'd come by. Thought maybe you'd feel . . ." He paused looking for the right word, "Tired."

Benny was a shirtmaker turned entrepreneur who owned a tailor shop, the disco, dabbled in Ultra-suede exporting and found time to serve as the president of the Lion's Club of Hong Kong. Once more we stared at the embodiment of more biographical paradoxes than we'd run into in a year back home.

We asked Benny how business was.

"Not bad," he rasped. "Not too good. It would be better if we had a liquor license."

We looked at our beers, at the XO cognac bottle on the next table (Hong Kong also leads the world in per capita consumption of cognac), at the densely populated bar.

"You don't have a liquor license?" Kelly asked.

Benny stood up to leave. "Not officially. That's why it's so expensive." He smiled, rubbed his thumb over his fingertips and walked away.

No more than a few minutes passed before we had more company.

"You friends of Benny?" We looked up. Finally, two guys our age, one a fleshy Oriental, the other an unshaven *gwailo* ("foreign devil" in Cantonese). We told them to pull up chairs.

Once we explained what we were doing one of them confidentially told us, "You probably want to write about me."

His name was Roland Tseng, and he shouted above George

Michael's voice that his father had been the mayor of Shanghai.

"The mayor?" We were impressed.

Roland nodded and explained that his lineage allowed him to be an important link between the United States and China as the Bamboo Curtain began to fall. He said he lived near Hollywood but that an airplane was his real home.

"What kind of work are you in?" Like Benny King, he was an "entrepreneur"—a little of this, a little of that.

"I'm a film producer," he finally decided. "Tom and I just came out. We were negotiating a big deal," he said referring to his companion. (His adjective was unnecessary; we had yet to meet anyone in Asia who was negotiating a little deal.)

He wasn't finished. "I'm also an author. I wrote a book on aerobic self-defense," he wanted us to know. "Look, I'll give you my card and if you want to get your book published just let me know. We are staying at the Regent if you want to get together while you're here."

Roland added that he was doing many meetings, though, and wouldn't have much time for us. He sipped a 7 and 7. "You know how it is. A lot of companies are coming to me with my connections. I can open all kinds of doors for them."

We asked Roland where he was going after Hong Kong.

"Taiwan," he shouted. "A lot of business there too."

"You have good connections there?"

He gave us the thumbs up sign. "The best. My father was one of the original Flying Tigers. He knew Chiang Kai-shek real well."

Yeah, and we were the King and Queen of Romania.

One of the advantages of Hong Kong over Korea and Taiwan was that we had plenty to read while we waited in our hotel room for return phone calls. Literature about Asia, by Westerners, fell into strange clusters—little Singapore was the subject of many volumes while the Hermit Kingdom of Korea was virtually ignored. Taiwan, which had shared a place with Korea in Japan's empire, also was bereft of chronicles. Those places colonized by Europeans fared best, including Indonesia, which had been rendered by Dutch travelers.

But it seemed that no place had been written about as often and as well as Hong Kong. Little about the Colony's history went undocumented; statistics about all aspects of life were plentiful including, as we'd seen, cognac consumption. Even the pulp fiction, as exemplified by James Clavell and Robert Elegant, shined brightly in its richness of intrigue and historical integrity. Hong Kong had the sort of history that surpassed anything a novelist could make up. Even though we had been there only a short time we suspected what lay behind all this prose: Hong Kong served as a window for the West. The colony made comprehensible a small portion of the East. We set out to read everything written about Hong Kong knowing all the while that little was in our grasp. As Richard Hughes had reminded us, we would always be outsiders.

Hong Kong was born in illegitimacy, an island nobody wanted.

It is appropriate that Hong Kong, one of the greatest international traders of our day, itself was the currency used to resolve a Sino-British trade dispute. Late in the 18th century, English merchants searched their empire, frantic to solve the horrendous balance of payments problem caused by the Mother Country's voracious appetite for Chinese tea, silk and rhubarb. They faced a problem the United States would realize nearly 200 years later: Asia wasn't interested in anything they had to sell.

The British eventually found the trade equalizer in India—Bengal opium. The Chinese called it "foreign mud," and they took to it like kids to candy.

The East India Company, which monopolized British trade in the Orient, funneled the drug up the Pearl River, between Hong Kong and the Portuguese colony of Macao, to its banks at Canton. There, 13 factories were established, each owned by a separate foreign company and each a self-contained area for the storage and maintenance of opium and its smugglers. Recalcitrant public officials were "squeezed" with some profits, and they left the illicit trade alone. It flourished.

Clavell writes about the dazzling success of this trade ploy:

> Opium became the inbound staple of trade. The Company quickly monopolized the world supply of opium outside the Yunnan Province and the Ottoman Empire. Within twenty years the bullion traded for smuggled opium equaled the bullion that was owed for teas and silks.

At last the trade balanced. Then overbalanced, for there was twenty times more Chinese customers than Western customers, and there began a staggering outpouring of bullion that even China could not afford.

The purveyors of the dream-inducing substance inspired a British equivalent of The American Westerns. Tales of heroism and kindness about the trade rose up where in reality there was only corruption and poison, both actual and spiritual. Instead of Jesse James and the Dalton Gang, the British feasted on the exploits of William Jardine and James Matheson, two smugglers of such skill that the company bearing their names has survived 200 years atop a Hong Kong business world where scruples and success are inversely proportional.

Clavell fictionalized these larger-than-life characters in *Tai-pan,* a historic novel about the colonizing of Hong Kong. Dirk Struan, a giant Scotsman, his face weathered by a hundred storms, and one-eyed Tyler Brock, a man as hard and as permanent as the iron he had been forced to peddle in Liverpool as a youth: These were the contestants of the title of *Tai-pan* (which roughly means "the boss") in Clavell's world. He writes:

> The opium smugglers became known as China traders. They were an intrepid, tough vital group of individualistic owner-captains—English, Scots, and some Americans—who casually drove their tiny ships into unknown waters and unknown dangers as a way of life. They went to sea to trade peacefully: to make a profit, not to conquer. But if they met with a hostile sea or a hostile act, their ships became fighting ships. And if they did not fight well, their ships vanished and were soon forgotten.

Hostility arose to meet these colorful men. The emperor realized that even the millions of pounds of bribes that flowed through officialdom could not offset the loss of customs revenues. He decided that the only way to staunch the flow of currency from China was to halt the opium trade and shut down Canton.

The British tried to preempt the Chinese in 1833 by taking voluntary steps, but in doing so they bumbled. Lord Napier, superintendent of trade, wanted British subjects to obey Chinese laws. But the royal servant committed a diplomatic faux pas by trying to see the viceroy of Canton about the matter. He tried to present a letter instead of a "petition," as protocol demanded. The insulted Chinese ordered a halt to all trade with the British barbarians.

Lord Napier, under pressure from the traders, ordered two frigates up the Pearl River to remind the Chinese who was boss, and he received a lesson of his own. The ships came back with their sails between their legs.

Emboldened by the British weakness, Lin Tse-hsu, who had been appointed viceroy of Canton, confiscated 20,291 chests of opium belonging to foreign merchants. He shut down the 13 factories. And he wrote to Queen Victoria, asking why her subjects should be allowed to peddle in the Orient that which they could not smoke at home. She didn't reply.

The British retreated to Macao, where the Portuguese governor, eager to stay on Lin's good side, made them feel less than welcome. Some ships also dropped anchor off the rocky, nearly uninhabited island of Hong Kong, whose name means Fragrant Harbor.

Richard Hughes traces the immediate events that gave birth to the Colony to a particularly raucous wine tasting on Kowloon in 1839. At the bacchanal, "visiting American winebuyers as well as British sailors and Chinese fishermen were involved, and a Chinese was killed." Lin politely asked Charles Elliot, Napier's replacement as superintendent of trade, to turn over the culprit for a public strangling. Elliot refused, but did punish some hung over sailors and paid compensation to the widow.

Lin felt humiliated and ordered retaliation, striking the British at their Achilles heel: He instructed all Chinese servants to quit British homes in Macao. And he asked the friendly Macanese governor to cut off food and water to the English. Elliot, anticipating Churchill at Dunkirk 100 years later, responded with an evacuation of all subjects from Macao in whatever vessels could handle them. They laid anchor off Hong Kong. Oddly, Lin didn't want to defeat the British; he just wanted a national kowtow to the emperor and an agreement that trade would be conducted by Chinese rules.

The British either misunderstood this Oriental subtlety or just refused to bite. The smell of war filled the fragrant harbor. On September 5, 1839, three British Navy cutters skirmished with three Chinese junks off Kowloon. Elliot followed up by sending a couple of fighting frigates to a duel with 29 Chinese men-of-war. Both Lin and Elliot reported victory, but it was four months before Elliot's word reached the ear of Viscount Palmerston, the foreign secretary. During this time, and even before, Jardine and Matheson had been lobbying Parliament for a strong sign of British superiority.

Palmerston ordered a force be sent from India to Hong Kong to ready itself for war with China. The British also came armed with a list of demands that, unsurprisingly, fit in very well with the commercial concerns of Jardine and Matheson: an apology, payment for the costs of the expeditionary force, payment for the confiscated 20,291 chests of opium, a free-trade treaty at five ports and recognition of British consuls as equivalent to a mandarin.

Richard Hughes reports on the efforts to inform the Chinese of these terms:

> The British ships moved up the China coast and tried vainly to serve their demands on the terrified Chinese at Amoy under a Western-style white flag of truce (which the Chinese thought must mean that there were dead aboard, probably cholera victims, as white is the Chinese funeral colour).

Unable to announce their terms for surrender, the British seized one of the approaches to Peking. It was then that the emperor realized that Lin's dispatches of hard-fought Chinese victories contained a bit of fiction.

Lin was put in chains; a Manchu mandarin, Kishen, was appointed to deal with the foreign devils. He persuaded them to forget about visiting Peking and return to Canton, where he hoped to set a trap for them. Instead, the British smelled a rat and went on a rampage. Their military might was so superior to the Chinese that within six weeks Canton was on its knees.

So, Kishen asked for peace, finally, and on January 20, 1841, the Convention of Chuen Pi was negotiated, giving the British a lot of money and a piece of land known as Hong Kong.

But the pact was never signed. Neither the emperor nor the queen was pleased. Palmerston dismissed Elliot for being weak and excoriated him for obtaining "the cession of Hong Kong, a bare island with hardly a house upon it."

The Chinese hierarchy proved equally daft.

The emperor repudiated the agreement. Sir Henry Pottinger replaced Elliot, and another round of fighting began. The English won again, and in 1842, the Treaty of Nanking was signed, providing for the opening of the five ports and China's payment of six million dollars for the opium that Lin had destroyed.

Tai-pan begins on the first day of British sovereignty over the island, January 26, 1841, although its ownership did not officially change until the treaty was signed. The book starts with the observation that not only was England unimpressed with what Elliot had wrestled from the Chinese as war booty, neither were the local merchants: "A pox on this stinking island," Brock said, staring around the beach and up at the mountains. "The whole of China at our feets and all we takes to be the barren, sodden rock."

The British proved to be more adept at conquest and colonizing than at grammar. An odd combination of naked greed at its most productive transformed the island from a tent town to a bustling mart. Hong Kong replaced Macao as the West's entrance to China, and with the opening of the new ports, trade flourished. The colony found itself wracked by malaria, coolie discontent and isolation, but in the end profit conquered all.

From time to time, the Chinese foolishly challenged the British, whose stronghold at Hong Kong provided a base for their warships. In October 1856, the Chinese boarded a British commercial ship named the *Arrow,* and Britain, displeased by the delayed reopening of Canton, sent a fleet up the Pearl to bring back their boat. After some foreigners were roughed up by local gangs the fleet went in again, and in December 1857, Britain captured Canton.

This time peace came in the form of the Treaties of Tientsin, which gave foreigners the right to travel throughout China. These pacts were followed by the Convention of Peking, signed on March 26, 1860, in which the point of Kowloon, facing Hong Kong island, was ceded in perpetuity to England. And to end the bad year, the Chinese, who lost yet another battle in October, ceded more land in Kowloon and a small island in the harbor.

What Britain had at the end of 1860 was land it was supposed to have forever, 36 square miles of territory whose population even at that time was 98 percent Chinese.

What happened next in the land-grabbing department marked Britain's first non-perpetual conquest and effectively set the alarm clock for the end of the British Empire.

France, always competitive with the limeys, had secured rights to a coaling station along the South China coast. Britain was in a huff—these were the headiest days of the empire—and made its displeasure known by demanding that China lease it another 250 square miles of territory, including 233 more islands, for a period of 99 years beginning July 1, 1898.

And thus, what we commonly know as Hong Kong took shape: the island, Kowloon, the New Territories (the land between Kowloon and the Mainland) and the outer islands.

This was a time when "the lowliest Briton was virtually a lord compared to the Chinese," so noted Mary Osgood, the heroine of Robert Elegant's *Dynasty*. The British Empire had peaked, and China's empire was on its last legs. The West was in ascendancy. But Osgood's observation really only reflected Western smugness and a misunderstanding of what lay below the surface. To a civilization that flourished before Britain was even born, the loss of territory meant only a temporary inconvenience. In 99 years, a matter of historical minutes to the Chinese, the leases would end and most of Hong Kong would be China's again. And as if to drop a reminder, riots and strikes broke out periodically throughout the years in protest of some bureaucratic bungle or just to let the Britons know they lived on borrowed time in a borrowed place.

Until the coming of the Second World War, Hong Kong's history moved in tandem with that of China. When xenophobia swept China during the Boxer Rebellion at the turn of the century, it swept Hong Kong. As trade with China increased, so did Hong Kong's importance. When Sun Yat-sen overthrew the Dragon Throne, his fellow republicans plotted in Hong Kong. When communists agitated, British goods in Hong Kong were boycotted. When Chinese killed Chinese, all of Hong Kong mourned because everyone had a relative playing on the main stage of the tumultuous events.

Then the chaos in which Hong Kong thrived crashed to a suffocating quiet on Christmas Day 1941, when Japan captured this territory and held it for three years and eight months. The mean-spirited Japanese maltreated the Chinese and rounded up the Britons like cattle and stuffed them into Stanley Fort.

The occupation meant humiliation for Britain. And, the beginning of the end of the empire. The Chinese did not miss this last point: Asians now ruled the colonialists. In *Hiroshima Joe,* a novel by Martin Booth, these thoughts struck the Chinese women and children standing in doorways, watching European prisoners of war march to dig holes for the Japanese: "It shocked them that those who had made the world tick could be so reduced to such indignity, such loss of face." The Colony never would be the same again, as the myth of Western superiority, to the extent there was one, had been shattered.

The relationship between the rise of the native Chinese and the demise of round eyes appears late in Booth's book when a daring homosexual British soldier encounters a Chinese thug, who as a coolie had dug ditches for the Japanese beside him. The Englishman, now desperately in debt to his comrade in shovels, appeals to the memories of those World War II days of shared misery.

> "Does nothing of the past affect you? We were once equals, once in the same hell and we helped each other. In the trenches of Kai-tak. Against the Japs. We fought side by side."
>
> "No. We were never equals. We did not fight together. You were a prisoner, a slave worker. I was the fighter. I took the risks. I killed the Japanese, not you. You never ambushed Japanese in the New Territories. I did. You surrendered. I would never surrender."
>
> "But the circumstances . . ."
>
> "They don't count," Leung interrupted him. "You should have died—fighting. That's the trouble with you Europeans. You value life too highly. Life in the East is cheap."

Evidence to prove that last point lay mangled in bloody heaps littered over the plains of China during World War II and its murderous aftermath, the civil war between the communists and nationalists. Hong Kong provided the haven for the fearful and the lucky. Practically overnight, nearly one million refugees streamed into the colony, jerry-rigging tin cans, blankets or cardboard and calling the ensuing structures home. The Colony was being suffocated. And yet it survived.

• • •

We pressed on with our search for Our Man in Hong Kong.

The Israeli brothers had taken over the offices of a fabulously wealthy, notorious international financier, so we were expecting an interview conducted in rich leather chairs, our feet hidden up to our ankles in plush carpet, and paneling of some exotic wood from the Bornean rain forest. Instead, the door was ajar and the air filled with sawdust and the noise of construction.

"Is anyone home?" we shouted.

"In here."

We walked over drop cloths to a small alcove. Oded Cohen was sitting at a telex machine, wearing headphones and speaking what sounded to be Chinese. Without pause he told us he'd be with us in a moment.

We watched as his secretary berated two men for placing a desk in the wrong place. She held a diagram in her hand and carefully scrutinized it as they moved the furniture.

Oded finished and gave us a warm welcome. "Shalom. Shalom, my friends."

He held up his cassette player. "I am trying to learn this damn language but I find it very difficult. My brother—you know Yakov?—he speaks Mandarin, Cantonese, you name it. All I ask is for a few words of Cantonese." He sounded exasperated, a feeling with which we could empathize.

"Sit, sit," he sounded like a Jewish mother. There were only three folding chairs set up on drop cloths. He shouted over the noise of an electric drill to his secretary. "What do you want? English tea, Chinese tea, Coca-Cola? What do you want? You must have something." We ordered drinks.

"So," he wanted to know. "Your first visit to Hong Kong, no?"

We told him about the previous evening.

"Leon and Diane are very rich, very successful, no? I think she is a very shrewd businesswoman."

And we told him we had gone to Chicago.

He looked pained. "Mark, Brian. Why don't you call me? Chicago is for little—what do you call them in English, the Yiddish word is *vances*. You know what I mean. Why didn't you call me? We go out. Have a nice meal. Go to disco with some stewardesses from Singapore Air. Why didn't you call me?"

We apologized and told him that we were looking for someone to show us Hong Kong and we wanted to give everyone a fair shake. We said he came highly recommended.

"You know I am flattered. Surely." But, he demurred. "What you need is a Chinese. Me, I can tell you where to buy a camera—by the way, when we finish here I take you to my electronics store. I'll tell them you are my friends. That's very important in Hong Kong. But what do you want me for? I am an Israeli. A Jew. Are you looking for *latkes? Latkes* I know where to find, but you want something more, no?"

He excused himself to read an incoming telex. Something about a project involving wood going from the Philippines to China to Australia to the States. We were learning that people in Hong Kong either intentionally complicated their professional résumés so we wouldn't understand, or that there was no such thing as a simple job description in the place. Oded described two other deals he was working on, each involving commerce among five countries.

He pointed to his telex machine. "That is all you need for business in Hong Kong. I sometimes sleep here in the office, depending on what time it is where I am doing business. There is no need to go out to see customers. People sometimes come to see me, but mostly all I do is talk by telex."

We wanted to know about all the construction. After all, the former occupant of the office surely had the funds to make the place comfortable. "Why are you tearing it up?"

Oded smiled. "You know how much trouble he is in?"

We said we had read the newspaper.

"You know what joss is?" He stopped himself. "Joss is luck. He had bad joss."

It seemed surprising that Oded, who had attended college in California, believed in such a thing.

"Of course, I believe it. And there are nearly six million people in Hong Kong and they believe it. You are in the East, remember that."

"So you tear up a man's office because he had a run of bad luck?"

Oded's eyes opened wide; he shook his head as if he had seen his favorite dog run over. "A run of bad luck? Yes, yes, I'd do anything to change that. This is Hong Kong. People will cut throats—not really, but you know what I mean—to make a buck, an extra half cent on a yard of piece goods, a penny on a ton on panel board. This is the most competitive place on earth and you don't need to make your odds worse by ignoring joss."

He told us that the first step to good joss was to hire the best *fung shui* adviser money could buy. "What you might call a witch doctor, a sorcerer. I call her a genius. The one we hired gets thousands of dollars. She goes to California often to advise the Chinese there, and they fly her first-class and put her up in the best hotels."

Oded's adviser recommended that the entire office be gutted, walls torn down, furniture discarded.

"Then she drew a diagram to place everything right." That is the essence of *fung shui,* the Chinese geomancy system that governs the order of physical surroundings. Those who subscribe to *fung shui* believe that everything must be in its proper place. We had read one description, written by a German living in Laos: "To be in the right place facing the right direction doing the right thing at the right time is a cross between being practically efficient and being ritually correct. It is being in tune with the universe."

And it is not taken lightly. Oded explained that he had to book his adviser months in advance. The adviser's job is to order all of the elements of nature—heaven, water (oceans), fire, thunder, wind, rain, hills and earth—with the goal of putting you and your enterprise in harmony and keeping the wrong sort of dragons out. Doors must be in the correct place, buildings must sit at the proper angle on a site, desks must be positioned just so.

Examples of a failure to follow proper *fung shui* abound. The popular *Insight* travel guide noted a few:

- Cathay Pacific Airways, a major Hong Kong carrier, didn't bother with getting advice before starting a new administration and engineering building. Employees began falling ill. A *fung shui* ceremony quickly took place, and no one got sick again.
- A superintendent in the Royal Hong Kong Police Force was concerned about his division's low morale. The men complained that the station house had bad *fung shui* because the building across the street had a low slanting roof with two wooden spirals aimed at them. A geomancer

was brought in and suggested mounting a pair of old cannon at the station's entrance. Police morale soared.

• The awesome view of the harbor from the Regent's lobby came about because the hotel's *fung shui* adviser had determined that the hotel's site was where a dragon entered the harbor for his bath. The solution was to design a see-through lobby so as not to disturb the dragon's ritual.

Oded gave us some advice. "When you are here don't dismiss anything as silly. People come here and they buy a cheap camera or find a nice suit, and they go home and they say, 'We did Hong Kong.' No, they did nothing; they understood nothing."

And that's why he said he was the wrong person to show us Hong Kong.

"What I know is so little. I have lived here for two years. When you leave you also will know so very little. But if you are lucky you will have learned a lot."

Oded clearly would not be persuaded, so we headed off to an electronics store to buy miniature Walkmen. Then he took us to get our fortunes told.

Hong Kong's emergence on the world's trading scene started in the late 1950s when the "Shanghai influence" began to take hold and entrepreneurial businessmen found great use for the abundant source of cheap labor. Into the 1960s the Colony welcomed anyone who could touch down there in flight from China. But then the load became too much for the tiny place to handle, and in 1962 an odd game of Ping-Pong took place with the border as the net.

Clavell depicted this scene in *Noble House,* where he wrote:

> For some unknown reason and without warning, the PRC border guards relaxed the tight control of their side and within a week thousands were pouring across daily. Mostly they came by night, over and through the token single six-strand fence that separated the New Territories from Kwangtung, the neighboring province. The police were powerless to stem the tide. The army had to be called out. In one night in May almost six thousand of the illegal horde were arrested, fed and the next day sent back over the border—but more thousands had escaped the border net

> to become legal. The catastrophe went on night after night, day after day. Tens of thousands of newcomers. Soon mobs of angry sympathetic Chinese were at the border trying to disrupt the deportations. The deportations were necessary because the Colony was becoming buried in illegals and it was impossible to feed, house, and absorb such a sudden, vast increase in new population . . . .
>
> Then, as suddenly as it had begun, the human gusher ceased and the border closed. Again for no apparent reason.

What these spasms of immigration made clear was Britain's tenuous held over the Colony. As quickly as the Colony constructed public housing—and it was success in this area that has made Hong Kong an urban showpiece—the supply was slurped up by families who had waited for years as squatters and were not about to let the newcomers push their way in.

Despite the tremendous demand on public services and the hardships caused by overcrowding the Colony continued to thrive. Cities like Mexico City or Lagos, bursting at the seams, have nearly keeled over from the weight of migration. Not Hong Kong. Almost from the start, labor was Hong Kong's primary resource and the businessmen reasoned that it had to be properly stored.

Which is not to say there weren't problems. In 1967, perhaps the greatest crisis of all hit: riots. Not the kind that arose out of a labor dispute or an extension of xenophobia like that which had occurred in the Boxer Rebellion. (These manifestations of discontent were endemic and recurred every once in a while.) The year 1967 was different for Hong Kong, because it was different for China. The Cultural Revolution swept the country, bringing it into psychological and political civil war, and from time to time, violence erupted. No one in China escaped the profound turmoil brought about by Mao's last grasp at its social and cultural fabric. And Hong Kong, notwithstanding the Union Jack flying over Government House, is, was and always will be China.

The 1967 riots apparently were well organized with one goal in mind: create chaos. In Hong Kong children and students threw rocks and bombs, workers sabotaged factories. China's window on the world was closing. But before the bamboo curtain fully dropped, those in Peking who recognized the importance of the great entrepôt prevailed over the radicals in Canton who wanted to bring Hong Kong into ideological line.

Mary Osgood, *Dynasty's* star, gave us some insight on how this adversity finally was overcome in Elegant's historical novel:

> "Reminded me of the riots of 1900 and 1909, particularly the political riots in 1900. It's frightening the way these clashes between Chinese and British recur. In 1900 the Boxers besieged the Legations in Peking. In 1967 the Red Guards besieged the Russian Embassy and burnt the British Embassy. Chinese and foreigners just can't seem to get along. The Maoists in Hong Kong again stuck up placards demanding: Crush British Imperialism. Kill the White Skinned Pigs. One couldn't really leave then, could one? Besides our own people were in danger."
>
> "Our own people, Mother?"
>
> "Yes, our own people. Millions of decent, hard-working Chinese who've been exploited for generations by both foreigners and their wealthy blood brothers. One simply couldn't leave them to the gentle mercy of the Communists. But it's really over now. I'm buying land as fast as I can, before everyone realizes the threat is finished and prices rise again."

From that moment on prices did rise, and Hong Kong's stock soared. While the United States slogged it out in Vietnam, soldiers on R & R enlivened Hong Kong. Our material needs enriched Hong Kong, and the "Made in Hong Kong" label began to dominate toy stores, electronics outlets and clothing racks. Britain, eager to display resolve that was sorely tested in 1967, opened the first tunnel connecting Hong Kong and Kowloon, and threw a municipal party to celebrate the Colony's survival.

Building continued apace. Entire new cities of public housing and accompanying service industries sprouted up throughout the New Territories. Land prices in the Central district on the island soared to world records as business returned to normal. All kinds of shocks rocked the Colony on the surface, but none interrupted its march to prosperity. For example, Britain's beleaguered pound was finally allowed to float; corruption became the middle name of Hong Kong's law enforcement authorities, revealed in spectacular cases of high officials turning out to be communist agents and in an exposé of English sergeants who had become multimillionaires on a copper's salary; OPEC disconnected the fuel tanks of the economy and droughts put unpleasant strains on its water tanks, and Richard Nixon made the improbable journey over the Great Wall. Hong Kong took notice, but it really didn't pause.

Around the mid-1970s, very quietly and nearly imperceptibly, an alarm went off, and the mood of Hong Kong became downright frenetic, as if suddenly everyone realized there was so much to do and so little time in which to do it. Maybe the trigger was the nostalgic trip of Queen Elizabeth and Prince Philip—whose favor the rich Chinese in search of a title sought but whose pageantry could not have been mistaken for influence. More likely, the twin communist corpses in 1976—Mao and Chou—caused this tiny kingdom of capitalism to recognize its own mortality. For to their successors fell the responsibility of deciding what to do when the leases ran out on the New Territories in 1997. This decision loomed as no minor event in the lives of the five million or so residents. Nearly every one of them had some personal experience with landlords from Peking. It was what drove those refugees to Hong Kong in the first place.

As Leon had alerted us, the sale of passports and the accompanying rights of citizenship to countries like Paraguay and Tonga became a new industry. Relatives in Canada and the United States started receiving savings from Hong Kong and built up bank accounts for the day when an exit could be made. Anyone with money was busily creating a second life in another part of the world. But one reaction more than any was most typical of Hong Kong: The economy really took off. Land was swapped at a dizzying pace, each sale bringing huge profits and setting records. Factories were set up in China to exploit cheap labor; Hong Kong would be the brain, the Mainland the arms and legs. So much happened so quickly; Diane's analogy was appropriate: It was like a game of musical chairs played to a tango at 200 rpm. It was also a game of chicken, because the stakes were so high. Sooner or later the music would stop, the Red Army would march to its posts and someone would be left holding the bag.

As if they tacitly acknowledged the ultrathin line between panic and prosperity, the Chinese and British governments made great strides to prove that Hong Kong was not a moribund morsel about to be eaten, but an animal that had to be sold in the prime of its life. In 1978, a new reservoir opened and the perpetual rationing of water ended. In 1980, an new subway system commenced operations, and it worked beyond everyone's wildest optimism. The landscape of the New Territories became the proving ground for instant cities, each of them apparently a stunning success and each of them erasing a squatter camp. What was once unthinkable was becoming true: There was room for everyone. China opened her doors to foreigners, to foreign investments, to the ideas that Hong Kong could headquarter much of her trade. And reverse psychology was at work, as communist enterprises moved into Hong Kong and took up the beat of commerce.

But still the big question had not been answered. And until it was, not matter how smooth the surface of life appeared, those nagging doubts still lingered. John Le Carré captured that apocalyptic vision so well, the one that must have caused so many of the Colony's citizens to leap from their beds in the dead of night and slip some more cash into the envelopes they directed overseas:

> It's the Colony's last day, he decided. Peking has made its proverbial telephone call. "Get out, party over." The last hotel was closing; he saw the empty Rolls-Royces lying around like scrap around the harbour, and the last blue-rinse, round-eye matron, laden with her tax-free furs and jewelry, tottering up the gangway of the last cruise ship; the last China-watcher frantically feeding his last miscalculations into the shredder; the looted shops, the empty city waiting like a carcass for the hordes.

By September 1982, everyone could hear the alarm, and its loud, nagging bell clanged throughout the Colony for the next two years. Margaret Thatcher's trip to Beijing in that month wiped out a few soothing messages that had been sent to calm jittery nerves. For example, Deng Xiaoping had told Hong Kong's governor in 1979, "Investors should set their hearts at ease." And in July 1982, lending banks had agreed to extend loan repayment terms on property in the New Territories for more than 15 years, i.e., after lease expiration.

Couldn't an emerging reformist China just sign a lease

extension with the British, raise the rent and continue business as usual? For reasons enough to fill a book: no! Hong Kong had to come back. The lapse of the leases signaled an expiration date for the humiliating memories inflicted upon China by foreign devils—English, French, American, Russian. Assertion of sovereignty over Hong Kong meant Deng feared not the outside world or the complex task of parenthood. And unless China handled the Hong Kong issue with calm and skill, it stood not a prayer of ever again seeing Taiwan in its fold. National pride, the intrinsic value galore of Hong Kong, and the opportunity to make a statement to the world about China's superiority—one normally reserved for victors of wars—were just some of the reasons Maggie stood no chance of departing Beijing with a promise for status quo.

The negotiations brought together two mind-sets as opposite as the worlds that produced them. The Iron Lady already had lived up to her nickname many times. And Deng had not exceeded the normal political life expectancy by kowtowing to prevailing winds or burying his head in the tea. He had been purged and rehabilitated, purged and rehabilitated. And those who had done the purging came to understand, once he rose to power, why it is that when you shoot at the king you'd better not miss: By 1982, the Gang of Four was really the Gang of Zero.

To let Maggie know he meant business, Deng essentially put up wall posters that said, "All of Hong Kong or all of Hong Kong." The Chinese were in no mood to listen to Britain's legal analysis about how Hong Kong and Kowloon belonged to the Crown in perpetuity and thus the negotiations would be limited to the New Territories—the land between Kowloon and the Mainland and the 233 islands. As door prizes for coming to China, Deng figuratively handed out maps of the Colony. "Look at them," he invited his guests. "Without the New Territories you will not have the following: your agricultural land, your largest container port and planes using the airport could not take off or land because you couldn't overfly our territory." Keep your island and keep Kowloon, blared the message, and you'll own a score of abandoned tailor shops and skyscrapers that may or may not achieve their scrap value: all of Hong Kong or all of Hong Kong.

Maggie left China to visit Hong Kong and appeared not

to hear. She reaffirmed Britain's loyalty to international law and the treaties. She said nothing had been ceded, nothing decided. She kept a stiff upper lip. And in the meantime her audience knew who she was dealing with and on what terms. Maggie had warred with the Argentines over sheep to protect British sovereignty, but would she really take on Deng, could she? The stock market and property market provided the answers. The slump had begun.

In fact, China would not even go on to the next phase of talks until Britain recognized Chinese sovereignty over all of the land. A face-saving diplomatic message to this end sent the talks into motion in the summer of 1983. And they still floundered.

Britain used the massive popular anxiety as an excuse for proceeding slowly and taking a tough stance. China countered with evidence; it orchestrated a public relations campaign through the press it controlled in Hong Kong and through its friendly unions. Britain pointed to the dying Hong Kong dollar as proof of its position; China claimed Britain was manipulating the currency.

Imagine, by the way, how the nearly six million pawns in this chess game felt.

Actually, the sense of doomsday's coming left nothing to the imagination. On September 24, 1983, after another inconsequential round of talks ended, fear reared up. The Hong Kong dollar, already way down, plummeted. Food stocks disappeared from stores. Trading businesses shut down, because no one could do business in a worthless currency.

China held firm. Britain didn't. All of her efforts to save the Colony were ruining the Colony. Only if Deng wavered would there be a silver lining in the cloud. And he stood steadfast.

Having given up on sovereignty, Britain did her best to save face and put in some safeguards to avoid the inevitable accusations of a sellout. After all, Maggie despised weakness: Let the Chinese beat you up, and the labor unions at home will strike the hell out of you.

The talks continued in Beijing and every now and then a bombshell landed in Hong Kong. Jardine Matheson, the Noble House itself, announced it would move its holding company to Bermuda. Deng let it be known that, of course, the People's

Liberation Army would be stationed in Hong Kong. A taxi strike led to violence and concern that if lame-duck Britain could not control events then China may have to move up its entrance. Britain finally publicly announced that after 1997, she'd no longer be there in any capacity, administrataive or honorary. All of Hong Kong would go back to China.

On September 24, 1984, the two countries signed "A Draft Agreement on the Future of Hong Kong." Britain agreed to return the Colony to Chinese sovereignty in 1997.

For a moment it looked like a fine compromise. But was it? Britain, inescapably, was going to pack up its bags and leave. Only China's assurances in 1984 would stand between the Colony's *modus vivendi* and the life from which most of them have escaped. And ultimately they were the assurances of Deng Xiaoping, who made these promises already as an old man and would not live until 1997.

Paranoia was running deep. This was the Hong Kong that we visited, a little place living on little time.

By the process of elimination and, it turned out, good fortune, David Wang became Our Man in Hong Kong.

That day we had lunch in the Luk Yu Tea House in the Central business district, a neighborhood hangout that seemed to be a thousand years old. The hardwood tables bore the stains of a million sloppy tea drinkers; spittoons stood strategically throughout the ground floor, and we were grateful no one bothered to use them.

We told the headwaiter we wanted *dim sum* (practically translated as "little things that go by in a cart"), and we think he asked us if we had reservations. We told him no, and we think he told us to get lost. There were plenty of empty seats when we arrived, although each table had what we thought was a card with someone's name on it. We waited. We think the headwaiter told us not to bother, but we waited anyway. Everyone seemed to know each other—the busboys laughed with customers, the headwaiter slapped more than a few on the back. Tables emptied again, and still we waited.

Finally, we did an extraordinary thing. We walked past the headwaiter and sat down. And sat there. The *dim sum* car pushers ignored us. The busboys serving a spectrum of teas passed us by. That is, until we starting grabbing them as they went by and basically shanghaied our lunch in Hong Kong. It was ugly. We felt lousy, although the food was great. We had learned a valuable lesson about survival in Hong Kong.

However, we are not that pushy by nature, and if that's how we were going to have to get by—it made us that more anxious to enlist David Wang.

His office was in the same complex as Oded Cohen's and contained practically the same equipment: a few desks, file cabinets and the almighty telex machine. We didn't ask David about the *fung shui* of his office, although we saw little red charms and paper cutouts in odd crannies of the place. His desk was cluttered with the catalogs of the U.S. retail chains: Sears, JC Penney, and K-mart. "I must keep up with the markets," he explained.

"You want me to be your guide? Fine," he offered. "But I lead an exceptionally boring life. All I want to do is make money and get laid, and I am not being very successful at either one."

We asked what the problem was.

"Making money, I think the problem is just bad timing. Not getting laid? Well, you'll see tonight. We'll have dinner with my parents and you'll see." David asked us what he could do for us.

We told him we'd like to meet his friends. We'd like to use his secretary to make calls and reservations. We'd like to see parts of the town that Westerners didn't frequent.

David said he would have no problem representing us. "Maybe it will help my social life if you write about me," he muttered.

He invited us to dinner to celebrate his father's birthday. The restaurant was just off Nathan Road, and we walked over. (We discovered one of the drawbacks of David's company; Hong Kong's streets were so crowded it was impossible to walk more than two abreast on the sidewalk so one of us always lagged behind and shouted, "What'd he say?" and scrambled to write down the conversation while navigating through the throng.)

On the way over, David warned us what to expect. "My mother will only talk about my social life. She will want to know if you are married, how you met your wives, how you think I should act in order to attract women."

We asked why she was so obsessed.

"Why do you think? I'm 30 years old. I have no brothers or sisters, so our family will die if I don't do something. This is very Chinese, for her to be worried."

David's father came from an extremely wealthy Shanghai family. They owned flour mills, fishing fleets and ice houses. Every winter the family had employed 30,000 people to chop ice out of the ponds and lakes on their property that they used to store fish and make life in Shanghai's sticky summers tolerable. David's father was an only son, and he and David's grandfather slept in the same room so that the bond between them could strengthen at all hours.

"It's unusual," he noted, "that my father was an only son and I am an only son. There isn't much of an insurance policy." As if to prove the point he darted across Nathan Road just ahead of a bus turning a corner.

When the Communist victory appeared inevitable in 1948, David's father was sent to Hong Kong with a large part of the family fortune to safeguard. Instead of living a gentleman's life, his father became enamored of the communists and blew the family's wad on several ships to support the cause. Then he returned to Shanghai—a hero to the Party, a goat to his family.

But eventually David's father grew disillusioned with the new system, and fell out of favor with those he had helped. Once the scion of an industrial network, he was sent to the floor of the family's flour factory to do menial work. He also was "rehabilitated" a few times. One day, he escaped back to Hong Kong, though this time the wealth he carried was one Hong Kong dollar.

His father found work in a cloth factory, where he labored all his waking hours. Eventually, he saved enough money to start a small trading house, and he became Exxon's representative in Hong Kong.

For the next four years David and his mother lived in Shanghai, the memory of his father fading. One day in 1965 a letter arrived with enough money for train tickets to the border, where his father was waiting for them.

"I think I was just about the last refugee out before the Cultural Revolution," he recalled. "They closed the border just after I left, and it never really opened again."

David left Hong Kong in 1975 to go to college in the United States, the University of Mississippi of all places. He said he knew someone who knew someone who went there, and that was his reason for going to the Deep South. After graduation, he returned to Hong Kong and set up an import-export business with his father.

"Now I'm specializing in curtains," he said as we arrived at the restaurant. "Who knows, maybe on your next visit I'll be the Curtain King of Hong Kong. I'm planning a joint venture with the United States and China to build factories, and I'll show you on the map the stores I have planned for the New Territories."

We noticed there were no other *gwailos* in the restaurant. David's parents hadn't arrived yet, so while we waited he explained his social dilemma.

It was hard to find women while living at home, and he couldn't move out. First, he was an only child and his parents needed to be proximate to him at all times. Even when David sat in his office, cluttered with curtains and venetian blinds, his parents sat with him. They watched him, nothing more, for hours on end. When he traveled on business they succeeded to the power of the trading company and acted as they thought David would. Invariably, employees would quit during his absences, and David would rehire them on his return. Friends and business acquaintances had told him his parents were nice but not exactly the docile caretakers he'd hoped they'd be. After all, he only had to look back at what his father had done when left in charge of his family's fortune.

Another of David's problems was simply time. He never stayed in Hong Kong long enough to cultivate a relationship with a woman. For him, as for most traders in the Colony, the most familiar site was Kai Tak airport's security zones. Manila one day, Taipei the next, and an afternoon in Canton—David never stood still, lest his competitors worm their way into his contacts. After all, these traders did not market well-developed skills—how else could he be in fertilizer one day and the Curtain King the next; they capitalize on access to markets, knowledge of cheap sources of supply and where the consumer market was going.

Plaintively, David posted the question, "How can I get a girl if I'm never here?"

His mother had tried out one stratagem. They had a neighbor (David and his folks lived just off Boundary Street in Kowloon in the only district with a decibel level below the intolerable range) who, along with her two brothers, had inherited their father's business of exporting cheap televisions from Korea into China. (Because South Korea and China don't have direct relations, Hong Kong acts as a transhipment point, much as it does with Taiwan-China trade.) The girl and David's mother grew very close. But David didn't like her; he said she giggled too much, complained too much and was too ugly. He told this to his mother and told her to drop any intentions she had of making a match. Undeterred his mother arranged for a formal Chinese rite wherein the neighbor swore obedience to David's parents and thereby became their daughter.

There was one final impediment to David's getting married, and this one stood so far away from his parent's imagination as to be totally incomprehensible. As a meek and wiry Oriental sapling David had observed life at Ole Miss from a distant sideline. "I never really fit in," he confessed. "To the blacks I was white. To the whites I was black." Most of it passed by without his giving a nod or a look of envy.

With one major exception. He blushed as he articulated it. "I am truly obsessed with black women. You know, like Grace Jones. I want one of them to use me as her love tool." He paused, "Now how can I explain that to my mother. How can I tell her I can't marry until I have black love?" There were times in our journey when we were speechless, unable to fathom how the world had nurtured such complexities.

David's mother and father arrived with a young woman in tow. David winced and whispered to Kelly, "That's my 'sister.' The dog. That's what my mother wants me to marry."

They all seemed pleasant enough. Neither of his parents spoke English, although they appeared to understand a few words. His father was about 65 and older than his years; David explained that he had been taking medicine for high blood pressure that caused mild depression as a side effect. His mother was very much as advertised: She barely took her eyes off her son. His "sister" was extremely attentive to her "parents," marching inexorably on their good side.

Needless to say, the conversation was severely limited. We discussed the origin of the thousand-year-old eggs we were eating, evidently marinated in a tarlike goop that causes their yolks to turn blue. We also discussed the skinny pigeons on our plates and the chicken livers with orange-flavored bread. David kept us entertained with a few sayings from Confucius: "The sister-in-law who sits on her brother-in-law's lap makes it hard for her sister."

When the meal was ending, David told us that his mother wanted to know if we were married and, if so, how we had met our wives. "I told you so," he announced.

His mother pinched his cheek and told us that she was upset that David had not been lucky. The "sister" busily shoveled food and pretended not to hear.

London then said something that David refused to translate. "No, you will only get me in trouble."

London insisted. "Tell your mother that we met a fortune-teller today when we went with Oded Cohen. Tell her the woman knew everything about us."

David didn't believe that.

"It's true," London said. "Just tell her."

She reacted immediately and blurted a message to David for us. While he translated she talked excitedly with her husband. The "sister" gave us a dirty look as if to tell us to keep our noses out.

David appeared fatigued. "She wants to know the name of the fortune-teller, where she is. She is telling my father we should all go there tomorrow."

"You see, David. We can be of some help."

He appeared annoyed. "All you do is get her hopes up. She thinks a fortune-teller is going to find me a wife."

"This one might." We still were spooked by what we had heard that afternoon, and we told this to David's mother. The fortune-teller had told London that he had been in the hospital six weeks earlier with stomach pains, a foreshadowing, she said, of a difficult year. She was right on both counts. Kelly's life had changed with a phone call a year earlier she surmised, something about a job offer he couldn't refuse. Right again.

We suggested to Mrs. Wang that this woman could spell the end to David's barren life. We left the restaurant in the very good graces of his parents, who had decided we represented a good omen.

David was downcast. "Come on," he said. "You come with me to my club, and you'll see what you've done."

We walked back to the New World Centre. (Except for our

trip to the fortune-teller we had spent our entire visit so far within a five-block radius, yet believed we had traveled so much farther.) We went in an elevator to the third floor, walked past two burly guards to an elegant entrance adorned by a chandelier reflecting off a polished marble floor.

A breathtakingly beautiful woman, dressed in a sequinned gown, beamed when she saw David and hugged him. David, grinning like a Cheshire cat, turned to us. "Meet Alice. She is your mammasan."

Alice shook hands with us and sized us up. She told David to wait just a few moments.

David seemed to have grown nearly a foot since dinner. "My mother doesn't understand this. If I get married then I have to stay home and watch television. Come in, you will see the difference."

At first, we had thought the Club de Luxe was merely a fancy nightclub. Robert Lomax, the lovestruck artist in *The World of Suzie Wong* had made the same error of judgment when he checked into the seedy Nam Kok hotel and bar in the Wanchai District across the harbor from where we stood.

> I watched them cross the hall, grinning to myself. Well, I am an idiot, I thought. I ought to have guessed from the clerk's face when I asked for a room. A room for a month! I suppose he's only used to letting rooms by the hour. And I turned and went through the swing door into the bar.
>
> Inside it was dim after the daylight of the hall. The windows were curtained and the room lit like a nightclub with rosy diffused light. I paused while my eyes adjusted themselves. Then the scene began to take shape; the bar counter in the corner; the huge walnut-and-chromium jukebox playing "Seven Lonely Days"; the Chinese waitress carrying trays of beer amongst the tables; and the sailors at the tables; and the girls.

The Club de Luxe existed in the same genre, but on another level. Technically, it is called a hostess club, where the mammasan finds you a date, pretty enough to make your heart stop. You talk to her, dance with her and leave with her if you want, but if you do it costs an extra "exit fee."

We had no intention of leaving with the women Alice introduced to us; instead, we wanted to marry them. The one intended for Kelly was tall and dressed in a strapless pale blue gown.

"She is from Mongolia," Alice explained. "And funny, very funny."

London was set up with Wanda, who was from Hong Kong and had told her parents that her waitress job was so lucrative that she was able to buy the entire family a new flat.

David didn't take a date. We asked him why. "Tonight I'll just watch. I'll pay the bill, talk with the girls and be a big shot. Why I brought you here is so you understand why I don't get married."

Alice apparently didn't understand David's stratagem. She brought over three different women, all of whom David treated to drinks then discarded by telling Alice he was bored.

Kelly asked his Mongolian Joan Rivers what she thought of her customers in general.

"I like Americans and Chinese the best. But the problem is more and more there are Japanese."

"Don't you like them?"

"I do and I don't. You see, for you to leave with me costs 1,000 Hong Kong dollars I tell the Japanese man it is 3,000 Hong Kong dollars, and he says okay. But then it is very boring with him. They are not very funny men."

Kelly asked her who the funniest customers were.

"The Indians," said the Mongolian comedienne. "We charge them 1,000 Hong Kong dollars just to talk to us, and when we say good night. That is very funny."

We danced with our dates to the sound of a disco band until nearly closing time. David chatted with some friends then sent us off in a cab. As we drove away we noticed he walked back into the building and disappeared in the elevator.

Wong Tai Sin is a Taoist temple that sits lost among the chaotic uniformity of tens of high-rise public housing residences. The temple is among Hong Kong's largest and is a favorite in part because of its excellent *fung shui,* as it is located between the shadow of the looming Lion Rock and the sea. Another of its positive attributes is its namesake, the god Wong Tai Sin, who could turn boulders into sheep.

The main altar area of the temple serves as the arena for a motley crew from nattily attired businessmen to women wearing aprons, all waving smoking joss sticks, prostrating on the ground and rattling the *chim,* a cup filled with numbered sticks that is shaken until a stick falls out that is then taken to a fortune-teller who builds a tale based on a single digit.

We shortcut this route and headed directly to the narrow, dark corridor to the side of the temple where tens of fortune-tellers ply their trade. Each sits behind a small counter, the walls adorned by pictures of a favorite relative, ancestor or deity. Each of the stalls has a small back room where tradition gives way, and the refrigerator and television are kept.

Our soothsayer wore horned-rimmed glasses missing one arm. She was balding and her face sported numerous liver spots that we accepted as signs of wisdom. She wasn't tough to find.

Hong Kong is populated by the superstitious, and each family has its own method of calling up the spirits to deliver important messages or order their lives so they could receive them. In *Monkey King,* a novel by Hong Kong–born Timothy Mo, the amahs, skeptical of their master's prowess and eager for tots to care for, went off to a certain place for help:

> Meanwhile, unknown to Wallace, others were labouring on the family's behalf. At least three of the joss sticks that had smouldered before the tree by Christmas had been spontaneous intercessions for May Ling by the amahs. Subsequently, Mrs. Poon had also bribed the servants into making the pilgrimage to the phallic rock and leaving food before the suggestive spur of granite. It had been a long walk for an old woman. In fact, repenting of her access of goodwill, Ah Doh snapped one of the brittle yellow sticks of incense they had planted in a cave underneath the rock—a fell stroke that drew a feeling wince from Ah King.
>
> If Wallace had felt a twinge, he had not shown it, and the marriage continued to provide food for malicious speculation in the servant's quarters and amongst the tenants.

Mrs. Wang, faced with a similar concern, sat David on the barroom stool in front of the fortune-teller and explained his problem to the elderly clairvoyant. She wanted a daughter-in-law. She wanted grandchildren. And, of course, she wanted her son to be very, very rich—after all, this was Hong Kong.

The fortune-teller nodded and sucked the arm of her

glasses. Then she stared intently at his face and asked to see his hand.

"What day was he born? What year? What time? Was it a rough birth? Was it supposed to be a boy?"

These questions she asked of Mrs. Wang, who was all too happy to supply the information. David's father chimed in with his recollections. David rolled his eyes in futility. A few passersby stopped to listen to his life story and, no doubt, to see how much these predictions would cost.

The fortune-teller explained to David's mother that she would concentrate only on his love life and leave his health and wealth, to the extent they were unrelated to romance, to another session. That was all right with the Wangs.

She consulted a dog-eared book filled with flimsy pages of incomprehensible columns of Chinese writing. She spoke in bursts of truths, it seemed, nearly knocking over David's mother with some of the revelations. The more she told the more David's mother wanted to know. His father held his wife as he listened and often asked what we assumed was, "Are you sure?"

David, who prides himself on being a thoroughly modern man, buried his head in his hands. When he did this his mother sent him a strong elbow and reminded him that the reader might want to consult his face at a moment's notice.

As the session intensified, the crowd thickened until no one could maneuver the thin passageway.

The message was trouble, but there was hope. David had to be engaged to be married by the following March (this was September) or two things would occur: He would go bankrupt and he would never marry.

The crowd looked upon him sympathetically. Their compassion would have been limitless if they understood the challenge that David faced: He had no prospect of getting married—he didn't even had a girlfriend—and without his beloved money he would wish himself dead. Oh, what a kick in the crotch he had suffered. He glowered at us, we who had brought him to this perspicacious woman.

We implored Mrs. Wang to find a solution. "Isn't there anything that can be done? We just can't leave so hopeless." She asked the question to the fortune teller.

David listened to the answer and mumbled to us, "Now you've done it."

Apparently there was a prescription, the woman was saying. David's father was writing it down. David would take it the next day.

We spent the rest of that day sightseeing in David's new Jaguar. "Enjoy it now," he winced, "because it'll be gone by spring." He was exceptionally gloomy, and he held the steering wheel tightly, pretending no doubt it was our throats.

"I can't believe you did this to me," he said.

"David, it's only a fortune-teller."

"You don't understand. My mother believes these things. All Chinese believe these things."

"We do too," we confessed. After all, this soothsayer had surfaced secrets that we believed were unsalvagable. "But not you, David. How can you go bankrupt just because you're not married? If anything, single life is cheaper."

He was unresponsive. He told us we were driving near the Walled City of Kowloon. "Perhaps my good friends who have betrayed me would like to have a tour," he said snidely. "I'll wait here."

He couldn't fool us on that score. No *gwailo,* and very few cautious Chinese ever ventured into the Walled City. The section of town had become a no-man's land; the British never claimed sovereignty over it, either because the lease maps were bad or because they assumed the Chinese had retained it, and it wasn't worth fighting over. Consequently, the area did not share Hong Kong's water and sewer systems, police protection or public housing opportunities. It sported an infestation of crime so thoroughly lawless that it appears in nearly every fictional account of Hong Kong. For example, Robert Ludlum sent the intrepid Jason Bourne there to test his mettle:

> The Walled City of Kowloon has no visible wall around it, but it is as clearly defined as if there were one made of hard, high steel . . . In squalid corridors crippled beggars vie with half-dressed prostitutes and drug peddlers in the eerie wash of naked bulbs that hang from the exposed wires along the stone walls. A putrid dampness abounds; all is decay and rot, but the strength of time has hardened this decomposition, petrifying it.
>
> Within the foul alleyways in no particular order or balance are narrow, barely lit staircases leading to the vertical series

of broken-down flats, the average rising three stories, two of which are above ground. Inside the small, dilapidated rooms the widest varieties of narcotics and sex are sold; all is beyond the reach of the police—silently agreed to by all parties—for few of the colony's authorities care to venture into the bowels of the Walled City. It is its own self-contained hell. Let it be.

"No thanks, David. We'll stick with you." Later, we regretted not daring him into dropping us off there because soon after, the British and Chinese governments announced a joint initiative to raze the entire seven-acre enclave and replace it with a park. No doubt, it soon will be replaced by another city or high-rise apartments and shopping centers; at least, David could add another outlet to his imagined chain of curtain stores.

We went on toward the harbor. Traffic was bearable; the pace of the day seemed to have slackened in the lengthening shadows of the afternoon. The populace had been braced for Typhoon Wayne, and the Royal Observatory warned that the storm packed a punch that could devastate the islands. Already, it had killed dozens of people in Taiwan, destroying millions of dollars of property in the process. When these late summer threats reared up they were taken seriously. Now, the word we heard on the car radio was that Wayne would not be visiting after all.

David offered to take us by car ferry from Kowloon to the higher elevations of the island. The harbor was filled, as it always is, with a range of vessels from a small family junk to a near supertanker. We were mystified at how each plied its route without crashing into another. And on this very unscientific 10-minute journey we confirmed one of Richard Hughes's observations: "But there are no seagulls in the harbor: Hong Kong throws away nothing that can be eaten or sold." Which means Hong Kong throws away next to nothing. It is said of the Cantonese that he will eat anything with legs but a table. And, in our sojourn along Nathan Road we had seen that he also will sell you almost anything that could fetch a price, no matter how small.

We toured though the Central district, feeling tiny among the skyscrapers glistening in the late afternoon sun. Along the water loomed the Connaught Centre, headquarters of many foreign companies as well as the trading firm of Jardine Matheson, as old as Hong Kong itself and run by the founding British family. The building is dotted with rows of windows, which we assumed were meant to suggest the portholes of Jardine's once mighty shipping empire. The locals have another perspective; they call Connaught "the building of a thousand assholes." Actually, there are 1,573. The newly constructed Hong Kong–Shanghai Bank building looked like the innards of an aircraft carrier standing on its end. (The bank actually issues the currency of Hong Kong, and for obvious reasons is Hong Kong's most powerful private institution.) The towers of the stock exchange shined like silver bars on end, and we couldn't help but wonder what assurances Beijing had made before so many millions of dollars had been sunk into the soil; the land alone had cost $700 million. We passed the construction site of the Bank of China, an intricate web of bamboo poles put together precariously, it seemed, and easy prey for a nasty typhoon. This building would be the tallest in Hong Kong, thereby making a statement rich in conflicting symbolism: Did the commies cherish money so much that their bank was their cathedral; were the commies just saying we can be capitalists, too, or were they saying that from now on the money will be red, and you will never forget that?

As we wound our ways above the towers on the switchback roads the air grew cooler, more pleasant, the view of the harbor more dramatic, and the quiet increased. We were reminded that Hong Kong's geography, like so many other cities', mirrored its social strata: The higher up you lived the more important you were. We crossed to the flip side of the peak toward the fishing village of Aberdeen to visit its harbor stuffed with a ramshackle flotilla of homes and fishing vessels. Thousands of Hong Kong's citizens literally live on the water all the time. There are hawker junks on which to buy junk, restaurant junks and even brothel boats.

The land-based town of Aberdeen is known as Little Hong Kong and for good reason. It is almost a miniature version of the city, with a few tall buildings and apartment houses, but its pace is so downscale it reminded us of a more staid place like Kansas City.

We drove along the shore toward Repulse Bay and passed cliffside homes with a view of a quiet sea. It was hard to believe that just on the other side of the peak a maddening den of activity cackled with commerce. Yet, the modern age finally had made it over the mountain: The Repulse Bay Hotel, the last holdout of airy colonial hostelries, had been razed, soon to be replaced by an apartment house and an exclusive private club. The vestiges of colonialism lay victim not to any political movement but to the almighty dollar and the desire to build new things with central air rather than ceiling fans. In the cramped town of Repulse Bay we shopped hard in the narrow alleyways and emerged with a booty of brand name knockoffs that we bought for a song.

The next morning we met David at his home and prepared to tackle his problematic future. He explained that his father had gone ahead to purchase the items prescribed by the soothsayer and that we would meet him at a temple in Mongkok, a section of Kowloon that, with 170,000 people per square kilometer, is believed to be the most densely populated area in the world.

As we waited for a cab we noticed an elderly couple a half a block away doing the same. We told David that they were first and we should wait.

"Nonsense," he said, frantically waving for a car. "This is Hong Kong. You don't give. You take."

Somewhere in the sea of humanity in which we were dropped lay the temple of hope for David Wang. We asked countless passersby for directions. No one had time to stop. They all were shopping, talking, hustling somewhere.

Finally, we found the San Tai Tzu temple squeezed among dilapidated low-slung apartment buildings. We read the plaque:

> In the 1890's a terrible epidemic broke out in Shanshuipo. The Hakka people brought the image of their patron deity San Tai Tzu (the 3rd Prince) from their native place to Shanshuipo to help suppressing the epidemic. The image was paraded throughout all the streets in the area. As a result, the epidemic subsided. The Hakka attributed this to the divine power of San Tai Tzu. In memory of him they built this temple in the 24th year of Kuang Hsu (1898). The San Tai Tzu festival is on the 18th day of the 3rd moon.

We asked David why he had chosen this particular temple to relieve him of his predicament.

"I didn't. The fortune-teller told me to come here. I think she gets a commission," he offered.

David's father came along shortly bearing a shopping bag. He emptied the contents on the small counter on one side of the small dark room along whose walls stood statues of tigers and funny little people.

"Oranges, pears, eggs, nuts and pork fat," he counted off. "Okay. We are ready." He clapped his hands and a teenage boy wearing a ragged T-shirt, black shorts and clogs made of Marlboro cartons emerged from a side room and took his place behind the counter. He had brown conked hair and tattoos all over his arm and looked like a sallow Chuck Berry, miniature version.

He studied the edibles. "Marriage?" he asked David's father.

"And money. We were sent from Wong Tai Sin."

For the next half hour the young lad shuffled from his back room to the counter, from the street to the counter (undoubtedly a nearby store was a source of supply). He built a pile of cheap paper goods of all colors, each bearing an animal likeness or some Chinese inscription.

Every time he added to the pile he barked instructions to David's father.

And so the rite to find a wife and stave off bankruptcy began.

David strode around the room carrying a bunch of joss sticks, which resembled the "punks" we used in summer camps to keep the mosquitoes away. He knelt in various places around the room and inserted them into pots of dirt. Then he lit two candles and put them in pots of dirt.

He returned to the counter, lit paper plates with animals on them, waved the fire about and ran outside into a courtyard and threw the fire into an oven. He picked up a hammer and banged a bell next to the oven. He did this three times.

Then he lay two pears and three eggs before a tiger statue. To make sure they'd be eaten he surrounded the foodstuffs with paper tigers.

All the while we were choking on the smoke.

David grabbed another bunch of joss sticks, lit them and deposited the bunch, three at a time, in a pot near all of the feasting tigers. He then put toothpicks in the food (the eggs, it turned out, were hard-boiled) in case, we figured, the tigers were in the mood for canapés.

The tattooed teen lit a lantern near the tigers, and we could clearly see David on his knees trying to figure out how to get the inanimate objects to start eating and help him out of his jam.

The kid told him to prostrate himself before the statue and clasp his hands together tightly.

Then from a dark corner emerged an old man with a saxophone, and he started to play *My Favorite Things.*

Through the thick smoke we saw David start up, wondering, no doubt, if an ad in the personals would be more promising.

The kid told him to stand up, quickly put pork fat on toothpicks and shove the lot into the statue's mouth. Then, David had to light more plates, wave them around, run outside and beat the bell.

David was exhausted and was having difficulty breathing. His father stood nonplussed near the counter. The sax wailed on.

"Am I done?" David asked.

The boy shook his head and brought up a bag of cookies and a red plastic bowl from under the counter. He dropped an orange in the bowl and told David to put it in front of the goddesses of marriage.

David lay it in front of 15 small dolls and looked for further advice.

"Joss sticks," the boy waved them.

Again, David circled the room filling the pots of dirt with the smoking sticks.

He was handed the remaining papers tightly rolled. He was told to kneel before the dolls, then kneel before 38 figurines of what looked to be eunuchs and to fill his head with wishes. Then he lit the papers and waved them at the dolls, the eunuchs and ran toward the oven. The sax built to a crescendo. David screamed. He had stumbled on his way to the oven and singed his hand.

The music stopped. He dragged himself back into the room, coughing and panting.

"Almost done," said the kid. He handed David a cup filled with 64 sticks. He told him to take it in front of San Tai Tzu and shake it until one fell out, to bring him the number and he would tell David what the rest of his life would be like.

David had to make a quick trip to Taipei, and we decided that we'd spend our free evening at the racetrack. Having visited a fortune-teller and a few Taoist temples made us feel lucky. Also, David told us he had a friend who had just won $2 million Hong Kong dollars. "But that's the first time I ever remember him winning. And he's probably spent 80 percent of his salary for the last 10 years at the track," he said.

We wanted to go to Happy Valley to watch the races, because that was the older of Hong Kong's two tracks, occupying a site that has been used for horse racing since the founding of Hong Kong. The track sits in an area of the island jocularly named because the English settlers thought it to be a nice place to live. Then they discovered malaria, and the only permanent residents of Happy Valley became horses and dead people. Today the track is surrounded by cemeteries and apartment houses, its land as valuable as gold. But somehow no one has ever suggested that the track be torn down and sold to real-estate developers.

As it happened, the night we wanted to go the races took place in the New Territories at Shatin, a track completed in 1978 on reclaimed land at the world record price of $100 million U.S. dollars. No one in Hong Kong has suggested that the Jockey Club, which runs the tracks, overpaid, for horse racing is in Hong Kong what praying is in Rome.

The high priests of this religion are the 12 stewards of the Royal Hong Kong Jockey Club, the largest private employer in the Colony. The Jockey Club is not permitted by law to keep the take, so it has built a score of hospitals and recreational facilities. To even know a steward in the Jockey Club is fodder for bragging, especially to visitors, i.e., "My friend, Y.T.—did I tell you he is a steward—well, the other morning he went to the loo."

More is bet on a single day of races in Hong Kong than in all of the tracks of England combined. (In 1985, H.K. $20 billion were wagered on horse racing, about U.S. $400 for every man, woman and child in the Colony.) On Saturday afternoon it is impossible to hail a taxi and those that cruise do so with the radio blasting news of ponies. Often whichever of the two tracks is idle fills up with spectators who watch the races on large television screens.

To get to Shatin we mounted the MTR, another Asian enterprise that mocked American know-how. Construction began on the Mass Transit Railway, Hong Kong's subway, in 1978, and the first line opened before schedule in February 1980. The system carries 42,000 passengers per route kilometer, about the same as Tokyo's; New York, by comparison, carries about 15,000. Most remarkably, the system, which is graffiti-free, pays for itself.

We climbed aboard at the Tsim Sha Tsui station and rode to Kowloon Tong station, where we transferred to the KCR (Kowloon Canton Railway). On both trains we were the only *gwailos.* The cars were packed but that didn't really bother us as we stood a head taller than anyone else.

The Jockey Club naturally has a swank enclosure for the privileged, but we weren't invited so we stood along the rail with thousands of nutty bettors. We barely understood the exotic bets available and finally out of exasperation bought a few quinella tickets.

After the race frenzy subsided, we faced the task of figuring out whether we had won. No one spoke English. We stopped a few people and showed them our tickets. Finally, one man pointed excitedly to one of them and pulled out a wad of money. His companion pushed him away and made a gesture that we assumed meant he was offering more money. A crowd assembled, and we were enjoying the role of auctioneer until it dawned on us just to go to the ticket window and cash it in for what it really was worth. As we walked away we could swear that there were more than a few racetrack goers who were amazed at how dumb the *gwailos* could be.

One Saturday afternoon we met David at the Fragrant City restaurant, near Boundary Street, which divided Kowloon from the New Territories, to take a *dim sum* and visit some blocks where tourists don't and would not want to go. One thing we had learned about Hong Kong restaurants: It's not easy finding a table for three. The Fragrant City served as a case in point. The clatter of dishes and cackle of children called up sound effects from an earthquake. Mothers grabbed their tots out of the way of the young girls who pushed the carts containing the little plates of food. The place, done tastefully in fire-engine red and gold lamé, went on without end; if it had four walls we didn't see them. And every table, most of them accommodating eight or more, was full.

"Maybe we will have to share a table with a family," David advised, "because no one comes in as just two or three."

We had no problem with that. In the end, the diners shunned us. (Why would anyone want to sit with us on their free afternoon out?) Our concern on that day was that due to bad cash management; we only had $4.80 among the three of us. Yet, we ate with abandon and managed to leave with 30 cents in our pockets.

We walked over to the Golden Arcade that David had advertised as the world's largest cut-rate computer mall in the world. He was right. All we had heard about Asia's disrespect for copyright laws stood on display in this three-story maze of high-tech hawkers. Programs that fetched $700 in the States could be had for $12 before any bargaining ever began. Hardware, too, was available for a fraction of the price we were used to.

"One day they'll shut this place down," David predicted. "It is so well-known and so successful that the day they want to make a showing against counterfeit items this will be the first place they will come."

Most of the clientele was in their teens, and although we couldn't eavesdrop we guessed that their heated conversations with the proprietors belonged well into the technical category. We proudly called ourselves computer literate because we could input a manuscript onto a disk; these kids, some of them young enough to be our children, apparently were arguing over far more sophisticated levels of literacy. What also was surprising was that there were many hipster teens around us, the type we saw in line at the Chicago disco. In the United States their counterparts spent a Saturday at a different kind of shopping mall discussing subjects other than how Lisa didn't work. Had we finally found a place where it was cool to be smart?

We went on. Between the Golden Arcade and the container port stand endless rows of well-worn 10- and 12- story buildings that reminded us of municipal prisons in the States—except the sound emanating from them were not complaints over our criminal justice system but the monotonous hum of machinery occasionally broken by the rumble of a passing truck. On this Saturday there was no foot traffic to speak of—just two tall blond guys and their kinetic host.

"This is the plan," David strategized at the entrance to one of the buildings. "We'll walk to the top and then stop on every floor on the way down. I'll give whoever is in charge my card and tell them you are buyers from the States and I am your representative."

"What are we buying?"

David was impatient. "Come on, you'll see as we climb up."

We stopped at the first landing and opened the fire door. We saw a sign that had someone's name followed by "Textiles." David turned, "On this floor you'll be textile buyers."

We started climbing again. "But we don't know anything about textiles."

David looked back, "Make it up."

"But we don't know enough to even fake it."

He stopped somewhere between the fifth and sixth floors, put his hands on his hips and looked down at us. "You two? You two could fake anything. You're the biggest bullshitters I ever met. You faked my parents out."

"How do you figure?"

"You told them you knew nothing about Hong Kong. Then you take them to a fortune-teller, and now they think you know everything about Hong Kong."

"If we did, then why would we need you? Did you tell them that?"

David had started climbing again. "Sure, I told them that. I told them you spent one day in Hong Kong and were lucky enough to find a fortune-teller. They shouldn't be impressed."

"What'd they say?"

He scowled, "They said that if you were that lucky in one day then I should spend more time with you."

We started on the 10th floor with a huge room filled with sewing machines, each manned by a young woman oblivious to the distraction we created.

We stood there for a few moments until a young man came over and introduced himself in a not so friendly manner. David explained that we were buyers from the States looking for new suppliers.

The manager reacted quickly. "Sorry, exclusive. Exclusive. No sale," he said and showed us to the door.

"Good strategy, David."

He held his palms up. "How was I to know they make exclusive. They don't want you to see their new line." He bounded down the steps. "Come on, we'll stop only at the even floors."

On the eighth floor another warren of women were at work. This time they were making uniforms for Swedish waitresses. We presented no threat to this operation, and the manager happily showed us about."These American gentlemen represent a very large restaurant chain," David assured him as he handed over his business card.

On the sixth floor they were making toys. The manager really didn't believe our story, and said that no one was allowed on the factory floor because of the number of spies in the industry. Instead, he showed us a year-old catalog and said if we'd leave our business cards he'd send the new one when it was ready. David saved us by donating his card and telling the manager to work through him.

"I know you're not seeing much," David apologized as we worked our way down. "But let me assure you that this is the heart of Hong Kong's industry."

"How can all these one-floor factories add up to that?" we asked.

"Because there are thousands of them. Everything here is textile or electronics or trade. Something fast that doesn't require a lot of capital or long-range planning."

We were witnessing the secret of Hong Kong's success—its abundance of well-managed, cheap labor in a flexible setting. While the Mainland and India could bury Hong Kong in sheer numbers of laborers, no other place stood ready to match Hong Kong's ability to produce top-quality new lines at a moment's notice. Velocity, flexibility and quality, above all, were Hong Kong's trademarks.

We had reached the ground floor again and meandered around a number of shipping containers. "You see," David said. "They put the items right in the containers and they go out on ships. We don't have room for warehouses, and we don't have time to build inventories of items that either will go out of date, or once they're hot they'll be made more cheaply someplace else."

We walked toward another factory area. Along the way we passed businessmen whose suits ranked with the finest in the world and ancient inhabitants of the streets, pajama-clad, their withered faces bent over tin rice bowls. Here was a McDonald's, and here was a hawker selling hairy chicken's feet. Here was a newspaper reporting on the financing of a proposed airport, and here was a barber cutting hair on the sidewalk. Here was a street with shops selling only birds—house birds, lucky birds, pretty birds, and here was a customer in a Mercedes stopping to buy some. Here were the crackling sounds of mah-jongg tiles falling, and here were the jackhammers of a new city of public housing. Here was David Wang educated in Mississippi, and here was the son of a fretful mother desperately concocting ways to beat the March marriage deadline.

Above all, here was a seriousness about industry. And we saw it again in a cinder-block square building stuck in the shadow of a high-rise apartment house.

"This is interesting," David warned. He leaned against a rusted oil drum, playing the tour guide of the bowels of commerce. "This building is a factory, too, but everyone only has one room, like a closet. And they all live in the public housing across the street. I bet not one of them has even been on the Star Ferry. Their whole world is on this block . . . just going back and forth."

There hung a decided stench of sweat in the darkened corridors of this factory building. Many of the cubicles held small printing presses, and we slalomed through stacks of calendars and instruction books. One man and his son were gluing rubber soles onto shoes. Another was punching a design mold into a small metal box.

"These people work all the time," David said. "And when they don't work someone in their family is working for them."

"Do they make much money?"

David asked one. "He said no. But I don't believe him. Everybody here lies about money."

After about 20 minutes David stopped us. "Rest time," he announced. We sat on the concrete steps of a landing.

"Too bad we can't afford a Coke," London lamented.

"Do you think you can panhandle us some change, David?" Kelly wanted to know.

His jaw slackened. "Sure, these people will feel sorry for you." He paused. "Are you nuts?"

"We can try."

David shook his head. "Come on, let's keep going. I hope you're not serious. Charity really isn't a word we use in Cantonese."

There were about 30 rooms per floor. Inside them, we glimpsed a metal stamping machine, a sewing machine to put labels on shirts, a stamp to adhere two halves of a cassette tape.

We stopped to chat with a few men at work, but no one really wanted to waste time with us. David was right about the working hours, though; most of the shops stayed open about 18 hours a day in shifts worked by various family members.

"There are six buildings in this complex," David said. "Thirty factories per floor, five floors per building times six buildings." He asked a printer if he could borrow his calculator. "That's 900 businesses right here in front of you. And each has an entire family working in it."

David stopped us. "Listen," he said.

We told him we heard nothing unusual.

"The ticking. You hear it?"

We told him we didn't.

He pointed all around, at the factory buildings and the apartment houses. He smiled. "That's funny. I hear it. And I bet they all hear it too."

Once there was a time when our trip to Lok Ma Chan, a small hill in the New Territories, would have gained a special place in our memories. David drove us there one day, then pointed to a pair of pay-for-the-scenic-view binoculars and told us that for 10 cents we could see China.

"You heard about how Hong Kong is the window," he said. "Well, for years this was the only view."

There was little to see. Certainly no allegedly paper mansions as we had seen through the mists of Quemoy or the Korean DMZ. Just an expanse of farmland with a few roads. Still, we felt some excitement as if we had tasted an illicit fruit. We could imagine how many thousands of American tourists had visited this spot in the 1970s and returned home bragging, "And I saw Red China."

Fortunately, we could get closer. David sent us to get visas at China Travel Service, the official tourist representative in Hong Kong. (We found it odd that such a function would be carried out by an apparent travel agency; still odder, however, was that Beijing's leading emissary to Hong Kong was not an ambassador or minister but the head of the official news agency, Xin Hua.) We found the visa process remarkably efficient; the price depended on how quickly you wanted results, and we received ours in a matter of hours.

We traveled to the border on the Kowloon Canton Railway, passing the Shatin racetrack and the gleaming planned urban satellite cities that sat in the shadow of the mother country. How ironic that so many had come so far only to go *back* again. He wondered about the feelings that permeated these places—fear, nostalgia, fatigue, anticipation. Would the captors be liberated, or would history repeat itself, this time with nowhere to run.

The train, as with everything in Hong Kong, was crowded. David appeared fidgety.

"What's the matter?"

"Nothing." He was lying, we could tell. After the factory tour he had been elated and told us how much he liked palling around—"I'd never go to these places if it wasn't for you," he confided. We had celebrated over a goose dinner alongside the San Miguel brewery, where the beer was fresh and plentiful. The place, which specialized in greasy but tasty goose, was a hangout for cabdrivers, and we could tell that David actually was relaxing, away from the telex and his parents. But now on the train he seemed downcast.

His mood deepened even more as we reached the Lo Wu station. He answered our usual battery of questions with monosyllables, without his customary sarcasm and sprite.

We barely could exit the train, the platform was so thick with travelers. "I think about two hours," said David surveying the throng.

"Why do so many people want to go back?"

"To visit relatives, bring gifts. Do business. Many reasons."

As we reached the enclosure we could see a very narrow river with rolls of barbed wire on each side. Yet, the physical unfriendliness of the border contrasted with the thousands of visitors going back and forth.

David had become downright sullen. He told us that he would have to go to different immigration lines from us and that we should meet him at the taxi stand.

"If I'm not there before it is dark, then go to the hotel without me. I'll catch up with you," he said.

"Why would you be delayed?"

"Because this is China, not Hong Kong. It may not be different for you. But it is very, very different for me."

"How so?"

We were carrying on a conversation in loud whispers as our lines diverged. David surveyed the line of humanity of which he was a part. "Because if they decide to let us across and then decide we can't go back, then I am history. You have lost your guide, and I am a coolie."

"You're serious, aren't you?"

He said nothing, but the expression on his face answered for him.

We walked over the wooden bridge into Shenzhen and waited. Hundreds of people walked past, many of them bent low to the ground with the weight of television sets and other electronics ware. We looked intently for David and began to worry. We thought he had been kidding in order to add a touch of melodrama. The afternoon wore on, however, without any sign of him.

We thought about what to do if in fact he had been detained. Obviously, the American consul would be of no use. Even though he had gone to school there, David couldn't even get a visa because of American fear of an exodus from Hong Kong. The British authorities in Hong Kong? Would they really demand the return of a Chinese-born citizen at this time? Wouldn't they pretend he had gone quietly in the night? The Chinese probably would claim we had made up the whole thing. These were the imaginings we had. Who knows the scenarios which David played out in his head.

Finally, he showed. "Sorry, guys. The line was long. I was hoping you'd wait. I hope you weren't worried."

"No, not at all."

There was little to distinguish Shenzhen from Aberdeen:

they both were miniature Hong Kongs. Skyscrapers appeared here and there; the noise of construction filled the air. One unusual sight, however, was the number of bicycles. They all lined up at a traffic light ready to pounce ahead in a flash.

"Shenzhen is not China," David said. We were riding in a taxi weaving among construction barriers. "Get that idea out of your heads right away. It is a special economic zone set up as like a classroom for the rest of China to see if they can tolerate capitalism."

"Who pays for all this," we wanted to know. The place was booming.

"Mostly Hong Kong money. A way to hedge your bets in case China decides to use Shenzhen in place of Hong Kong. And if not, at least these guys will have gotten on the good side of the government." David looked somewhat relaxed and added, "This is where my curtain factory will be."

All of the signs in our hotel lobby were in English. We told David our first stop had to be the restaurant because we were dying for a plate of noodles. Unfortunately, the closest we could get was spaghetti and meatballs.

"I can't believe this," London complained. "We finally get to China and we can't have Chinese food?" We could have had hot dogs (the American kind, not what is usually associated with China), milk shakes or steaks. But nothing Oriental.

"Ask them to cook up a plate of noodles," London asked of David.

He refused.

"Why not?"

"They will lose face. They think this hotel is what Americans are looking for when they come to China. If you complain about the food they will be insulted."

A coquettish teenager eating ham and eggs with an older man caught our eye. David noticed.

"Forget it. Forget it," he waved his hand in front of our eyes. "Don't even think about it."

"About what?"

"Sex. That's what. She's probably for sale. That's her pimp. You take her to your room and I go to jail."

"David, you are paranoid."

"No," he insisted. "Just careful." He saw two men standing

at the restaurant entrance looking lost. They wore blue shirts and matching pants and stood out from the customers because of their drabness. David excused himself.

We waited for him in the lobby, where we had to shoo away endless requests from bellboys and waiters to get something for us.

David returned. "My business is done."

"What did you do?"

"Those were my suppliers from Manchuria. One I gave a tin of cookies, the other a carton of cigarettes. They are happy."

"That's it? That's why you came here?"

He nodded. "We do business by telex. But they wanted a chance to come to Shenzhen, so they asked me to telex them about an important meeting. Just an excuse to get away."

We asked about the gifts.

"I can't give them money, and they don't drink. They can't get cookies or American cigarettes, so they are happy. They will be away for days and go back with an order that they already had before they left."

We went sightseeing the next day. We asked a cabdriver to take us as far as he could in an hour, and we ended up in a small village with no paved roads. Animals and children kicked up dust. Two-story cement houses stood behind gray walls. Everyone stared as we walked by. Women sat on stoops and beat their laundry. A little girl defecated in our path. (Was she trying to tell us something?) There were no cars, only bicycles. Nothing was colorful, nothing pretty. We had been in literally 50 towns like this in Brazil and always had found a bar, a pool table and fast friends. Here we found nothing but a quiet place we were sure we did not understand.

David sensed the eeriness. "It's like stepping back in time," he said. "This is old China. For you this may be interesting. Not for me. Maybe this will become the new Hong Kong. Maybe Hong Kong will become the old China. You can go home and wait for the answer in the newspaper. I can't."

A man named George Tan had cropped up in a lot of conversations during our visit. Even at that first meal at the New World Centre, Leon had assured us, "You will want to see the trial of George Tan. You will learn a lot about how business is done if you follow his story."

David urged us often to visit the courtroom to bring him

up to date on the case. Hong Kong observed English law, which prohibited reporting of an ongoing trial. Those who followed the Tan trial did so from clippings sent to them by friends and relatives in places like Taiwan or Singapore. "If I went I'd probably be lost in what they were saying. But you go, and then we'll have a dinner with some of my friends. You can practice your journalism with them," David promised like a parent.

The Tan trial began on February 27, 1986 and was predicted to last for more than a year. We weren't in any hurry, and we figured we'd find out what was going on before we went for a visit. It was one of a thousand business scandals that plague fast-and-loose Hong Kong. Only, as we were to discover, it was juicier than most. We became obsessed with the details.

It had begun to unfold in early 1983 with the discovery of the body of Jalil Ibrahim, a 33-year-old assistant manager of Bumiputra Malaysia Finance, a bank controlled by the Malaysian government. Jalil had been sent from Kuala Lumpur to Hong Kong to help work out a complicated series of bad loans the bank had made to several local companies. He found it frustrating, lonely work and, as he wrote to his wife, he felt he was not getting the cooperation he needed from his colleagues.

One night in July he was asked to do a favor for a man introduced as a prominent Malaysian businessman. The man wanted to buy $5,000 in travelers checks and asked Jalil to come to his room at the Regent. There, in as fine a hotel room as money can buy, Jalil was strangled to death.

Two days later, police found his body stuffed in a suitcase that had been dropped in a banana grove in Taipo-Kau, a waterfront town deep in the New Territories and not far from the Chinese border. They quickly discovered his identity and learned through sources that one of Jalil's last acts had been to hold up a loan intended for one of the myriad holding companies owned by this man George Tan, who at the time was a rising star in Hong Kong business circles.

After Jalil's body was found, the police decided to take a closer look at Tan and raided his office to seize records. As a result the bank's intended bailout of Tan's companies was scuttled.

A few months later, the body of John Wimbush, one of the most prominent lawyers in Hong Kong, was found at the bottom of his swimming pool with a manhole cover tied around his neck. Friends say he left a note suggesting that his death was suicide. He had been depressed about business. As senior partner in the firm of Deacons, his primary client was George Tan.

We visited a prominent solicitor, a friend of Wimbush's, who was a senior partner at one of Deacons' rival for prestige among the British firms of Hong Kong. "When I first heard of John's death I thought it was murder," he told us. "I very well couldn't see him so bloody depressed to do something like this.

"But," he added. "The six-page letter. No murder victim I know of writes letters of remorse before dying."

We sipped tea and looked around his wood-paneled office. No trace of the empire's demise had intruded into these quarters. The top partners still had English names and schooling. Our companion would be leaving that night to spend the summer months in Britain.

"I think John killed himself, if that's what he did, because so many people lost so much," he said. "Not George Tan, mind you, or the Carrian people. That was the name of Tan's company, you know. Carrian. Always reminds me of carrion. It was ordinary people who had invested in these deals. And I don't think they were structured soundly."

We asked him if the Tan trial really stood out as an exceptional event.

He leaned back in his rich leather chair and stared at the ceiling. "Yes and no. When you get down to it all it was was land speculation. The Chinese, you know, are gamblers and great speculators. They know how to squeeze the last penny out of a piece of property.

"But Tan, you know, may have the added an element of greed. Money is so terribly important to Hong Kong. Tan made so much so quickly people worshipped him. Money is what this place is all about, you know."

As Tan's saga unfolded to us it bore some similarities to a fictional American success story—that of Jay Gatsby. Once he began his fall people became uncertain about the phenomenon and when they actually first had heard of George Tan and where he had come from. That was unusual for Hong Kong. Despite its population explosion, Hong Kong really is a small town. From the highest to the lowest level of commerce, men still do business with people their families have known for generations. A handshake will seal a million-dollar loan.

"A British banker here will ask what assets you have to secure a loan," the British lawyer explained to us. "An American banker will ask if you have the cash flow to service the debt. But a Chinese banker will ask who was your father."

Hong Kong is really the capital of a country that appears on no maps. Call it Overseas China, a loose federation of refugees including many astute businessmen who have set up shop in places like Singapore, Malaysia, Thailand and Indonesia but find common ground in the financial markets of Hong Kong.

When Tan arrived in the mid-1970s as if from behind a curtain, people assumed he was part of this mysterious world of Chinese high finance. He was a rare character in Hong Kong, an outsider who rose to the top. Still, we heard that Tan passed himself off as a protégé of the wealthy Chung family, so many assumed he was a distant relative. (We later learned that he was born to a Hokkien merchant family in Sibu, Sarawak on the island of Borneo.) He had studied engineering in England, then started a series of businesses in Singapore, the last of which reportedly went bankrupt. In 1971, Tan set his sights on Hong Kong with a very simple notion of supply, demand and the velocity with which money could be made.

George Tan apparently also had one other attribute: an iron stomach. He learned quickly the psychology of the Hong Kong market and realized that with the wildly escalating prices of the late 1970s, bankers barely had time to appraise the underlying value of a real-estate asset. Banks were awash in cash and eager to lend; you could name the amount. Tan wasted no time. He gave life to the exaggeration often heard in Hong Kong: It's the only place you can land your plane at 10 o'clock, form a company by noon and start trading on the stock exchange by 2.

In 1977, he formed his main company—Carrian Holdings Limited—which would give birth in short order to a corporate family tree that resembled the electrical circuitry for a nuclear power plant. Tan's first foray into the financial pages occurred in 1979 with his acquisition of Mai Hon Enterprises, the property subsidiary of a watchmaking company. As an indication of what he was capable of, Tan purchased a piece of property for

$200,000 and several months later refinanced it with the Chinese Bank of Communications for $3 million. But that was not real money, at least by Hong Kong standards. And besides, there were some signs the property boom was running out of steam. When the frenzy died, so would the hope of pyramiding profits. Tan decided to create his own frenzy, but he needed a Big Deal—and fast.

One of the properties on that golden strip of Central land that we had toured with David Wang was called Gammon House, a 42-story structure also built by Jardine's that somewhat resembles the Building of 1,000 Assholes, but with square windows instead of round, giving it the appearance of a computer punch card standing on end. The old-line British managers of Hong Kong Land Co. had made a mistake in 1978 by "going Chinese," as those who like to maintain the proprieties of the Colony say, and gave in to speculation fever. They purchased Gammon House from Jardine's for $100 million and quickly discovered that given the cost of funds and rental yield, it was a money-losing proposition. With the boom dying, it looked like they would end up the greatest fools. Then Tan, who was nobody's fool, heard of their plight.

With funds he said came from overseas Chinese investors, Tan used Carrian Holdings to buy Gammon House, paying the astonishing sum of H.K. $998 million or about U.S. $140 million.

He then *gave* the building to Mai Hon, which he had renamed Carrian Investments, Ltd., sending the stock market into a frenzy and tripling the price of CIL shares.

Finally, he announced the sale of Gammon House to another group for U.S. $200 million—a profit of $60 million for CIL, which he controlled.

People took notice.

Almost singlehandedly, Tan had refueled the property boom. He went from obscurity to stardom in record time; in his first major-league start he threw a no-hitter. What did it matter that no one had heard of him or knew where his money came from or even understood the terms of the sale? The hard-working folks of Hong Kong don't keep their money in mattresses; they gamble it in one form or another, and Tan had got the game rolling again. He was adored by widows, orphans and bankers alike. The Chinese phrase they attached to him was, "Rain in the right season." The only question that mattered was, what will he do next?

"Carrian brings together some of the world's wealthiest overseas Chinese," the Hong Kong *Standard* wrote of the holding company that consolidated Tan's enterprises, "and reportedly has access to vast Middle Eastern funds." Other stories said Carrian was investing funds for Philippine President Ferdinand Marcos and even the Soviet Union's Moscow Narodny Bank. Under Hong Kong law, he didn't have to say where the money came from and he coyly did not.

Almost immediately after the Gammon House deal the cream of British colonial finance began to climb on board. Vickers da Costa, a respected brokerage house, wrote a gushing report predicting that Carrian shares would "continue to be highly rewarding" and added, "One thing of which Carrian Investments can not be accused is being a dull share." Hong Kong Land, happy with its profit from Gammon House, embarked on a series of deals with Tan, each at a more astonishing price than the last. This is when the late John Wimbush and his law firm of Deacons signed on as solicitors and Price Waterhouse was retained as auditors. Wardley investment bankers came in as advisers and finally the mighty Hong Kong Shanghai Bank began lending money.

"Once Hong Kong Bank was in, everyone wanted in," our solicitor friend told us. "They are the bluest of blood in this part of the world and who could question their judgment?"

The credit tap was open for Tan. Barclays Bank syndicated one loan, as did such multinational giants as Commerzbank and Westdeutsche Landesbank of West Germany, Banque Paribas of France and Bankers Trust, Crocker National and Bank of America.

Tan continued to do a series of real-estate deals, always buying at a hefty premium, but he also began to craft a conglomerate that included one of the Colony's largest shipping companies, Grand Marine, an insurance company called China Underwriters, a taxi and bus fleet and a tourism company. He was bidding for an airline and hoped to gain a vertical monopoly that would allow Carrian interests to take a tourist from hotel to tour and back home. He also bought property in the United

States, including a deal that wowed the city fathers of Oakland with a promise of the tallest building in the West. By 1981, Tan commanded a work force of 33,000.

"Hong Kong's newest *taipan*," the *South China Morning Post* called him, conferring the traditional title for the handful of the Colony's great financiers. The press said Carrian represented the birth of a new hong or trading company, a worthy home-grown successor to the declining British fortunes.

His image was mysterious and mythic. He gave few interviews and his rare comments were, for the Chinese, appropriately humble. "There are no heroes in Carrian," he said once. He shied away from the social scene and claimed a 20-hour workday.

"I believe in the simple life, sincere, honest. I enjoy going to the food stall for a bowl of noodles and a cup of coffee costing 30 cents," Tan said. He did, however, evidence a passion for Rolls-Royces, purchasing five of the Colony's preferred automobiles of status. He lavished gifts on business associates, often starting meetings by handing out Rolex watches. His offices were decorated with what visitors said were extraordinary European paintings and antiques, and he even purchased the Star of Asia diamond for $2.8 million in cash from Van Cleef and Arpels.

He was a devoted follower of *fung shui*. On the advice of his personal *fung shui* adviser, he refused to travel over water and agreed not to leave Hong Kong until after his 45th birthday. He adhered to his lucky numbers, 3, 6, 8 and 9, such as in the H.K. $998-million purchase price of Gammon House. (Eight is a particularly lucky number in Hong Kong because its Cantonese translation—"paat"—is very close to the word for prosperity—"faat.")

While Tan was on his rapid rise, one of the few dissenters in the press was Philip Bowring, deputy editor of the *Far Eastern Economic Review*, who asked on several occasions, "Who controls the group and what is the source of its apparent limitless supply of money?"

His money, Tan finally said, came from four Tan families in Malaysia and Singapore with interests in shipping and timber.

Then Bowring posed the more important question. Given that most of the real-estate deals seem to be trades among a small group of companies, "Where do the profits come from?"

There was no answer forthcoming, though shortly after the churlish question was asked one of the dailies ran a story headlined, "Booming Carrian Outgrows Its Critics."

The reason no one looked too deeply at Carrian was because that isn't the way business is done in Hong Kong.

We visited Philip Bowring in his cramped, dusty quarters in a walk-up on Gloucester Road in the Wanchai district of the island. Bowring's magazine occupies an odd place in Asian journalism. Under the editorship of Derek Davies, the *Far Eastern Economic Review* probably is the most respected business journal and perhaps the most abstruse. We found it possible to wander through many stories without understanding what they were talking about, only to soon meet someone who raved about it. We often wondered if we were missing an inside joke or if the rituals of Asian business were beyond us.

Bowring wore no celebratory crown as many American muckrakers do when their prey finally falls. He said that once he began looking at Carrian the house of cards was pretty much evident. "You've got to understand that there's an easy-money attitude here to begin with. Couple that with the Carrian boom and the identity of those aboard and you can imagine the auditors weren't auditing too closely."

"But still, how could all of these sophisticated law firms and banks be fooled?" we asked.

Bowring interrupted us to quickly edit a piece. "They were fooled because they wanted to be fooled. Tan hired two of his own auditors at Price Waterhouse to work for Carrian. And Deacons? How much do you think they collected in fees? Millions."

It just seemed odd that so much could go on in plain sight without anyone blowing the whistle, we told him.

"I guess that's the problem still with Americans," Bowring sneered. "Too many virgins. Think about it. Whoever stopped doing business with Carrian had to say in effect, 'This boom's not for me.' And who is going to do that? In Hong Kong?" He gave us one of those how-stupid-can-you-guys-be looks that we were getting accustomed to.

Besides purity, another difference between American business and Hong Kong's is that Hong Kong has almost no securities regulations and disclosure laws. Those on the books are rarely enforced. Major corporate transactions are often not reported. It is a simple matter to incorporate, and many companies, including those publicly traded, are held in nominee names, protecting the real owners. The public often does not know who owns what, and as the Tan case revealed, neither do the bankers.

Banks are allowed unlimited secret reserves from which they can draw to smooth out earnings, making published statements meaningless as a gauge of performance. Even the Hong Kong government has a secret reserve fund for bank bailouts, recently estimated at $5 billion (or about one-third the size of the United States's Federal Deposit Insurance Corporation) after being tapped for a series of failures.

Inside dealing, as broadly interpreted in the United States, whether in stocks or real estate, is not a crime in Hong Kong and carries no penalties. And in a Confucian culture where you trust a third cousin with your life, there are a lot of insiders. The laws have some provisions against banks making loans to directors or related companies, but they also are rarely enforced.

Tan took advantage of it all, and then some.

Had anyone really paid attention, they would have noticed that the supposedly brilliant Gammon House deal was a death-defying high-wire act that almost ended up on the floor. Although Tan publicly announced the sale and entered it on his books at a profit, in reality the deal never went through. The group Tan was selling to could not come up with the cash, if in fact they ever intended to, and Tan had to do some scrambling. His solution was masterful. He patched together a complex rescue, selling off individual floors, first to the Bank of America, which paid $124 million in cash for 15 floors and the right to put its name on the building, then to other banks to whom he owed money. Eventually the banks were the losers when the market decided that the price for the sum of the parts was not worth more than the whole.

Tan, of course, was on to other things. His method was this: Pay top dollar, but on deferred terms. If he bought a company, he'd secure the loan with Carrian stock—a seemingly wonderful asset appreciating by the day. If he bought property, he'd mortgage it, then borrow against the increase in value again. In a rising market, everybody can be happy and Tan's schemes aren't so uncommon in Hong Kong or elsewhere in the world. What was unique, though, was that the market was rising *because* of all the activity Tan was creating. He was a one-man typhoon of transactions, a market-maker.

Tan would use his latest borrowings to pay interest on earlier loans and make tiny down payments on new property. By paying a premium price, he found lots of sellers. Meanwhile, each purchase boosted the value of Carrian Investment stock, which he then leveraged mercilessly to wrest more money from the banks.

Along the way he created a web of hundreds of companies, most with no assets. He bought and sold assets among those companies in a series of paper transactions that created the illusion of profit. For instance, he announced the sale of a block of Union Bank stock on December 31 and booked a tidy profit—no matter that the buyer was a company he controlled and the deal never closed. Sometimes he would have one company guarantee a loan for a second company, though neither had any real assets.

Tan also raised funds from the stock market with some clever sleight of hand. He sold to a group of investment bankers a new offering of shares that Carrian Holdings, the private company, would be willing to repurchase at a premium the following year. Carrian Holdings, however, had no cash to repurchase anything; its prime asset was the Investment's shares. As Bowring had said, a lot of sophisticated people believed because they wanted to believe.

Tan's challenge was to keep up the illusion until either the real-estate market caught up with him and he could actually sell the overpriced property, or until his productive enterprises, such as shipping and tourism companies, began to produce enough cash flow to service his debt.

In our search for Tan's skeptics we looked up Raymond Sacklyn, publisher of a local financial newsletter called *Target,* who made a career of unearthing Hong Kong's financial scandals. Sacklyn told us that he had breakfast each morning at the Lee Gardens Hotel, a moderately priced tourist hotel in the Causeway Bay district, and that's where we could find him. He warned us on the telephone that he left promptly for work at 8.

He had a reputation as a respected gadfly, and we expected him to lash into Tan and the Hong Kong business community for its hypocritical support of the scoundrel. Instead, Sacklyn surprised us; he defended George Tan. "Maybe he did some things wrong, but George Tan wasn't just a scam artist. I believe his intention was always to create a real operating company. He just moved too fast."

Sacklyn fielded a phone call that undoubtedly had been planned in advance to give him a graceful exit if he wanted to ditch us. Yet, he returned to his scrambled eggs and continued as if he had never left off. "Tan sent his taxi drivers to Tokyo to take lessons on how to behave politely. He spent a lot of money cleaning up all the buses. You wouldn't do that if you were just going to skim off all the money. He wanted a real empire. He once told me he wanted to be bigger than Jardine's. And who knows? If only he could have kept ahead of the money."

Sacklyn stroked his beard and looked at us carefully. "You guys seem to know what you're doing. Forget Carrian, that's history." He reached into a pile of papers he'd been reading when we arrived. "You want a big one from me? West German bank, Far Eastern investors?"

We told him we would be happy enough to piece together the Carrian story.

"I've got one here," he pulled out another sheet. "Eighty-five million defrauded. They bought up television stations."

No thanks, we told him. Just Tan.

He looked disappointed and dove back into the eggs. "I knew George Tan. I think he was done in by his middle management. They just couldn't keep up with him."

We asked Sacklyn about the high-priced talent surrounding Tan. "I told Tan that just because a guy's white doesn't mean he's competent or honest," he told us between bites.

We apologized to Sacklyn for keeping him after 8. He waved us off. "No problem. You sure you don't want a scandal?"

We assured him we didn't and stood up to leave.

"Sit down just for a moment," he insisted. "Then what about me? Do you want any information? I'm a millionaire in anyone's country. There's no one I don't know."

One of Sacklyn's observations seemed right on point: Tan was the speed king of Hong Kong's finance. For him velocity of money was the key. In one sense, Tan was managing an elaborate check-kiting scheme, using a small amount of money to keep paying off a vastly larger debt. When one loan came due, he pulled the cash from any enterprise that had it to make the payment or borrow from someplace else. Others have tried the same sort of superleveraging, but rarely on such a scale. That he kept it up for as long as he did was remarkable. But then for all the risk, Tan was performing with a secret safety net.

As later became apparent, Tan had tapped into one of the all-time mother lodes of free money. Despite all the myth and rumor about Tan's original source of funds—because even with all the borrowing, there had to be a substantial trove of cash somewhere—his sugar daddy was the strange institution called Bumiputra Malaysia Finance.

Bumiputra means "sons of the soil" in Malay and refers to native Malaysians. Since the British granted independence to its onetime colony in the 1950s, there has been a long and sometimes violent dispute between the overseas Chinese, who control much of the nation's wealth, and the native Malays. BMF was started to rectify the situation. How or why the Hong Kong branch, which was supposed to be attracting deposits and funneling them back home, ended up loaning vast sums to a Chinese enterprise is one of the untold stories. But it became clear that BMF's loan decisions were not being made on the basis of rational business judgments.

Though no one knows whether the relationship extends back to Malaysia, Tan developed close friendships with several of the BMF officials in Hong Kong. He called general manager Lorrain Osman "Uncle Lorrain" and other officials said Tan was like "a member of the family." Tan would give them cars, including a Daimler, a Mercedes and a Rolls, and sometimes blocks of stock in one of his companies. Several of the BMF officers served as officers of Tan companies. The *Asian Wall Street Journal* reported that Tan once guaranteed a million-dollar loan for one top BMF official.

In return, it seemed, Tan could have all the money he wanted. At various times he borrowed more than a billion dollars from the bank, much of it just on a signature. He could tell BMF what a property was worth and they'd mortgage it for him. As it turned out, BMF wasn't much more gullible than any of the other bankers—just more deeply involved.

But for a time, it seemed all the maneuvering wouldn't

matter. In early 1982, Tan was certainly no more than one step ahead of his creditors, but he was moving forward, which was what counted. His businesses were generating cash flow; the real-estate market, while not leaping ahead, was still stable. And the Hang Seng stock index—the Dow Jones of Hong Kong—was strong, with most observers expecting it to top 2,000 by year end. It seemed that by force of will, Tan would become the king of Hong Kong. For a short time, a few months at most, he was worth over a billion dollars. In two years, he had gone from virtually nothing to become one of the richest men in the world.

And then came an event that even the imaginative George Tan could not control: Maggie Thatcher's visit to Beijing in September 1982, and her insistence that Britain would stand by the Treaty of Nanking and hold on to Hong Kong and Kowloon. The Chinese, who already had adopted all the leases-or-else posture, were offended. Fear of a scorched-earth reaction filled the air in Hong Kong. The stock market began to tremble.

In a week, the Hang Seng index fell 280 points, wiping out over 25 percent of the value of the shares; it would close the year at half its opening quote.

The real-estate market died even faster. Who wanted to own something the communists were going to take over in 15 years? A lot of people were at risk and lost a lot of money. Carrian and George Tan lost the most.

Tan had loans coming due continuously. There was no market to sell property, and, with the plunge of stock prices, bankers were calling for more collateral for stock-backed loans. If that weren't enough, the world shipping market suffered a disastrous plunge because of overcapacity and Tan's Grand Marine shipping company became a money loser.

The bankers finally began to look closely at Tan's empire and gasped. But as the saying goes: If you owe a banker $10,000 and you can't pay, it's your problem; if you owe $10 million, it's his problem. Led by Hambro Pacific Ltd. and Wardley, Ltd., a subsidiary of Hong Kong Bank, money men from around the world tried to effect a workout of Tan's debts. These things were done quietly in Hong Kong, all the more important in a case as large as Tan's which had the potential to pull the entire market down. By the spring of 1983, a rescue plan was ready.

It was a complicated plan that required a lot of cooperation. But one serious snag was the new young assistant manager at BMF, Jalil Ibrahim. He was holding up a $4 million loan that would have triggered the sale of some key companies. Testimony at his murder trial revealed the loan was a key to restructuring Carrian. A lot of big banks and George Tan himself were hanging on that loan.

When Jalil's body was discovered, the dominoes began to fall.

Police raids sank the bank bailout plan and left bankers from around the world holding probably a billion dollars in unrecoverable debt.

Tan himself was indicted—along with Bentley Ho, his right-hand man, two Price Waterhouse accountants and two businessmen—on nine counts of fraud, essentially related to an alleged conspiracy to defraud creditors and shareholders of Carrian Investments, Ltd.

He was released from jail on a $7 million cash bond.

The trial of George Tan took place in Courtroom No. 4 of the Supreme Court, a mere stone's throw away from Gammon House, which had started it all. The courtroom was completely redesigned for the trial in order to accommodate the six defendants, their counsel, the nine jurors, the wigged judge and the 1.5 million pages of evidence seized during the case.

On our day in court Tan's bookkeeper, Florence Ho, was testifying. She told a translator that millions of dollars had flowed into Tan's companies, but she didn't know the source. She said she had assumed the Bumiputra Bank had lent the money, but she said she also had heard that funds had come from the Philippines.

Where were the books of one of the subsidiaries? the wigged prosecutor asked from his seat in the front row of desks.

Florence Ho, a woman of about 35 with the air of a woman hiding her child from her ex-husband, told the translator that they had disappeared.

It was very dry stuff. Florence scowled a lot; the prosecutor never lifted his eyes from the thick looseleaf before him. At least to two Americans, the judge and the attorneys in their wigs and silk gowns looked silly. The jurors—seven men and two women—looked thoroughly bored, as if they'd somehow landed in calculus class without having taken algebra. Florence

Ho's insistence on a translator of course meant that her testimony would take twice as long.

No one stood up to ask questions or object; there barely was room, what with all the desks covered with binders of documents.

In the second row behind defense counsel, sat a small man with buck teeth, thick glasses and disheveled hair. He didn't react to any of the testimony, or even confer with his attorneys at the breaks. He had a faraway look in his eyes, as if he was wondering how to make this all go away.

After the trial we met David for dinner at a Chiu Chow restaurant in a Kowloon basement. We toasted our journey through the travails of Hong Kong's business world with a thimbleful of Iron Maiden tea, which is the customary starting and finishing touch to all Chiu Chow meals. This food is the specialty of the Swatow port district of Guangdong province; the most famous dishes are shark's fin soup and a dozen preparations of bird's nest, which allegedly keeps you young. One of the most popular Chiu Chow restaurants was owned by George Tan and called Carriana.

David ate up our report of the trial, which we assured him was a rather boring event.

"No, no," he objected. "It's something we don't have time to see; it's interesting. And I probably wouldn't understand it anyway."

We asked him if it was so interesting why didn't he just take a few hours to visit the courthouse.

He scoffed, "A few hours? To hear history? I would rather you spend the time for me." His face collapsed into a smile. "That's our deal isn't it—I show things to you and you tell me what I see?"

We asked him if he resented George Tan for what he did.

He shook his head. "I don't think anyone resents him, except maybe some of the shareholders. I think it was silly to be so public and to get caught. But, if anything, I think people feel sorry for him."

"How so?"

"Because we have about 10 years left to make money. If you are good you can make or lose a fortune three times in 10 years." With his chopsticks he grabbed some bird's nest and added, "But not if you're sitting in a courtroom going over ancient history."

We remembered the look in Tan's eyes as he sat there, the one we had assumed meant remorse, shame. We asked David what he thought was going through Tan's mind.

He chewed with gusto. (You need a good set of choppers to eat Chiu Chow food.) "Guilt? Shame? This is Hong Kong. The only shame Tan is feeling is that he got caught. What he was thinking is what we all are thinking. How do I make money next? I am sure of that."

One of the age-old ways of making money in Hong Kong is to play the stock market. It is also one of the fastest ways ever invented to lose money. When the stock market in New York rises or falls 10 percent in a day it is the stuff of banner headlines; in Hong Kong it's just another day. Not only is the Hong Kong market subject to the normal vicissitudes of profits and losses, but as we learned in the Tan matter it also serves as prey for clever manipulators and for the political contest over who runs Hong Kong. In any other part of the world such an exchange probably wouldn't exist because of all of its inherent volatility. But this condition mirrored the mood of the investing public; they gambled in Hong Kong, and if the game was fixed they still stood a chance to win. That's what living on borrowed time is all about—taking chances.

The guardian over the exchange was capping off his career when we paid him a visit. In 1969, Ronald Li and 10 Chinese colleagues founded the Far East Stock Exchange, challenging the dominance of British investment houses that had run the market as a private gentlemen's club in which insiders held an enormous advantage. By the late '70s there were four exchanges in all, Li's being dominant. Headquartered on the eighth floor of a downtown office building, the pit was little more than an oversize storage closet, cramped with hundreds of telephones and scores of runners in red jerseys with large gold numbers. The technology of Li's exchange belonged to a bygone era.

But in 1986, he engineered the merger of the Colony's four exchanges and moved the Hong Kong Stock Exchange into the sleek new skyscrapers sitting on the waterfront's most valuable properties. Those were heady days for Li, as Hong

Kong shared in the worldwide bull market, and its state-of-the art technology and trading opportunities attracted foreign institutional investors.

We visited Li during the physical transition from the littered uproar of the old quarters to the antiseptic clean of the new. By this time Li was accustomed to interviews. Most of Hong Kong's mega-multimillionaires are totally inaccessible to the press, including Stanley Ho, C. H. Tung and Li Kaxing, reportedly the richest of them all. Even the voluble Sir Y. K. Pao, when he went native, closed the zipper to the media. A man named Henry Fok once was considered Beijing's unofficial representative among the truly rich of Hong Kong—whatever Fok did was assumed to have been done with communist money. None of these men wanted to vie on best-seller lists with Donald Trump and Lee Iacocca.

Li was different. The maturation of the stock market gave him the opportunity to be seen and heard, and the audience he played to sat in Beijing. He told us he wanted to maintain a high profile because he wanted the Chinese to understand that when they realized they would need a stock exchange there only was one man to run it.

Li himself was a formidable businessman, and as he watched 1997 approach he fancied himself one of the bridges between capitalism and communism. An accountant by training, Li inherited a family shipping business and immediately sold off the last vessel, bought stock and started an accounting firm. His wealth reportedly is scattered worldwide, including U.S. real estate, Canadian movie theaters and a share of the Bank of Canada. When we met him, Li's net worth was estimated at U.S. $1 billion.

Li looked to be in his early 60s, tall, thin, his face beginning to sprout liver spots. He spoke rapidly without much prompting. We asked him if one exchange would be better than four and why.

"The unified exchange is what Hong Kong deserves," he answered. "Because it is a place of people intensely disinterested in politics and interested only in economics."

Li told us that his great accomplishment in creating one exchange was in allowing money to move through the markets much faster than before, which in turn allowed businesses to find capital quickly; after all, there loomed a deadline after which no one knew how private business would fare. "And," he added. "Hong Kong markets now have respectability. We are one of the great markets of the world. Before it was too difficult to persuade big investors from overseas that we were anything more than local."

We asked Li about the future of the exchange after 1997. He sprinkled his speech with Americanisms learned during college and graduate school in the United States. "If I told you I wasn't nervous I'd be lying through my teeth," he said. We thought this to be an odd statement from one attempting to curry favor with China. He continued, "But it's not a dictatorship that frightens me. It's democracy. In a democracy you're ruled by the masses. One nose, one vote. And there are more stupid noses than clever noses."

During the unified exchange's first year of operation Li ruled it with a velvet fist. He tightly controlled the 21-member committee of directors, excluding from them representatives of the large international brokerage houses. He himself chaired the listings subcommittee of the exchange that controlled the access of new issues to the market.

In the eyes of most observers, Li acted as an autocrat over his creation, which might have been perfectly normal, except this man swore to us that his personal motto and that of nearly everyone else in Hong Kong was: "Goddamn it, leave us alone!"

Li hurried through tens of phone calls while we sat in his office. Between each one he shot a sentence at us as if we were watching five-second commercials on Hong Kong capitalism. Finally, he grabbed Kelly by the elbow and told us to ride down the elevator; he had a big deal to attend to. (As always, no "little deals" were in the offing.)

Li assured us that we already must have seen the essence of what made Hong Kong work. "These people," he pointed to some of his red-jerseyed runners who shared the elevator with us, "have escaped from places where people were trying to take away their money. Here whatever you make you jolly well keep most of it. No social security, no minimum wage, no regulations. People can watch out for themselves. There may never be another place like this in the world again."

Li actually had become known to the outside world for a reason other than his stewardship of the exchange: a new issue that was awaited with great fanfare. Known as Volvo Entertainment Enterprises, Ltd., the company's principal asset was Club Volvo, the largest and splashiest hostess club in Hong Kong. It made our Club de Luxe look like a sixth-grade dance. On any night about 800 hostesses entertain patrons who are whisked through the club in a custom-made lavender electric Rolls-Royce. Computers keep running tabs, so that patrons can cut off conversation before the next $18 hour begins. The "take-out charge" was $135 paid to management. All in all, Club Volvo brought the world's oldest profession into the computer age and its shares into the hands of schoolmarms and grandmothers.

Public issuance of the shares promised a bonanza for the owners of Club Volvo, who included Loretta Fung, sister of American Taiwan-lobbyist Anna Chennault and none other than Ronald Li himself. Li defended the transaction by stating, "I will list anything under the sun that's both profitable and within the law." (Interestingly, Beijing's top official in Hong Kong, Xu Jiatun, had attended the opening of Club Volvo. When you consider the owners, the type of establishment and Xu's background as a former provincial party secretary, you can begin to understand why Westerners have such a hard time understanding the politics and sociology of this part of the world.)

One person sure not to invest in Club Volvo was David. He was irate over Li's plans. "He makes a joke of the two things I take most seriously—making money and sex." We were on our way to our reward meeting for having covered the George Tan trial for David. We were finally about to meet some of his friends, ostensibly to talk to them about Tan, although we had another topic on our agenda. This promised to be an opportunity to discuss 1997 with people our own age who would be coming into the most productive years of their careers. For Leon and Diane, the alarm clock would sound when they already had picked many of the fruits off the trees they had planted. For David and his friends the trees probably only would be blossoming by 1997.

One would have thought the hard-fought custody battle over Hong Kong would have provided some apparatus for an orderly transition from West to East. But the angel of order wafted high over Hong Kong, headed in a beeline for places like Japan, and just never alighted in the Colony. The Joint Declaration really didn't make things predictable or calm. In fact, what was to be a manifesto and a map had become a muddle. Hong Kong continued to be Hong Kong.

The catchwords of post-1984 life are deviation and convergence. According to the letter of the Joint Declaration, the Colony obviously belongs to Britain until 1997. But everything Britain has done has received public notice from Beijing: Either there has been illegal deviation from the Joint Declaration or convergence with its principles.

It's been a conundrum for Britain, which has over the centuries developed a tradition of decolonization through a process of democratizing the political structure and grooming local leaders for the task of governing. Britain rarely has pulled out of a place without trying to leave behind at least some semblance of a system of free elections and self-determination. It wanted this for Hong Kong; it insisted on this for Hong Kong. The Joint Declaration provided for Hong Kong to have its own governor and elected legislature, its own laws and independent courts to enforce them and the freedoms of speech, press, assembly and religion. The treaty did not have a prayer of passage in parliament without these basic democratic safeguards.

But implementing them has been something else, and Britain's commitment to them apparently has eroded since they were enunciated.

The pas de deux occupied center stage with the release in May 1987 of the "Green Paper" or blueprint on political development. Prior to publication Britain, through its governor, had embraced the concept of speedy elections in order to begin the establishment of a democratic structure. The litmus test of "democracy now" was support for a ballot in 1988 for members of the legislative council. Instead of making the recommendation for these elections, the authors of the Green Paper said public opinion polls should determine if and when direct elections should take place. Britain was accused of copping out, because no one doubted China's control over the apparatus that shapes public opinion: media, unions and prominent civic leaders.

China opposes any basic changes to the political structure until 1990, when it expects to promulgate the Basic Law or "mini-constitution" for Hong Kong. The precedent of direct elections prior to that time would force the laws' drafters to embrace the ballot box, which China apparently doesn't want to do, or repudiate them, which would cause indigestion in Western political bodies. China wants nothing created without its say-so. So Britain has punted.

What China apparently wants is no change. Imitation is the sincerest form of flattery, and the irony is that Britain has created a political structure that China wants to inherit lock, stock and barrel. The British colonial system in Hong Kong stands as one of history's great anti-democratic institutions. All of the political power lies in the governor's hand. There is no voting, no representative government, and an ability to snuff out basic freedoms with the stroke of a pen. China only needs to replace a handful of leaders, and the Colony could go about its business.

Britain has tried to leave behind a government and code of law vastly different from that which existed before, and its articulated willingness to do this gave birth to a "democracy lobby" composed mainly of middle-class educated citizens. For the first time in the history of Hong Kong, self-determination had a chance.

But only a chance, because the new child's full name would be Hong Kong, China, and the parent sharing that last name holds other ideas.

Direct elections was just one issue on which China's strong ideas overwhelmed Britain's well-intentioned but ineffective—no matter what, the Union Jack will fall on June 30, 1997—proposals and the meek voice of dissent among the Hong Kong citizenry. In July 1986, a flap arose over China's plan to build a nuclear power plant at Daya Bay in Guangdong province, only 35 miles from the Central business district. One need only look at the radius of destruction surrounding Chernobyl to see how close the Building of 1,000 Assholes stands to ground zero. The issue achieved prominence as a test of Hong Kong's ability to influence internal Chinese decisions that nonetheless had a definite impact on Hong Kong. In the end, the feelings of the Hong Kong populace apparently mattered not. Even Britain sat on the sidelines for this one, because it easily understood what the construction of a nuclear power plant and resulting development could mean to its own commercial interests in the East.

Another storm arose in March 1987 over the enactment of a new press law that on its face greatly liberalized what had been on the books, which allowed the government to close newspapers, seize printing presses and ban imported publications. Instead of winning kudos for a display of democratic impulses, British action was denounced as another concession to China's demands. What bothered the new law's critics was the introduction of a new measure that makes it an offense to publish "false news that is likely to alarm public opinion or disturb public order" without requiring the government to prove malice. In effect, the burden of proof shifted from the prosecution to the defendant, who now has to prove his innocence. Hong Kong's press, which had flourished despite the old laws *sans* teeth, now faced a measure that it was sure would be exercised. And the government injected more jitters that spring by revealing that it had been illegally censoring films that it feared would offend Beijing.

Chimera can inspire a lot of people to hope that Britain will institutionalize democracy before it departs, but that would only be wishful thinking. At the same time, a culture that measures history in centuries not seconds repeatedly has shown the patience and resolve to wait until July 1, 1997. The so-called economic revolution of China carries the country forward but still light years away from Hong Kong. China knows this, and it is not about to adopt a child it cannot control.

This logic shakes the Colony to its roots. Exodus fever has spread pervasively, and applications for visas to Canada, Australia and the United States have reached the saturation level. (The number of "no criminal conviction certificate" applications, a prerequisite to the issuance of a visa, jumped 162 percent from 1983 to 1987.) Anyone who can afford to buy a passport from another country is doing so, and has stuffed it in the mattress in case the world reverts to 1967 and everyone is asked to answer for every belief he or she has ever harbored.

David had told us to try to find out from his friends whether or not they had passports from other countries. "No one talks about it," he said. "Everyone assumes that the other guy has one."

"But you don't, do you?"

David said nothing.

We met his friends at a comfortable community center in Kowloon that had tennis courts, a swimming pool and a restaurant. We sat with David and his lawyer-friend, Kenneth Lee, and waited for two others to join us.

Kenneth was an associate at Deacons when John Wimbush killed himself, so he wasn't much interested in what we had learned about George Tan. "You're only unraveling what my colleagues raveled in the first place," he kidded.

David and Kenneth had been friends since childhood; their fathers had been friends since their childhood in Shanghai. Kenneth has gone to law school at the University of Manchester in England, and he was leaving in two days to take his younger brother to enroll there.

We asked him what he was doing to prepare for 1997.

"Nothing." He picked at some noodles that had arrived at our table and told the waiter they were cold. He ordered more food and two Coca-Colas. "That's what you should always remember when they talk about the decline of the West. Coca-Cola still rules the world."

We told him we took great comfort in that. "Where will Deacons be after 1997?" We pressed on.

"I don't know. I left there, you know. About six months ago and joined a Chinese firm."

"Why?"

He smirked. "Not what you're thinking. An insurance policy, that's what you're thinking."

We smirked back.

"No, my senior partners now would disappear faster than those at Deacons if there was a rumble," he assured us. "I went there for the simple reason they pay me more money."

David interrupted. "Kenneth's worst nightmare is they will close Club de Luxe."

"Ah, CDL," Kenneth gasped. He held his Coke up to the light. "If CDL would drop off the map I would like to go with it." Then he turned to David, "By the way, you told them you are the king—Alice's boy, they call him."

David blushed. He was saved by the others just coming in from tennis; they looked light years away from those two manufacturers from Manchuria whom David had met in Shenzhen.

Both Vigor Liu and Aubrey Chang had gone to college in California. Vigor was David's accountant and Aubrey worked for his father's construction business.

"Nineteen-ninety-seven?" Aubrey opined. "So what. They're still going to need roads, buildings, houses."

"But they may not need you to build them," we offered.

"Then we'll take our business elsewhere. It's just not that big a deal."

David added, "It's not a big deal to these guys because they already consider themselves Californians."

That was apparent—in their pastel tennis clothes, in the Perrier they sipped, in the haughtiness of their mannerisms. Vigor assured us that he had nothing to worry about because "most of my clients are in Canada or the States anyway."

In fact, there seemed to be only one worried soul at the table—David Wang. The others obviously had thought out their route to and after 1997. David couldn't get beyond that point. We knew, despite his attempt to be inscrutable, that he held no second passport. Why else was he so frightened crossing the border? And we had known it from a day when we sat in his office with his father when David was in Taipei and tried to assess whether a passport for Belize could be worth $25,000.

Kenneth said that he believed China would respect the "one government—two systems" pledge. "They always honor their treaties," he said. "Although this one is subject to enough interpretation to suffocate it."

"I still say it won't pay for them to kill Hong Kong's businesses," Aubrey said.

Vigor disagreed. "What do they need your construction company for? They could have a thousand of their own. They use you for five years, you teach them and they then rehabilitate you."

They all laughed except for David.

Aubrey noticed. "Come on, David. Just think how many more hostesses they'll have at Club de Luxe."

"How many girls they have on the Mainland," Vigor pondered. "Five hundred million?"

Kenneth was polishing off his reheated plate of noodles. "Enough politics," he announced. "Let's concentrate on 500 million women."

There was a moment of silence.

David was preoccupied as he drove us back to the Marco Polo. We were to fly out the next morning.

"What's wrong?" we asked.

"Do you see what I mean about them. They have what I call passportmania. They can be maniacs because they have passports. I don't like it."

We were parked in front of the hotel. The doorman held open the door. David told him to shut it. "Let's drive around the block again."

"What's the matter, David, you going to miss us?"

His mouth crumpled into a smile. "Yes. Maybe. You see, I don't have many friends. You saw my friends tonight. Imagine what this will be like in the future."

"How so?"

"I predict as we get closer to 1997 my friends and I will fall apart. They will have condominiums in California, and I will have a headache."

"David, it's not a death sentence. Things will work out."

"Easy for you to say. You're leaving tomorrow."

SINGAPORE

WE CAME into the city-state of Singapore the same way the Imperial Japanese Army had come 45 years earlier—from the north. Singapore dangles from the end of the Malay Peninsula like a diamond earring. A thin causeway connects the Malaysian city of Johore Bahru with the northern coast of the 240-square-mile island where a legendary tiger-infested jungle has been replaced by forests of 20-story public housing complexes. There is also on the north side a magnificent shipyard, remnants of a British naval base that once supported the mightiest fleet in history as it steamed about Asia to protect the interests of the empire.

That base and Singapore's location along the narrow passageway between the Indian and Pacific oceans made it one of the great strategic ports in the world and the object of Japan's desire as it began to colonize Asia. All the shipping between those two vast oceans had to come through the Strait of Malacca and then past the even narrower Strait of Singapore, 10 miles wide. Those ships that didn't stop in Singapore to refuel or unload still had to parade past the watchful eye of whomever controlled the city.

So in the early part of the century the British, who had claimed Singapore in 1819, did a very British thing and built sturdy gun emplacements on the highest points of the island. Set in reinforced concrete bunkers were five 15-inch cannons that could target a passing ship and sink it in minutes. For smaller vessels, there were six 9.2-inch guns and 18 six-inch guns. Inside the hills were honeycombs of ammunition stores and supplies enough to keep the gunners happily firing away for months at a time. The British called Singapore "the Gibraltar of the East." John Gunther, the breathless travel journalist whose *Inside Asia* shaped the views of a generation of

Americans, called it a "bigger and better Gibraltar, one of the most formidable concatenations of naval, military and strategic power ever put together anywhere." Except for one small problem.

The guns were all pointed the wrong way.

All the cannons were aimed at the sea which, the British felt, was the only place from which any self-respecting enemy would attack. At the end of 1941 the Japanese came from the land. "The little men," as the British overlords used to call them, rode bicycles as fast as their little legs would move down the length of the Malay Peninsula and arrived to find a handful of Tommies with rifles eyeing them from the north end of the island. All the serious hardware was waiting to blast a Japanese fleet that was occupied elsewhere in the destruction of the U.S. Navy at Pearl Harbor.

Still, the Japanese continued at a disadvantage. They were attacking a well-defended island, outnumbered perhaps 30,000 to 60,000—though the British didn't know that at the time—and they were stretched to the limits of their own supply lines. If they didn't get a surrender quickly, they were going to be in trouble. Winston Churchill, appreciating the importance of Singapore, cabled, "There must at this stage be no thought of saving the troops or sparing the population. The battle must be fought to the bitter end and at all costs."

The fierce Japanese commander, General Tomoyuki Yamashita, decided to go for broke and staged an all-out assault aimed at the heart of the city. After several weeks of bombing, the fabled British resolve faltered. Unaware how desperate the Japanese were and fearing a slaughter of the civilian population, General A. E. Percival quickly decided to call it quits.

On February 15, 1942, with Percival looking frail in his blousy khaki shorts and knee socks and the bull-necked Yamashita looking like a Las Vegas pit boss, the British agreed to an unconditional surrender—one Churchill called "the worst disaster in British history." In his definitive history of Singapore, C. M. Trumbull quotes one of the British commanders as writing, "It was a case of British academics fighting Jap realists. They are *not* bloody marvels, but they *are* intensely practical and keen, and therefore aggressive and very, very fast." Yamashita later wrote: "My attack on Singapore was a bluff . . . I was very frightened all the time that the British would discover our numerical weakness and lack of supplies and force me into disastrous street fighting." To those with the strongest stomach went the spoils. When the flag of the Rising Sun was hoisted over Singapore, the age of white man's imperialism was ended in Asia.

"Now Lee, he would have starved before he surrendered," an Asian historian who first told us the tale said when he finished. "That's the difference. The British were the old world. Lee is the new world. And he's a lot tougher."

Lee is Lee Kuan Yew, the diminutive prime minister of the minuscule city-state of Singapore and the most respected, reviled and quoted figure in Asia. Its first and only prime minister, Lee has ruled Singapore since 1959, shortly after its independence from the British. He is said to be that rare bridge between East and West, a Cambridge-educated son of upper-class Chinese who was raised to revere British ways but adopted them to Asian culture. Whether from Cambridge or Confucius, Lee has learned not to point all the guns the same way and has survived one of the longest tenures of any head of state in the world.

He had been variously described to us as brilliant and ruthless, as a man who had effected the greatest of all the Asian miracles and as a vicious despot who had created the prototype for a modern totalitarian government.

"Singapore is an evil place," a British investment banker had told us in Hong Kong. "It has all the cleanliness and efficiency of an operating room. That's because of Lee. But nobody in Asia is smarter or knows more about this part of the world. You ought to try to have a chat with him."

We were trying. We had come to Singapore to see what this last, most curious of the Four Little Dragons was all about and to see if we might be able to meet the P.M., as his countrymen called him. Clearly it would not be easy. Lee was not a fan of the press and rarely gave interviews. He had become, though, a sort of Holy Grail for us. The man with the book of wisdom. Time and again we had heard that "Lee understands Asia," "Lee can best explain the New World." We had spent months traveling in Asia and we felt no closer to being able to answer some of the questions we started with: How were these Dragons different from the West? What was the secret to this hybrid economic system that was not capitalism and not communism? Was Asia really becoming the dominant region of the world and what did that mean for the United States?

What we had read and heard of Lee made him seem one of the most remarkable leaders of the 20th century. He embodied most of what is good and bad about Asia. He is highly educated, driven, clever, resourceful, enduring, paternalistic, anti-democratic and above all, pragmatic. What he had created had hints of Utopia and the Brave New World, and it was, on balance, thought to be very successful. The rest of Asia, and in particular the reform-minded rulers in Beijing, were watching his experiment most carefully.

Some said it was only too bad that Lee had such a small country to work with. Others said it was just as well.

The scenery out the window of the taxi was like that along the entrance road to Disney World. The tropical shrubs and flowers lining the highway were not just well-tended but *manicured.* A topiary hedge in the shape of Mickey Mouse would not have been out of place. The litter-free road twisted gently under scrubbed concrete overpasses and past new sun-washed white apartment towers growing from palm groves on either side. Alongside us were white-sand beaches fringed with more palms.

At one point another cab passed us going in the opposite direction with a flashing blue light on its roof. We asked our driver what it was.

"Oh, that's for speeding," he laughed sheepishly. "If you go more than 55 kilometers an hour, the light goes on so the police can see it and arrest you."

His own speedometer stayed a steady hair under 55. We had heard about the famous Singapore laws: $500 fines for spitting (a habit the older Chinese affect for luck), throwing trash or wearing your hair too long. Our cab had several official government stickers on the dashboard; one said, "Be loyal to Singapore," another reminded of the "service attitude" that said "Provide a pleasant journey, take pride, be honest, patient and understanding." But the blue light took rules to a new dimension. This was self-policing.

"That seems silly," London said. "Don't people just disconnect it?"

"No, no, sir," he said, turning serious.

"Don't all these rules drive you crazy?" London baited the hook.

"No, no sir," the driver said, staring straight ahead and ending the conversation. We learned later that the penalty for a cabbie criticizing the government was loss of his license.

We checked into what was then the world's tallest hotel, the Stamford Westin at Raffles City, an I. M. Pei–designed tube that stuck 73 stories into the blue equatorial sky. A room was $50 a night, ludicrously low by international standards and the result of a glut of hotel rooms begun in the early 1980s when the economy was growing at a more than 10 percent annual rate. At the time it appeared that Singapore would achieve its stated goal of becoming the Switzerland of Asia by the end of this century instead of early in the next. But even this superheated country had to obey the humbling laws of economics, it seemed, and when the supply exceeded the demand, the price of a room dropped.

From the 55th floor we viewed the organized sprawl of a city that was more modern than any we had seen in Asia—and maybe even the United States. If there was a comparison, it might have been to Dallas or the core of downtown Los Angeles. Spreading along the shore of a harbor dotted with freighters was a cluster of 30- and 40-story office towers of varying styles of undistinguished modern architecture. Most had been built within the last 10 years. Amidst them was a bright green field surrounded by the ornate granite structures that once housed the colonial government. This was the Padang, the greensward where the British once played cricket and gathered on the verandas of the surrounding clubs to drink pink gin and complain about the scheming little men of Asia.

Farther out, there was not the usual urban sprawl but tidy clusters of apartment towers and single homes set in lush patches of green. Dotted everywhere were the sharp aqua swatches of swimming pools and the rusty red of clay tennis courts. And toward the ocean we could see where vast areas of land had been reclaimed and now supported several office and hotel complexes. In fact it was apparent that the site of our hotel had once been on the harbor but was now almost a mile in. Before us were millions of cubic feet of new concrete and churned earth representing billions of dollars of investment.

What was remarkable was that the people of this country had accomplished it all in 20 years.

Just near the base of the tower we could see a curious old building, a tin-roofed square surrounding a murky pool. It stood untouched amid a whirlwind of construction activity on surrounding blocks. We asked the bellboy if he knew what this solitary temple was.

"That is the Raffles Hotel," he said quickly. "It was the most famous in Asia."

As he left the room with five Singapore dollars in his fist, he added, "Now we are the most famous."

The hotel was at one end of a "tourist belt" that ran north along Orchard Road. The neighborhood was almost pristine, lined with sparkling hotels and shopping malls set back from palm-shaded sidewalks. What became immediately apparent as we wandered around was what Singapore did *not* have: It had none of the stench and crowds and noise of the rest of Asia. Singapore did not smell of urine or rotting food, mangy dogs did not sleep in doorways, steaming noodle carts jammed with soup-slurping patrons did not line the curbs. The sidewalks, while busy, were not packed shoulder to shoulder with people elbowing their way upstream like spawning salmon. And while the wide streets were busy with auto traffic, it was not jammed bumper to bumper in the midst of a cacophony of horns. Even the ubiquitous scooters seemed quieter.

In search of a snack, we felt close to home. Too close to home. Tucked amid the shopping splendor were familar fast-food temples such as Orange Julius, Pizza Hut, McDonald's, Burger King, Ponderosa Steak House and Hardee's ("You have Hardee's in the United States too?" asked an astonished young woman we asked for directions).

We went native and picked Big Rooster, a local entry in the fast-food world, that featured "BBQ Chicken" in a blaring environment of blue-and-yellow plastic seats and continuous reel Madonna tapes. "Get into the groove," she sang as we tried chicken sandwiches that were just as reconstituted as anybody else's.

At the Centre Point Mall, the well-stocked Times Bookstore sported a window laden with success books. *Corporate Pathfinders, Going for It!* by Victor Kiam, *What They Don't Teach You at Harvard Business School.* The stores were stuffed with the staples of consumerism: slim black stereos, giant-screen color televisions, tiny tape recorders and giant boom boxes, cool white kitchen appliances—from food processors to coffee grinders to G.E. frost-free refrigerators—clothing for children right out of the fashion magazines, Steinway pianos, Guess jeans, silk dresses, lingerie.

We had seen much of this elsewhere in Asia—Hong Kong had malls, even Kuala Lumpur had a new one, which approached the status of a national museum—but nowhere else was there that gleaming new feel and smell and indeed the moderately bored clientele of the high-priced spread in the United States. This could have been Chicago's Water Tower Place, Houston's Galleria or Washington's White Flint. The requisite well-barbered guys scuffed along sockless in Gucci loafers with bright yellow sweaters tied around their necks, women in simple silk shirtdresses and just the right amount of gold jewelry for the afternoon rolled their eyes at the prospect of wading into yet another sale on Papagallo shoes. The store clerks were polite but distant. Despite the Asian tradition, one did not bargain for anything here. "The price is as marked, sir," said the man in the high-end stereo store as he stood impassively by as if to add, "It doesn't matter to me whether you buy it or not. Someone else will."

We didn't know how they learned it, but these Singaporeans were more like us than we were.

Not far from Orchard Road was a small reminder that if the Singaporeans were like us, it had not been for long. Tucked in among the soaring office towers was the 15-square-block enclave of Chinatown, all that remained of the old way of life. For a century and a half, while the British carried on in their colonial bubble, the back end of Singapore was a teeming ghetto of shops and packed apartments. When Sir Thomas Stamford Raffles of the British East India Company bought the island from the Sultan of Johore for $8,000 a year—in a deal that rivaled Peter Minuit's purchase of Manhattan Island from the Indians—he laid out a plan. All the buildings of importance were clustered majestically front and center on the harbor while "the ethnics" were confined to quarters shoved off to the sides—one for Chinese, one for Indians and one for Malays.

From the time the British took hold in 1819, what had once been a Malay trading post (Singha Pura is Sanskrit for Lion

City) became a predominantly Chinese city as people in search of work migrated from the mother dragon down the Malay Peninsula, stopping at the end and rarely daring to continue on to the unknown Moslem wilds of Indonesia. Many had come as indentured laborers looking for the pot of gold that was not to be found in China. A handful of prosperous merchants managed to lead lives of privileged "Queen's Chinese" with their own servants, but the rest lived not unlike they had in their home villages. Young men were as likely to end up as rickshaw pullers or dock workers and pay a few cents for a straw mat in a crowded tenement. Mostly it was the cleverest merchants who survived the intense back-alley markets of this crossroads city where everything was available and everything was for sale. The underground economy of Singapore was one of small shopowners who lived over the family store with a dozen relatives.

Urban renewal changed all that, as slums and even the well-preserved old parts of town were torn down with remarkable thoroughness. Now all that remained was this toy village—again, like a Disney exhibit—where aged men and women with faces like weathered wood squatted over bowls of noodles and carried on commerce while the generation of their grandchildren came to gawk. It might, in fact, all be gone if the government's cleanup campaign hadn't suffered a disastrous drop in tourism as a consequence. The city that was known as "Sinapore" in the early part of the century for its brothels and opium dens, now had little besides shopping to offer tourists. Five thousand food hawkers had all been moved into government-regulated centers where they occupied numbered stalls and customers sat at tables in a common central area. The market, too, had been moved to a vast central location that had none of the charm of the many open-air markets we had seen throughout Asia. The sampans, or houseboats, had also been banned from the once-virulent Singapore River, which was now clean enough to fish. The floating city had looked great in old photographs, but few would argue that cholera epidemics were a fair price to pay for charm.

What was left of Chinatown looked like every other Chinatown we had seen, though not so big or dense and thus not so foreboding. Down every side street one could see the outline of nearby skyscrapers. The result was that that sense of being lost in a maze—an anxiety central to enjoying any Chinatown immersion—was absent. The shuttered, fading building fronts were splattered with large Chinese characters. The second-floor windows oozed signs of life—laundry, plants, songbirds in cages.

Within the open storefronts were dark realms of baskets and barrels filled with pungent medicinal herbs and foods, such as the usual ground deer's antlers, powdered snake bile, duck claws, dried squid, black thousand-year-old eggs, cages filled with live pigeons, rabbits, turtles and snakes. There were barbers and calligraphers as well as funeral merchants who sold giant paper replicas of dragons and other animals to be burned on the death of a relative.

More horns honked on one block of this time-warp zone than in all of downtown Singapore. A fat man in a blood-smeared apron shouted angrily at a truck driver. The fishmonger pulled a long black carp from his tank and whacked it with a board four or five times until its skull broke with a loud snap. Then he handed it to a customer. On a corner, a hunchbacked old woman sold incense sticks, twisting herself awkwardly to hand them up to buyers. Above her a government poster showed an attractive young Chinese man and woman wearing tennis clothes and smiling at each other. It was part of the campaign to eliminate the various Chinese dialects and get everyone to speak Mandarin, the most formal. "I speak Mandarin," the guy was saying with enough of a leer so that we all knew what was really on his mind.

Just to the east on Serangoon Road was another cultural flashback, this time Little India, where the 7 percent of Singapore's population who had migrated from the overcrowded shores of Sri Lanka and the south Indian coast came for a taste of home. Again, small shops predominated though the goods were completely different. Instead of the thousand-and-one medicinal herbs and potions, there were baskets of spices whose aroma combined to give the scent of a strong curry sauce. In fact all the smells were alien, as if we had walked into a stranger's house. The sounds as well. The high-pitched pings of sitars and wailing nasal voices came from cassette players. But most disorienting were the colors. At the steaming restaurants, impossibly brown Tamil waiters spooned iridescent yellow curry onto Day-Glo green banana leaves. Women wore shocking pink saris while the men preferred saffron-colored dhotis that showed their skinny brown legs from mid-calf down. Shopfronts exploded with piles of fabric or garlands of flowers in hot pinks, oranges and yellows combined to shock rather than soothe. Most jarring of all was the Hindu temple, called Sri Mariamman, with its gate entwined by hundreds of deities painted in garish cartoon colors: pink skin, black eyes, red tongues. The walls were lined with glazed cows, a tower over the entrance stacked with all manner of unfamiliar figures from elephant-headed men to women in soaring gold headdresses.

As we walked we heard a melodic chant being broadcast from a loudspeaker. It was the *muzzein* calling the Muslim faithful to 4:30 prayer. Perpendicular with Serangoon Road was Arab Street, the third triptych of Singaporean culture. This much smaller shopping area didn't really serve Arabs as much as Malays, the natives of the archipelago that stretched from the Philippines to the end of Indonesia and comprised dozens of distinct ethnic groups. They were united by their Islamic faith—the only common ground they had with Middle Eastern Arabs. The Malays, whose fishing village originally caught Raffles's attention, made up about 15 percent of Singapore's population. Their relaxed lifestyle was reflected in the relative torpor of Arab Street, in contrast to the freneticism of Chinatown and Little India.

The Malays had the reputation of caring far more about their families and religion than material possessions. This made them superfluous in a money-obsessed society such as Singapore's and from the days of the British they had been pushed out of the mainstream of commerce. Until recently most have lived in traditional stilt villages called *kampongs* scattered through the island. Inexorably, though, they were being packed into housing towers, sometimes with members of their extended families, sometimes not.

Arab Street shops were laden with baskets and wickerwork as well as piles of printed batik cotton and costume jewelry. But as far as the shop owners were concerned, you could buy or not buy. Besides, at 4:30 people were either entering the gold-domed Masjid Sultan Mosque or unrolling their prayer rugs and turning toward Mecca.

In an afternoon's tour, then, we had found the parameters of Singapore: the glittering facade of success and the quaint relics of its soul left behind. Each of the three ethnic sections represented strong cultures that often had existed for centuries in exile without assimilating. The streets with the shops and the newspapers and the gossip from home were a link to one's roots, just as such neighborhoods had been for American immigrants for decades past. And it was for such reasons that the government had been eager to tear them down. For Singapore wanted a melting pot in the most complete sense of the word. It wanted a homogenized national identity, not Tamils and Hakkas and Javanese with competing interests and mutual mistrust. In the New World there was no accommodation for such a waste of energy. The ethnic enclaves were totems to be destroyed; the secular religion of capitalism was to be encouraged. That the three enclaves were allowed to survive as tourist geegaws meant that the purge was successful.

That night we had a date. A Singapore Airlines flight attendant we had met invited us to a rock concert. She promised to bring along some friends and, given the just reputation of Singapore Air girls for lithe, exotic beauty, we accepted. Unfortunately the only friend she could muster was her boyfriend, a Frenchman named Hugh, who had conceded to the Chinese pronunciation of his name: Oogh. Karen and Oogh picked us up in his Peugeot and we raced along the harborfront highway into a setting sun that silhouetted the palm trees and made us think that this place indeed had some comparisons to paradise.

We discovered that the concert was in an office building, the 15th-floor auditorium of the World Trade Centre to be precise, no doubt the usual site for ponderous seminars on such subjects as New Tariff Practices of the ASEAN Nations. It seemed that tonight, too, the seminar barons were in charge. Uniformed ushers escorted a polyglot crowd of softly giggling teenagers to their seats in front of a harshly lit stage. No special effects for this show. The auditorium, which sat perhaps 2,000 people, quickly filled up.

"Not a bad crowd," whispered Oogh. "Last year when David Bowie came to town they booked him into the soccer stadium. It seats 45,000. They sold 3,000 seats. Nobody could understand it because he had been selling out all over the world."

Without a warm-up act, the hottest band in Paris took the stage. Charlelie Couture, they were called, and Oogh said they really were big, though one would have been hard-pressed to find confirmation in the polite applause from the crowd. They might as well have been playing chamber music. What they did play was a sort of updated '50s jazz, like Miles Davis on electric guitar.

The lead singer, in beret and shades, hunched over the microphone and slithered out some tunes that may have been hip but weren't exactly danceable. Not that the impassive crowd would have known the difference.

On one side a knot of French kids tried to spark some fun. A blonde girl in tight white pedal pushers and pink high heels stood up on her seat and clapped rhythmically. An usher immediately came over and asked her to sit down.

"*Pourquoi?*" she asked with astonishment.

"No standing during the performance," he said simply.

She sat and pouted.

After 40 minutes the show was over and the pride of Singapore youth clapped for a few minutes, then filed quietly out to the elevators and through the atrium lobby to waiting buses.

We learned later that the show had been sponsored by the Banque Nationale de Paris. Usually concerts were sponsored by the police department.

Karen was apologetic.

"The problem with Singapore is that there's nothing to do," she said. "Everything is so perfect."

We had dinner at another government creation that was, in fact, pretty perfect. It was called the Seafood Center, a collection of the best fish restaurants that had been moved to a single oceanfront site by the Urban Development Management Corp.

We chose the Red House and had a feast of chili crabs, sweet grilled prawns as big as lobsters, steamed clams, curry noodles and scallops in tangy black-bean sauce. The food was fresh, hot and probably the best meal we had. In six months of travel throughout Asia, our stomachs knew the joy of a rigorous health code. We were scarred with the memories of rancid ox tails in Penang, old clams lurking in the soup in Seoul, cabbage dredged from the *klong* in Bangkok and Shanghai pigeon that tasted like it had been marinated in motor oil.

But the Red House made it all better. And so did the fact that everyone spoke English, no one was trying to cheat us, the telephones worked flawlessly, the hot water was hot and the taxi driver was insulted when we offered him a tip.

We sat and watched the lights of hundreds of ships in the harbor—another whole city at anchor—and wondered what was so bad about a place that made things work the way they were supposed to work. Singapore was like a fussy waiter who cleaned the ashtray after each flick and crumbed the table between courses. Was that wrong?

On the way to breakfast the next morning, we got on a moderately crowded elevator and plunged to the 27th floor. There the doors opened and a young Chinese couple stepped on, at which point the safety buzzer went off. Now this is not an uncommon occurrence on elevators in the United States and it is safe to say that neither of us had ever seen anyone actually get off. The buzzer stops in a few seconds and the elevator proceeds. Not this morning. The couple was mortified. They shuffled backward, apologizing as they went, and bowed deeply as the doors began to close.

We started breakfast with steaming bowls of rice porridge and a news fix. This was one of those days—and we had had quite a few—when it seemed that East Asia was serving all the anecdotal material you could eat. The little stories and the big stories were all about the dynamism of this part of the world. The business pages were full of accounts of deals and new factories and joint ventures with the West. The life-style pages were about how to buy the right things to make yourself and your home look good. The ads were for expensive clothes, second homes and airline tickets.

The English-language daily in Singapore is the *Straits Times,* a stuffy, oversize broadsheet with the sort of bold headlines and confused typography that make it appear to be produced by old-fashioned printers locking up great blocks of lead type. The advertising would have been at home in any local daily in the United States: a full page touted the arrival of American-style gluttony in the form of a "Big Gulp" soft drink at the 7-Eleven convenience stores; an ad for a luxury singles' apartment complex featured a young, career-oriented man and woman exchanging meaningful glances under the words, "Make the Right Start at Clementi Park"; a sale at the John Little department store was "Bursting with super buys at the lowest prices!!"

The lead story, however, was one that would not occupy the front page of any American newspaper we knew of. The biggest news in Singapore that day was about the students who had scored the highest on the recent university entrance exams. There under the headline "Exam Scores Announced," was a dramatic sidebar and photos about the top scorers in the grueling test. "Chiat: Had recurring nightmares," read one caption beneath a smiling, hollow-eyed youth. "Dang: Seven hours of study a day for weeks before the exam," read another. This was the sort of treatment Americans were accustomed to lavishing on high school football heros, but front page treatment for grinds? Nerds? Dorks? Weenies? Where were their priorities?

The *Straits Times* also quoted from a survey of world banks, noting that of the top 10, seven were now Japanese; Citibank, the largest in the United States, was No. 9. The education minister of Malaysia reported that tensions between the Malays and the Chinese—something the Singaporeans feared immensely—were at their worst level since just before the 1969 riots when 2,000 Chinese were killed and their shops and homes looted. A dispatch from Taiwan talked about the increasing number of teenagers there being killed in motorcycle crashes during races. Teens quoted in the piece attributed it to the need for excitement in their usually boring, austere lives.

And there was one other piece of note. Deep in the paper in the local briefs was an item about how the death of a 23-year-old student had been ruled a suicide. He had hanged himself from a tree at the Jurong Country Club after he failed his second-year exam in architecture.

Our first meeting was with the Prime Minister's press office. The sun was just burning off the night's moisture as we walked across the glistening green *padang* to City Hall, a squat gray-stone sprawl of a building topped by a distinctly phallic-shaped bell tower. On one side were the regimented Greek columns of the Supreme Court. Across the way was the Singapore Cricket Club with its brown beams and sweeping porches looking as if they belonged in a London suburb. This neighborhood, once the center of British domination, was now the seat of government for the Republic of Singapore, to the extent that any place was the seat. Government departments were spread throughout the towering office buildings, many of them built with government funds for one agency or another. Lee kept an office here in City Hall, but did most of his work at his residence, the former home of the British governor-general. We gathered that Lee was comfortable with things British.

The P.M. was the product of a British education and an Anglophilic household. He was a fourth-generation Singaporean, the great-grandson of Hakka Chinese immigrants. By Lee's birth in 1923, the family was of the reasonably prosperous class called "Straits Chinese," meaning they were more rooted in the British Straits Settlements than in Mainland China. Lee's father dreamed that his son could be the equal of any proper English gentleman and sent him to the exclusive Raffles Institution and later to Raffles College, where he was a freshman when the Japanese invaded. After the war, he went to Cambridge on scholarship, where he read law and earned several academic distinctions.

The P.M.'s press office, however, bore no resemblance to the elegance of Whitehall. Brutally functional might have best described the austere room lined with gray metal desks and barely cooled by a wheezing air conditioner. Young men in white, open-necked shirts paused from tapping on manual typewriters to stare as we were ushered in. In a country that existed by oiling the cutting edge of technology, the prime minister's office got by on carbon paper. There was a Confucian mandate that the ruler must maintain the trust of his people to preserve his legitimacy. One way Lee interpreted that was to mean that he and his government must not live in opulence.

We were greeted by Lee Geok Suan, a small woman with a firm handshake and the thick glasses and taut hair of a strict elementary school teacher. She took us into a conference room that was cooled to freezing, opened a folder and began to ask a series of terse questions.

"When did you hope to meet with the P.M.?"

"This week."

"Hmmmph.

"Your first book sold how many copies? How many of that was hardcover? How many copies were bought in England? Were they hardcover or soft? Why do you not have the same publisher? Mr. Kelly, what is the circulation of your magazine? Who reads it? Mr. London, what type of law do you practice? Who are your clients?"

The questions went on, precise, detailed enough to craft a chapter on each of us and, it seemed, more than any press secretary could possibly care to have answered. Her eyes would drop to the folder for ammunition, then she would look up. Eventually she seemed satisfied that we were who we claimed and began to ask what questions we intended to ask of the Prime Minister.

"They must be precise questions," she said. "He will not be interested in speaking in generalities. You must know exactly where the interview is going."

We did not. We never did. We started every interview with a few questions and then saw where things went. We wanted to get a sense of the man, to encourage him to open up. But one look into the withering glare of Lee Geok Suan and we moved to Plan B.

"Sure, uh, we've got specific questions," London began tentatively. He tried a few.

"We'd like to ask him why he thinks Singapore has been so successful and what you have to do to keep it up. What is it about the Asian way of doing things that is better than the Western way? How do you decide where to draw the line between running the country efficiently and giving rights to the citizens? How should the United States try to deal with Asia?"

"Those are very broad questions," she smiled. "Perhaps you can make them more specific."

She handed us several sheets of paper and a pencil.

"I'll give you some time to write them down," Lee Geok Suan said as she rose and, with a barely perceptible bow of her head, left the room.

So we put down some specific questions that we thought sounded good, even if we didn't particularly care about the answers. What specific incentives did Singapore use to attract foreign business? What specific advantages were there for a business to manufacture products here than, say, the United States? What religion do most Singaporeans practice and specifically how does that influence the style of government? That sort of thing. We listed a dozen or so.

In exactly 20 minutes Lee Geok Suan reentered the room and picked up the questions to study.

"Ah," she began. "These are very particular questions."

We beamed. She frowned.

"I'm not sure you need to talk to the P.M. to get these answers. I think we could find people in the various specific departments who would be better able to give you detailed information. I'll see what I can do and get back to you."

Then she was gone. And we knew that these people were either a lot more clever than us or a lot more stupid. We feared we knew the answer.

The next evening we crossed the road from the polished marble excess of our multi-use hotel-retail-office complex to the dirty white pile that bore the logo Raffles Hotel. Buried among a concoction of additions, there was the outline of a once-majestic building done in a sort of tropical French Renaissance style with a procession of rounded windows and ornate friezes topped by a green tile roof. Framing the entrance were tall travelers palms with straight trunks opening out to delicate fans that rustled in the breeze. A parade of trishaws—bicycle-powered rickshaws—lined the circular driveway, their aging drivers smoking and joshing each other in gutteral Chinese. A stiff fellow in a red jacket and white pith helmet opened the hotel door for us.

Now we were getting somewhere. This was the bastion of empire we had been anxious to find. This was the exact point where the roads of the Raj in Asia had crossed, immortalized by Maugham and Kipling. It was a name that breathed the perfume of exotica. Raffles: A place where tiger hunters came to swap stories with wealthy rubber planters from up-country, where the bored wives of colonial administrators langorously eyed the ne'er-do-well sons of earls and dukes on holiday.

"Raffles," said Maugham, "stands for all the fables of the exotic east." He wrote several of his novels while staying at the hotel and gathered much of his material in its public rooms. He was famous for eavesdropping on conversations at the bar and using the stories of travelers as the basis for his bitter, ironic sometimes funny tales of Europeans in an alien world.

If the E&O Hotel in Penang was a branch office, this was

the headquarters of empire. Raffles was opened in 1886 at a time when the British controlled the Malayan Peninsula to the north and the vast island of Borneo to the east. Taken together they were the greatest sources for rubber and tin,which in turn had become two of the most valuable commodities for a world in the second stage of industrialization. Farther to the north, Hong Kong and Shanghai were the outlets for the wealth of China, which was also routed through Singapore.

In the 1930s, there were perhaps 5,000 Europeans in Singapore controlling this vast sub-empire. They and a handful of Chinese lived lives of extraordinary luxury. It was an era of spacious homes set on grounds manicured by a dozen servants. The "white" section of town—anchored at one end by Raffles, at the other by the cricket club—was a tidy wonderland of clean streets and imposing buildings. Surrounding them were half-a-million Asians, most working for subsistence wages and living in fetid, disease-ridden slums.More so than tin and rubber, they were then, as now, the great resources of Asia.

The British believed that rule was enforced as much by image as by might. That's why their colonial capitols, customs houses and banks were built to be both opulent and permanent. Raffles Hotel was such a symbol, a stronghold of the stiff upper lip. In its prime, Raffles was *the* clubhouse. Each evening the various coloreds could stare through the hotel's portico and watch their betters swirl on the dance floor, men in short white dinner jackets, women in crinoline gowns. Even during the Japanese siege, Raffles kept up the side with dinner dances each night, the ballroom properly blacked out and the orchestra playing until midnight. The scene must have astonished the Asians whether for its arrogance or its naiveté. For their part, the dancers were no doubt puzzled, but not too concerned, about the growing indicators that they were about to be taken over by these curiously aggressive yellow men. Whatever, the civilized dinner dance was damn British, thank you, and they hadn't managed to acquire half the world by abandoning their customs and going native. In this part of the world a man still bathed regularly, wore stiff collars and dressed for dinner.

As we pushed through the doors of the hotel, reality slapped us down in the form of the first object we encountered: the rather ample backside of an Australian woman which was straining the seams of her red shorts as she bent over to tie her sneaker. Her ensemble was completed with a T-shirt and straw hat, which matched that of her florid-faced husband who was proposing, "C'mon, duck, just one more 'a them sling things." Surrounding the couple was a scene befitting a bus terminal before a holiday weekend. Luggage from a just-arrived tour was piled on the floor. People in colorful garb and laden with shopping bags pointed still and video cameras at each other. The English tourists, a doughty lot, played their role by wearing sensible shoes and long pants for the men, flower-print dresses and seemingly identical shoes for the women.

The lobby played to the crowd, offering several souvenir stands selling Raffles ties, T-shirts, bags, pennants and curry mix. Over the ballroom hung a long banner which read, "Home of the Singapore Sling." People posed under it for photographs.

We were met in the Writer's Bar by the hotel's general manager, Roberto Pregarz, a suave European in a dark suit who appeared oblivious to the scene around him. He called to the barman behind the handsome mahogany bar to mix a round of slings.

The drink, he explained, was invented in 1915 by a Chinese barman.

"It may be the most famous drink in the world," Pregarz said proudly. "It is one of our best marketing tools."

The hotel served 1,000 a day at $4.25, though not made, we noted, by the painstaking hand method. The barman held a white plastic bottle and sloshed out measures of red liquid that most closely resembled Hawaiian Punch. He then inserted into the glass an orange wedge, pineapple spear, cherry, plastic straw and plastic swizzle stick in the shape of the travelers palm with the words Raffles Hotel on the fronds. The glass was then put before us on a Singapore Sling coaster, which Pregarz encouraged us to keep as a souvenir.

The drink was sticky sweet, but fortunately they hadn't held back on the gin. We later learned, not from the hotel, that the recipe was a half-measure of Beefeaters gin, a quarter-measure of Peter Heering cherry brandy, a quarter measure of fruit juice—lemon, lime, orange—a dash of bitters and a dash of Cointreau. Not that we planned to be making it at home.

While we let the buzz of gin wash over us—drunk before noon, now *that* would be proper colonial behavior!—Pregarz told us about the history of the hotel. It was originally a tiffin room, a place where the British gathered for a light lunch such as a Europeanized curry over rice. In 1886 the three Sarkies brothers from Armenia turned the site into a hotel, which they named for the founder of Singapore. Fame came quickly when the roving journalist Rudyard Kipling was looking for a meal and stumbled upon Raffles.

"You know, Kipling once said, 'When in Singapore, feed at Raffles,' " Pregarz told us in a tone that was properly reverential for a quote that had given the hotel 100 years of great publicity.

Actually, we found out later, Kipling had a little more to say. The quote was from his 1889 book *From Sea to Sea* and the full version is: "Providence conducted me along a beach in full view of five miles of shipping—five solid miles of masts and funnels—to a place called Raffles Hotel, where the food is excellent as the rooms are bad. Let the traveller take note. Feed at Raffles and sleep at the Hotel de l'Europe."

Kipling's photograph graces the wall of the Writer's Bar as do pictures of Noel Coward, Joseph Conrad and, that greatest of all Raffles publicists, W. Somerset Maugham.

"I will admit that the hotel is not what it was," said Pregarz. "But we have such a legacy. We sell atmosphere." He paused to wave his arm in the direction of the photos of great men. "And inspiration."

We were interrupted by the voice of an American woman.

"Look, honey, Billy Dee Williams stayed here. Here's his picture. . . ."

"In 1905, we were the Savoy of Singapore. We plan to bring those days back . . ."

". . . and that guy McGarrett from Hawaii Five-0 . . ."

". . . to re-create the grandeur of a very elegant time . . ."

". . . and the whole Osmond family. Look there's Donnie when he was little and Marie. . . ."

The woman would perhaps have enjoyed the hotel's official brochure that notes, in the same breath, that, "Somerset Maugham, Noel Coward and Rudyard Kipling wrote about Raffles Hotel and the film "Pretty Polly" with Hayley Mills and Trevor Howard was produced in the hotel in 1967."

Raffles was owned by a local bank, the Oversea-Chinese Banking Corp., and a government economic development agency, which viewed it as a strategic asset.

"One of our tourism consultants said that around the world, the name Raffles Hotel is more famous than Singapore," Pregarz explained. When the bankers heard that, they decided to come up with money to refurbish the hotel to the way it was in its prime. There was some dissension in the government because for many native Singaporeans, Raffles was still the symbol of colonial rule. Some said that since non-whites were excluded in the old days, why should they patronize the hotel now? But in the end pragmatism won out, as it usually does in Asia, and the decision was made to certify Raffles as a landmark.

The restoration hadn't started when we were there. Pregarz took us for a tour of the musty rooms walled with cheap paneling and acoustical tile ceilings. The carpets of the most famous hotel in the world were worn. Even the proudly advertised high ceilings seemed ungainly and out of proportion to what we were used to.

On the ground floor, Pregarz took us to the billiard room, where there were blue tiger's footprints painted on the floor.

"That's supposed to be the path of the famous tiger who was shot under the table in 1902," he explained. "It had terrified the town. Then C. M. Phillips, the headmaster of Raffles Institution and a crack shot, came and got it."

Tigers were once serious business in Singapore. In the mid-1800s, they killed dozens of people a year. But by 1902 there were few if any left on the island. Actually this unlucky specimen had escaped from a circus. And as the skin on the wall attested, he was closer to a large cat than a Bengal man-eater.

Still, Raffles wasn't all phony. Some of the grandeur was on display, such as the tons of polished brass, the marble floors, the ranks of prized Hainanese waiters whose relatives had poured whisky-and-soda *stengahs* for the British and now efficiently served whatever tour group the travel agencies had booked for the week. In the Elizabethan Grill there was a magnificent sterling silver roast beef cart that a waiter had buried in the Palm Court when the Japanese invaded.

The Palm Court itself, which was ringed by the guest rooms, was an impressive space. White wrought-iron furniture sat on green lawns framed by frangipani, palms and bougainvillea. Though the lawn was as frayed as the carpets, if you squinted, you could imagine what the scene must have been like. Just as Singapore was, from the mid-1800s to the Second

World War, a great crossroads, so was Raffles. If you traveled by ship in Asia, you *had* to come through here. In a quieter time when the distance between two points was measured in weeks, not hours, Raffles was an oasis of civility and comfort. If you had to wait five days for a ship, why not savor three-hour lunches, teatime and leisurely nightcaps in the bar with strangers?

On a given evening, people would be waiting for a table at the captain's station and craning their necks to see who was dining with whom. The sound of string music floating through the perfumed air would be a soft backdrop to the rumble of meaningful conversation and gay laughter. The cream of the colonial power structure would have been here: rubber barons and bankers, ship captains and fleet owners, colonial governors from the wilds of Borneo whiling away a few days until their ship left for home leave, tin mine managers from up-country spending a few days in the company of people who spoke English. On the dance floor, elegantly turned-out couples waltzed under giant ceiling fans to the best orchestra in Asia.

Just then a plump, naked German boy dove into the pool, splashing us and ending a sentimental reverie. On a chaise nearby was what appeared to be a very large, trussed and uncooked Thanksgiving turkey but what was actually his mother in a string bikini.

And it was a good thing he brought us to our senses. For how much of this place was really grandeur and how much arrogant nonsense?

Wasn't it in large part racial bigotry and the absolute conviction of their own superiority that doomed the British? Didn't Raffles more appropriately stand for the worst of Western culture and wasn't its shabbiness a reminder of what happens to those afflicted with hubris?

"Singapore remains a figure of all that was fustiest and snobbiest in the colonial empire, all that went with baggy shorts and ridiculous moustaches," Jan Morris, the chronicler of the British empire, wrote. "Singapore was the archetype of Somerset Maugham's Empire, Noel Coward's Empire—an Empire that had lost its purpose, its confidence and its will: when it fell to the Japanese in 1942, in effect the Empire fell too, and the idea of Empire, too."

In an introduction to Maugham's *Malaysian Stories,* Anthony Burgess talked about the typical European's contact with the world he was administering: "When a European paid a visit to the East Indies, the only Malays, Indians and Chinese he would meet were coolies on the rubber estates, houseboys and cooks in bungalows, barmen in clubs and hotels . . . He tended to regard them as mere colorful 'extras,' with no opportunity to star in the drama of Oriental life."

Maybe Roberto Pregarz's vision of restored glory is the wrong idea. Why not go the other way and hire poor British nobles to come and perform? Forget the Malay dancing show. Get a couple of old cockers in mustaches to eat roast beef in 85-degree heat and talk about how the playing fields of Eton really formed the measure of a man. Leave the carpets frayed and the tacky signs in place. Let Raffles be a warning that if you don't watch out you end up selling your birthright to fat German ladies.

We stepped from the hotel lobby into the night and gazed up and up at the 73-story white-and-silver Raffles City across the street, lit like a beacon. Rarely in Asia had we seen the future and the past so disproportionately arrayed.

As a final homage to the ghosts of empire, we decided to tour the town by trishaw and engaged two of the drivers in front of the hotel. Five dollars for a half-hour spin around downtown. A few minutes after we started, we wanted to stop.

The trishaw—along with its foot-powered precursor, the rickshaw—was one of the great symbols of old Asia. It was all about the cheapness of life. One man pulling another for money. One man's life so far removed from the other's that all he had to sell was the same as a horse. The man's advantage, in the narrow streets of Singapore or Hong Kong, was that he took up less room and could maneuver more easily.

In 1920, there were 25,000 rickshaws in Singapore, mostly pulled by Chinese peasants who had come looking for a pot of gold and found themselves at the bottom of the barrel. They were all young men because no one lasted very long pulling a rickshaw. Occasionally the newspapers would make civic pleas not to beat the pullers if they didn't know where they were going. The "rickshaw wallahs," as they were called, earned a few cents a day, which was about what it cost to rent a straw mat in a packed dormitory somewhere in the twisting innards of Chinatown. A man would pull heavy Europeans or his lighter, more prosperous fellow Chinese, until he was exhausted and then crawl home for a bowl of rice and, if he had saved, a pipe of opium. Eventually, disease and fatigue would catch up and he would be too slow to compete with the younger pullers. The syndicates who owned the rickshaws would take it away from him.

Still, there was no shortage of young legs. With succeeding waves of immigration in the early part of the century, rickshaws replaced ox carts and *gharries,* or pony carts, as modes of transport. It was not until cars and buses became commonplace in Singapore in the late 1930s that the government officially banned rickshaws and allowed the more humane trishaws.

Trishaws were now only for tourists, but they were becoming more popular. We couldn't understand why. Our drivers were skinny old men with yellow, gap-toothed mouths who strained to keep up speed as we moved away from Raffles along the *padang*. They sweated and wheezed as we rolled past the brightly lit skyline of the financial district and around toward Chinatown, which glowed in eerie green from the giant neon Fujitsu Film sign.

Gamely the trishaw men cut off taxis and maneuvered among the traffic, grunting and swearing. Elegant Asians stared at us with what we perceived to be disdain through the windows of air-conditioned Mercedes sedans. We were humiliated. We made the trishaw drivers drop us off 15 minutes early and walked back to the hotel.

Later that night we went to find one more monument. We had heard the stories of Bugis Street and had to see for ourselves. "Boogie" Street was the way people pronounced it, instead of the correct boo-geese, and given what went on there, the name was appropriate. This was said to be one of the great connoisseurs' spectacles of Asia. In a manner befitting this crossroads city, Bugis Street was the capital of cross dressing.

It was in the Arab district near the harbor. The street was named for the Bugis tribe, once the greatest sea traders of the region, who came from Macassar in the Celebes, now called Sulawesi. Each fall, 5,000–6,000 Bugis would travel by boat to Singapore to barter exotic goods they had collected on their travels through the region: ebony, camphor, ivory, coffee, parrots, sarongs and antimony. What they mostly wanted in exchange was gunpowder and opium.

In keeping with the raucous tradition of the Bugis, over the years a number of street-side cafes had sprung up. The street became a haunt for sailors and, therefore, prostitutes—or was it the other way around?—as well as tourists with adventurous spirits.

But the real show came after midnight when lithe, hairless young Asian boys dressed as glamorous women made a nightly strut for all to see. They jiggled silicone-enhanced breasts and blew pouty red kisses to their audience. Usually the night would build to a climax featuring an impromptu striptease show at the municipal fountain.

"It's pretty much all in good fun," an American friend who had traveled the region told us. "It isn't high-pressure, commercial sex like Bangkok or sleazy like the Philippines. It's kind of friendly, actually."

We followed the map and headed off, passing through some of the shop districts we had seen earlier, finally coming to the intersection that we knew was the heart of Bugis Street.

What we found was broken road and piles of earth looking like someone had dropped a thousand-pound bomb. Had they blown the place up? Was this how Lee Kuan Yew dealt with the eccentrics of his society?

We asked a dark-skinned man passing by what was going on here.

"Subway," he replied with a wide smile.

"Huh?"

"This will be a subway stop. Very big. With new shops and offices."

"But what about the nightclubs?"

"All gone."

Damn. Another place about which people could gloat, "You should have been here two years ago. That's when it was *really* interesting."

We learned later that the Urban Redevelopment Agency had decided that Bugis Street was not in keeping with the image of the new Singapore and figured a subway station was the easiest way to eliminate the problem. So in came the wrecking ball and out went another memento of old Asia.

Only a lot of people weren't happy about it, we discovered.

Pushed by those who worried about plummeting tourism revenues, there was a movement afoot in the government to bring back Bugis Street. Even before the subway was finished, we heard the Urban Redevelopment Agency had set aside a grant to recreate the seedy strip in a kind of gross parody of urban renewal. Disneyland goes drag.

By this point, we were not surprised. Like Raffles Hotel, Singapore would pick and choose the history it wanted to enshrine. The legacy of Singapore would be what the central planners said it should be.

The question we asked ourselves, while sipping cocktails on a warm evening as we watched a fiery sun drop below the palm trees and the orderly parade of commuters returning home in their shiny cars, was this: What's wrong with Singapore? At the moment, the obvious answer was "nothing." Singapore was doing pretty well at being an urban utopia. The city worked like a well-chipped personal computer. There was little crime, people had enough to eat, families lived close to each other, the economy was strong. From our own experience, everyone other than the Prime Minister's press assistant had been pleasant, well-mannered and intelligent. Still, something about the place made us uneasy. That night we had dinner with Susan Lee and her friend Jimmy and we began to understand why.

We drove to Little India in Jimmy's BMW and entered a brightly lit curry house where the waiter plopped rice onto fresh banana leaves and spooned an incendiary fish-head stew on top. Susan, who had worked in the United States, used a fork. Jimmy, in polo shirt and Brooks Brothers khakis, took the traditional route and scooped with his right hand.

We knew Susan from the States. Jimmy was an old friend of hers; they were not, she had explained earlier, dating. But dating was indeed the subject of the evening, as in, "How come I can't get a date?"

"Since I've been back, this place is worse than the U.S.," Susan lamented. "This is becoming a city of yuppies. Everybody works too hard and doesn't know what to do with their free time. I come home at night, watch TV for an hour and fall asleep."

"We are infected with the success ethic," Jimmy explained.

"The P.M. tried to put the fear of failure into us and now we're stuck with it. Even in my generation, there is this sense that if we don't do exactly as we're told, the whole country will fall apart."

Both were in their early 30s, both came from educated parents, had good jobs, made decent salaries and still lived at home. The lives they described were ones of high anxiety prompted by lifelong incantations to succeed from their parents and their government—a government that was seeming to us more and more like a surrogate parent.

Dating stress was only one symptom of a rigid society that encouraged the material success ethic of the modern world along with the chauvinism of the old world.

"Smart men don't want to date smart women," Susan said. "They still want docile wives who stay home."

"My problem is that most of the women I know have more education than me," Jimmy added. "There are twice as many women in graduate school as men."

"So what does the government do?" asked Susan. "They set up an official matchmaking service. Then they give financial incentives for women with a college degree to have children. The government is worse than a grandmother."

The government also had a habit of changing its priorities. "When I was growing up," Susan said, "women were told they couldn't have more than two children. Now I'm being told I've got to get married and have four children or I'm letting my country down."

"Everything is so controlled here," Jimmy said. "Sometimes the rules make you crazy."

The same topic dominated dinner conversation the next night with Lau Saum Wing and his wife, Jeannie.

"Singapore is an efficient place," the young entrepreneur told us. "It is made for doing business. It is run by and for those who know what that means."

And that does not mean whining about the lack of a social life. That was inefficient. Lau had gotten over his dating problem by marrying soon after graduating from college. Jeannie shared his distaste for social games. They liked working hard and making money. For that, Singapore was the perfect place—as long as you didn't spend all your time there.

"My interests are all over the world," Lau explained readily. "This is a great place to be based, but it isn't big enough for everything I want to do."

Lau owned a printing company founded by his father, which he had expanded with substantial business from the United States and Europe. He also was heavily involved in real-estate deals in Southern California and Canada—mainly shopping centers.

"We put together syndicates with the older rich guys who aren't real comfortable investing their money abroad. I understand America so they trust me."

Then he added: "There's an awful lot of money lying around this island in mattresses."

He was a sort of Chinese Duddy Kravitz, a young guy on the make with the gleam of burnished bullion in his eyes. Jeannie was not far behind. They thrived on anxiety: Mercedes with car phone, fax machine, personal computers, telex links to Los Angeles and Toronto. The world couldn't move fast enough for them. Everything was deals and sales. It was a language Singaporeans understood. For instance, Lau's print shop worked two 12-hour shifts a day because that's what his pressmen wanted.

"I pay them U.S. $1,000 a month, but they want the overtime. Thank God, 12-hour days are still no big deal in Singapore."

As we drove across the island, Lau explained the way things worked here.

"Your average Singaporean lives in a little box."

"See, like pigeonholes!" Jeannie pointed out with a disapproving scowl as we passed a block of high-rise housing units. Lau and Jeannie lived in a private home.

"It can be a very regimented life. That's fine for most of the people here. You have a highly skilled work force that is well taken care of. They have their own homes, even if they are apartments in the sky, the government tells them how to save their money and how to behave. Government transportation gets them to work. They pay into a government health care plan. Life is okay. The hard part comes in trying to keep things interesting for the most skilled people."

Singapore, which lagged in cultural life, such as music, theater and museums, needed to stimulate what was becoming one of the most highly educated populations in the world. Typical was the problem of male-female social life, or, as Lau put it, "the dating problem."

"We hear a lot about it from friends," Jeannie laughed. "It seems kind of silly."

"No, no," said Lau. "It's serious. My friends want to go to Los Angeles or San Francisco to meet girls. They're smart guys who can make money anywhere. But they can't meet girls in Singapore. And then what happens to Singapore if none of the smart people have babies anymore?"

"So the government provides what they think is the answer," Jeannie said with a sneer. "They start a Department of Dating."

"It's called the Social Development Unit," Lau explained. "One of the P.M.'s pet projects. He started it when he saw that the birthrate among mothers with graduate educations was dropping. The idea is to get the right people to have babies."

Not that he thought there was anything wrong with such a policy, Lau said. It made sense. Singapore was a small place that had to be kept in balance. Everything about the country required control and continual fine-tuning by the handful of people who knew how to do such things.

Jeannie had her own ideas. She was not comfortable with the government controlling that aspect of her life—to say nothing of the way they went about it.

"Can you imagine that the government sponsors moonlight cruises to get people to marry and breed?" she said. "SDU cruises. I call them the Loveboat for Single, Desperate and Ugly."

Lau frowned at his wife, but said nothing.

We decided to investigate this Social Development Unit, which sounded more like something out of Brave New World than Utopia. The reactions we heard to it ranged from amusement to mild resentment. One member of parliament with whom we talked smiled and called it "socialized sin," others admitted to being a little uneasy but felt assured by the P.M.'s insistence on the importance of the program. In Singapore, we were learning, there was no question that the P.M. knew best.

We scheduled a meeting with Dr. Eileen Aw, director of SDU, at her office in a new downtown high-rise office building.

As we hissed up 40 floors in the quiet, antiseptic elevator, we prepared ourselves to confront the underbelly of modern Asia, where human considerations were discarded in favor of the coldly rational calculations of social engineers. Birthrates were things to be managed precisely. The poor and the ignorant were encouraged not to propagate; only the cream of the race should multiply. And Dr. Eileen Aw, Big Brother's Director of Mating, was the one who made it all work.

Her office was a vast, neon-lit open area lined with ranks of desks and cubicles manned by dozens of prim women in white blouses and dark blue skirts. In the waiting room sat several men in their early 20s, shifting awkwardly in their chairs and avoiding eye contact with each other. Occasionally one of the women would come back and usher a man to an enclosed office.

We were taken to one of those offices where we looked out over the omnipresent harbor and waited. Suddenly the door opened and a woman in a white lab coat said, "I am Dr. Eileen Aw."

She was about five-feet tall, close to 50 years old with graying hair, twinkly eyes and a gentle smile that was all out of proportion to what we expected. As we sat and talked we discovered that she was a physician for the health services at the National University of Singapore—19 years of dealing with mysterious diseases on the day before exams, an unplanned pregnancy here and there, stress-related insomnia. She even had two children of her own.

We were expecting Nurse Ratched and we got the Chinese equivalent of a Jewish mother who wants her daughters to marry doctors. Only in this case, Eileen Aw thought of her daughters as every marriageable woman in Singapore.

"The P.M. asked me to take this job in 1980 after a report he commissioned showed that our women weren't getting married. Thirty percent of those who graduated from the university weren't married by age 30. I knew this to be true. I had many friends who were not married but who did want to get married."

She smiled sadly and continued, "I couldn't very well say no. We are talking about a lot of very unhappy people.

"We also knew that the trend was going to get worse. Thirty years ago, the ratio at the university was four men to one woman. By 1986, it was two women to one man. That is an astonishing change.

London asked why this was so.

"It shows that women study harder than men," Aw said with a smile. "It also shows the power of the Chinese mother. In Singapore, we put no restrictions on who can go to university. If you pass the tests—which aren't easy—you're in. Chinese mothers want all their children to do well. They push and push. The girls take the pushing better."

Further studies confirmed that all these newly educated women weren't getting married while the educated men were marrying less-educated women. It was a wild exaggeration of the syndrome some American professional women complain of. "We had 40 percent of graduate women unmarried and 40 percent of uneducated men unmarried. We also found that it never happens, and I mean never, that educated women marry uneducated men. So what we have tried to influence is people marrying like-educated people."

The task had been daunting. "We found we had to start from the bottom and work up. We don't have much high school dating here. Pressure to get into the university is so intense. We have people who are 30 and have never dated. One young man came to me and told me he didn't know where to begin."

The life-style she described for young Singaporeans was much like that of Susan Lee. "In Singapore we work too hard. Young people go from 7 A.M. to 7 P.M., then watch TV and go to sleep.They are at a loss for what to do on a Saturday afternoon. So they call a buddy, because they have no energy to socialize. That's a very typical pattern.

"So we organize tea dances, outings, cruises—all so they don't have to organize their own social lives.

"For the quiet ones, we also have a matchmaking service. It's very personalized. They apply. They come in for an interview—maybe you saw some in the waiting room?—then their record is put into the computer and compared for like interests.

"But the hardest thing we've had to do is to change attitudes. We found that it wasn't the men as much as it was the women who were unwilling to get involved. They are financially independent and think they don't need men or marriage.

"Women are influenced by Western ideas much more than

men—which makes sense because the West allows women more freedom. Why should a man be Westernized when the East is best for him? Women don't want to just settle for a man. They don't need marriage for marriage's sake. They want to wait for Mr. Right, even if it's unrealistic. Women read more than men, they've been influenced by Western novels.

"Then one day they are 30 and alone and they are unhappy. I know too many women like that."

When Aw took over SDU, there had been private matchmaking services, but they were discredited when it turned out that only a few guys did all the dating. So Aw decided to become the matchmaker of last resort. "Singaporeans feel that if it is a government agency, they have confidence."

And has it worked?

"Over three years, starting in 1984, we have 300 married couples," she beamed.

As soon as students graduate from the National University, they are invited to register with SDU. Of 4,000 graduates, about 1,000 register.

"This is not a coercive program," Aw said. "It's just a service that they can use or not use. This is not the government being manipulative. A lot of people have a problem. Why not help if we can?"

But isn't there a hidden motive in all this, Kelly asked.

"It is government policy that the family unit is very important and must be preserved," she agreed. "A society with too many singles is unstable."

But there was another aspect to SDU that went beyond tea dances and matchmaking and strayed into the realm of genetic selection. The ultimate goal, after all, was to encourage only certain kinds of women to have children. Nobody was looking to find dates for Malay shopgirls or Indian dockworkers.

In 1972, the government said all Singaporean women were having too many babies. "Stop at Two," became the slogan. And the population increase slowed. But a decade later, Lee realized it was the educated women who weren't having children.

The first step was to discourage the poor, mainly through providing financial incentives to have women sterilized after two children. Goh Chok Tong, the deputy prime minister, stated the government's policy this way: "As long as you can provide the proper education, environment and parental care, then you can have three children."

But this did nothing to encourage the better-off to procreate, so Lee hammered home the point in speeches. "At least two, better three, four if you can afford it."

In addition to the dating campaign, a graduate mother's program was set up offering tax incentives and a promise of preferential treatment for the youngsters once they reached school age.

Lee, ever a creative thinker, even toyed with a radical solution that he raised in a speech to students at the National University. He suggested that maybe Singapore would be better off going back to the old Confucian custom of polygamy for the elite. "The way the old society did it was by polygamy," he said about the birth problem. "A successful man had more than one wife." Then Singapore remodeled itself on Western ethics. "It was wrong, it was stupid." He cited the example of modern Japan, where men have mistresses and wives stay home and take care of the children. He noted that former prime minister Kakuei Tanaka had a mistress and said, "The more Tanakas there are in Japan, the more dynamic will be Japanese society."

Public opinion was not with the P.M. on this one and he dropped the issue. But he has not relented in his desire to find a way to mold Singapore's future generations. "You can take the cowardly way out and say, 'Very touchy, leave it, let's think about it,' " he said in another speech. "I am accused often of interfering in the private lives of citizens. Yes, if I did not, had I not done that, we wouldn't be here today."

But when we suggested to Dr. Aw that this was all pretty ominous stuff, she seemed hurt. None of this was about tampering with nature, she said. It was just trying to give the natural urges of boys and girls a little government-sponsored nudge.

"What I do isn't social engineering," she said with that gentle smile. "I just try to make some lonely people happier. How can that hurt?"

One thing we were discovering about Lee Kuan Yew was that he didn't need anyone to interpret his thoughts. He said what was on his mind. When he said he intended to interfere in the private lives of his citizens, he meant it. One had only to read the signs throughout the country to get an indication of what Lee considered the model Singaporean. One who: didn't smoke or spit, didn't litter, smiled, spoke Mandarin, had three children, was courteous, wore short hair, brushed his teeth daily, kept his place in a queue, knew the words to the national songs and sang them in public.

Each of these standards was, at one time or another, the subject of publicity campaigns engineered by the Department of Psychological Defense, a curious unit within the Ministry of Communications run by Richard Tan Kok Tong, who, if not a full-fledged member of the Thought Police, was certainly a few steps closer than Eileen Aw.

Tan, too, had a mission that, by his description, was totally innocent.

"Our job is to win the hearts and minds of the people," he said with an expectant smile. "You remember that phrase from the Vietnam War, don't you? It was a good idea, it just didn't work for you."

Tan was a short, intense man. He met us in his conference room surrounded by six female assistants whom he periodically sent scurrying for one prop or another. Soon the room was filled with the tools of Tan's trade: brochures, posters, leaflets and videocassettes.

"We actually adopted the idea from Sweden and Switzerland. They consider it a matter of national security that people have a sense of their nation. That they think of themselves as belonging. It is doubly important for us. We are a small nation in an unstable region. Events in other countries nearby can affect us. The minute there is cleavage in our society, we are in trouble."

Then Tan explained the carrot-and-stick approach he implemented on behalf of the P.M. "We try to make people feel good about their nation, to give them confidence. But we also remind them of our vulnerability."

We thought of Susan Lee and her worry that if she didn't have four kids, Singapore would fall apart. Whatever Tan was up to, it was succeeding. Yet as he talked on about the various campaigns, we got the impression that most of it was pretty benign or even useful. An anti-spitting effort may seem silly, until you contemplate the notion of two million Chinese in a confined space, many of whom spit habitually for luck.

Typically, the campaigns were based on appeals to public spirit, not negative incentives such as taxes or laws. Confucianism stresses obligations, not rights, and group spirit, not individualism. "We place society above the individual," Lee says. Singaporeans see the role of government as someone who establishes social values, and as long as the government is legitimate and fair, the people must obey it. One particular area of success was the recent "no smoking" campaign. The PM was a chain smoker who quit then turned on the evil weed with a vengeance, vowing a nation of non-smokers. Despite estimates that three-quarters of Chinese men overall smoke, Singapore has few smokers, and the government said the number was steadily declining. The proof was in the fact that while the American tobacco companies were straining to get into the lucrative Korean and Taiwan markets—virtual smoker's paradises—nobody cared much about Singapore.

Tan sensed some of our unease at so much state-driven propaganda. "It may seem like a lot of manipulation. But in America you have so many powerful symbols that you take them for granted. You have great men like Abraham Lincoln and Washington. You see your heritage portrayed in the stories on the Walt Disney TV shows. That is what nation building is all about. Like you we all come from different roots, but it is so sudden. The idea of Psychological Defense is to provide the social glue."

The techniques were at least as creative as Walt Disney. There was, for instance, the stylized drawing of a lion that the government hoped to make into a national icon ("strength, courage and excellence"). It was designed by the BBD&O advertising agency in a 1986 international competition and looked suspiciously like the one used for many years by Harris Bank in Chicago—but if Korea could use Tony the Tiger for the Olympics, why not? Then there was the national song, which resulted from the National Song Competition sponsored by a local soda bottler, proving conclusively the conjunction between pop and patriotism the world over. McCann Erickson, another giant ad agency, won this one with "Count On Me, Singapore" ("Count on me, Singapore/Count on me to give my best and more/You and me, we'll do our part/Stand together, heart to heart").

"We place a great emphasis on songs because people can

participate," said Tan. There was only one problem. Singaporeans are too shy to sing in public. The solution? Yes, a "Sing, Singapore" campaign.

Still, even Richard Tan, the master manipulator, was not sure that the propaganda machine could crank much longer. When his assistants left he told us an interesting parable.

"I see the world composed of sheep, goats and horses. Sheep must be led. Goats can be pushed from behind. And horses do mostly what they want. In the United States, you are horses. Lee Kuan Yew uses fear to motivate—the sheep have to have fear of the wolf around the corner. But now we are becoming goats very quickly. The next generation of leaders has added more hope, more of a sense of goals ahead. Goats need hope.

"But I think the time of the horses will come even more quickly. People read a lot, they travel, they want more say. When we are horses here," he shook his head, "I don't think we will be able to control things with songs and slogans. I'm concerned. There are a lot of things about horses I don't like."

After we left the great goatherd, we decided to go to the zoo. We needed a break from the mental gymnastics of trying to figure out what Singapore was up to. The explanations all seemed so logical, so comfortable. These guys made sense. After the cacophony and barely controlled chaos of our own democracy, here was a government that ran on the basis of a comprehensive plan executed to perfection.

The Singapore Zoological Gardens wasn't yet world-class, though it had the potential, given its location in a region with so many exotic animals. Singapore was the logical exhibition point for creatures lurking in the Borneo rain forests, the remote islands of Indonesia and the deep-sea trenches off the Philippines. What it lacked in quantity of animals, it made up for in the authenticity of their habitat. Located along the Seletar Reservoir in the middle of the island, the lush grounds evoked the dense jungle that once covered the entire country. Most animals were contained by natural barriers, and there were few cages and fences.

Roaming freely was a tribe of orange orangutans, the ugly but intelligent apes who were capable of sitting at a table and drinking tea with a zookeeper. A caretaker who introduced himself as Dr. Roy said that the giant mammals, about two-thirds the size of a gorilla, are facing extinction in the vanishing forests of Borneo and Sumatra. They normally live in small groups up in the tree canopy that arches over the forest.

"There are maybe 4,000 in the wilds now," Dr. Roy said. "We have 19 here, the largest group in captivity. They are happy here and they have reproduced because we have taught them a new way to live. We have induced them to live together in a large colony. They have responded by creating a whole new social hierarchy of their own. They may not have the freedom to roam wherever they want any longer, but we have made them much better off."

That afternoon we discovered we weren't making any progress with the Lee interview. But we were starting to learn more about the man. When it came to maintaining his power he was cleverly ruthless. His enemies were much more likely to end up discredited, humiliated or a member of Lee's party than they were to be imprisoned, executed or "disappeared," as the Latin Americans like to say.

What seemed important to Lee was that he *have* enemies. Like each of the other Dragons—Korea with the North, Taiwan and Hong Kong with China—Lee had to have his bogeymen. Whether he believed them to be a real threat or not, Lee, like many enduring leaders, had convinced the population of sheep that there were wolves out there and that only he knew how to keep them at bay.

Sometimes the bogeymen took strange forms. While we were there, the government was obsessed with rooting out what it called a Marxist cell of young college graduates. Stories appeared in the press about what the Internal Security Department called "a Marxist conspiracy to subvert the existing social and political system in Singapore through communist united-front tactics to establish a communist state."

At a time when most other Asian nations had stopped finding communists lurking under the beds, Singapore staged the largest roundup in a decade, eventually arresting 22 suspects and holding them without trial under the sweeping provisions of the Internal Security Act, the law that allows Lee to do pretty much anything he wants under the guise of national security.

"It is not a practice, nor will I allow subversives to get away by insisting that I have got to prove everything against them in a court," Lee said in defense of the security law. And, indeed, we learned that one Lee opponent named Chia Thye Poh had been held in jail for 21 years under ISA, never having been charged, tried or convicted of any crime.

When their identities were known, the subversives turned out to be a bunch of do-gooders. All were associated with religious, experimental theatre or public welfare groups. Several came from the Geyland Catholic Welfare Center, which, among other things served as a sanctuary for runaway maids. Others were involved with Third Stage, a theatre group known for its recent satire, *Oh! Singapore* that, while tame by American standards, had upset some local officals. Sample song line: "Have trust in *us*/and do what we want you to do/just work hard, play hard, but don't think too much/let *us* decide what's best for you." The theatre's president, Chang Suan Tse, had said at the time of production, "I think it's good that we can look at ourselves and laugh. I suppose it's part of being mature."

Those arrested claimed they had been made to go days without sleep, kept standing for hours in freezing rooms and threatened continually by police. By all accounts, they weren't innocent school kids. During their college days some had been affiliated with Marxist groups. But more recently they had published papers that called for more democracy in Singapore, a freer press, independent trade unions—things considered subversive in few of the world's prosperous countries these days.

Perhaps they were due for some criticism by the government, but as their attorney, Francis Seow, head of the local bar association, put it, "You don't use a steamroller to crack a nut."

The real problem, several people we spoke with suggested, was that Lee felt betrayed by these young upstarts. They were the best and the brightest of Singapore's family—several had advanced degrees and had studied abroad, one at Harvard—and now they were throwing it all in the face of their long-suffering papa. We already knew that Lee took the events of Singapore personally. Now we had an example. These children had all the benefits of education and good homes that Lee's carefully structured society provided, and this was how they repaid him?

Eventually they were all released. But from several paranoid young people we talked to we got the clear sense that Lee's point had been made: Let us decide what's best for you.

And just as our own paranoia was feeling nicely stoked, there was the magazine hunt. We went from hotel lobby to bookstore to kiosk looking for *Time*, the *Far Eastern Economic Review* and the *Asian Wall Street Journal*—three staples of any traveling businessman—before someone was kind enough to tell us that they had been banned. The actual Singapore term was "gazetted," which meant that only a handful of copies could be distributed under government control. Lee's philosophy was: We don't mind if people in Singapore read your magazine, we just don't want you to make any money in the process.

The foreign press, it seemed, was Lee's most reliable bogeyman that, again with seeming irrationality, he attacked at the slightest provocation, using the provisions of the Undesirable Publications Act. Clearly it did no good to the country that hoped to be an international entrepôt center and sophisticated regional headquarters depot to ban major international publications. The same could be said for a country with a thriving printing industry that sought to become a regional center of printing. Yet ban they did.

When the *Far Eastern Economic Review* ran an article about the sudden strength of a Lee opponent, the P.M. declared that the magazine was meddling in domestic politics and slashed its circulation. When the *Straits Times,* the largely captive local paper, criticized the government's action, its editor, Peter Lim, was removed from his job. Later, *Time* angered the P.M. when it refused to print, verbatim, the government's letter of reply to a critical piece. The *Asian Wall Street Journal* earned Lee's eternal ire by cutting right to the heart of the matter. In an editorial, the *Journal* called a series of court actions against one of Lee's opponents "official harassment." The editorial continued, "We don't know if Mr. Jeyaretnam is guilty, but even if he were, many Singaporeans wouldn't believe it because court actions and especially libel suits have long been used in Singapore against opposition politicians."

We gather that the next sound heard was the steam coming off Lee's forehead. The next act was a cut in the *Journal*'s circulation from 5,000 to 400, followed by an exchange of letters in which the government demanded corrections and an unedited reply.

When we started asking government officials about the press disputes, we were given as the definitive response a copy of a speech made by B. G. Lee, son of the P.M. and heir apparent. "We recognize no First Amendment right to freedom of the press," Lee said bluntly. "We do not aim to approximate U.S. practice as an ideal." The careful, articulate speech pointed out that no foreign publications had a right to circulate in Singapore and that if the government thought a publication was stirring up trouble, it would be cut off. The reason, Lee said, was because Singapore was a small, volatile country and passions, or riots, could be inflamed by outsiders.

Made sense to us. At least for a while. But in the end, the issue wasn't just the press. It was appearances versus reality, which was the whole puzzle of Singapore. Here was an example of how so much lay under the surface in Singapore. Things appeared fine. There were lots of magazines on the newsstand—all you could want. Unless you happened to want something the government didn't want you to have.

The magazine hunt led us to the person who could be considered the largest bogeyman in Lee's recent years, goading him, taunting him, sending him into apoplectic fits, reminding him of his insecurities and finally, needing to be destroyed. His name was J. B. Jeyaretnam and when we called his law office to ask for an appointment, he got on the phone and said, "Oh, sure. Come on this afternoon. I don't have much to do these days."

His office, in a decaying modern building a block from City Hall, smelled of the musty books that cluttered its shelves and desktops to an impenetrable depth. Two secretaries sat idly chatting. From behind a glass partition emerged a man who was a palette of brown: skin beyond cocoa almost to mauve, peach shirt, tan tie and brown suit. Sweeping silver mutton-chop sideburns gave him the look of a Dickensian barrister, but the shiny gray eyes that smiled in advance of the mouth made clear that this would have to be one of Dickens' more mischievous characters.

"I am Jeya," he said, extending his hand. He was also, as we quickly learned, a little depressed these days. The windy standard-bearer of the beleaguered Singapore opposition had met the full force of Lee's displeasure and it took his breath away. Lee had finally brought out the heavy artillery against Jeya and slammed him with damning sanctions.

"They've finally got me out of parliament," Jeya said a bit wistfully. "Can you believe that Lee views me as the greatest threat to his continued rule?"

His stooped shoulders shrugged into his frayed shirt collar in a gesture so pathetic as to leave some doubt that the P.M.'s paranoia was ill-directed.

"And I can't comment on whether they are trumped-up charges," he said as the final humiliation, "because then they will get me for contempt of parliament."

Jeya had just lost a four-year legal battle over charges he fraudulently used party funds. The government lost the first trial but won on a second try. Jeya's sentence was a month in jail, but more important he was stripped of his seat. Lee was still threatening to seek disbarment proceedings, depriving Jeya of a livelihood. Whether the charges were trumped up or not, the *Wall Street Journal* was correct in assessing that everyone believed they were. Part of what Lee had wrought was a legal system with little credibility when it came to "political" crimes.

The financial cost to Jeya was also high. "My practice has suffered. A lot of work depends on government. You need a license to do anything. That's how he keeps the legal profession in line. If a businessman uses the wrong lawyer, he won't get what he wants."

J. B. (for Joshua Benjamin) Jeyaretnam was born in Sri Lanka of parents living in Johore, just across the causeway in Malaysia. He studied law at University College in London, while Lee was at Cambridge. They both returned to Singapore to practice as barristers and Jeyaretnam was one of Lee's political supporters as he moved up the ladder.

"He was for the rights of the individual and the worker. In 1959 when he took over as P.M., I was in favor of him. I saw that Lee had the interests of Singapore at heart, but also that he was very personally ambitious.

"In 1965, after we were thrown out of Malaysia, he shed tears in public, but he was principally responsible. If he couldn't be P.M. of all Malaysia, then he wanted complete control of Singapore. He lost no time in undermining the institutions of society: trade unions, the press, the courts. He did what Hitler did. And I was completely disenchanted. He was moving toward totalitarianism."

It wasn't until 1971 that Jeya decided to try to do something about Lee. He became active in the Workers Party and began a long and lonely battle to be elected to parliament. Finally, after six tries, he was victorious in 1981. It was a blow to Lee's People's Action Party, which had lately been winning all the seats, but Lee tolerated the colorful, eccentric speeches of Jeya until the 1984 election, when the PAP's vote total slipped to 63 percent and Lee reportedly flew into a rage and considered a change in the voting laws. He said that perhaps one-man, one-vote was wrong for Singapore, as it sometimes gave "freak" results.

Suddenly, Lee was more threatened by Jeya. He began challenging him on the floor of parliament, he cracked down on news outlets that were sympathetic to him and he pressed the criminal case against him.

"He can't find a legitimate peg to hang me on," Jeya said. "He can't call me a communist or even a Marxist, because I'm not. Everything I do is in the open. All I want is some more democracy, a more open government.

"It would be churlish to say he hasn't accomplished some good things. But they have been bought at a price. What has happened is that we are a nation designed to benefit the elite. Everything is the emphasis on excellence. There is no place for the ordinary people. And less than ordinary. The government has admitted that 15 to 20 percent of the population has fallen out; they are in poverty. But they are Singaporean too. Don't we have to do something for them?"

We went to see Augustine Tan, a sitting member of parliament and sometime critic of the government who nonetheless answered Jeya's question with an emphatic "no."

"We all started as social democrats, but we learned more about human nature," said Tan, who taught economics at the National University. "Maybe all but Jeyaretnam. The welfare state doesn't work. We have learned that lesson and we don't need to go back and relearn it.

"Singapore is a success because we have a work ethic—if you don't work you don't get anything. And we have a subtle but firm authoritarianism. But to understand why, you have to understand where Lee came from—where we all came from. We came out of the chaos of World War II. Our generation has seen close up what the world can be like, so we work to keep the chaos from coming back. Lee is the way he is for a reason. But there is only one bottom-line question: How can you argue with success?"

While we waited for word on an interview that was looking less and less likely, we learned these things about Lee Kuan Yew.

There is a story some Singaporeans tell in hushed tones that when Lee was 11 years old, he asked an uncle if he could have one of his canaries to keep as a pet. When the uncle refused, Lee supposedly plucked all the feathers from the tiny bird.

In his critical biography of Lee—which, remarkably, is on sale in Singapore bookstores—T. J. S. George quotes a former shipmate of Lee's who recalled how he quickly made a name for himself when he was traveling to England to attend university. There were six passengers to a cabin and each morning the steward brought a ration of three buckets of water per cabin. Lee, however, would wake up before dawn and use all the water for himself—and sometimes go looking in other cabins for more. "This, of course, made him quite unpopular," the passenger recalled. "But he didn't seem to care."

Professor C. Northcote Parkinson, an Englishman who taught for many years at the University of Singapore, describes Lee this way: "Utterly without charm, his expression is one of barely concealed contempt; for his opponents, for his followers, perhaps for himself. . . . One cannot imagine that he is even capable of friendship."

George himself writes of Lee, "When he talks of creating a new Singapore, he means, of course, creating a new society that will justify his own attitudes to life . . . partly it is a way of compensating for his alienation by making a society in his own image—the projection on to the national scene of an individual's complex psychological problems."

But then there was this quote from former president Richard Nixon: "The fact that a leader of Lee's breadth of vision was not able to act on a broader stage represents an incalculable loss to the world." Henry Kissinger went further, calling Lee "the smartest man in the Western world."

Lee was a complicated man who elicited strong reactions, that much we knew. But there had been few attempts to probe his life. His past was that of Singapore's; his identity and the country's had become one. His legacy surrounded him—in concrete and glass as well as flesh and blood—and he felt no need to promote his triumphs. He was, we had been told, contemptuous of most journalists. He rarely granted interviews and the one semi-official biography, *Lee Kuan Yew,* by Alex Josey, was mostly a collection of speeches. All the many stories about Singapore contained few anecdotes about its prime minister and little insight into his personality.

From what we could gather, Lee treated government service like something of a priesthood. His dedication was total. His only hobby was golf, at which he was said to have a nine handicap. He never read books for pleasure, didn't listen to music or watch movies. A gaunt man, he nonetheless exercised every morning to keep his weight down. He ate lightly and never touched bread or rice. In his early days in politics, he gave up beer and the Cambridge-acquired pipe, realizing that he would have to be in top shape to endure the grueling round of community meetings and speeches that were so crucial to his first successes. From those days on, he characteristically carried with him a thermos bottle of green tea that he sipped incessantly.

His dress became the uniform of his People's Action Party: white short-sleeve shirt with open collar, tan pants and, occasionally, a sport coat. He was compulsively clean, changing his shirts several times a day and washing his hands repeatedly.

His office was austere and functional, befitting a civil servant. His public manner was stern bordering on arrogant. He was known as a superb debater, picking apart the arguments of his rare opponents in clipped British-educated tones.

He was, by all appearances an incorruptible man who seemed immune to the politician's common sins of greed and lust—though pride seemed a constant companion. Alone among Asian nations, Singapore in the almost three decades of Lee's rule has never had a high-level corruption scandal. He had built an extremely wealthy society, yet seemed uninterested in enjoying any of the fruits of that wealth. It was as if there was no need to hoard cash for the future because for Lee there was no future. Despite his talk of succession, he planned to control the destiny of Singapore until his death, unless, as Jan Morris wrote, death hasn't been banned in Singapore by then.

From a variety of sources we managed to piece together his career. Lee Kuan Yew was born September 16, 1923—probably in Singapore, though some accounts say in Indonesia—to a middle-class Chinese family that had lived in the city for a century. They were originally Hakka Chinese, a group that settled in the southern Chinese province of Kwangtung but scattered all over Asia as they fled the various hard times and persecutions of the Chinese empire. The Hakkas had a sense of adventure and would rather pick up and move than stay and suffer. They were respected as tough businessmen and known for their arrogance, determination and energy.

From its founding, Singapore had been a Chinese island in the middle of a Muslim world. Malaysia to the north and Indonesia to the south shared the Islamic religion and a suspicion of the Chinese who, as far back as the early 19th century, were viewed as outsiders with an uncanny ability to make money. One reason was their commercial alliances with the British, who seemed more comfortable dealing with a Chinese who was motivated by money than a Muslim who was motivated by religion. Lee's great-grandfather and grandfather both had worked as go-betweens for British business interests and had become Anglicized to the point that they were part of the so-called community of King's Chinese.

Lee's parents were Lee Chin Koon, who held a high status but not necessarily high-paying job with a foreign oil company, and Chua Jim Neo, an intense woman of Chinese and Malay descent. Both parents revered the British, then at the height of their powers, as did Lee's grandfather, Lee Hoon Leong, who vowed on the birth of his grandson to make him the equal of any Englishman. He was given a Chinese name—it means "the light that shines"—but his family used his English name, Harry, which was logical since his mother raised him on the English language.

As is still the custom with Chinese mothers, she also pinched pennies on household funds so her son could go to the best schools. Lee was admitted to the British-run Raffles Institution for high school and quickly rose to the top of his class. He also won a partial scholarship to study in England and was set to go when the war intervened.

"The war was a traumatic experience for Kuan Yew," wrote T. J. S. George. "He was a naturally sensitive boy and he was an impressionable 19 when the conquerors arrived. He was to say many years later that the Japanese 'never knew what they did to a whole generation like me. But they did make me, and a generation like me, determined to work for freedom from servitude and foreign domination. I did not enter politics. They brought politics on me.' "

Lee's political epiphany began when he lost faith in the Brits, after the Japanese made their legendary conquest of Singapore. As the stunned British and Australian troops, including Governor Shenton Thomas in pressed white ducks, were herded the 14 miles to Changi prison, Lee was one of those who watched in disbelief, silent and uncheering, confounding the Japanese who had hoped to be received as liberators.

Lee, like the rest of Singapore, had no more faith in the Japanese. The lesson he learned was not to be subjugated by anyone. The Japanese may have tried to portray themselves as Asian kindred spirits, but their conduct in Singapore during the war demonstrated that yellow men could be even more imperious and racist than the British. Behind their rhetoric of the Greater Asian Co-Prosperity Sphere, the Japanese saw themselves as the only truly superior men. But Harry Lee knew better.

During the Japanese occupation, Singapore, renamed Syonan, was a horror both physically and psychologically. The *kempeitai,* Japanese military police, ruled the town through fear and suspicion and came down particularly hard on the Chinese. While Indian and Malay petty criminals were usually released with a warning, the Chinese were routinely decapitated, their heads put on public display. Males from 18 to 50 were regularly rounded up and interrogated as subversives. Hooded informers pointed out those they said were anti-Japanese, or those they merely didn't like. Boatloads of Chinese were taken out to sea and shot or drowned. The Japanese admit killing 5,000 Chinese this way, but other evidence suggest the number may have been many times higher.

Treachery and survival became an art form as various

groups competed against each other and lobbied the Japanese for favorable treatment. Malays turned against Indians, the Chinese-born were suspicious of the natives. As the black market raged, values were turned upside down. The sleaziest people prospered. Racketeers and gamblers were kings; informers and secret agents were role models for survival. The educated and wealthy were targets for blackmail. And then, in the torturous final weeks before the war's end, municipal services collapsed, the lines for rice became long and anarchy reigned in streets filled with the sick and homeless.

Finally, on Sept. 5, 1945, Lord Louis Mountbatten accepted the Japanese surrender and the myth of Japanese invincibility was destroyed—just as the British myth had been destroyed almost four years earlier.

It is unclear exactly how the war affected Lee and his family, but the boy who would become known as an ultimate pragmatist appears to have made his own early bargain with the devil. He quickly learned Japanese and went to work as a translator for Domei, the Japanese news agency. There is interesting speculation that what he may have been doing was working for British intelligence.

One reason for this speculation is what happened immediately after the war: Lee was given free passage to England on a crowded troopship at a time when any transportation was hard to come by. He was also given an upgrade on his scholarship, transferring from the London School of Economics to Cambridge. There he yet again showed his relentless nature by convincing the master of his college to allow him to live off-campus in order to be closer to his fiancée, Kwa Geok Choo, who was studying at another Cambridge college across town.

"It was the story of his life," wrote British journalist Dennis Bloodworth of Lee's manipulations. "When he wanted something he would display the cool cheek of a man whose very will to have his own way made him self-confident. And what he wanted was not always easy to get, for he was a worrier and a perfectionist, forever metaphorically lining up papers with the edge of the desk."

He worried himself into high honors in law at Cambridge, which led to an oft-repeated quote that would have made his grandfather proud: "I speak to Harold MacMillan [British prime minister] and Duncan Sandys [colonial secretary] as equals. At Cambridge I got two firsts and a star for distinction; Harold MacMillan didn't."

Singapore after the war was a universe away from the placid, medieval quadrangles of Cambridge. Like all the countries of Asia, it was a broken place with a tottering economy, hordes of refugees, rationed food (four ounces of rice a day for men, three for women) and streets ruled by thugs and, increasingly, communists. The uneasy wartime alliance the British had made with communist guerillas in Malaya had returned to haunt them as they now faced a seasoned, armed opponent intent on driving them out. The year 1948 began what the British diffidently called "the Emergency," a vicious guerilla war that was to take 12 years and 3,000 civilian lives before it ended. Largely because of the communists, the British made Singapore, Malaya and the states of Sabah and Sarawak on the island of Borneo into Malaysia and announced their intention of granting independence. It was just a matter of how they would extricate themselves.

Lee returned from Cambridge in 1950 and soon opened the husband-and-wife law firm Lee and Lee, Advocates and Solicitors, in a shabby second-floor office on Malacca Street. But it was his wife, called Choo, also an honors student, who ran the firm and bore three children while Lee pursued politics. He came to public attention in 1953 with his defense of student journalists at the University of Malaya who had been charged with sedition. It was, ironically, his fervent defense of civil liberties and a free press that won him notoriety.

Whether he believed what he argued was not the point. As British journalist Noel Barber noted, "He started as he meant to go on, with no scruples about allying himself with enemies he despised if it suited his purpose, or jettisoning allies if they became tiresome or dangerous."

Lee formed his own People's Action Party in 1954. He took in the communists, leftists and anyone else outside the mainstream just to become a credible opposition party. It was a dangerous strategy because it is doubtful his sympathies ever lay with the left. The thesis of Dennis Bloodworth's book, *The Tiger and the Trojan Horse,* is that Lee decided to ride the tiger of communism to gain power quickly while the communists saw him as a Trojan horse to get them into mainstream politics. In the end, Lee executed a masterful strategy of using the communists, keeping them in check until he consolidated power, and then crushing them by exiling their leaders or throwing them in jail. Some argue that it was this dangerous flirtation, which almost backfired, that has given Lee his paranoia about communists under every bed and prompted his occasional irrational crackdowns.

Lee was elected the first prime minister of the new state of Singapore on June 3, 1959. He called for "a social revolution by peaceful means" and all the fears that the British had of renewed labor unrest and radical, anti-capitalist reforms were quieted. Lee moved quickly on many fronts. His ministers were due at their desks by 8 A.M., not the customary British start at 10. He announced that anyone who threatened the fragile peace between management and labor would be jailed. He also started his paternal quest to clean up Singapore's morals and habits, going after the city's seamy side by eliminating juke boxes and striptease shows. Singapore, he said, suffered from a "sex-obsessed yellow culture" and he intended to put a stop to it. He also quickly began to implement his philosophy of an egalitarian, multiracial society that would be rid of the castes and classes that had infected Asia from its earliest history. Egalitarian, though, meant that everyone was to be given equal opportunities. Lee was by breeding and inclination an elitist who most certainly did not believe that all men were created equal when it came to intelligence or productivity. He was convinced from the start that Singapore had to be ruled by a small group of exceptional men. The cream would rise to the top.

"We are born unequal and we've got to make the best of the lot," Lee once said in a speech. "And whether it is fruit trees, whether it is race horses, whatever it is, this is the way nature works. . . . Don't we want to use some common sense and say to ourselves, 'The more we have of people who can run this economy better, the better it is for everybody'? "

With a few exceptional men in place, he turned his attention to the economy. With Goh Keng Swee, a fellow student from his days in England, he set out to turn this sloppy, shattered backwater into an industrialized nation. Creation of jobs would be the ultimate accomplishment and Lee and Goh decided that as tiny as it was, Singapore had to follow the model of Japan after World War II and become a factory. Bodies were the only natural resource, so a way had to be found to encourage foreign companies to set up shop in Singapore. Lee's goals were, especially in the early days, socialist. He wanted the state to provide for the needs of the population. But his methods were capitalist. The rule was not that citizens contributed what they could and were given what they needed, but rather, the more they contributed, the more they received. Enterprise and the free-market system were ideas Lee believed in at a time when they were unpopular in most of Asia. The state would create a livable environment and would coax businesses along, but the individual was on his own. His success or failure was up to him. "The government has to be the planner and the mobilizer of the economic effort," Goh explained. "But the free enterprise system, correctly nurtured and adroitly handled, can serve as a powerful and versatile instrument of economic growth."

But before they could do much on the economy, they had to deal with a crippling array of social problems that kept Singapore on a par with Third World countries. Lee's hoped-for work force was hungry, sick, uneducated and living in hovels. Lee moved quickly on all fronts. Through the astute courting of international organizations such as the United Nations, public housing was thrown up, roads built, health care improved. Lee also cracked down hard on the unions, gutting their power by jailing the most militant leaders and threatening the others. If he was going to sell the sweat of Singaporeans on the international market, he was going to have to be able to guarantee the price as well as a stable environment in which to do business.

"The excesses of irresponsible trade unions are luxuries we can no longer afford," he said. New laws allowed longer hours, fewer holidays, less overtime and fringe benefits, and no strikes.

But if low wages were to be the stick, Lee also had a carrot. He promised Singaporeans that if they would follow his vision and build a nation, they would be rewarded. He and his minister of culture, Sinathamby Rajaratnam, worked to instill a common purpose in the motley assortment of races and cultures that found themselves shipwrecked on the tiny island. The clean-up campaigns, the no-spitting laws, the national songs all took on new significance in the context of an effort to make people think of Singapore first and themselves second. The intent, Rajaratnam said, was to create "a Singaporean of a unique kind.

He would be a man rooted in the cultures of four great civilizations but not belonging exclusively to any of them." Only together, Lee would say, can we succeed. Pick yourselves up. Take pride in your country and your work, and we'll survive in a cruel world. He urged discipline and ruggedness and decried corruption. Soon after he took office he pointedly warned one notorious corruptor of Third World officials, the United States, "You are not dealing with Ngo Dinh Diem or Syngman Rhee. You do not buy and sell this government."

He also offered concrete benefits such as an increase in employers' contributions to pensions, which became a powerful tool of fiscal policy, allowing the government to rebuild the island's infrastructure.

The strategy worked. Foreign companies began to come. Shell Oil opened a $30 million oil refinery and textile companies set up shop in the vast industrial park called Jurong. As the skill of the work force improved, more sophisticated companies such as television and computer makers found Singapore a hospitable place to do business. Eventually local entrepreneurs also began to participate and start-up companies succeeded. But always there was the fine hand of the government controlling the process, setting wage rates, adjusting tax levies, allocating bank credit, demanding that citizens save and using the savings to build new housing. It was a system that few socialists would recognize, though hard-core capitalists would be equally astonished at the government meddling. This "free market" economy was run more like a giant corporation with Lee Kuan Yew as chairman of the board. It was a high-risk, hybrid economy that put incredible responsibility on those at the top to make the right decisions. But somebody must have been guessing right more often than not because the experiment worked. From the 1960s through the 1980s, Singapore's annual growth rate has averaged close to 10 percent a year.

Iron-fisted politics was also part of the plan. How necessary it was isn't as clear as the evidence of economic success. Could the Singapore miracle have been accomplished without the repression? The curtailment of civil rights? The cowing of the population? In the early days, it was clear that order and stability had to be maintained. The Singapore that Lee and his brain trust inherited was riven with violent strikes and various bombings and assassinations that spilled over from the feuds of its neighbors in Malaysia and Indonesia. The Internal Security Act of the British rule was strengthened. Public assemblies of more than five people were not allowed without police permission. Those who tried to topple the system were jailed. It was harsh medicine, but it worked. Singapore was viewed as an island of stability in a sea of turmoil.

"I am also a realist," Lee explained. "The magnitude of what one terms license, or civil liberties or personal freedom has got to be adjusted to the circumstance." Recalling the 1955 bus strike riots in an interview with Dennis Bloodworth, Lee said, "It is vividly etched in my mind; and every time anybody starts anything that will unwind and unravel this orderly, organised, sensible, rational society and make it irrational, emotional, I put a stop to it—and without hesitation."

But as time went on, the conceit of Lee and his chosen technocrats evolved to a belief that without them, Singapore was doomed to fail. Order became synonymous with their own tenure. Only they could manage this unique economy they had created, so they rationalized that whatever kept them in power was good for Singapore. Soon, it wasn't just bona fide subversives, but any who opposed Lee who were jailed without charge and released at his whim. Politicians who spoke out against him were sued for libel, investigated and prosecuted for making false statements. Some perhaps deserved jail, but the legal proceedings made it difficult to know the truly dangerous from the bothersome.

The last major event in Lee's consolidation of power was Singapore's independence. Lee probably started in politics with the notion that he would first be prime minister of Singapore and then head of the much vaster Federation of Malaysian States, the collection of onetime colonies that Great Britain was gradually weaning into an independent nation. What Lee wanted, he said audaciously in the early 1960s, was for Singapore to be "the New York of Malaysia." It quickly became apparent that this was not to be, as the Malays decided they didn't want a bunch of Chinese pushing them around in their own country.

Not that Lee wasn't in turn suspicious of the Malays. Often on his mind was the word "amok," which *Webster's Dictionary* defines as "a murderous frenzy that occurs chiefly among Malays." The journalist Noel Barber wrote: "It is the fearful, inexplicable outburst of demented frenzy that causes the people of Malaya to run amok—for no apparent reason to attack, maim, kill anyone near them during a period of frenzy that lends them an almost incredible strength." We had no idea whether there was any truth to this notion—the idea of one culture being plagued with irrational outbursts seemed a little farfetched—but the Singaporeans believed it. The history of Singapore shows that from the early 1800s, the island has had a number of instances of seemingly unmotivated Malay riots, most seriously in 1964 when 35 people died and 600 were injured.

That year there seemed to be a reason, however: A deal to unify Singapore and Malaysia was in the works between Lee and Tunku Abdul Rahman, the Malay prime minister. There is wide dispute over whether Lee ever wanted the merger to go through. Publicly he supported it, though he antagonized the Tunku at every turn, refusing, for instance, to give up the title prime minister. Certainly the riots made Lee realize that the goal of one nation was unrealistic. The Tunku eventually drafted a bill to make Singapore an independent nation and, in August 1965, Lee signed it. At the age of 43, Lee had total control of a nation with industrial peace and political quiet.

While we were in Singapore, we discovered that the Tunku was still alive. Retired since the late 1960s, he was living on the island of Penang, off the northwest coast of Malaysia. We decided to see if, given age and distance, the Tunku would be one person willing to talk candidly of Lee and 1965, the critical turning point in his career.

Penang, at the north end of the Strait of Malacca, was another former British outpost that had been recolonized by Chinese immigrants. The road along the sea was lined with crumbling mansions that had been built by opium dealers and the sister hotel to Raffles, the far more authentic E & O, still commanded a stretch of oceanfront. But Penang, too, was prospering. They called it Silicon Island for all the semiconductor plants that had sprung up. The inescapable names of Hitachi, Sanyo and National were all over town.

The Tunku lived in a small estate guarded by several plainclothes policemen. He may once have enjoyed the privacy due the "father of Malaysian independence," but a suburb had grown up around him made of large houses occupied by Japanese electronics executives.

We were escorted down a long hall stocked with the trophies of a great career. The walls were adorned with tiger skins and skulls. Glass cases held a huge collection of walking sticks, silver cups, plates, plaques, scrolls and photos commemorating the birth of a nation. One showed him waving to the crowd on Merdeka Day, independence day, 1957, when the British relinquished control of their former colony. Everyone including the British wore ornately silly hats, the Tunku was in an elaborate fez. It could have been a scene from the Marx Brothers in Freedonia if the business at hand hadn't been so serious. In fact, as much as it was easy to view Malaysia, with its oversize mosques, sultans' palaces and Islamic-Chinese culture, as a bizarre place, they, too, had accomplished a great deal in 20 or 30 years and the Tunku was responsible for getting them started.

We waited in our socks until we were ushered into the Tunku's den. The father of Malaysian independence sat in a rocking chair watching American Saturday morning cartoons—specifically, Muppet Babies. There were children's toys scattered around, but no children. An aide whispered into his ear and the Tunku turned to us with a smile.

"So you are going to see my old friend Mr. Lee?" he said with what could have been sarcasm or just the bonhomie of a veteran politician. He was 84 years old and loose dentures garbled some of his words. But his voice was strong and his mind clear.

We said that we weren't sure if we'd get to see Lee, but that we were interested in knowing more about him.

"He is a strong character, a man of real determination who could control the Chinese people—which is something not many have succeeded at anywhere. I didn't want to take Singapore as part of Malaysia. I resisted for many years. But when Mr. Lee came along, I decided to see if we could reach an agreement."

The Tunku had been the great conciliator. He had persuaded the British to grant independence, had forged alliances between the Chinese, who were about 30 percent of the population, and the Malays, about 50 percent. A son of the sultan of Kedah, he had the stature to bring each of the other sultans—who acted as a sort of shadow feudal government—into the agreement. He even brought the remote states of Sabah and Sarawak on the island of Borneo into the Malaysian federation. But the nettle in his side was always Lee.

Singapore was part of the original federation, but Lee quickly became a controversial figure in the Kuala Lumpur parliament. The Malays feared that he was plotting a Chinese takeover of the country. He personified all that the docile Malays detested about the Chinese: He was aggressive, ambitious and arrogant. More conservative members of the ruling party pressured the Tunku to force Lee out or even arrest him.

The Tunku told us that at first he resisted and tried to work out a compromise. But during a trip to London in June 1965, he became ill and had to be hospitalized. While he was gone, the campaign against Lee, fueled by Muslim fundamentalists within the party, had already sparked riots in which several dozen people were killed and hundreds injured. From his hospital bed, the Tunku decided that either he would have to overthrow the government of Singapore or expel the state from the federation. When he returned to Kuala Lumpur, he told Lee that unless Singapore went its own way, he would not be able to prevent the bloodshed.

When Lee went on television to announce to the nation the separation, he wept, saying, "All my life, my whole adult life, I have believed in merger and unity of the two territories." He called Singapore's expulsion "a moment of anguish." But the Tunku later portrayed his performance as crocodile tears. "I don't know why Mr. Lee acted like that," the Tunku said. "He was quite pleased about it."

The Tunku's theory was that Lee either wanted to be prime minister of all of Malaysia or to pull Singapore out so he could at least have total control of the city-state. In the end, Singapore seemed the victim, but Lee had pressed so hard for power in the first months of the federation that the Tunku became convinced he was trying to provoke a confrontation. "He saw himself as the legitimate leader of Malaysia," recalled the Tunku. "He even spoke Malay better than I did." Lee, he laughed, "was too clever by half."

In his history of Singapore, John Drysdale quotes the inscription the Tunku wrote to Lee when he sent a copy of his memoirs: "To the man who worked hard to form Malaysia, but who worked even harder to break away."

But 20-some years after Lee stopped being a daily source of pain, as he sat in his frayed den with a Barbie Doll commercial chattering in the background, the Tunku said he was no longer sure who had made the better deal. "Lee has created a true multiracial society. He has one state. His people are united."

Not so in Malaysia, where tensions between the Malays and the Chinese were as high as they had been since 1969 when the Muslims turned on the Chinese, wrecking their shops and killing several hundreds.

"We started out in a very happy way," he mused. "We ended British rule. We fought off the communists. Despite Mr. Lee, we tried to get the Chinese and the Malays to get along. Now I see things slipping back."

He talked of the laws that discriminated against the Chinese, but how, despite all the favoritism, the Malays were unable to make economic progress. Of the resurgence of Islamic fundamentalism. Of the government crackdown on the press and the courts. Of the recurrent government financial scandals.

"Mr. Lee has avoided that. He has done well."

And after thanking us for coming, he turned back to his cartoons.

Whether Lee truly had designs on splitting from Malaysia or not, in August 1965, he had no choice but to make it on his own. Always the master of manipulating the public mood, he used the hardship as a way of spurring unity and productivity. In a remarkably short time, he had implemented his plan for remaking Singapore in his image.

What he created, and continued to refine for the next 20 years, was something hard for the West to understand. Or, at least for us to easily capture. The historian C. M. Trumbull calls it "pragmatic socialism or paternal capitalism." Jan Morris, mulling the Lee miracle, wrote of his philosophy, "It is a sort of mystic materialism, a compelling marriage between principle and technique which neither capitalism nor Soviet communism seem to have achieved." As Lee himself put it, "A society to be successful must maintain a balance between nurturing excellence and encouraging the average to improve. There must be both cooperation and competition between people in the same society."

In Singapore, the state did not own all the means of production. But private industry didn't own it either. The government was an investor in many large companies and, like many substantial investors, didn't involve itself in running the business day to day. But when things weren't going well, the executives knew that they ultimately had to answer to Lee Kuan Yew. The government also planned the overall economy, deciding which businesses would get favorable loans and tax breaks and which would have to survive on their own—or fail.

Singapore was not a welfare state that taxed the rich in order to dish out benefits to everyone else. If you didn't work, you didn't eat was the philosophy. Yet the government had an intricate system for forcing people to save their money and thus provide for needs such as housing, medical care and retirement benefits. A workingman in Singapore would have to be an idiot to so badly manage his life that he ended up destitute.

What would be considered intolerable government meddling in the United States, and cruel government complacency in some of the socialist nations of Europe, worked in Singapore because of the wide acceptance of the Confucian philosophy.

"Looking back over the last 30 years," Lee said in a 1987 interview with the *New York Times,* "one of the driving forces that made Singapore succeed was that the majority of the people placed the importance of the welfare of society above the individual, which is a basic Confucian concept." It also gave Singapore the discipline to work hard in return for future gratification, Lee said. His nation avoided the strife of many developing nations that were too eager to enjoy success "before there are many fruits to distribute."

What he feared was the Westernization of Singapore, the corrupting influence of his citizens reading "too many American magazines or British textbooks that instill the belief in the rights of the individual." In the West, "the state and the individual are put on par. This is not acceptable in Confucianist societies."

It was this social contract that Lee worked so hard to preserve. He was the stern papa, all right, but he didn't drink, gamble or womanize so the kids stayed in line. He and his key people lived modestly and worked hard, which convinced the people of Singapore that the government had the people's best interests at heart. Thus Lee could give speeches such as this: "I say without the slightest remorse that we wouldn't be here, would not have made the economic progress, if we had not intervened on very personal matters—who your neighbor is, how you live, the noise you make, how you spit (or where you spit) or what language you use. . . ."

Or, as he once put it more succinctly, "We decide what is right. Never mind what the people think."

There was one other speech of Lee's to which we paid close attention. He delivered it while we were in the country, at a celebration of National Day, an occasion he chose to recap some of his accomplishments. In 1959, he said, 90 percent of the people owned no property. "Twenty-eight years after we took over control of Singapore, 80 percent own homes—and soon it will be 94 percent. Every home has a telephone, refrigerator and television set. Our society has become 80 percent middle class. Our people have important stakes in Singapore's stability and prosperity."

The accomplishments were truly extraordinary—beyond those of Korea, Taiwan or, for the average man, even Japan. Something we had noticed from reading the old stories about Lee was that criticism was nothing new. He had been slammed as an authoritiarian since the 1960s, called a merciless despot, compared to Idi Amin and Hitler. The difference was that now he didn't seem to feel the need to justify his methods or to explain them. Singapore is not the West, he now said with pride, and, we sometimes felt, the implication was that Singapore was better than the West. His Asian neighbors, who had been so suspicious of this arrogant, disciplined ruler, were now seeing the outcome and they liked it. It was not a coincidence that Goh Keng Swee, the father of the Singapore economy, was a regular visitor to Beijing and that some China watchers felt that if Deng Xiaoping had his way, he would remake China in the image of Singapore. The marketplace of ideas had voted and it said that Singapore was a success.

Ironically, while Lee was fearing the encroachment of the West, we feared the opposite. The very success of Singapore troubled us in a perverse way. Of all the Asian nations we had visited, Singapore was at once the most Western on the surface, but the most Eastern underneath. We bristled at the authority, the rules, the conformity—all concepts tolerated only in small doses by those who grew up in the last half of the American century. Singapore's success—which was symbolic of the other Dragons—said to the world, "The rules are changing. Freedom is not top priority." After her own travels, Jan Morris offered this chilling thought: "Could Lee Kuan Yew be right, in claiming that in Singapore, at least, the rich man was happier than the free? How long would you pine for liberty if you had never sampled it?"

Even Goh Keng Swee mourned what Singapore had given up in order to make the machine run efficiently. "We have in Singapore intellectual conformity in place of intellectual inquisitiveness," he once said, "and the sum total is a depressing climate of intellectual sterility."

Yet it is a wonderfully comfortable confinement Lee has created. Singapore is on the verge of becoming the ultimate yuppie society with all the toys and baubles of all the world's glittering malls available to any Singaporean who wants it. The only price was their souls.

We were finally told by the P.M.'s press office that he would not see us. But they had a surprise. His son would. We were not disappointed.

Lee Hsien Loong, known to everyone in Singapore as B. G. Lee, was the first son and annointed successor of Lee Kuan Yew. In his mid-30s, he had been groomed for great things, from an education at Cambridge, Harvard and the U.S. Army General Staff College, to a series of top military and government posts. Hsien Loong, whose name meant "heavenly dragon," was not guaranteed the prime minister's post when his father retired, but it was assumed that eventually he would fulfill his destiny.

We had been told that he was a formidable intellect and a man as aloof and arrogant as his father. One profile of him in *Asiaweek* magazine recounted a story that could just as easily have fit the patriarch. While he was a mathematics major at Cambridge, classmates recalled that B. G. Lee had an annoying habit when taking exams. When he would solve a problem, one classmate said, "He'd sort of snap his fingers to show he'd got it and give a smile of satisfaction. He used to annoy everybody because he'd have signaled three times when all the rest were still working on the first problem."

He spoke English, Mandarin and Malay as well as some Russian. As a soldier he quickly rose to the second-highest rank in the army—the B. G. was for brigadier general—and once directed a dramatic helicopter rescue of 13 tourists trapped in a cable car. He joined the government in 1984 and was immediately put in charge of a special economic commission that was supposed to find a way to pull Singapore from its first major recession. B. G. Lee's plan was implemented and within a year, the economy was soaring again.

The son provided at least anecdotal evidence of the father's belief in the supremacy of genetics.

The Heavenly Dragon greeted us at the door to his expansive 50th-floor office with a view like that from the bridge of a giant ship: Singapore harbor, the boat-specked straits and the shore of Indonesia beyond. The furniture was cool and modern: leather couches, thin black lamps and, behind a rosewood desk, the blinking green screen of a personal computer. This domain would have well-suited the CEO of a Fortune 500 company and contrasted startlingly with the photos we had seen of his father hunched over a gray metal desk in the middle of a barren office.

"Thank you for coming," he said with unpredicted modesty. He gestured to deep leather chairs arranged around a glass table set with coffee cups.

"Or would you prefer tea?" he said in a soft voice accented with the precise diction of Cambridge. He wore a gray pinstripe suit that hung on his lean, six-foot frame. His black hair was cut close in military fashion. His face was angular and intelligent, though with none of the reptilian cunning that showed through in his father. Leaning back comfortably in his leather chair, a hand on each armrest, no one would mistake B. G. Lee for a cobra about to strike.

We said that we wanted to ask him the same questions we had hoped to put to his father. We wanted to know why Singapore was governed the way it was, what he saw for the future of his country and how he saw the United States fitting into an Asian century, if such an ascendancy was really happening. The three of us talked for almost two hours, but mostly the two of us listened.

"Asia is not necessarily the center of the world, but it is not a part of the world that you can afford to neglect. These are countries that are growing not just economically but in terms of sophistication and purchasing power. Their success is not a zero-sum game. Just because we win doesn't mean you have to lose. If we do better, you can do better as well. You can sell to us.

"But you cannot just sit back. If, say, the Japanese are able to make cars at half the cost of Detroit, then you have two solutions. Either Detroit emulates the Japanese and does as well or you change your currency values and declare the U.S. dollar to be worth half as many yen as it used to. You are now recognizing the problem and lowering the dollar—which is better than not recognizing it at all. But is that a good solution for a power that has for several decades dominated world affairs?

"The only solution you have to your trade problems is to become more competitive. It is a buzzword in Washington, but what it means is that the quality of your output has to go up, investments have to be put in. If the Japanese work like zombies, well, if you want to be in the same league, maybe you have to work like zombies too."

He laughed at that without smiling.

"You have to understand, we're all on a treadmill in this world.

"The world is a competitive place. The name of the game in the international economy is division of labor. When you see a powerful economic force arriving on the other side of the ocean, is that not a spur to work harder and an opportunity for trade and doing business? Sure the Japanese are cheating on import restrictions and finding many ways to cut you out of the market and sometimes being quite blatant about it. But they have done that for a long time and it did not previously stop the Americans from succeeding. So what has changed? Your attitude?

"What's important is not just the cost of labor. The key is total productivity. There's the labor cost, infrastructure, inventiveness of the leading edge of technology and the quality of your production process. Not just individual workers but the way whole plants are organized and structured and efficiency is squeezed out of fallible human digits.

"A friend of mine who sells a line of Japanese office machinery here visited a plant in the United States—Connecticut or somewhere—and the manager showed him around and said, 'We are the leading edge.' But it was just sloppy stuff lying around, people sauntering about, work in progress piled up in stacks. He considered himself at the forefront of the business, but obviously he's not looking ahead of him.

"It's not just the quality of work force that matters, it's the ability to organize groupwise. That is something that is difficult in the United States. In Asia, I think there is a group instinct. In the case of the Japanese there is a unique culture. In the case of the NICs, a combination of sound government, hard-working populations and for most of the countries political stability, providing a stable place for foreign companies to come and operate. It is something that's a basic precondition for business to succeed but not available in many places in the world.

"You can see the difficulties that China has providing these preconditions. They are the same stock as us, the same culture—but a different system. And they can't break the system. They're trying very hard, but how do you abandon two generations of Iron Rice Bowl and comfortable bureaucratic mentalities? Iron Rice Bowl means we all eat from the same bowl, which means, performance, that's up to you; it doesn't matter. Rewards, you get it as a group. And if you do badly you can't be fired, if you do well you need not be rewarded.

"We are the very opposite. We start from the basis that there is no Iron Rice Bowl in the world. Nobody owes us a living and if we don't perform we will get nothing. Similarly we believe that the best way to motivate people is to have a fair system where rewards are in line with performance and opportunities are denied to nobody. Because with 2.6 million people, the pool is small and everyone who can make a contribution must be given the maximum opportunity to do so.

"There are more people lying on the social safety net in the United States than there are people in Singapore. I don't want to comment on your system, but welfare benefits once granted are irremovable. We have minimal public assistance in Singapore, no unemployment benefits. We do believe in looking after our people well, making them self-reliant. So although there is no state retirement pension scheme, we make sure that each person has made provisions in his working life to save up for his own pension funds under the Central Provident Fund. We used to have heavily subsidized health care. We are moving toward MediSave, which is not like your Medicare, but personal savings put aside for health care. I think the more we go to that it will, first, encourage individuals to use services more efficiently, and it will give people a choice to decide whoever provides them the best service.

"In Singapore we have an appreciation for how fragile we are. Why are we here? There is nothing special about this island. It is just one of 18,000 islands in the region. But here you can do business. You have banks, telephones, airports that work, factories that are up and running in six to nine months. What makes it special? The only thing which makes it special is that the place is revved to 99 percent of what it is capable of. And unless you can always run at that efficiency, you'll just sink. There's no reason to be here. Do we have hydroelectric power? Timber, tin, gold, gas? We have none. But if we want to continue to be here, we have to be special.

"That's the treadmill. Everyone in the world is on it, but some people see it more clearly than others. Korea has 40 million people, that's a critical mass, enough to be a major industrial power. Taiwan has 20 million. Hong Kong has a hinterland—all of China. Our hinterland has to be the whole world. We have to trade with the Chicago Mercantile Exchange, to link up by satellite to London financial markets. We have to be fast and clever.

"The only question is, can we keep it up? When you are new, the first generation, the challenge is still fresh and the response from people is readily forthcoming. When you have to continue this into a second generation, the challenges are less obvious, but their potential for turning from challenges into threats still remains. Can a population continue to be aware of them, to continue to perform as well as it did? That's the difficulty.

"There is, for instance, political pressures for liberalization. People travel all over now. They come back and say, 'We look like Dallas, why can't we become like Dallas?' But we are not. In Dallas, you don't get covert groups sharpening knives and daggers and preparing for racial conflict and needing to be picked up by the security police from time to time. You don't have anybody plotting to start mass movements to confront the government and cause bloodshed and violence. Well, we do because we are in a different part of the world and we are not surrounded by the whole of Texas and then the whole of America. We've got to understand that.

"So the government has to be able to get its point of view across, as we have tried very recently with the 16 Marxists—it's a small group, but it makes the population understand that these are the sorts of threats we are still going to see even though this is a different Singapore than in the 1950s and '60s.

"There is a Chinese phrase. As your skill rises, so too does the power of the devil rise to match it.

"The situation with the foreign press is an example. We look at it from two perspectives, one of wisdom and the other of legal right. Is it wise for an open economic and political system to allow foreign newspapers to have a strong influence on the domestic political process? In other words, to take positions that agree or not with the government, to campaign for or against particular policies or particular parties and try to cause different outcomes within the country? I don't think it is unreasonable to conclude that we wish to set our own destiny and we don't wish to have that determined by foreign influences, whether malevolent or benevolent.

"On the question of legal rights, we start with the basis that nobody has the right to circulate in Singapore. You are a foreign newspaper, are you entitled to be here? No. Who is not here: *Pravda* and *Renmin Ribao.* No American newspaper has ever raised a fuss on behalf of them.

"If you are reporting the rest of the world to us, you can report anything you like. If you are reporting Singapore to the rest of the world, you can write anything you like because it doesn't disturb us. Tass has a correspondent here. So does Xinhua. But if you are going to report Singapore to Singaporeans, we have the right to ban you.

"What the new press laws allow is that we restrict the number of copies so that means you do not profit from the circulation or the advertising. If anyone wants to make photocopies and disseminate the information, we don't mind. Now, let us see, given those rules, whether you reveal your preference to be campaigning for the truth, in which case you'll happily continue to print what you used to print, or whether it matters to you how much money you earn, in which case the editorial line will change. And I think the events have proven that the second is a more powerful motivation.

"It is not just a prickliness that leads us to do this but a whole record that shows the dangers newspapers can cause. There are many cases of inflammatory articles causing riots and subversion—so many events in the last 30 years that have led us to this conclusion. Would people here by happier if they had to read photocopies of their *Wall Street Journal* or if they could read the full *Wall Street Journal* but had to ride in a bullet-proof car to work?

"We do not have the same democracy as you. The way that populations articulate their aspirations and arbitrate their disagreements is not easily exportable. Even Westminister democracy is not the same system that the Americans have. We are not Anglo-Saxon. We have to make our own arrangements. We have a system that is patched together.

"There is no plausible alternative government for Singapore—no opposition governing team. We have combed the country for the best possible talent. Anybody who is able to make a contribution and agrees with us on the fundamentals is in. We are a small country. If you want to depend on having two teams—one in, one out—well, you're no longer running at 99 percent capacity but maybe 50 percent capacity.

"At the same time, we have to find ways to air doubts and arguments. It is not healthy to suppress them. There will be opposition members of parliament. They speak up. If they make sense, if they offer arguments, we offer answers. If they are right we follow them, if they are wrong we point them out. If they are malicious we demolish them and if they are criminal we prosecute them. But the system must find a way so that everyone whether in or out feels he has a say. Some species evolve toward extinction. In so many other countries that started out voting fair, they have broken up. We have no unique secret virtue that immunizes us.

"We always believe our success is fragile and we think, for good reasons, that it can be wiped out in a stroke. For all his problems, it took Mr. Marcos 15 years to come to his end. It will take us less. And the Philippines can still get back on their feet. We will never get back on our feet. Once Singapore is misgoverned, either through corruption or incompetence, you must assume every talented Singaporean will be scattered in either Vancouver, or San Francisco, or Stanford or Harvard. They're not going to come back. So that's the end.

"Your success is less fragile. You've got wealth and confidence. Take education. You've got some of the best educational institutions in the world. They not only attract bright people but teach a certain sense almost of manifest destiny. Which is good because in America you go out and change your world. In Singapore we are different. For us, education is a basic way to survive. If we were not educated, we would be as cheap as anybody else in the Third World. We don't want to be cheap, we want to be valuable.

"In America, though, there is now a sort of non-competitive, stop-the-world-I-want-to-get-off sentiment that you have to get rid of. Because you can't get off. So you start to talk of protection. These pressures for protection have been around since long before David Ricardo. And every generation has to learn this for itself. I mean you can prove it in the textbooks and demonstrate in mathematical theorems that protectionism leads to depressions but each generation doubts this not quite so strongly. You may have to learn this lesson again and things will get much worse for you before you reach equilibrium.

"You see, in Singapore, we don't have your sense of manifest destiny. We have a sense of survival. It remains to be seen which skill the world will most value in the years to come."

And he smiled for the last time, a thin but sincere smile. He saw us to the door and wished us well.

We left humbled. David Ricardo, indeed. Here was a politician comfortably quoting 19th-century English economists as easily as if they were in that morning's newspaper. And fatalistic economists at that, which was in keeping with the words that still rang in our ears. "Treadmill. Zombies. Survival." B. G. Lee was not as arrogant as his father was reputed to be. He was just a very smart man with a firm grasp on how the pieces of the world fit together, trying to explain it to a couple of guys who had trouble balancing their checkbooks.

What was humbling was the clear logic of his unromantic view of the world. We had set out to Asia carrying all the baggage of the quintessential post-war Baby Boom American. Happy and complacent, we didn't exactly grow up preoccupied with questions of survival. Who did we know who talked about the world being a treadmill? But here was someone our age who has seen the world from our side as well as his own. From his perch overlooking Singapore Harbor, B. G. Lee was in a rare position to observe such things. He helped manage a society that lived by its wits, a shrimp that made a science of watching where the whales were swimming. Now he was telling us to watch out, and the scary part was that he was right.

Our morning with B. G. Lee brought back a parade of images from thousands of miles of travel. Grim faces set to a task in factory lofts from Seoul to Taipei to Bangkok. Frantic traffic at 7 A.M. Students in pressed uniforms arrayed in school yards. But mostly it brought back the looks of hungry aggressiveness we had seen in the thousands of faces that hurried past us on the streets. The Asians weren't supermen, but their accomplishments had shocked us. They were smart, disciplined, motivated and they knew an awful lot about the American market they were in the process of invading.

As we packed to head back to Bangkok and then home, it occurred to us that we knew a lot more about them than when we started, but not nearly enough.

THAILAND: THE NEXT LITTLE DRAGON

WE WEREN'T SUPPOSED to be in Thailand. When we started this odyssey, it was just a place on a map more or less between two destinations. The Four Little Dragons were Korea, Taiwan, Hong Kong and Singapore. Thailand was another story. For another day, another time.

Then it seemed that after Singapore, Bangkok would be comfortably decadent and anonymous. In Singapore, everyone cared about your business; in Bangkok no one cared. And at this point, we were sick and tired of anybody caring. We were exhausted by questions—asked by us or of us. We were sick of moving. And we were, in fact, experiencing a kind of depression; we had the unremitting sense that we had seen the future and it didn't look all that promising for the U.S.A. Beyond all that, we were looking at a grueling 33-hour journey home, during most of which we would be stuffed in a hermetically sealed United Airlines canister. We needed a few days by the pool, a little sightseeing and some blistering Thai food with lots of beer to make it all better.

But in Bangkok some things happened that stirred our curiosity one more time. We tried very hard not to notice, to put our minds on strike, to have fun and not to worry about GNP, levels of productivity and whether or not our children would have to learn Mandarin or Japanese in order to speak to their employers. But idleness just wasn't in the cards. Thailand was a seductive place—not in the infamous sense, but intellectually; Thailand was a developing Dragon.

What attracted us immediately was the incredible energy being produced by Bangkok itself. The town that the travel writers all described as exotic, sensuous and sleepy was a honking, screeching, hollering machine of commerce that, as one Thai told us, "could be the fifth Dragon—if we wanted to." If we needed further proof of how profound the Asian transformation had become, Thailand was it. Still, Thailand had its own charms and the newly muscular economy wasn't as obvious as the spanking skyline of Singapore or the grittiness of Korea.

Shortly after we arrived, we sat at the terrace bar of the Oriental Hotel, which overlooks the chocolaty Chao Phraya River. We sipped icy Kloster beer in the sweet humid air and studied the patrons who ranged from rich German tourists on a sex holiday to pinstriped investment bankers in deep conversation with trim Thai executives, all arrayed against the backdrop of a river churning with rice-laden barges, houseboats and all manner of small craft darting downstream. The far bank was a silhouette of stilt houses, temple spires and factory smokestacks behind which a fat orange sun slid languidly to the horizon.

This was not the same Asia to which we had become accustomed. Bangkok was no less crowded than the other Asian metropolises, but there was grace and beauty to the place and the people. Thais were soft-spoken—loud chatter, we were told politely, is for monkeys—raising their voices only to laugh, which they did frequently. As we stood in the hotel lobby, we watched two bellboys standing next to a pile of bags at stiff attention but all the while trying to knock each other down with discreet kicks to the back of the knees. Finally one fell and both giggled until a sharp word from the bell captain riveted them back to attention. The captain walked off trying to conceal his own smile.

On a slow ride across town, a taxi driver turned to us with a smile that was genuine, not leering, and said, "So what kind of sport do you guys want? Girls? Boys? Both? Other things?"

He handed over a pile of color brochures for various massage parlors, hostess clubs and bars. When we said we leaned toward girls, he offered his critical analysis of the clubs. One was "all Japanese, not for you," another got a disdainful "uh, Indians go there," a third was deemed unsuitable because the girls were too old—that is, more than 18 years old. We told him we'd have to get back to him on this. We had another date that night. With the King of Bangkok. Not the real king—Rama IX, also known as Bhumibol Adulyadej the Great, a benevolent monarch whom the Thais revere as a demigod—but a man of equal imperiousness.

The King picked us up in his Bentley, an incongruously large car in a city of tiny Toyota taxis and three-wheeled motorcycles. He cruised in air-conditioned stateliness as he drew on a briar pipe, the perfect English gentleman, a modern version of a Kipling character moving with lordly presence among the natives. A fine picture except we found out that he was an American who had come to do business during the Vietnam War and, like so many Americans, stayed on to enjoy life where a modest Western income was princely and business was an easy game if you knew the right people. He was a big man in Bangkok, but he made us think of the saying, "In the land of the blind, the one-eyed is king." And we told him so, a little more delicately.

"Used to be," he said as he looked into the distance and nodded to himself slowly. "Used to be. But not now. These Thais are becoming damn good businessmen. This is no lazy tropical paradise anymore."

We knew what was coming. The old "you should have been here five years ago" routine. We heard it everywhere we went. "Oh, those were the great days. . . . Lobsters were a dime . . . Hotel suites went for 10 bucks. . . ." That sort of thing.

And he did, more or less, tell us how wonderful Thailand had been in the '70s when the handful of Americans were revered like Great White Rajas. A man could be pampered by women from cooks, maids and mistresses to a Thai wife—all of whom came from a culture that made pleasing men a virtue for women. The idyllic beaches were uncrowded and there was game enough in the north hills for a hunting party whenever the mood struck. Drugs were, well, available if that was one's preference. Money could be made running small businesses or acting as agent for foreign interests. There was opportunity, but nobody was in too much of a hurry.

"In those days," he said as we stopped dead in the middle of a clogged intersection and horns erupted all around us, "the problem in Thailand wasn't relaxing tension. It was building up enough tension to get anything done."

No more. Bangkok was boomtown.

"Just look around."

And we did. By twilight the city was a remarkable amalgam of old, new, ornate, garish, tasteful and atrocious architecture all slapped down in a random pattern with no real center. A

20-square mile sprawl had office buildings standing adjacent to market stalls, slum housing and city estates behind whitewashed walls.

"The Thais don't like rules," the King explained, "and that includes zoning."

Neon signs hummed to life, blaring out an alphabet from Mars. Thai script, unlike any other in the world, is made of looping strokes and short accent marks and is wholly unintelligible to one who hasn't studied it. English is not prevalent in Thailand, except to announce FOOD, BAR and MASSAGE.

The street scenes slid past the car windows in silence, like a movie with the sound turned off. Hawkers sold noodles from great steaming pots or skewered beef cooked over glowing red barbeques. Strollers browsed tables piled high with T-shirts, jeans, costume jewelry and bootlegged cassette tapes. Knots of men, their knobby elbows poking from baggy short-sleeve shirts, conspired on corners, smoking and laughing.

The Bentley was surrounded by tuk-tuks, three-wheeled motorcycles that served as cheap taxis. Each had a canvas roof and was elaborately adorned with paint and Christmas ornaments in an individual statement of its owner's taste. The tuk-tuks—so named because of the sound they made idling in traffic—darted from lane to lane and between cars and trucks with terrifying speed. Built for two, some carried five or six passengers or a dozen boxes of cargo.

"It's always been a great town at night," The King observed. "The difference is in the daytime. People really work now. It's been an incredible transformation."

Why the change?

"I think it was that fucking Pol Pot. He put a blowtorch to their asses. Ten years ago everybody thought this place was the next domino in Asia. They had an active Communist Party. They were feeling pressure from all sides. But when they saw those sorry survivors from the communist experiment in Cambodia come pouring across the border, when they heard about the madness, they straightened up."

We had dinner at a quiet seafood restaurant where the prawns were as big as lobster and every dish was a cacophony of spices and heat. Small portions of beef or chicken were served with vegetables and combinations of basil, coriander, ginger, chili, mint and coconut. Each bite exploded in the mouth, sometimes causing our eyes to water or the lips to go numb. Yet after a mouthful of Singha beer, we had an uncontrollable urge to shovel in another forkful.

"Couple things about the Thais you should know," the King said as he drained a beer and smacked his lips. "They've never been conquered. Never. They'll all mention that to you at some point, but it's a big deal. In 800 years they've kept the Western powers and their own unruly neighbors at bay. Freedom and independence are very important to them. Your basic Thai wants to be left alone.

"The truth is," he mused as he examined a giant garlic prawn on his fork, "this country conquers you."

The second important lesson about the Thais was to learn the meaning of the word *sanuk.*

"Roughly, it means fun. And if something ain't *sanuk,* it ain't worth doing. The Thais divide the world into two parts. *Sanuk* and *mai sanuk*—not fun. Eating, drinking, parties, sex—all of those are supposed to be *sanuk.*"

"So work is *mai sanuk?*" London inquired.

"Not necessarily. *Sanuk* doesn't mean the Thais are a bunch of goof-offs who won't work. They will. They're tough people. But they're not machines. Life has to be more than a paycheck or it's not worth it. I've heard several stories of Japanese factories starting up with all their employees standing at attention and singing company songs. All that Mickey Mouse. The Thais laugh at it. They think it's stupid. You stick them in front of a machine all day and they won't work.

"So the Japanese got smart and they played music in the factory. They had more breaks and they started all kinds of games for the workers. Suddenly, work became *sanuk,* or as *sanuk* as it could be, and productivity increased.

"Now this place is the favorite spot in the world for the Japanese to build factories. Hundreds of millions of dollars of Japanese capital is pouring in. All because of a little *sanuk.*"

We sipped our beers and smoldered for a while.

"Well, are you ready for some *sanuk?*" the King laughed at last. Who were we to argue?

We drove to Patpong, the city's most famous nightclub district where entertainment of a sexual nature could be found on three short, parallel blocks—Patpong One and Patpong Two catered to heterosexual tastes while Patpong Three was frequented by homosexuals.

The atmosphere wasn't exactly wholesome, but it wasn't so sleazy, either. The humid air smelled of sizzling *satay* while roadside carts displayed counterfeit Rolex watches, Gucci purses and Vuitton luggage. The streets were filled with couples and groups of young people—Thais and foreigners—laughing and drinking. Blinking neon announced dozens of clubs with "go-go dancing," "striptease," or "topless" as the featured entertainment. Cold air blew from the open doorways as pitchmen gestured invitingly to glowing interiors. Most of the clubs were similar: loud disco music, strobe lights and a stage upon which anywhere from one to 10 girls in bikinis danced with bored expressions, some with numbers pinned to their suits. The King explained that it was possible, though not easy, to order by number and buy a girl away from the bar for an hour or the evening.

There were some genuine hookers on the street as well. Tiny girls who teetered like birds on too-high heels, some with lipstick smeared as if they'd put it on for the first time. They were funny and sad.

"Country girls," the King explained. "They have no work up north so they come down to the big city. Prostitution pays a lot better than working in a factory.

"Let's try this place," he suggested.

We walked up a flight of stairs to Queen's Castle. Inside the large room, the atmosphere resembled a boisterous college bar, and was not at all like the somber, desperate sleaziness of a strip bar in the United States. There was the din of loud talk and clinking glasses.

We settled into a corner table and the King began a seminar on the Thai economy. A few minutes passed until we realized that on a stage in the center of a circular bar a man and woman were engaged in a very erotic dance that seemed to be moving in a direction that most choreographers only hint at.

"The main reason for the success is the Chinese," the King said without taking his eyes off the stage. "The Thais leave the ethnic Chinese alone and they drive the economy." He said as much as one-third of Bangkok's population was of recent Chinese descent.

A couple of pretty young girls in evening dresses that looked absurdly like they belonged to their older sisters came to the table and asked if we'd buy them a drink. They blocked the King's view of the stage and he waved them away.

"Everybody else hates the Chinese. In Burma and Vietnam they kicked them out. The Malays and Indonesians have all kinds of restrictions on them. The Cambodians killed them. But the Thais tolerate them. The Thais tolerate anything as long as it's good for the Thais.

"But as this country gets organized, what's happening is that they're pricing places like Taiwan out of the market. A university graduate will work for $200 a month here. A factory worker for a few dollars a day. My Taiwanese clients tell me that a Taiwan worker costs six times what a Thai worker costs—and he's only four times as productive. So who wants to make shoes in Taiwan?"

It was the treadmill B. G. Lee had described in Singapore. However smart you thought you were, however cheap, however clever, there was always somebody coming up behind you. And if you slowed down, you'd get stepped on. It had happened to the Taiwan shoe industry in an instant when its wages became too high. Today it was the Thais turn. Tomorrow, maybe Sri Lanka would overtake them, or Malaysia, Indonesia, the Philippines. If we didn't believe it when Lee told us, we just had to ask the lithe young couple onstage, by now performing a very convincing reenactment of hot and heavy sex in front of an audience of drunk, shouting foreigners.

Excuse me sir, madam? Is this really such a dog-eat-dog world? Do you honestly feel such competitive pressure that you'd do anything to earn a hundred dollars a week? Couldn't you have gone to trade school instead?

The King saw us staring and understood the irony.

"They get well paid for that," he said with authority. "Ask some 14-year-old kid who works in a garment factory for four or five cents an hour how tough life is. He'd love to fuck onstage for a hundred bucks a week. Hey, the minimum wage in this country is 35 cents an hour, whenever anybody bothers to enforce it."

We had come in at the crescendo of the first show. After a brief intermission, the warm-up acts started again. The girls in string bikinis came on, some with eerily beautiful faces that were part Asian, part American. Most striking was one girl who was part black, part Thai. She had a muscular body with full breasts and a tight Afro. They'd be about 18 years old. One last American legacy before we licked our wounds and headed home from Vietnam.

The King talked of diversification. The Thais had more natural resources than any of the other Dragons, a population of more than 60 million and a greater number of industries. "They won't allow themselves to get caught depending on a few products. They're going to be big in seafood, canned pineapple, frozen chicken. They've got assembly plants to produce motorcycles, appliances and electronic components. They make their own cars.

"You're talking about steady, controlled growth of 7 percent of GNP each year . . . export sector pumping out about $14 billion . . . $13 billion coming in so you've got a net surplus . . . foreign debt. . . ."

As he talked on, the stage cleared and a girl walked on displaying a magic marker and a large sheet of white paper. Then she sank down on her haunches and began to rock to the music. The crowd at the bar stood up and we couldn't see what was going on, but the fans loved it. She swayed and twisted in a kind of jerky rhythm.

"Where did she put the marker?"

"But you've still got an agrarian economy," said the King. "I mean 80 percent still live on the farm . . . land of a million rice fields . . . rice bowl of Asia."

"She's writing something, but not with her hands."

"One of the five largest net food exporters in the world . . . A really great place to do business."

Then she held up her handiwork for the crowd to see, parading it around the stage to applause and laughter and finally turning it toward the table in the corner. The paper read: "Mark and Brian: Welcome to Queen's Castle!"

King, you devil.

"Jeezus," said Kelly.

"Nice penmanship," said London.

"All in good fun," said the King.

If it seemed that we had sex on the brain, it wasn't our fault. Sex was big business in Bangkok and no one let you forget it. Seventy percent of the tourists who came here were male, including the infamous German sex tours and the Japanese "boom-boom" groups. In the age of AIDS, that was starting to change and the government was promoting many of Thailand's other wonders—while not quite discouraging the more traditional entertainment.

Thailand has spectacular palm-fringed beaches and lush mountain jungles filled with exotic wildlife. There is a rich, deep culture, much of it evident in the unique artistry and architecture of the temples and palaces scattered through Bangkok. In the harsh light of day, Bangkok was even more exotic, more foreign than at night, if that was possible. The skyline of the city is speared by temple spires rising from wide bases to needlepoints that, against a nicely polluted yellow sunset, look like sets from a Flash Gordon movie.

The temples themselves are marvels made of beaten gold and semiprecious stones painted with dragons and gods. Wat Phra Keo held the Emerald Buddha, the most sacred object in Thailand. The carved figure sat atop a 30-foot gold altar, bathed in a mysterious radiant light. At Wat Trimitr there was a five-ton Buddha made of solid gold that had only recently been discovered: It had been covered with plaster 200 years ago to keep it from the invading Burmese.

The streets were as much an open-air market as Seoul or Hong Kong, but the goods offered were more plentiful and varied. Food was everywhere, whether it was cooked snacks for sale from carts or produce arrayed in baskets. The fruit alone suggested the bounty of the country: durian, mangosteen, rambutan, coconut, papaya, mango, plantain, lychee. Then there were piles of red, yellow and green chilis, whole chickens and ducks, slabs of beef and hogs.

Bangkok was fast becoming the shopping mecca of choice for tourists, surpassing Hong Kong, which was pricing itself out of the bargain range. A stroll down any street revealed silks, porcelain, antiques, lacquerware, precious stones and ancient wooden artifacts. There are hundreds of gold shops in Chinatown, each with hundreds of thousands of dollars worth of burnished 24-carat wares displayed in the window—each priced at a slight markup from the day's market price for gold, the workmanship being virtually free.

We tried to soak up as much of the intoxicating place as

we could in a few days, but Bangkok didn't make it easy. The city had one major liability and it was a consequence of progress. Bangkok had few competitors when it comes to traffic. It was not merely bad traffic but astonishing traffic, snail-like traffic, claustrophobic traffic that could make anyone with a pulse rate above catatonia scream in exasperation. Pick the wrong time of day and it could take three hours to go a few miles across town. And just when it seemed it couldn't get any worse, the rains came and the real tie-ups started. Not that we could get out and walk. Bangkok is an incredibly complicated city of alleys and lanes, many of which aren't on maps. And even if you knew where you were going, it could take 20 minutes to cross a busy street.

More than an annoyance, traffic was a symbol of the price the Thais were paying for progress. The country did not have the infrastructure—from roads and ports to schools and hospitals—to support rapid growth. A lot was going to have to change if the Thais intended to compete in the big leagues. From what we had seen, it wasn't clear to us if they wanted success badly enough, if they were willing to pay the price.

We talked about the dilemma over lunch with Suvit Yodmani, a government official whose title was director of the Office of National Identity.

"The title is a little strange," he admitted. "It sounds like we're trying to find our identity, and that's not the case. We're not like Singapore. We know who we are. We're Thais. But we have a complex culture and sometimes we have to explain it to ourselves and to the outside world."

Suvit was in the propaganda business. A former government press spokesman who had a doctorate from Boston University and credits from Harvard and MIT, he started the office in 1981 because he thought Thailand was getting too much bad press, mostly centering around prostitution and drug production in the notorious Golden Triangle in the far northwest.

"Our press is very free here," he explained. "We don't hold back the bad news. But I try to balance it. To tell people here and abroad all the good things we have."

And they have a lot.

Besides the natural beauty and the resurgent economy, the Thais have their irrepressible attitude which was, as the King prophesized, conquering us.

"Thais hate tension or confrontation," Suvit said. "It comes from our religion. We are mostly Theravada Buddhists. We take very seriously the rule that you should do to others as you would have done to you. That makes us very tolerant of other people and their behavior. When we see someone who is dark-skinned, usually a Hindu or a Muslim, we ask if he takes beef or pork, and then we forget about it. We also believe that you will be rewarded in a future life for the good you do in this life."

Sort of like Christianity only with all carrots and no sticks.

"Of course the negative side of being so tolerant and free is that we are undisciplined. We are not very good at planning. I don't know if you can get by in the world anymore without being more aggressive and thinking ahead."

It seemed that this was already happening in Thailand. Wasn't the government pushing the country to become the next NIC? Suvit sighed and smiled weakly. He was thin and nervous with a very un-Thai ailment: an ulcer. When we ordered lunch, he told us that he couldn't share his, because he couldn't eat spicy food.

"It's not necessarily a good thing. You have to make sacrifices. We watch the other Dragons, we have seen the sacrifices they made. We have such a good quality of life. You don't want to lose that.

"Thai Buddhism stresses the middle way. It does not stress feverish economic activity as Confucianism does. Buddhism seeks a balance. I don't know if you can succeed and keep that."

Suvit frowned as he stirred his tea and thought about how painful it would be for his adolescent nation to grow up. He patted his wounded stomach and said, "Maybe this is the future."

One night we had dinner with a friend-of-a-friend who told us about a place that we had to see. For several years he had worked for the U.S. government and private relief agencies at the refugee camps along the Thai-Cambodian borders. These were the camps that received the human flotsam of the boat people escaping Vietnam as well as the dazed survivors of the Cambodian genocide when that country was ruled by the maniacal Pol Pot. More recently the Vietnamese were exerting their imperial intentions in Cambodia and people were still fleeing.

"The camps tell another story of what can happen in this part of the world," our host said. They were the most current symbols of centuries of wars, revolutions, feuds and economic depressions that have swept over Asia and forced millions of people from their homes. Our friend, who had been here since the early days of the Vietnam War, reminded us that combining the words "stability" and Asia" had only been appropriate for about 10 of the last 5,000 years.

We decided to see if we could get permission to visit.

"A little advice," he offered. "Be careful of the black shirts. They're called Task Force 80. They run the camps. They look like Thai military but they're not. Some of them are just bandits. They're paid a dollar a day. Life hasn't been very kind to them so they're not kind to anyone. And get out of there before dark. The roads along the border are anything but secure."

A pass to the border usually took weeks to get, but after two days of intense lobbying at the U.S. Embassy and several Thai ministries, where hangdog looks and fervent pleadings had more of an impact than in most bureaucracies of the world, we received stamped permission slips. We hired a taxi and set out.

Bangkok before dawn pattered soothingly on us. The heavy dew in the air eased the tension lines of sleepiness in our faces, the musky aromas of a fresh day filled us with expectations and the quiet orchestration of early-rising shopkeepers assembling their wares brought this massive urbanity down to a human scale. Slumped in the backseat of a taxi, we marveled at how easy it was to navigate the streets that within hours would be cluttered with too many people, too many cars, too much energy.

As we passed beyond the city's force field, the humming chaos quieted to a rustle. In a few miles we traveled backward a hundred years. Where Bangkok dropped off there started miles of luminous green farmland, interrupted occasionally by refineries, power plants and incongruously gaudy temples lost in the middle of nowhere. We were tempted to stop and explore but our driver was firm that we barrel through the countryside because our trip would be a long one and its danger would increase in proportion to our distance from Bangkok. We had to be away from the border before dark, he insisted with a note of urgency in his voice that made us believe.

At the town of Prachin Buri we stopped to ask directions. The driver's queries were met with puzzled frowns and responses along the lines of, "Why do you want to go there?"

Obviously the border made the Thai on the street no less uncomfortable than the political leaders in Bangkok. Amid the friendliness of Bangkok it was easy to forget about the venom that surrounded Thailand—in Burma, Laos and Cambodia, all communist-controlled countries with some of the harshest, most enigmatic governments in the world. Cambodia at the time was occupied by the Vietnamese, who still hinted at fulfilling the ancient dream of a grand Annamese empire under Hanoi's influence—and including Thailand. The Thais had a realistic respect for the Vietnamese fighting machine, which sometimes spilled over the border and engaged Thai troops, but always ostensibly in pursuit of Cambodian rebels. One day, the Thais feared, the Vietnamese would keep coming.

Also of concern was the growing presence of Pol Pot and his fanatical Khmer Rouge followers. Like some severed head from a horror movie, the architect of the genocide that has come to be known as "the killing fields" had regenerated himself and his army and now stood astride the border, waiting for a chance to retake the country. For the Thais, Pol Pot was indeed the enemy of their enemy, a situation that centuries of astutely pragmatic diplomacy had taught them to cultivate. Still, to do business with a man best compared to Adolf Hitler was testing even the Thais' tolerance of amorality.

The ripe green rice fields and the solitary farmers prodding water buffalos seemed more fragile than ever as we sped on to Aranyaprathet, the closest city to the border. The camps string along the C-shaped border like a gulag. We were heading for a camp called simply Site 2, and no one seemed to know what that meant. Someone volunteered directions to Khao-I-Dang, one of the first camps set up in 1979 to receive the flow of misery from Cambodia. We had been told in Bangkok that Khao-I-Dang was closed, although we had also heard that 20,000 refugees still lived there.

Outside Aranyaprathet the road lost its pavement and the flow of cars thinned to a trickle. We bounced along uncomfortably for a few miles before we came to our first military roadblock. While the stone-faced sentry with the bayoneted M-16 checked our credentials, the driver again asked directions.

"Site 2 is about one hour from Khao-I-Dang," the driver said. "They say we must leave the camp by five o'clock. The road closes then."

Kelly told him to ask why.

"Bombing. The Vietnamese bomb the road after dark." He looked at us in wide-eyed astonishment like some burlesque straightman who's just had his pants pulled down. This was turning out to be a little more for him than a fare to the airport. We were afraid he might be eyeing an exit stage left.

"Don't worry, we're with you all the way," said London, by way of reassurance. "If you die, we die. And we wouldn't be going if we thought that were going to happen." Would we?

It hardly calmed him, but at least he threw the car into a forward gear and went on.

We passed a cluster of buildings advertising themselves as the headquarters of Task Force 80. We had heard more about the black shirts, including stories of torture, robbery and rampant corruption. We had heard that at night they allowed Thai gangs to enter the camps and loot and rape in return for a share of the booty. The stories persisted, but there was no way for an outsider to confirm them because of the strictly enforced curfew. The Thai government had no desire to do anything more for the refugees than allow them to remain cordoned off in a small no-man's land. They were officially not refugees eligible for resettlement in Thailand or other countries but displaced persons merely waiting to return to their homeland. Many had been displaced for 10 years. The Thais feared that any other strategy toward the diaspora would attract even more lost souls.

We reached Khao-I-Dang and tried to enter, but were rebuffed because, as a guard told us, "Khao-I-Dang is closed." As we drove by we saw teams of small boys playing soccer in this camp that didn't exist.

We passed convoys of water tankers, olive-colored troop carriers and an occasional vehicle sporting a logo from various international relief agencies. More roadblocks. More checkpoints. More stony faces. We were in a war zone.

At last, after five and a half hours, Site 2—a collection of neat, thatched bamboo huts and barbed wire fences that seemed part Boy Scout jamboree and part concentration camp. The rows of huts stretched to the horizon. We could see children darting back and forth across the paths between the huts, kicking up plumes of dust in the hot, stagnant air. The camp was well kept, without the usual blights of rancid garbage and insect clouds.

The reaction of the driver was most telling. He looked around with the same amazement as if he had stumbled on a lost civilization. Here in his own country was a city of foreigners. Indeed, there were about 165,000 people jammed into the two-square-mile Site 2, more Cambodians in one place than anywhere but Phnom Penh. And they had all come at once. In November 1984, Vietnam launched a sweep of resistance camps sprouting just inside Cambodia, driving most of the civilian population out as well.

The camps along the border divided along political lines. Five of them housed Pol Pot's Khmer Rouge followers and were largely outside the control of foreign relief agencies and the Thai government. Much of the aid they got, particularly military equipment, came from the Chinese who detest the Vietnamese even more than the Thais do. The enemy of my enemy. The politics of Asia.

Site 2 housed the largest contingent of displaced persons, most of them supporters of the Khmer People's National Liberation Front, founded in 1979 by Son Sann, a former prime minister, who is aligned with Prince Norodom Sihanouk.

We wandered into a section called Phnom Dongrek and met an assistant camp administrator, a tall thin man in a blue polo shirt, fatigue pants and sandals who introduced himself as Keo Lundi. He had been an electrical engineer in Phnom Penh when the Khmer Rouge took over but managed to pass himself off as a laborer—the alternative being execution for being an educated man. He survived for three years under the Khmer Rouge then escaped across the border. He was 45 years old, but looked 60, his weather-beaten face etched by canals of anxiety.

"I lost three children to the Khmer Rouge," he said without emotion. "I hate them."

When Pol Pot took over Cambodia, right after the United States pulled out of Saigon in 1975, his twisted vision was to scour the country of all corrupting urban influences and create a rural society that was the essence of communism. If there was ever a shred of rationality to the idea, it quickly dissolved into a nightmare. Cambodia became a giant slave labor camp ruled by the capriciously violent soldiers of Pol Pot's guerilla army. All schools, churches and hospitals were shut down. Any trace of Western culture was eliminated and that included anyone educated in the West or even anyone who spoke English or French. Nineteen seventy-five became Year One of a lobotomized nation.

Lundi's story was typical of many of the country's seven million residents. With thousands of other city dwellers, he was marched from Phnom Penh to a rice-growing area and told to farm. Never mind that no one knew anything about farming. If you didn't work, you were killed. And work meant every day, all day, an endless cycle of monotony where weeks and months ceased to mean anything. Only those who tapped deep reserves of physical and emotional strength survived. And those who were the strongest—or the luckiest—escaped.

Lundi said he still had hope that he would return to Cambodia and push the Vietnamese out. He didn't know what he would do if the Khmer Rouge came back. "I think they're finished," he said vaguely. We wondered if he understood the complexity of all this—that within a hundred miles lived 300,000 or so refugees unified only by their place of birth and their hatred of the Vietnamese. As a whole, they had been the perpetrators, victims and witnesses of the darkest holocaust of recent memory, and nothing appeared to temper the likelihood that it could all happen again. The Vietnamese had announced a withdrawal from Cambodia in 1990, and if they were to be believed, Lundi would be running into the maelstrom again. The free-for-all would be decided by the side with the most guns, and that meant Pol Pot would be back.

The Thais and the Chinese had made a pact with the devil by allowing the Khmer Rouge to reorganize. In the sort of intricately rationalized diplomacy that has long been practiced in this crowded part of the world, they reasoned that only the Khmer Rouge could put pressure on Vietnam to withdraw from Cambodia. So they gave them vast stocks of arms and training bases in Thailand. Who would fill the vacuum once the Vietnamese pulled out was a question left unanswered. But since the Khmer Rouge had shown a desire to subjugate and abuse only their own people, perhaps the Thais and Chinese didn't care.

We walked to a dusty square surrounded by larger huts. This was the municipal center. Lundi took us to the school and we watched a woman write words on a blackboard while ranks of bony, big-eyed children stared quietly ahead.

"Education is difficult," Lundi whispered. "The Khmer Rouge killed most of the teachers. We have no young men to teach because when they are 18 they become soldiers. They go back across the border to fight. So we have a few women who went to high school and now they teach high school. We have a generation of people who do not know anything."

He pulled us out of the doorway and lowered his voice.

"Many, many people have problems of the head," he said, tapping his temple with a finger. "Even me," he shrugged. "They killed my children. They forced me to pretend I am stupid. And every day I live in fear that they will kill me."

Now that he mentioned it, there was something odd about Lundi. His eyes were cloudy and lethargic. They didn't move in synch with the rest of his body but instead drifted off on their own as if slowly focusing on something far away. In Vietnam veterans they used to call it "the thousand-yard stare." We could only guess at the trauma buried behind those eyes—and behind the eyes of all the children in the schoolhouse.

Life in the camp was warped. Cambodians were doing very un-Cambodian things. Those who knew the old Cambodia described it as a gentle place, sort of like Thailand without the energy. Family and home were sacred. But in the camp, women were selling themselves as prostitutes. Men were drinking and beating their wives. Mothers were beating their children. Teenagers were forming gangs for protection.

Class let out while we talked. Swarms of children in torn but clean clothes danced around us, laughing and pointing, tugging on pants legs and demanding attention.

"They still know how to laugh, how to be happy," Lundi said. "It is sad because they will soon forget these things."

Lundi said he marveled at how hope tended to evaporate a little more each day. "These people have survived Pol Pot. They have survived the Vietnamese. They come here, at the end of a journey for freedom. Then they stop. They have nowhere to go.

"Sometime there is shelling by the Vietnamese. Last month five people died. At night we can hear the fighting. But that is not the real danger. The real danger is that we are losing hope. People here want to go to America. Maybe I want to go to France. Or back to Cambodia. But now we are nowhere."

Tucked in a corner of Site 2 was a separate camp for Vietnamese refugees—those who had made their way out by land instead of sea. Many were ethnic Chinese who were singled out for harsh treatment and special "reeducation" by the Vietnamese. Ngu Thoung Chieu introduced himself as the mayor of the camp.

"I welcome you," he said stiffly. "I have been here five years, two months and three days. You come in."

We began to walk through the streets, getting waves and smiles. Several people came up to tell us their life stories.

"We like Americans," Ngu said. He didn't need to add that most everyone here wanted to go there as well.

"I was a soldier fighting with GIs," Ngu said. "But I have no documents to prove it. Soon they will find out and I can go to America."

At the sewing school, Truong Minh Hien barked out instructions to a roomful of middle-aged women hunched over new Singers.

"They will need skills in their new countries," she explained. "Sewing is a good thing."

There was not the same feeling of lassitude in the Vietnamese camp, perhaps because even among those who had been there for four or five years, they knew they had a chance to leave.

Truong, a stocky woman with a square Chinese face, had arrived in 1984, after walking through Cambodia.

"I was a nurse, a midwife," she said. "My husband was an acupuncture doctor. Soon we will live in America."

How was she so sure?

"I have a brother in Wichita, Kansas. Soon everything will be ready."

And when she arrived?

"My sons and daughters. I will send them to medical school. They will be doctors in America. That is the greatest thing."

She savored the thought for a moment with a smile, then excused herself and turned back to her class.

When we left the sewing school, we were grabbed by Nguyen Van Nhuc, a stiff-backed man in military fatigues whose eyes were as overly bright as Lundi's had been dull.

"I am the most worthy of the United States," he wanted us to know. "I speak English and I am a fighting man for you."

Nguyen invited us to his hut and sat us down for tea. The hut was decorated for Christmas, even though it was August, and a mournful picture of Jesus hung on the wall, the kind where droplets of blood can be seen oozing from beneath the crown of thorns. He said he had become a minister in the Seventh-Day Adventist Church.

"I am a Ranger captain," he told us. "An American hero."

From a footlocker he pulled out a folded piece of paper. It was a citation for bravery signed by General Creighton Abrams on March 28, 1971.

"I get this in Laos," he laughed. "Laos? America doesn't even know there is a war in Laos. But I fight there against the communists. I fight the communists from 1956 to 1973. Then I get a head wound and I stop."

We asked Nguyen what he had been doing for the past 14 years.

"Hiding. Hiding from the communists. Finally, I get two pieces of gold to buy a boat. But they steal it. So I walk instead. Across Cambodia."

What troubled him, he confessed, was that he was being denied his just reward for a lifetime of fighting communists. Nobody was letting him into America.

"I am here since 1983 and I am miserable. I don't know why I cannot go. I have an uncle in San Jose, California. I take any work, any job. Driver, mechanic."

We asked if he ever thought about going back to Vietnam. He cringed as if he were going to throw up.

"I must go to America. I am the freedom man. I am the freedom man!" He stood up and saluted us. "Yes, sir, I am the freedom man."

Our driver nudged us and pointed to his watch. Unless we planned to spend the night with Nguyen, we had to get moving.

The old soldier escorted us to the gate, and after we said goodbye, he snapped off another salute. The Freedom Man, who was partly crazy but very sincere, was still at attention when we rounded the corner.

• • •

We drove back along the border. To our left, only a few strands of razor wire separated us from Cambodia. To our right, tanks and armored personnel carriers were dug into bunkers every mile or so. Sometimes in a clearing we caught sight of soldiers in combat gear eating their evening meal from tin plates and wondering whether tonight was the night the Vietnamese would surge into Thailand to claim their birthright.

It was on this precarious strip of land that we ended our trip. Asia, as well, ended here—and began here. To the left, for over a thousand miles, lay the ruins of centuries of conflict—tribal, international and regional—and peace seemed as elusive as the day Marco Polo first brought news of a remarkable land to the East. Just a few years ago, while the rest of Asia watched in silence, a million people were executed or worked to death in an act of Dark Ages barbarism unequaled in the second half of the century. Behind us lived 300,000 souls yearning for a moment in their lives when fear would be an alien concept and hope would flourish.

And beyond the camps lay the new Asia. If the eye could see that far, there would be the exploding energy of Bangkok. There would be B. G. Lee atop his glass skyscraper proudly parading the numbers that proved Singapore's greatness—and rightfully so, for when he was born, Singapore's future was not any more certain than Keo Lundi's. And we would see W. P. Chuang in Taiwan, whose prize memory was that four-day reign of peace in August 1945; now his steel mill towered over nearly any America had to offer. In Hong Kong, Ronald Li professed his hard-eyed vision of the city as a lifeboat in a cruel world where the strong should prosper and the rest need not be cared for. And we would see Lee Yong Ho who had leaped from a diet of tree bark to a doctorate at Yale, compressing hundreds of years of development into less than a lifetime.

So many had come so far. The landscape of Asia not long ago was barren—from Hiroshima to Seoul to the swamps of Singapore. As we rode that fortified road along the border, we wondered: What next? Our journey had convinced us that we stood on the doorstep of the Asian century. The commitment to education, to hard work, to a purpose beyond self-interest brought Asia to the brink of global dominance. How the mantle had passed from Europe to America to Asia, and why, are questions best left to scholars of history. But it had.

Yet this thought bothered us. The dominance of Europe had produced a mother lode of art as well as profound political and social concepts—liberté, égalité and fraternité—that had endured for centuries. America had learned those lessons well and built upon them.

We had toured this continent as it was emerging, maybe at the same stage as de Tocqueville had toured ours. We questioned whether we had found the same spiritual richness that he had. Where de Tocqueville found the equivalent of naive enthusiasm, boundless in its vision to change the world, we found a cynical, calculating approach to survival. Asia wasn't trying to create a new, improved society, it was trying to figure out how to best exploit the old one. In months of travel, no one talked to us of making the world a better place. They talked of a color television set and a car in the garage—or at least a car for their children.

There is an atheism in Asia that is disturbing. Confucianism is a system well-suited to the harsh realities of the new global economy. In a worldwide marketplace, there are immutable laws that say good things will flow to those who are disciplined and efficient. But there was, we thought, more to life. We wondered if beyond the trade numbers, the housing projects and the Olympics, somebody had a plan for how our lives would be enriched by the Asian century. What were the truths that lay self-evident in Asia?

Site 2 suggested that there may not be any. As long as there stood in the shadows of the Four Little Dragons and Japan a man, snapped to attention, proclaiming, "I am the freedom man," then the mantle will not pass gladly. That man is surrounded by the barbed wire needed to segregate a volatile, suspicious part of the world. As long as he calls to America for opportunity and peace, Asia will not be a worthy heir. This may be the region with the greatest foreign reserves and lowest deficits, but it still had not convinced us that it was truly rich in heart and mind. For each of the successful Dragons, there was a Cambodia, a Laos, a North Korea. And there was China, imitating for now its successful neighbors but mindful that just

20 years ago, it had been swept clean of its progress during the insane Cultural Revolution.

We had been intimidated and impressed throughout our journey by the accomplishments we saw. We had been apologists for America's glaring weaknesses. Yet, as darkness closed in on that dusty, dangerous road, we found great comfort in our one secure asset: We had what the freedom man wanted.

EPILOGUE

IN THE MONTHS since we left Asia, the pace of change has been furious. Each of the Dragons is bigger and more formidable than when we started. Some of the changes have been surprisingly promising—Korea and Taiwan today are freer societies; some have been disappointingly predictable—Singapore is clamping down. The total U.S. trade deficit with the Dragons grew to about $30 billion in 1988, about half the size of our deficit with Japan, which has begun to fall. The economies of each of the Dragons are growing at an amazing rate and it seems inevitable that, taken together, they will have the impact of a new Japan sometime in the early 1990s.

Korea is seeing the most spectacular change. The gathering storm clouds we had witnessed turned into a violent, purging deluge that resulted in free elections and a new, reform-minded president. A virtually bloodless revolution culminated in December 1987, with the election of Roh Tae Woo as president. A former general and crony of President Chun Doo Hwan, Roh has made believers of the cynics who feared he would continue the same military repression. He has allowed democracy to take hold on all levels in what, so far, is an extraordinary political transformation.

Some of Chun's relatives and friends were tried and convicted of corruption—which proved to be as pervasive as everyone suspected—and jail terms were handed down to many feared former officials; Chun avoided an embarrassing trial by agreeing to self-exile in a rural monastery. Even the open-wound of the Kwangju uprising was the subject of a parliamentary investigation.

Kim Dae Jung did not become president. He did run, however, stubbornly keeping himself in a three-way-race with another opposition candidate—with the result that Roh's victory was assured. Kim now serves in the legislature and is said to be keeping alive the dream of another try at the office he feels is his destiny.

Along with political reform has come industrial reform. Union restrictions were loosened and almost immediately the country was hit with thousands of strikes. But this time protests were met with big pay boosts instead of big sticks.

The Olympic Games came and went without significant political incident, giving Korea at least some of its hoped-for international recognition. But the Games also laid bare the Korean character in front of millions of viewers who witnessed such scenes as Korean boxing officials pummeling a referee after a disputed call and a Korean boxer sitting alone in a ring for an hour in public view as atonement for losing a bout. The Koreans hated the media from the United States—the Elder Brother—for dwelling on the incidents. But in the end, so much of what they did was conduct precisely appropriate to a Little Brother.

North Korea remains a menacing mystery. While many in the South began to openly call for reunification, officials from the North agreed to a series of bizarrely unproductive meetings that featured speeches, posturing and insults, but no proposals. The betting was that the North would eventually have to get in step with the reform movements in China and the Soviet Union, but war or peace still seemed equally possible. The North did not disrupt the Olympic Games, as it had hinted, but several months before the games, it did blow up a civilian Korean airliner, killing 115 people. The CIA raised its estimate of the size of the North Korean military to one million troops, the fifth largest in the world.

And through it all, the Korean economy soared. As Japan found itself squeezed by the rise of the yen—and the resulting rise of its prices—Korean cars became the fastest-selling imports in the United States and brand names such as Hyundai, Samsung and Goldstar became as common as Sony and Panasonic.

The changes in Taiwan were nearly as dramatic. Those fistfights in parliament portended good things to come in the political arena.

President Chiang Ching-kuo brought political spring to Taiwan in his final days, so much so that the earth must have churned around the grave of his father, the Generalissimo.

Press restrictions were lifted, anti-government demonstrations were permitted. Opposition parties were allowed to campaign. Martial law was lifted after 38 years. Perhaps the most startling announcement came in November 1987, when the government said citizens of the Republic of China could visit relatives on the Mainland. In 1988, more than 400,000 people went. Taiwanese also began to question the deification of Chiang Kai-shek and calls were heard for investigations into some of his imperious conduct, including the long-suppressed story of a massacre of thousands of Taiwanese at the hands of Chiang's troops in 1949.

Chiang the son died at the age of 79 of a heart attack at the beginning of 1988 and was succeeded without incident by Lee Teng-hui, a former mayor of Taipei who had been educated at Iowa State and Cornell. Most significantly, Lee had been born in Taiwan. He continued the process of political liberalization. Among the reforms: an offer of almost $150,000 to any aging legislator who would retire. The goal was to encourage a new generation in the legislature and shed the ancient warriors who came from the Mainland and still thought they would return home in triumph.

Taiwan's economy showed no signs of slowing from its superheated pace. Wages rose, as did per capita income, almost to the level of Singapore. While the Taiwanese still had the world's highest rate of saving—about a third of what they earned—for the first time they began to spend. As tariff barriers with the United States fell they started to consume such items as refrigerators, washing machines, designer clothes, cigarettes and even, surprise, American cars. The Taiwanese stock market rose more than 700 percent as the man on the street began to invest.

The spending spree helped ease the trade deficit with the United States, but for 1988 it was still about $15 billion. To even things out, Taiwan was buying huge stocks of gold from the United States. At last count, in the spring of 1989, Taiwan was sitting on cash reserves of more than $75 billion—second only to Japan's $90 billion. The world was waiting for Taiwan to follow the Japanese lead and start investing that cash abroad.

Meanwhile, the Chinese in Beijing looked on with envy and continued to talk of the need to have Taiwan return to the fold—peacefully, of course.

• • •

In Hong Kong, people watched Beijing with a more immediate concern. The subject of every discussion was July 1, 1997, and there was no consensus on what would happen, just a lot of nervousness. Foreign passports and foreign bank accounts remained popular. Both wealthy businessmen and their skilled mid-level managers were voting with their feet and leaving for good. About 50,000 left in 1988 alone.

Still, the other side of the 1997 puzzle could be seen in the factories sprouting all over southern China. For some the question was whether it wasn't Hong Kong that was taking over China. Whatever politics wrought, it was clear that economic reform would be hard to erase. There are those who believe that entrenched economic changes, as well as the return of thousands of U.S.-educated students, eventually will spell the end to the political hard-liners in Beijing. Honk Kong obviously counts on this happening. Yet, jitters, not confidence, permeates the Colony; Chinese governments from the beginning of time have shown a willingness to sacrifice their own people for the sake of their own survival.

The most important news from Hong Kong, though, was that David Wang got married. Shortly after his visit to the fortune-teller who told him "marry or go bankrupt," he received a phone call from a businesswoman from Singapore who was killing time on an overnight stopover on her way to the United States. Her name was Julie Chiu and she had met David several years earlier at a business convention. Was David free for dinner? she wanted to know. A month later they were engaged.

Also cheered by good news was George Tan, the wheeler-dealer who almost brought the whole economy down. His gigantic fraud prosecution was thrown out by a judge after more than a year of testimony and $12 million in costs. After hearing the government's case, the judge said it was too broad. The government huffed and said it would try again. Meanwhile, Hong Kong's real-estate market was as overheated as ever and the stock market was booming. There was sure to be at least another crash or two before regulating the world's freest free market became the problem of the Chinese.

Not faring as well was Ronald Li, the chairman of the gleaming new stock exchange who had given us such an education into the mentality of the Hong Kong businessman. He was getting ready for bed when the bottom fell out of Wall Street on October 19, 1987. Rather than face his share of the beating he knew was coming round the globe, Li chose to shut down the exchange for a week. The decision was disastrous. Once the market reopened, it crashed with a fury. People lost millions of dollars, firms went bankrupt and a number of top brokers were caught trying to embezzle clients' money to cover their own losses.

But nobody was hit as hard as Ronald Li, who was arrested and charged with accepting bribes from companies who wished to be given permission to float new issues on the Hong Kong exchange.

The crash had little effect on the beehive of factories in the colony in any case and the financial markets rebounded smartly. In 1988, the growth rate was almost 14 percent. The piles of goods for export allowed Hong Kong to overtake Rotterdam as the world's busiest container port. Analysts said that anyone who wanted to get money out before 1997 had already done it. The money that was left—and there was a lot—was risk capital. In the great business casino, the betting was that high rollers would keep throwing the dice with increasing intensity until the Chinese took over. Hong Kong over the next few years was liable to get really exciting.

Singapore was supposed to be the great beneficiary of the Chinese takeover of Hong Kong. Some observers—mostly Singaporeans—felt certain that corporations and financial markets would want to move to the more stable confines of their tropical paradise. The only problem was that while Lee Kuan Yew's neighbors saw the need for more democracy, he offered even less, seeing enemies under every bed and cracking down at the first whiff of dissent.

Lee picked fights with U.S. diplomats, and an ill-tempered rebuke on trade policy was delivered by an underling. He imprisoned critics, including the most attractive candidate for an opposition seat in parliament, Francis Seow, and even warred with an old colleague, Devan Nair, one of the original founders of the country. Even the Privy Council, the highest court in the British Commonwealth, had implied harsh words for Lee when it ruled on the case of his imagined nemesis, J. B. Jeyaretnam, who had been disbarred. The case was a "grievous injustice," the council said. The prosecution, inspired by Lee and suspiciously conducted, had resulted in Jeya and a colleague being "fined, imprisoned and publicly disgraced for offences of which they were not guilty."

Was Lee entering his dotage, people wondered? Was 30 years of power clogging his arteries? Was he just getting cranky?

But while much of the rest of the world may have been skeptical, Singaporeans were mostly content. Lee won 82 percent of the vote in the fall 1988 election. The perennial question was how long he would remain in power. The practical answer was: until he died. The betting was that he would be succeeded as prime minister by one of his deputies, Goh Chok Tong, with the likelihood that his son, B. G. Lee, would eventually take over. But Lee had a new plan. He wanted to create for himself the new post of president, a job which some people felt would allow him to maintain control.

From the standpoint of the economy, who was to complain? Singapore continued to refine things in its move toward a high-tech economy. All the indicators were in the right direction and besides, it was increasingly attracting attention—and cash—from one group who seemed to thrive on order and cleanliness and didn't mind the political restrictions: Singapore was becoming one of the favorite places to invest for the Japanese.

And in Thailand, which was becoming known as the fifth Dragon, with growth rates approaching 10 percent and investment capital pouring in from all over Asia, they talked about how the Khmer Rouge were consolidating their forces along the border and preparing to retake power in Cambodia. It was like a bad dream. The recurring Asian nightmare. It was impossible, everyone said. Yet it was happening.

Finally, there was China. As this book went to press, the Biggest Dragon writhed in turmoil. Scenes of prisoners with shaved heads—once the portrait of the Cultural Revolution—returned to our television screens. Death sentences were handed out to those who were deemed enemies of the state. The leaders reacted against any criticism from foreigners. Again, the window to China appeared to be closing, and the final pictures were not pretty. The Four Little Dragons obviously took notice and, no doubt, were reminded that the world indeed can be a treadmill which can go backward as easily as it went forward.

June 15, 1989

INDEX